# Bloodsuckers of the Commonwealth

Manchester University Press

POLITICS, CULTURE AND SOCIETY IN EARLY MODERN BRITAIN



This important series publishes volumes that take a fresh and challenging look at the interactions between politics, culture and society in early modern Britain and beyond. It seeks to counteract the fragmentation of current historiography by encouraging a variety of methodological and critical approaches to this period of dramatic conflict and change that fundamentally shaped the modern world. The series welcomes volumes covering all aspects of sixteenth, seventeenth, and eighteenth century history, including the history of Britain's growing imperial ambitions and global reach.

To buy or to find out more about the books currently available in this series, please go to: https://manchesteruniversitypress.co.uk/series/politics-culture-and-society-in-early-modern-britain

# Bloodsuckers of the Commonwealth

## Monopolies, petitioning, and the public sphere in early modern England

Ellen Paterson

Manchester University Press

Published by Manchester University Press
Oxford Road, Manchester, M13 9PL

www.manchesteruniversitypress.co.uk

British Library Cataloguing-in-Publication Data
A catalogue record for this book is available from the British Library

ISBN 978 1 5261 8908 0 hardback

First published 2025



EU authorised representative for GPSR:
Easy Access System Europe, Mustamäe tee 50, 10621 Tallinn, Estonia
gpsr.requests@easproject.com

Typeset
by Deanta Global Publishing Services, Chennai, India

# Bloodsuckers of the Commonwealth

## Monopolies, petitioning, and the public sphere in early modern England

Ellen Paterson

Manchester University Press

Published by Manchester University Press
Oxford Road, Manchester, M13 9PL

www.manchesteruniversitypress.co.uk

British Library Cataloguing-in-Publication Data
A catalogue record for this book is available from the British Library

ISBN 978 1 5261 8908 0 hardback

First published 2025



EU authorised representative for GPSR:
Easy Access System Europe, Mustamäe tee 50, 10621 Tallinn, Estonia
gpsr.requests@easproject.com

Typeset
by Deanta Global Publishing Services, Chennai, India

*For my late brother-in-law, Mark Hayes*

# Contents

# Acknowledgements

I have many people to thank for their help and invaluable support whilst completing this monograph. First, thanks are due to the staff and archivists of The London Archives, British Library, Guildhall Library, Parliamentary Archives, Bodleian Libraries, Hampshire Local Archives, Somerset Archives, Suffolk Archives, West Yorkshire Archives, Swindon and Wiltshire Archives, and to the Longleat Archives. Much of the research for this monograph was undertaken during the pandemic, and the tireless work of archivists and librarians who were able to provide digital copies of documents and scans of book chapters was invaluable. I am especially grateful to Jerome Farrell, Kate Higgins, Hannah Dunmow, and Penny Fussell for allowing me to use, and for guiding me through, the fantastic collections of their respective livery companies.

The completion of this monograph would not have been possible without the support of Keble College and the CMRS Career Development Fellowship, which I have been lucky enough to hold since October 2023. Writing and editing in the summer of 2024 were made even more enjoyable by the SCR and the incredibly supportive space the college offers for early career academics. I'd like to thank all of my colleagues at college, and at CMRS, for making me so welcome in its amazing community. In addition, the early modern community at Oxford (and especially the Early Modern Britain seminar) has been an incredible support network, and I'd like to particularly thank Lucy Wooding, George Southcombe, and Steve Gunn for their continued encouragement. I am also grateful to Mansfield and Oriel colleges where I spent a year as a Stipendiary Lecturer, and special thanks are due to Helen Lacey for her ongoing support.

I am so grateful to all colleagues who have read and commented on drafts of chapters, including Grace Heaton, Alex Beeton, Thomas Stevens, and Jana Hunter. I am also grateful to Grant Tapsell who offered invaluable advice in developing this monograph. I am incredibly thankful to Jason Peacey who offered encouragement and feedback for my research, and who has gone above and beyond to offer support and advice on all things petitioning.

My work has certainly been enriched by your knowledge and generosity commenting on earlier drafts. I would also like to thank Ed Legon for our various discussions on the cloth trade over the past year. The advice offered by the anonymous reviewers and the series editors at MUP was also incredibly valuable, and I would like to thank them all for their guidance and expertise. I'd also like to express my gratitude to the various Institute of Historical Research seminars for inviting me to give papers, allowing me to discuss my ideas whilst in the early stages of formation. Thanks are also due to the students I have been lucky enough to teach over the last few years. All errors remain my own.

Most invaluable of all has been the continued support of both Ian Archer and Alex Gajda – two incredible scholars who supervised me throughout my doctorate and who have continued to offer endless encouragement, help, and friendship (as well as reading numerous drafts). You have both gone above and beyond to support me, and I remain in awe of your boundless knowledge. I couldn't have wished for two better supervisors and friends.

Finally, thanks are due to my family, especially my dad and my mum who have supported me in my ambitions to be a historian from day one. My final thanks are for my greatest companion throughout this journey, my fiancé James Eaton – thank you for letting me talk endlessly about petitions, monopolies, and livery companies for the last few years.

# Abbreviations

| | |
|---|---|
| *APC* | J. R. Dasent (ed.), *Acts of the Privy Council of England, new series,* 46 vols (London, 1890–1964). |
| Archer, 'London Lobbies' | I. W. Archer, 'The London Lobbies in the Later Sixteenth Century', *Historical Journal*, 31:1 (1988), pp. 17–44. |
| Archer, *Pursuit* | I. W. Archer, *The Pursuit of Stability: Social Relations in Elizabethan London* (Cambridge, 1991). |
| Ashton, 'Conflicts' | R. Ashton, 'Conflicts of Concessionary Interest in Early Stuart England', in D. C. Coleman and F. J. Fisher (eds), *Trade, Government and Economy in Pre-Industrial England: Essays Presented to F. J. Fisher* (London, 1976), pp. 113–31. |
| Ashton, *City* | R. Ashton, *The City and the Court 1603–1643* (Cambridge, 1979). |
| BL | British Library, London. |
| Bodl. | Bodleian Library, Oxford. |
| Brenner, *Merchants* | R. Brenner, *Merchants and Revolution: Commercial Change, Political Conflict, and London's Overseas Traders, 1550–1653* (London, 2003). |
| BRO | Bury St Edmunds Branch, Suffolk Record Office. |
| *CD 1621* | *Commons Debates 1621,* W. Notestein *et al.* (eds) (7 vols, New Haven, 1935). |
| *CJ* | *Journal of the House of Commons: Volume 1, 1547–1629* (London, 1802), *British History Online*, https://www.british-history.ac.uk/commons-jrnl/vol1 (accessed 27 September 2024). |

| | |
|---|---|
| CP | Cecil Papers, Hatfield House. |
| *CPR* | *Calendar of the Patent Rolls preserved in the Public Record Office, Elizabeth I and James I*, various editors (London, 1939–2014). |
| DA | The Drapers' Archives, London. |
| GL | Guildhall Library, London. |
| *HMC Lincoln* | Historical Manuscripts Commission, *The Manuscripts of Lincoln, Bury St. Edmunds and Great Grimsby Corporations; And of the Deans and Chapters of Worcester and Lichfield, &c.* (Fourteenth Report, Appendix, Part VIII) (London, 1895). |
| *HMC Sackville* | Historical Manuscripts Commission, *Calendar of the Manuscripts of Major-General Lord Sackville preserved at Knole, Sevenoaks*, ed. A. P. Newton (2 vols, London, 1940), i. |
| *HMC Smedmore* | Historical Manuscripts Commission, *Royal Commission on Historical Manuscripts Report on the Additional Estate Papers of the Clavell and Mansel Families of Smedmore 1516–1874*, ed. J. P. Ferris and E. Allen (London, 1977). |
| *HoP* | *The History of Parliament: The House of Commons 1604–1629*, eds. A. Thrush and J. P. Ferris, 6 vols (Cambridge, 2010), accessed at history ofparliamentonline.org (accessed 24 July 2024). |
| HRO | Hampshire Record Office, Winchester. |
| Kyle, *Theater* | C. R. Kyle, *Theater of State: Parliament and Political Culture in Early Stuart England* (Stanford, 2012). |
| Lans. | Lansdowne. |
| Larkin and Hughes | J. F. Larkin and P. L. Hughes (eds), *Stuart Royal Proclamations* (2 vols, Oxford, 1983). |
| Leng, *Fellowship* | T. Leng, *Fellowship and Freedom: The Merchant Adventurers and the Restructuring of English Commerce, 1582–1700* (Oxford, 2020). |

| | |
|---|---|
| *LJ* | *Journal of the House of Lords: Volume 3, 1620–1628* (London, 1767–1830), https://www.british-history.ac.uk/lords-jrnl/vol3 (accessed 27 September 2024). |
| *ODNB* | Oxford Dictionary of National Biography. |
| PA | Parliamentary Archives, London. |
| Peacey, *Public Politics* | J. Peacey, *Print and Public Politics in the English Revolution* (Cambridge, 2013).*PP 1624* |
| *Proceedings in Parliament 1624* | *The House of Commons*, ed. P. Baker (London, 2015–2018), British History Online, https://www.british-history.ac.uk/no-series/proceedings-1624-parl (accessed 27 September 2024). |
| SP | State Papers. |
| SRO | Somerset Archives and Local Studies, Somerset. |
| Supple, *Crisis* | B. Supple, *Commercial Crisis and Change in England 1600–1642: A Study in the Instability of a Mercantile Economy* (Cambridge, 1959). |
| Thirsk, *Policy and Projects* | J. Thirsk, *Economic Policy and Projects: The Development of a Consumer Society in Early Modern England* (Oxford, 1978). |
| TNA | The National Archives, London. |
| TLA | The London Archives, London. |
| Withington, *Politics* | P. Withington, *The Politics of Commonwealth: Citizens and Freemen in Early Modern England* (Cambridge, 2005). |
| WSHC | Wiltshire and Swindon History Centre, Chippenham. |
| WYA | West Yorkshire Archives, Leeds. |

All dates are given in the Old Style Julian Calendar, as recorded by contemporaries, but the year has been taken to start on 1 January.

# Introduction: 'The courtiers craved all, the Queen granted all'

> Being by me moer p[ar]ticulerly Demaunded, why they repaired that day vnto the Court, In the end they confessed, That their purpos[e] was to haue exhibited a complaint vnto the L[ords]. The copie wherof (being in my opinion very slaunderous & scandalous...I herewith send vnto your L[ords][.][1]

On 23 July 1605, Thomas Sackville, the Earl of Dorset and Lord Treasurer of England, wrote to the Privy Council to describe an attempt by members of the London Dyers' Company to present a petition at Court. Whilst petitioning was perceived as an acceptable and legitimate form of communication, a means by which subjects of various degrees could express demands and grievances to authority, the Dyers' actions had clearly generated a degree of alarm amongst the Council. This led them to charge Dorset with the task of investigating their conduct.

The Dyers' Company were a livery company responsible for the government and regulation of the dyeing trade in London. A respectable and royally chartered body, deemed as providing order and governance to a flourishing industry, they were one of many livery companies essential to the economic and political life of the metropolis. Why, then, had their petitioning activity in 1605 caused such concern? Like so many other corporate bodies, the Dyers had found themselves vexed by the growth of an unpopular and intrusive fiscal policy: patents of monopoly. In the late Elizabethan and early Stuart periods, the cash-strapped Crown granted myriad patents to courtiers and projectors, both as a means to fill the royal coffers and to bestow patronage on loyal subjects.[2] In August 1604 a patent had been granted to the courtier Sir Arthur Aston, providing him and his syndicate with exclusive rights to make a new dyeing mixture from the commodity of logwood.[3] Despite the regular issuing of statutes and proclamations prohibiting its importation and use for the dyeing of cloths, James I was willing to allow its limited importation in the realm to colour other commodities – a decision sweetened by his choice to impose new customs duties on the product.[4] For the Dyers, the financial benefits this grant might have provided for

Aston or the Crown were not enough to convince them that it was beneficial for the dyeing industry. In their petition, they moved to express their concern that the patentees sought only 'their owne privat[e] gayne', imposing 'intollerable' prices for a dyeing mixture, the alleged benefits of which were merely 'p[re]tended to the comonwelth'.[5]

The Council was concerned with two main aspects of this protest: the nature of the complaint, and the way the Dyers had acted as petitioning subjects. Whilst on the surface the Dyers' protest appears to have been a simple rejection of an unpopular patent, a rather specific industrial concern, their protest saw them engage with the more contentious topic of the King's prerogative powers, under which all monopolies and charters were granted. Dorset was concerned that the Dyers had not merely expressed criticism with the way in which the patentees had exercised their grant, but had questioned 'the patent it self', a dangerous utterance which challenged James' authority.[6] Yet most of his letter was concerned with the means by which the Dyers had importuned authority. Crucially, this was not the first time they had approached the Court with their complaints. Dorset noted that their concerns had already been referred to the Master of Requests and the Attorney General for a hearing. Despite this, the Dyers had moved to lobby other figures in Court. Not only had they informed Henry Howard, the Earl of Northampton 'in private with some part of their greifes', but they had also sent a petition to Robert Cecil, the Earl of Salisbury, 'of on[e] & the same effect', for which they had received a 'iust & reasonable' answer.[7] Upon further questioning, the Dyers admitted that they had intended to exhibit a further petition to the Council, the copy of which was enclosed by Dorset in this report, though they denied that Salisbury had answered their previous suit. Regardless of the truth of these claims, their actions caused Dorset to classify them as incessant petitioners, and the Dyers and patentees were prohibited from troubling James or the Council with any further supplications until the following Michaelmas term. Their complaints, whilst burdensome for the Council, did not prevent them from having some degree of success. By November 1605, Aston's grant was re-issued under new terms on the basis that the charges he had imposed on logwood were indeed too high.[8]

The Dyers' continued agitation against various logwood monopolies throughout James's reign reveals the complexities of industrial conflicts and the ways through which these were negotiated and expressed via petitions. By James's final two Parliaments in 1621 and 1624, accusations would be levelled by the city's leather dressers that the company's protests to the logwood monopolies were nothing more than a self-interested ploy to allow them to monopolise and use the commodity for illegal purposes.[9] Rival interpretations of the state of the industry and the necessity of the product were articulated by current patentees, dyers, and leather dressers, as each crafted their own narrative of the state of the industry to appeal to MPs.[10] In this case, as in so many others, monopoly policy generated tensions and conflicts which received expression chiefly through supplications.

This episode, whilst certainly complicated, is merely one of many cases of anti-monopoly petitioning activity which occurred in the period 1590–1625, as Elizabeth and James's use of prerogative fiscal devices saw economic policy emerge as a central issue vexing subjects in a nascent public sphere. Whilst scholarship on the turn of the seventeenth century has so often been pre-occupied with tracing the existence of constitutional conflict or consensus, confessional divides, or the moral dimensions of the Court, this book argues for the need to re-integrate analyses of economic policies and trading conflicts into understandings of political culture.[11] Corporatism and monopoly politicised subjects, triggering engagement with such issues as liberties, property rights, and economic regulation which received debate through petitions. As Joan Thirsk has so aptly shown, a range of patents were granted to inexperienced courtiers in what was a 'scandalous' phase of monopoly policy.[12] This study offers the first in-depth exploration of anti-monopoly petitioning agitation to demonstrate the centrality of this economic issue to the lived realities and political activity of sub-elite groups in early modern England.[13]

Thirsk has argued that patents had some of their most negative effects in the city of London, where the sheer number of projectors and monopolistic schemes served to fuel hostilities.[14] The influence and established status of London's livery companies meant that they emerged as key opponents of new monopolies. Robert Ashton has argued that patents triggered 'conflicts of concessionary interest' in the metropolis, which saw battles fought, and unexpected alliances made, as companies and interest groups moved to protect or advance their own interests.[15] Meanwhile, older tensions between or within companies were given added impetus as opponents proved able to use the accusation of monopoly against industrial rivals. This book will focus especially on petitioning campaigns launched by, and against, London's various livery and overseas trading companies. As we will see, companies acted as important associational spaces, creating networks and fostering occupational identities which facilitated collective petitioning action. The Dyers' petition offers merely one example of a livery company protesting the intrusion on their established trades by projectors and courtiers, whilst the criticism against them levied by the leather dressers attests to the ways patents could divide industries. However, even outside of the city, this economic policy served to foster discontent and promote debate as groups of subjects reached for new corporate privileges and fought against monopolistic trading bodies, and more localised conflicts of concessionary interest were fuelled and created by the issues of corporatism and monopoly. Whilst scholars have done much to broaden our understandings of the intellectual contours of the monopolies debate, explored Crown and city relations in the early seventeenth century, and begun to construct a fuller picture of 'popular politics', an exploration of these issues in tandem has the capacity to offer a new perspective on the late Elizabethan and early Stuart periods.[16]

## Monopolies in an 'age of incorporation', 1590–1625

The granting of patents of monopolies at the turn of the seventeenth century is, in many ways, well-covered ground. Studies by John Cramsie, Linda Levy Peck, and Thirsk have revealed their importance to Crown financial policy.[17] The right to grant monopolies belonged to the Crown as part of the royal prerogative, a 'resurrected' power utilised to help combat the cash shortages faced by Elizabeth and her Stuart successors.[18] Generally, they fell into four main categories. The most legitimate were patents for new inventions or industrial processes, providing holders with the sole rights to use and produce their products. More contentious were grants which provided the holder with the sole power to produce or sell certain commodities, patents for the supervision of entire trades and industries, or grants which allowed the holder dispensations from the law (for example, in the form of licences to import or export prohibited goods).[19] The initial imperative to develop England's domestic industries through these grants, especially by bestowing them on skilled foreign inventors, soon gave way to the 'scandalous' phase in monopoly policy from the 1580s.[20] Their number and range greatly expanded, and inexperienced courtiers emerged as the main recipients. Such was their extent that one anonymous libeller writing towards the end of Elizabeth's reign jested that as the 'Courtyars craved all/ The Queene graunted all'.[21] The papers of William Cecil, Lord Burghley and of Sir Julius Caesar, Chancellor of the Exchequer from 1606–14, are littered with a number of proposals and petitions from would-be projectors seeking patents for new inventions, industrial processes, and offices over a variety of trades.[22] A list of projects compiled in August 1609 included 105 potential 'proiects of gaine'.[23]

Hitherto, scholars have demonstrated the extent to which the monopoly issue triggered discontent and debate in both Parliament and the law courts, with older scholarship using this issue to comment on Crown and parliamentary relations in the years preceding the Civil Wars.[24] That this economic policy allowed subjects to engage with broader issues of political and constitutional import has been illustrated by David Harris Sacks, Clive Holmes, and Nicholas Tyacke, demonstrating the ideological issues raised by their use.[25] More recently, scholars have also shown the importance of concerns with monopolists and the projector figure in popular culture more broadly, expressed through such forums as libels, broadsides, and drama.[26] Whilst petitions produced by projectors have been analysed, anti-monopoly petitions remain a relatively underexamined source capable of providing insights into the ways many subjects were politicised by this issue.[27] It also allows a move away from analyses focusing on the response of MPs, peers, and courtiers to monopoly as they battled with the constitutional issues they raised, showing the reactions of retailers, artisans, and craftsmen to this fiscal device.

Monopoly policy was contentious not only due to the constitutional questions it raised: it also uneasily overlapped with England's pre-existing and expanding corporate system. The period 1590–1625 has often been characterised as an 'era of incorporation'.[28] A variety of corporate institutions were created and chartered, from towns and craft guilds in the localities to new companies for overseas trade in a period of global expansion. Historiography has focused extensively on the chartering and activities of new and established overseas trading companies, including the Merchant Adventurers', East India, and Virginia Companies.[29] Often overlooked in comparison is the range of new companies for domestic trades incorporated in both London and the provinces.[30] As will be explored in Chapter 1, monopoly policy created jurisdictional clashes and tensions with older and established bodies. Ian Gadd and Patrick Wallis note that the monopoly and guild system 'overlapped': new charters and patents clashed with the rights of pre-existing institutions, generating contests and battles.[31] Further, the boundaries between a legitimate company and a monopolistic body were often unclear. Whilst the former provided order and regulation, the latter was seen as enhancing private profits at the expense of the public good. These distinctions were not so clear-cut to easily identify a monopoly body from a legitimate institution. These boundaries were constantly discussed and tested within petitioning disputes, as subjects of varying degrees moved to debate and negotiate this form of state power and its role in local economies. In this context, the topics of corporatism and monopoly emerged as key issues driving politicisation. The petitions produced, whilst on the surface centred around quite specific economic issues, allowed subjects to engage with larger issues surrounding liberties and the prerogative, as they simultaneously claimed for themselves a right to participate in the investigation of the realm's economy.[32]

## City politics – freemen and companies

The city of London and its livery companies were essential to anti-monopoly agitation. The city authorities worked both to organise and legitimise petitioning complaints and to investigate proposed grants, rendering it necessary to provide an overview of the structures guiding social, economic, and political life in the metropolis. Both the Court of Aldermen, the main executive body of the city presided over by twenty-six aldermen from each of the city wards, and the Common Council, consisting of councillors elected at wardmotes by freemen, were essential courts for petitioners.[33] Corporate interests were well represented in these spaces; at the beginning of this period, the Court of Aldermen consisted of members of the Adventurers' Company, but as Robert Brenner has demonstrated, they were gradually replaced in the course of the early seventeenth century by the rise of the East India–Levant combine.[34] The Lord Mayor, elected annually and usually the most senior alderman, was crucial for communicating company grievances to the Council and the Crown throughout the period.

In the mid-sixteenth century, three-quarters of adult males in the capital were members of one of London's companies, this being necessary to receive the city freedom.[35] The freedom was an important element of city life, bestowing on holders economic and political rights, including the ability to set up shop and to trade in the city as 'citizens'.[36] It could be achieved in three different ways: by patrimony, redemption, or through apprenticeship. The so-called 'custom' of London allowed freemen to practise any trade in the city.[37] As Phil Withington has shown, the politics of citizenship prevalent in corporate bodies throughout the realm was based heavily on humanist ideas of 'civility', creating a desire amongst freemen to participate in civic governance for the good of the broader commonwealth.[38] As such, those holding the freedom had a heightened sense of their role and rights as citizens, frequently appealing to customs and charter culture to defend their trades and to engage in city affairs. As we will see, these sentiments infused petitions sent by freemen from across the realm with invocations of liberty, encouraging them to protest any intrusions on their livelihoods.

The companies to which freemen belonged acted as important institutions regulating trade, drawing up ordinances for their members and serving as social and charitable institutions.[39] As many as seventy companies were in existence in London at the end of the sixteenth century.[40] At the top of the company sat its master, assistants, and wardens, all of whom were members of the livery, admission into which required high fees and which was thus reserved for the most prosperous members.[41] Companies also possessed a yeomanry element, consisting of journeymen and householders; in some companies the yeomanry had their own wardens and separate finances.[42] Householders ran their own businesses, hiring journeymen as wage labourers and keeping a set number of apprentices.[43] Apprenticeship remained an important route by which many acquired the freedom, with many younger sons of gentry receiving such training.[44]

London's livery companies were active and incessant petitioners and lobbyists. Ian Archer, David Dean, and Chris Kyle have demonstrated the processes whereby companies introduced bills in Parliament and petitioned the city and Court to protect and advance their own interests, sometimes without the approval of the wider city authorities.[45] Supplications presented in the name of entire companies, like the Dyers in 1605, could be discussed in general court meetings by members and penned by company clerks and lawyers. As will be seen in Chapter 2, specific lawyers could be chosen to infuse complaints with targeted rhetoric, creating 'hybrid' documents in which the concerns of company members, leaders, and lawyers fused.[46] It was not only company leaders who instigated this activity. Archer and Joseph Ward have explored the processes through which apprentices, journeymen, and householders petitioned their Court of Assistants, showcasing an ability and willingness to communicate with their leaders.[47] In companies like the Clothworkers, the yeomanry element frequently petitioned Parliament and the Council without wider company approval.[48] Through company court books and warden's accounts, insights into the mechanics of this petitioning can be gleaned, as specific campaigns can be traced through companies' extensive archives. Anti-monopoly petitioning will be shown to have involved a range of collaborations and processes, from petitions penned by company lawyers to subjects organising agitation outside of the auspices of company organisation. This provides a new perspective on the importance of both formal and informal spaces for petitioning activism and the varied means through which money was gathered to launch campaigns.

Livery companies stood at the centre of many of the anti-monopoly campaigns discussed in the proceeding analysis. As such, these campaigns allow us to advance pre-existing understandings of Court and city politics in this important era of change. The seminal works of Ashton, Brenner, and Valerie Pearl have done much to strengthen understandings of the alliances and conflicts between Crown and city interests in the early Stuart period, with the intention of tracing the later Civil War allegiances of merchants.[49] Monopolies and the creation of new and intrusive corporations have been seen as causing a growing divide between Court and city interests. Ashton argued for the range of 'conflicts of concessionary interest' in the city, arguing for a breakdown in relations between companies and the Crown, and their alliance with Parliament, by Charles's reign.[50] Brenner by contrast argues that new merchant elites in colonial trades were involved in an 'aristocratic colonising opposition' in Parliament, whilst old merchant elites in the city remained allied to the Crown.[51] This book will reveal that the reality of relationships was much more complex than a story of 'alliance' or 'conflict'. Instead, city relations were marked by a *range* of shifting and transient alliances which also occurred below the level of business elites and merchants, and even outside of company boundaries. These were myriad and particular: groups allied over one cause found themselves as opponents fighting a different monopoly only a few years later.

By drawing on overlooked manuscript petitions, we can advance pre-existing studies of city and Court relations, placing those touched by monopolies at the centre of analysis. These sources allow the realities of political life in the metropolis for subjects battling the real effects of monopolies to be gleaned. There is a need to pay greater attention to the physical spaces in the metropolis where these alliances and battles occurred.[52] Petitions provide a window into these realities. The great cloth market of Blackwell Hall in London allowed the fostering of connections, whilst taverns and halls provided spaces for discussion in local settings. In London, Common Hall, attended by liverymen, saw monopolies discussed and petitions penned. Alliances were also made *beyond* the confines of the city. Chapter 5 will show the ability for clothiers from different counties to ally with powerful merchants in the Staplers' Company whilst attending a new Commission for Trade. This book reveals the range of negotiations, bargaining, and alliances between courtiers, artisans, and syndicates in a landscape dominated by underhand deals and plotting.

Throughout this book, particular attention is paid to discourse, adding an important new dimension to studies of Court and city relations. The languages in supplications provide insights into contemporaries' perceptions of political processes and the frameworks through which they interpreted and sought to negotiate monopoly policy. Powerful cries against bondage and for liberty to trade were voiced by petitioners. By paying attention to this rhetoric, otherwise obscured alliances and deals made between interest groups can also be traced. Appeals to rights, including growing ideas that occupation was akin to property, were a feature of manuscript petitions; this did not merely emerge within widespread printed petitions of the later seventeenth and eighteenth centuries.[53] Further, the rhetorical strategies employed by petitioners reveal processes of 'feedback' between petitioners' demands and broader discourses articulated in parliamentary debates and government proclamations. At times, these were tactical strategies designed to win the sympathy of authorities. Yet in other cases they show a real engagement of subjects with issues pertaining to free trade, corruption, and the law – providing an insight into their ideological beliefs. A study of the rhetoric of petitions, a method deployed by scholars including Archer, Kyle, and Holmes, reveals subjects' exposure to these ideas and, at times, their use of tactical petitioning strategies to articulate 'rival truth claims' within trading conflicts.[54]

## Petitioning and popular politics in early modern England

Petitions are recognised to have been 'ubiquitous' at all levels of English society, deployed by a range of subjects to different centres of authority including Quarter Sessions, Parliament, and the Council.[55]

Petitions involved requests to authority, though as we will see, they could easily blur the boundaries with lobbying documents, or combine supplicatory language with allegedly 'neutral' reports on trade. Petitions could relate to private or public concerns. As Elly Robson has demonstrated, even those which were seemingly centred on local issues could generate a real engagement with broader national political concerns.[56] Whilst scholarship has highlighted the centrality of petitioning in early modern society, supplicatory activity in the late Elizabethan and early Stuart period has often been overshadowed by the torrent of studies focused on the rise of the printed petition or mass supplicatory activity during and after the turmoil of the Civil Wars.[57] However, imposing an imaginary dividing line between pre-political manuscript petitions and mass-printed supplications is unhelpful. It is not the case that earlier petitions were deferential requests, with subjects employing stock phrases or humble rhetoric in suits which did not engage with larger issues of the moment.[58] Manuscript petitions scattered throughout various archives demonstrate that economic concerns pushed subjects to engage in pertinent debates occurring in the political nation, even in supplications which did not amass a huge number of signatories and which were intended for a more limited audience than their later printed counterparts. Thus, the Dyers touched directly on the nature and scope of the royal prerogative in 1605 as they battled over logwood, generating concerns with their 'seditious' and 'slanderous' supplication.

As Brodie Waddell and Jason Peacey have recently noted, pre-existing studies of the use of petitions pay insufficient attention to the perceptions held by subjects of institutions and government, of their 'political imaginaries'.[59] Addressing these concerns, this book will analyse petitions against monopolies to provide insights into subjects' perceptions of political processes and institutions, as they criticised certain bodies for not heeding their plight, or expressed their hopes that others might prove more receptive to their causes. Chapter 4 will demonstrate the ways through which glassmakers in London appealed to the House of Commons' institutional memory to paint a picture of the body as sympathetic in their fight against the monopolist Sir Robert Mansell. In so doing, petitioners contributed to larger processes whereby MPs and peers perceived Parliament as responsive to the concerns of subjects.[60] Further, the volume of petitions sent against monopolies will be shown to have given rise to institutional developments, contributing to processes of 'state-building from below'.[61] As we will see in Chapters 4 and 5, temporary and permanent commissions emerged in response to petitioning complaints and to resolve problems created by clashes in monopoly policy, giving rise to new 'points of contact' for petitioning activity.

This raises questions as to what types of subjects were engaged in these campaigns, and how far down early modern England's hierarchical social structure they extended.[62] Which subjects were touched by monopoly policy? This book explores the participation of many freemen, many of whom were members of England's 'middling sort', and who had the resources and skills to set up their own shops and to participate as citizens in corporate spaces.[63] It will also examine the petitioning of subjects in the provinces as well as those in the capital, revealing the ways monopoly triggered action across the realm. Petitions sent from wealthy merchants, including members of the Adventurers' Company, who dominated city government in the sixteenth century, are analysed alongside those sent by merchants in outports including Ipswich and Bristol, who amassed quite large personal fortunes.[64] Retailers and wholesalers were involved in this activity, including wealthy liverymen in the Grocers' Company and smaller shopkeepers in towns like Southampton.[65] Artisans and craftsmen of varying degrees engaged in monopoly debates, including glassmakers such as Isaac Bungard, who we will meet in Chapter 4, a figure who had the financial resources necessary to supply London markets with glass. We will also meet petitioning clothiers based in the West Country, many of whom employed others on a putting-out system, with the capital to purchase raw materials and to travel to London to sell their cloths. Some were powerful figures in local society and just as wealthy as local yeomanry and husbandmen.[66]

However, this book will also trace the petitioning activity and politicisation of groups below the middling sort where possible, including poorer craftsmen, journeymen, and apprentices. This includes leather dressers and glovers in the suburbs of London, who frequently complained that they did not have the finances necessary to afford rents inside the city walls. Artisan tobacco pipe-makers also protested the restrictions on their trade imposed by a new corporate body, whilst fishermen in Devon and Cornwall lamented patents to courtiers. We will meet female spinners and apprentices in Chapter 4, who attended the House of Lords to voice their monopoly concerns. Outside of London, dependent wage labourers in counties including Wiltshire and Gloucestershire left their marks to sign petitions. Spinners and weavers complained of the actions of their clothier employers and the state of their trade in documents which display a remarkable awareness of key developments and debates occurring in the realm.

The range of subjects involved in anti-monopoly petitioning activity therefore allows a fuller exploration of the practices and characteristics of

'popular politics' at the turn of the century. Attempts to chart and explore the existence of a public politics in the early modern past have led to a wealth of studies exploring the various means through which non-elite subjects were exposed to news and the myriad ways through which they could actively participate in local and national politics.[67] The early modern state has been shown to have been de-centralised, relying on local office-holding and wider participation to function.[68] This created opportunities for subjects to be directly involved in the very processes of governance. Anti-monopoly petitions will be shown to have been a feature of this participatory state. City authorities, the Council, and Crown called on subjects to provide testimony on proposed projects or economic policies, wishing to draw on their first-hand knowledge of trades and industries. Further, monopolistic commissions, patentees, and companies saw the state reach further into the lives of subjects, triggering concerns with corruption.[69] By paying closer attention to petitions produced in response to these intrusions, those that might not have had mass audiences, we can gain insights into the processes of government in early modern society and the ways through which petitions were used to negotiate the structures of economic life at a local level.

## A 'public sphere'?

Chief amongst the arguments advanced in this book is the need to re-conceptualise our understandings of the early modern 'public sphere', to understand the role and place of economic issues within it. Jürgen Habermas's oft-cited model describes the processes in the later seventeenth and eighteenth centuries by which the public began to engage in rational–critical debate in spaces free from government interference.[70] Peter Lake and Steven Pincus have argued for the existence of a 'post-Reformation' public sphere between 1530 and 1640, dominated by discussions of religion, foreign policy, and 'evil counsel'.[71] This episodic public sphere witnessed high points of discussion, mobilisation, and public 'pitch-making'. Both Puritans and Catholics made appeals to the public through printed and manuscript materials, whilst members of the Elizabethan regime were prepared to appeal to public opinion to convince the Queen to adopt certain courses of action.[72] By contrast, David Zaret has argued for the development of a public sphere with the growth of printed and 'liminal' petitions in the 1640s, documents which served to mobilise public opinion.[73]

Perhaps more helpful is Alastair Bellany's concept of a 'pre-Revolutionary public sphere', marked by the increased circulation of materials including manuscript libels in the period 1580–1620.[74] This book will show that the charged issues of monopoly and corporatism, growing in contention between 1590–1625, fostered discussion and politicisation in this pre-Revolutionary sphere. Discussions of political economy are often seen as a distinctive feature of the 'post-Revolutionary' sphere, emerging post-1688 as the development of a manufacturing state necessitated the free circulation of economic information.[75] Similarly, Michael Braddick has discussed the ways through which a shift from a demesne state to a tax state by the end of the century led to a greater discussion of fiscal measures and their impacts on subjects' liberties.[76] This book will show that discussions of economic issues were central to the pre-Revolutionary public sphere. Rupali Mishra and Anthony Milton have already revealed the capacity for companies to use print in the 1620s to appeal to public opinion.[77] More recently, Alexandra Gajda has explored the ways in which trading concerns were central to the public discussions surrounding peace with Spain following James's accession; merchants lobbied and were consulted during diplomatic negotiations.[78]

Manuscript petitions show the ways through which the monopoly issue pushed company members and even non-merchants to negotiate with authorities, and whilst not intended for a larger public audience, still witnessed the deployment of specific techniques to allow a more limited 'pitch-making' to occur. These petitions were not only intended as an exchange between subjects and authority, described by Zaret as requests which went 'up the chain of command', but will be shown to have facilitated a dialogic culture, as counter-replies and rebuttals emerged as a central aspect of monopoly disputes.[79] Whilst not shared amongst a mass of subjects, petitions were copied and sent to a limited subset of audiences, including rival companies and MPs, in ways which allowed dialogues to occur *across* groups. Thus, in the case with which we opened, it was the logwood patentees who had provided Dorset with a copy of the Dyers' petition to Salisbury, complete with a note of his response to it, to foster a presentation of them as unruly petitioners contravening his judgement. However, the Dyers utterly denied that they had received such a reply, rendering their intention to petition the Lords again as justifiable as they questioned the credibility of the copy of the petition so supplied.

The monopoly issue allows us to reflect on another key area of historical enquiry: the revisionist and post-revisionist focus on 'conflict and consensus'.[80] The following analysis certainly reveals the existence of a range of conflicts and disputes within trade, many of which provided subjects with the experience of engaging with ideas and debates which would remain pertinent post-1625: legalism, the importance of property, and the relative balance between prerogatives and liberties were topics of wider discussion before Charles's Personal Rule. London was in many ways a place fraught with tensions, as interest groups battled over how best to manage trade, and the clashes caused by the existence of older and newly bestowed patents gave rise to conflicts which spurred subjects to engage with sensitive topics such as the authority of prerogative charters. Even outside of the city, those contesting or pushing for new charters were able to express their opinions on the consequences of the deployment of state power at the local level, whilst using petitions to participate in governance. The effects of monopoly policy even allowed subjects to engage in debates on colonial trade; Misha Ewen's study of the Virginia Company has highlighted how conflicts between colonial merchants and English subjects over tobacco monopolies and regulation gave rise to petitions by subjects, which engaged heavily with discourses on customary rights to trade.[81] Monopoly policy clearly caused conflicts, yet as we shall see, contests were articulated in shared discourses. Beliefs in the necessity of corporate regulation, coined here as the 'corporate principle', remained enduring even by the close of our period, despite calls for a 'free trade' being articulated by petitioners and MPs in Parliament.[82]

By returning economic issues into analyses of political culture, we can move away from Marxist-style interpretations analysing the Civil War through the lens of class conflict, or seeing all battles in corporate spaces as driven by handicraft-master conflicts.[83] Instead, this book seeks to trace the emerging ways in which subjects saw themselves as necessary agents in the making of economic policy, and traces the role played by economic debates in fostering a participatory culture in the early Stuart period. Both Archer and Steven Rappaport have shown the importance of the participation of freemen and non-freemen in London for the maintenance of stability in the city in the sixteenth century.[84] More recently, Jordan Downs has argued that London's inclusionary politics during the Civil Wars was essential for popular mobilisation.[85] The companies acted as important spaces for this activity, housing parliamentary committees and involving themselves directly in the war effort.[86] Anti-monopoly petitioning activity provides another lens through which to see the importance of a growing participatory culture in the city and in companies: petitions abounded, news on trade was spread, and networks were fostered, all of which set important groundwork for the processes which were fundamental to later mobilisation. The government's reaction to this process, much like its response to the Dyers, was often contradictory. Spaces were created facilitating petitioning, and discussion of matters of the economy was far more readily accepted than debate on religion or foreign policy. Petitions were welcomed by authority, but at times, petitioners could overstep the contested line demarcating acceptable behaviour from seditious actions, leading to punishment and rebuke.

This book borrows from the approaches of 'new social history' which has shown overlap between local social conflicts, customs, and economic cultures.[87] The politics of trade can be studied to provide insights into the ways in which seemingly narrow conflicts in industry gave rise to an engagement with ideological issues, overlapping with the broader public sphere. In some cases, this paved the way for groups to mobilise with the later onset of the Civil Wars. As Chapter 5 will reveal, this period saw the acceleration of the development of a more coherent national consciousness amongst clothiers, a group who would later be key to the parliamentary cause.[88] Through a study of these issues, this book aims to move post-revisionism forward. Lake and Peacey have argued for the need for historians to do so by looking to the practices and processes shaping political culture.[89] Analysis of the disputes generated by corporatism and monopoly allows a more effective insight into the developing participatory political and economic cultures of a range of freemen and subjects including clothiers, starchmakers, and glassmakers. The period 1590–1625, falling as it does in the age of the pre-Revolutionary public sphere and the era of incorporation, provides a particularly important moment to analyse the tensions generated by the expansion of monopoly policy. This is not to say that the contests generated by monopoly ended on Charles's accession, yet these were to evolve in character and nature as the Personal Rule transformed the political and economic landscape.[90]

## Sources and structure

The following analysis is based on an extensive use of archival sources, including manuscript petitions, company Court orders, and wardens' accounts. Most are contained within the records of individual livery companies and the records of the Corporation of London, the State Papers, the Cecil Papers, and the Parliamentary Archives. To uncover the mechanics of petitioning activity and to allow campaigns to be followed in their various stages, the case studies chosen are traced through the archives. Payments for scribes and lawyers can be found in account books, whilst correspondence between the Crown and localities allows us to uncover the importance of local authorities as intermediaries for petitioning activity. Underexamined personal collections by prominent MPs including Sir Robert Phelips and Sir Thomas Jervoise are also drawn upon, which provide insight into both parliamentary petitioning practices and, in the papers of the latter, the local political activity of clothworkers.

This book is organised both thematically and chronologically. Chapter 1 begins with an overview of the issues of corporatism and monopoly, assessing the ideological, constitutional, and economic issues raised by their use, and considering how these topics triggered petitioning activity outside of London. Attempts by clothworkers to form new corporations in Ipswich and Bury St Edmunds reveal the ways in which the age of incorporation provided opportunities for subjects, whilst the petitioning opposition provoked reveals the local conflicts generated by monopoly policy. Even in counties far removed from London, petitions were penned for the establishment of new corporations, and these could be met with resistance.

Subsequent chapters are each focused on specific anti-monopoly petitioning campaigns, examining different companies, contexts, and chronologies. They analyse petitions sent to different authorities, including the city and Crown, the Council, Parliament, and new commissions. Taken together, they allow an analysis of changes and continuities in this activity between 1590 and 1625, whilst each also provides detailed studies of campaigns. This approach allows attention to be paid to the discourses, processes, mechanisms, and outcomes of petitioning activity. A close analysis allows a fuller understanding of the complexities of specific industrial disputes and the actors involved and shines a light on the politics behind the organisation of petitioning protest.

Chapter 2 begins in the 1590s, during Elizabeth's era of scandalous monopolies, focusing on petitions sent to the Corporation of London and the Crown in this period of socio-economic tension. Companies reached for new patents and charters, generating concern in the city, whilst subjects from a range of trades were invited to comment on proposed patents through investigative commissions appointed by the city and Crown. Particularly contentious was a patent granted to the courtier Sir Edward Darcy for the searching and sealing of leather which prompted collective petitioning agitation from the Skinners' and Leathersellers' Companies. This campaign allows a reflection of the tactics deployed by petitioners in the fraught context of the 1590s, culminating in Elizabeth's issuing of her famous 'Golden Speech' in her final Parliament of 1601.

Chapter 3 moves forward in time to look to the early years of James's reign and petitions sent to the new King. Charters were granted to artisans and to profit-seeking syndicates hoping to benefit from the development of new trades. James began his reign with the public announcement that monopolies were a thing of the past, issuing a proclamation that would subsequently be used by different interest groups as they attempted to present their goals as linked to the new King's economic agenda. At the same time, older corporate bodies found themselves affected by new patents which conflicted with their rights in trade. The Grocers' Company were one such body, moving to petition against the incorporation of a Starchmakers' Company in 1608. Analysis of this campaign reveals the ways through which petitioners could play on the blurred distinction between legitimate company and dubious monopoly as they attempted to protect their own interests.

The final two chapters, focused on the later Jacobean period, examine petitions sent to two different institutions. Chapter 4 considers petitions to Parliament, focusing especially on James's final two Parliaments in 1621 and 1624. Whilst the prominence of anti-monopoly debates in both sessions has been noted, a torrent of manuscript petitions existent in MPs' collections and the Parliamentary Archives allow an analysis of the ways through which petitioners approached and even perceived Parliament as they referred their disputes to this great court of justice. Subjects from across the realm sent their anti-monopoly petitions, and attendance at committees drew a wide remit of subjects to the institution. As such, the process of petitioning Parliament served to foster politicisation. This chapter will also demonstrate the ways through which glassmakers approached the Commons in their effort to fight a key monopolist, Sir Robert Mansell. Their supplications appealed to the memory of past parliamentary decisions as they crafted a narrative designed to persuade MPs to support their plight at a time when its own institutional memory was developing.

Finally, Chapter 5 focuses on petitioning activity in the 1620s, primarily by participants in England's most important industry, the cloth trade. England was experiencing an economic depression and the need to find remedies for the crisis led to the discussion of its causes and potential solutions in Parliament and Council commissions. Petitions complaining of distress from clothing counties articulated anti-monopoly sentiments, blaming the realm's economic woes on the monopolistic control of the Adventurers' Company. In turn, these petitions gave rise to new institutions designed to receive petitions: the temporary and permanent Commissions for Trade. These commissions marked an important stage in economic policy, whilst the petitions sent to them would have a decisive effect on the attitude of Parliament and the Crown to the Adventurers' privileges. Wealthier clothiers and poorer spinners and fullers petitioned. In this context, a united and national industrial interest began to emerge.

Through an analysis of these lively and richly documented campaigns, the centrality of economic debates and issues in the politics of the period can be gauged. For now, it is necessary to turn to the main issues driving these debates and contests: corporatism and monopoly.

## Notes

1 CP 190/141, fo. 141r.

2 Thirsk, *Policy and Projects*; W. H. Price, *The English Patents of Monopoly* (London, 1906).

3 *CD 1621*, vii, p. 404.

4 *Ibid.*, pp. 132–3. The revenue-raising potential of the project was directly commented on by Lord Chief Justice Popham, see CP 106/68, fo. 68r.
5 CP Petitions 2090.
6 CP 190/141, fo. 141r.
7 *Ibid.*
8 C 66/1677, *CPR 3–5 Jas*, fo. 197r; *CD 1621*, vii, p. 405.
9 PA, Main Papers, Supplementary: James I, HL/PO/JO/10/13/9, fos 111–12.
10 *CD 1621*, vii, pp. 132–9, 156–64, 405–10.
11 J. P. Sommerville, *Royalists and Patriots: Politics and Ideology in England, 1603–1640*, 2nd edn (Oxford, 2014); A. Bellany, *The Politics of Court Scandal in Early Modern England: News Culture and the Overbury Affair, 1603–1660* (Cambridge, 2002); R. Cust and A. Hughes (eds), *Conflict in Early Stuart England: Studies in Religion and Politics, 1603–1642* (London, 1989).
12 Thirsk, *Policy and Projects*, p. 51.
13 Some analysis of particular campaigns has occurred, see Archer, 'London Lobbies'; N. Tyacke, 'Collective Biography and the Interpretative Challenge of Early-Stuart Parliamentary History', *Parliamentary History*, 32:3 (2013), p. 547; M. Ewen, *The Virginia Venture: American Colonization and English Society, 1580–1660* (Philadelphia, 2022), ch. 5.
14 J. Thirsk, 'Projects for Gentlemen, Jobs for the Poor: Mutual Aid in the Vale of Tewkesbury, 1600–1630', in J. Thirsk (ed.), *The Rural Economy of England: Collected Essays* (London, 1984), pp. 286–8.
15 Ashton, 'Conflicts'.
16 D. H. Sacks, 'Private Profit and Public Good: The Problem of the State in Elizabethan Theory and Practice', in G. J. Schochet (ed.), *Law, Literature, and the Settlement of Regimes: Papers presented at the Folger Institute Seminar 'Political Thought in the Elizabethan Age, 1558–1603'* (Washington, 1990), pp. 121–42; C. Russell, *Parliaments and English Politics, 1621–1629* (Oxford, 1979); Brenner, *Merchants*; Ashton, *City;* J. Peacey, 'Print and Public Politics in Seventeenth-Century England', *History Compass*, 5:1 (2007), pp. 85–111.
17 J. Cramsie, *Kingship and Crown Finance under James VI and I, 1603–1625* (Suffolk, 2002); L. L. Peck, *Court Patronage and Corruption in Early Stuart England* (London, 1991), ch. 6; Thirsk, *Policy and Projects.*
18 C. Holmes, 'Parliament, Liberty, Taxation, and Property', in J. H. Hexter (ed.), *Parliament and Liberty: From the Reign of Elizabeth to the English Civil War* (Stanford, 1992), p. 129.
19 H. G. Fox, *Monopolies and Patents: A Study of the History and Future of the Patent Monopoly* (Toronto, 1947), pp. 62–5.
20 Thirsk, *Policy and Projects*, pt. 1, ch. 4.
21 TNA, SP 46/26, fo. 148.
22 BL, Lans. MS 74; BL, Add. MS 10038; BL, Lans. MS 162.
23 BL, Add. MS 10038, fos 19r–22v.
24 D. Seaborne Davies, 'Further Light on the Case of Monopolies', *Law Quarterly Review*, 48:3 (1932), pp. 394–414; Russell, *Parliaments*; R. Zaller, *The Parliament of 1621: A Study in Constitutional Conflict* (Berkeley, 1971);

some to see the Company as attempting to restrict the export of white cloths to their mart town in Middelburg, and to a broader questioning of the need for corporate organisation in the industry, emboldening interlopers to pen a bill for free trade.[55] As we will see, regulated companies for domestic trade were also caught up in these tensions surrounding monopoly and free trade.

The importance of charters in linking bodies to the government via the royal prerogative explains the determination of many groups to seek them.[56] As Rupali Mishra has demonstrated, companies could claim to be state agents, using prerogative-bestowed charters to authorise their actions and providing the Crown with loans, although the relationship between Crown and company was one marked by negotiation.[57] Stern has shown that companies acted as 'company-states', as one of many overlapping bodies exercising their own sovereign authority in early modern England's decentralised state.[58] Charters bound their members into an 'artificial person' capable of holding land, being sued, and penning their own ordinances and regulations to govern.[59] The charter, often drawn up and displayed in company halls, was material proof of their authority. However, it could be subject to different and changing interpretations as a 'living document'; as clashes between chartered rights occurred in this period, varying perspectives on the meaning of patents became a key feature of petitioning disputes.[60]

Usually, charters were bestowed by the Crown, and groups could seek parliamentary confirmation of their grants. However, some groups appealed directly to Parliament for incorporation.[61] For example, the Cutlers' Company of Sheffield introduced an act for incorporation in Parliament in 1621.[62] They already had ordinances for the regulation of their craft, approved by the local Earls of Shrewsbury, yet this act expressed concern that these had been ignored by subjects who were without 'any Rule or Gouerment'.[63] The act expressed hope that incorporation would enable the number of apprenticeships to be controlled, whilst ensuring that knives and instruments were sealed with marks to attest to their quality.[64] Throughout the act, appeals were made for privileges to be bestowed 'by the Authority of this p[re]sent p[ar]liam[en]t'.[65] By 1624, they were successful.[66] Richard Hoyle notes that their decision to appeal to Parliament, rather than seek letters patent, may have been a strategic move, following the example of other groups who had similarly appealed to MPs and peers to alleviate problems in trade through statutory regulations.[67]

The Cutlers were not the only group to seek charters through Parliament; the Norwich Dornick weavers introduced acts for incorporation in 1621 and 1624.[68] At times, officials seem to have encouraged groups to approach Parliament. In 1621 and 1624, glovers and leather dressers residing within five miles of London introduced bills in the Lords for incorporation, hoping to separate from the Leathersellers' Company. They had previously petitioned James, but Lord Chancellor Ellesmere and the Lord Treasurer had certified that 'they thought their Request fit for the Parliament'.[69] Their act combined their request for incorporation with a desire for a more rigorous enforcement of statutes against forestalling and the making of pelts, as a necessary precursor for undermining the influence of leathersellers who were accused of dominating supplies.[70] In this case, appeals for incorporation were channelled through Parliament, likely because this issue touched so closely on pre-existing statutory regulations. Despite this, the Lords were reluctant to proceed without any 'Reference from the King'.[71] Clearly, incorporation through Parliament was attempted in this era of corporatism as groups sometimes sought privileges through the authority of statute. Ultimately however, it was the royal prerogative which was essential for bestowing so many with the authority necessary to create body politics to govern trades and industries.

## Contested boundaries: monopoly body v. legitimate institution

As a form of fiscal policy so intimately tied to the royal prerogative, charters and patents raised constitutional concerns. Crown and subjects generally spoke of the English constitution as consisting of a harmony and balance between the monarch's prerogative powers and the liberties of subjects, upheld by the central bulwark of the constitution – the common law.[72] The monarch was seen to possess both an ordinary prerogative, to be exercised through the common law, and an absolute prerogative to act in areas where the common law had less force or application, for example, in the sphere of international politics.[73] In the late Elizabethan and early Stuart periods, the range of extra-parliamentary revenue-raising devices used in peace time, including monopolies and impositions, triggered debates surrounding the scope of the prerogative and its relationship to liberties and property.[74]

These revenue-raising devices, granted outside of Parliament and without the consent of subjects, were perceived as an affront to liberties. In Elizabeth's final Parliament of 1601, MPs presented monopolies as an infringement on the property of her subjects, reducing them to a state of bondage.[75] Perhaps most famously, the case of the Levant merchant and grocer John Bate (1606) saw a forceful invocation of liberties, as Bate refused to pay the imposition on imported currants as a form of taxation without consent. Despite receiving support in the Commons, the judges found in favour of the Crown, arguing that the right to levy impositions was an essential aspect of the royal prerogative.[76]

Free trade debates in James's first Parliament also saw objections voiced to monopolies based on issues of 'natural right'. Those arguing for the free trade bill in committee expressed the argument that 'all free subjects are born inheritable to their Lands, so also to the free Exercise of their Industry in those trades, whereto they apply themselves and whereby they are to live'.[77] To deprive men of the right to merchandise was thus against the natural right of subjects. Similarly, many patentees were charged with collecting new fees or fines for such processes as searching goods for quality. This led subjects to protest that illegal impositions were being introduced on trade. As we will see, this generated an early expression of the need to defend trade and property from illegal exactions, sentiments which would be key to later pre-Civil War contests surrounding such devices as the Forced Loan and Ship Money.

Monopolies were also opposed through references to divine law. Within Elizabethan Parliaments, MPs objected to them on the grounds that they interfered with the God-given right of all men to exercise their labours.[78] For Nicholas Tyacke, this was part of a Puritan mode of politics, with influential radicals including the lawyer Nicholas Fuller emerging as vocal opponents of monopolies in Elizabeth and James's reigns.[79] As Puritans moved to criticise what they perceived to be illegal practices in the prerogative court of High Commission, particularly surrounding the enforced use of the oath *ex officio*, arguments pertaining to the subversion of Christian liberties and the undue extension of the royal prerogative became an important feature of discourse.[80] This fusion between religious and constitutional ideas from the 1580s would soon encompass economic concerns, as fiscal policies including impositions, wardship, and monopolies were attacked as encroachments on subjects' common law rights and as contrary to the law of God. As Christopher Brooks has argued, questions surrounding liberties were, for most subjects, intimately connected to economic issues.[81] Consequently, it is important to examine the monopolies issue as a pressing point in which constitutional and economic grievances combined. These languages, which have been extensively studied in their parliamentary context, were not merely articulated in the House of Commons. As petitioners from myriad social groups expressed disdain for specific monopolies or charters, they too engaged with broader issues of political and constitutional import, combining calls for liberties with a strong invocation of their common law rights.

Patents and monopolies also generated protest due to their practical effects, emerging as a more pressing social concern across the realm as their number and scope expanded. Patents for the sole production or sale of specific goods forced many subjects out of their life-long trades or required them to pay for licences from patentees for permission to continue them. Patentees and their deputies had extensive powers to search houses, workshops, and warehouses for goods produced or sold contrary to their patents, with authority to seize goods and fine offenders, sometimes acting violently.[82]

Even those subjects who were not directly involved in these trades could suffer from the effects of monopolies; they could cause increased prices and a decline in the quality of goods. These practical effects were seen to discern a legitimate corporate body or regulatory office from an odious patent. In 1586, an anonymous projector called for Elizabeth to grant a new charter to a company for the making of paper. They informed the Queen that 'the same is not monopoly', as this institution would provide employment for the realm's subjects.[83] It would thus serve the public good, and not reduce trade into the hands of one man only.

The boundaries between legitimate corporation and monopolistic institution were hazy, partly because, as Gadd and Wallis argue, the guild and monopoly system 'overlapped'.[84] Writing to Lord Chief Justice Popham on 8 September 1605, Salisbury grappled with the tensions raised by proposals for new merchant companies and the organisation of trade to France and the Levant. Specifically, he responded to petitions by merchants protesting plans for the incorporation of regulated companies to organise these trades. Salisbury stressed that any proposals for the trades needed to ensure that there was no 'iniurious Exclusion' of merchants.[85] Only this would ensure that there was 'noe wronge done to the Libertye of any other subiect'.[86] Imposing reasonable entry fines would allow merchants to join overseas companies, preventing any infringement on their rights to trade and helping to avoid the formation of monopolistic institutions. Popham in his reply was more pessimistic. For him, it did not matter what pretences merchants made when asking to be incorporated. Usually, their main desire was 'their privat[e] end[e]s'.[87] In a postscript, he advised that the best way to discern these motives was to request the merchants to set down the ways in which they planned to order trade. Only then would it become obvious 'what they earne in yt'.[88] Throughout the Jacobean period, demands for the establishment of a 'free trade' were increasingly articulated by subjects through petitions and by MPs in Parliament.[89] Yet often subjects were articulating a desire for the membership of merchant companies to be made more open, rather than expressing beliefs in the need for a laissez-faire trading system, or for the abolition of all such institutions.[90] As Astrid Friis has argued, even in Parliament there appears to have been a hazy sense of what could be properly termed a monopoly; in turn, petitions became important spaces where these distinctions were contested and negotiated, as subjects used the accusation to discredit opponents whilst presenting themselves as members of legitimate bodies.[91]

The evidence of legal cases provides further insight into the ways in which this distinction was negotiated, and specific by-laws of companies could allow them to overstep these boundaries.[92] In 1621 the Leathersellers' Company, opposing the incorporation of the glovers and leather dressers described above, suggested that it was 'daungerous' to create a new corporation, given that it was 'easy to build a Monopolie upon such a foundation, by the helpe of some by lawes & ordinances, amongest themselves'.[93] This period witnessed important legal cases investigating by-laws, indicative of the charged nature of this issue. As David Chan Smith has argued, the growth of corporations as forms of government for trade, as opposed to merely fictional entities, led to numerous cases questioning the extent to which they served the public good.[94] Subjects resorted to litigation to challenge what they perceived as monopoly, and judges were required to scrutinise and rule on how they could be determined in the law. Many of these cases dealt explicitly with infringements on the rights of subjects to trade, the issue which underpinned this distinction.

In 1582, the London Joiners' Company found themselves before the courts on account of by-laws which allowed them to search and forfeit the goods of joiners who were not members of their Company within the city.[95] Popham presented this as an infringement on subjects' rights, citing Chapter 29 of Magna Carta and the rights of all freeborn Englishmen to the laws of the realm. The Joiners could not 'prohibit any man from occupying this trade…for it might be advantageous to them to allow only a small number'.[96] This was in effect the first step towards creating a monopoly. In his defence of the Company, London's recorder William Fleetwood turned to the familiar ideas of good order and government. Such ordinances were intended only to allow 'a decent order and necessary government, and to avoid deceits in work'.[97] They were thus not an attempt to monopolise trade, but merely tended to the 'benefit of the people, and the public weal'.[98]

Similar ideas were explored in the case of *Davenant v. Hurdys* (1599). The London Merchant Taylors' Company found themselves subject to scrutiny before King's Bench. The cause of the complaint issued against them by one Edward Davenant was a by-law issued in 1575 which required each member to ensure that half of the cloths they put out to be dressed were given to other members to work.[99] Coke objected to this as a direct infringement of members' rights to decide for themselves who to put out their cloths to, which deprived other clothworkers of work.[100] Whilst the final judgement reached in the Joiners' case is unknown, the Merchant Taylors' ordinance was adjudged as void.

Patents granted to individuals also triggered legal investigation and saw the question of monopoly discussed. In 1596, a patent was awarded to the Groom of the Chamber Sir Edward Darcy for the sole making and selling of playing cards, with a licence allowing him the sole import of the same. This controversial patent was challenged by the Haberdasher Thomas Allen in the case of *Darcy v. Allen* (1602) on the grounds that the custom of London allowed any freeman to practise any trade in the city.[101] The patent was adjudged a monopoly in a case which defined some of the key features which helped contemporaries to distinguish legitimate patent from monopolistic grant moving forward.[102] Rather than serve the public good, this patent increased the price of cards and lessened their quality. Cardmaking was defended as a legitimate and ancient trade, which had employed many throughout the realm. By restricting the same, the patent deprived men of their industries. Contemporaries might approve of patents for new inventions or industrial processes, but they were critical of those which granted control of a pre-existing and widespread industry into a 'fewe mens handes', thus depriving other subjects of their goods.[103] Strikingly, Darcy's defence expressed a concern that the ill-defined term monopoly was but a 'hatefull name of late more comonly vsed then heretofore by manie that knowe not the trewe vnderstanding of the Worde'.[104] Even contemporaries were aware that the precise meaning of 'monopoly' could be contested, and that the term itself was increasingly loaded.

Legal cases focused not only on companies and specific patents in London, but also investigated the ordinances of guilds throughout the realm. Cries of monopoly were heard beyond the city, sometimes against pre-existing institutions. Guilds and merchant companies in towns could possess monopoly rights over trade, translating to a dominance in their town, and this could lead to protests which were articulated within the courts.[105] In 1615, a case was heard in King's Bench against the Tailors' and Clothworkers' Company of Ipswich. One William Sheninge brought a complaint against an ordinance of the Company which ordered that no one could practise the tailoring trade unless they had presented themselves before the Company and had proved that they had served an apprenticeship of at least seven years.[106] Sheninge was fined by the Company for tailoring in Ipswich without their permission. The judges found in favour of the complainant. In his later reports, Coke noted that this ordinance led to the 'oppression of young tradesmen, by the rich and old of the same trade', who aimed to interfere with their rights to trade.[107] Coke thus drew a distinction between those ordinances of companies which were 'against the common law, and the commonwealth', and those which were 'for the good order and government of men of trades and mysteries'.[108] However, discerning what amounted to a by-law intended purely for good order and one which was intended to restrict trade could prove problematic, especially as companies could use this widespread rhetoric of order and regulation to defend restrictive by-laws.

In 1617, a similar protest was launched against the Weavers' Company of Newbury. In this age of incorporation, the Company received a charter directly from Elizabeth in 1601.[109] A proviso within it ordered that no subject was to weave in the town before being admitted by the Company, a similar restriction as that questioned in Ipswich.[110] The Company issued an ordinance barring any from practising the trade unless they had been an apprentice in the town and had exercised the trade for five years prior to the passing of this ordinance.[111] In 1617 a complaint was brought against the Company by one Staps, who had been weaving in Newbury for five months without having served an apprenticeship and without the Company's licence. The judges ultimately found in his favour. The ordinances of the Company were found to be unacceptable; technically they excluded all who had been apprenticed to the trade since the ordinance passed, as they could not have been weaving for five years prior to its passing.[112] Sir Henry Hobart, Chief Justice of Common Pleas, produced a report on the case which repeated ideas that acceptable by-laws needed to be 'subject to the general law of the realm', whilst questioning the ability of new corporations such as this to make ordinances which served to 'exclude all persons to use an art or trade in their town'.[113] The case of the Tailors of Ipswich was directly cited in this judgement.

## Local charters and petitioning protest

It was not only through legal cases that charges of monopoly were articulated. Not all subjects had the monetary resources to launch expensive legal proceedings against companies in the courts as previously described. Whilst petitioning incurred expenses, including for the scribes necessary to pen suits, this was likely a more accessible means for many to articulate their monopoly grievances to authorities. This occurred throughout the realm. As Ewen has shown, tobacco farmers in Gloucestershire resorted to petitioning and even rioting to protest the intrusion on their trade by the Virginia Company in the early Stuart period.[114]

Across numerous trades, supplicants drew explicitly on arguments pertaining to liberty, commonwealth, and good order as they protested patents which were genuinely perceived as intrusive monopolies and as they challenged those which threatened their own dominant hold on trade. In towns across the country, subjects had the opportunity to hear arguments against monopolies, informing their protests. In both 1601 and 1621, Elizabeth and James issued proclamations which attacked specific monopoly grants, promising subjects that these would be reviewed by the common law and fostering the impression that both abhorred monopolists.[115] In 1601, Elizabeth delivered the so-called 'Golden Speech' to MPs in Parliament in which she attacked those courtiers around her who had misled her into granting monopolies, damaging the health of the wider commonwealth.[116] This speech would be printed, sharing these lamentations more broadly.[117] MPs in late-Elizabethan and Jacobean parliaments had heated debates on monopolies as they sought to represent the grievances of their constituents from throughout the realm, articulating anti-monopoly rhetoric which could be shared and absorbed, especially given the increase in the volume of parliamentary news in circulation and the sheer accessibility of Parliament in the early seventeenth century.[118] In more local settings, Assize Courts offered the opportunity for disdain against monopolists to be aired and heard. In 1606, Coke delivered a speech at the Norfolk Assizes, attacking monopolists and projectors in the realm who served

> To anoy and hinder the whole *Publicke Weale* for his owne priuat benefit: In which course he so well thriueth, as that by toyling some short time, either in *Starch, Vineger,* or *Aquavitæ*, he doth in the end thereby purchase to himselfe an absolute beggerie[.][119]

The language of protest against monopolists was powerful and articulated through numerous media, which increasingly included libels, satire, and woodcut illustrations.[120] These discourses would similarly be expressed within petitioning protests, as subjects sought the aid of the Privy Council, Parliament, and the Crown against monopolists and industrial rivals.

Larger town corporations and pre-existent livery companies emerged as petitioners against newly chartered companies. In the early seventeenth century, new companies were formed to govern one industry in particular: the cloth trade.[121] Broader changes in the industry and its enduring importance as a key source of employment likely account for the dominance of this industry in experiments for company organisation. For example, the growth of new and lighter cloths known collectively as the new draperies led to efforts to create new corporate bodies, as clothworkers called for regulation of this flourishing industry.[122] Spurred on by the spate of new charters being issued throughout the realm, subjects moved to create new, or to strengthen pre-existing, companies for the cloth trade.[123] In Reading in 1606, the borough corporation read out orders in their Guildhall prohibiting a recently established Weavers' Company from exercising their charter.[124] This had been bestowed on the Company by the King himself, but it appears as if a legal decision had seen the charter declared invalid. Two better-documented cases from early seventeenth-century Suffolk attest to these issues: the creation of a new Company of clothiers and clothworkers in Bury St Edmunds in 1609 and Ipswich's Tailors' and Clothworkers' Company, incorporated in 1606.[125]

The cloth trade was integral to Suffolk. Broadcloths and kerseys were produced in the countryside and exported through the town of Ipswich, and the county also served as an important space for the spinning of yarn and combing of wool.[126] In Ipswich, cloths were not only exported but also finished and dressed.[127] Bury was also an important centre for the trade, and in 1606 the borough had finally secured a charter of incorporation through the endeavours of its middling sort of subjects.[128] By 1607, they had established strict ordinances to regulate the industry which allowed the aldermen and burgesses to appoint six overseers, two weavers, two shearmen, and two clothiers to search cloths and to apply seals to attest to their quality.[129]

On 1 April 1609, the Company of Clothiers, Clothworkers, Woollen Weavers, and Tailors of Bury St Edmunds received a royal charter.[130] This had been granted upon the 'humble petic[i]on' of clothiers, clothworkers, tailors, and weavers in the town who had expressed concern with the poor workmanship and myriad abuses hindering their trade.[131] The incorporation was presented as a means to ensure regulation, and the language of the charter was saturated in appeals to order. George Unwin has argued that the creation of such institutions in towns was often driven by drapers and clothiers, 'local capitalists' seeking to dominate and organise trade through the towns, coming into conflict with town authorities and merchants who disliked these restrictions on trades.[132] However, in this case, officials of the town and some of those tradesmen involved in the incorporation of the larger borough in 1606 participated in this new corporate enterprise.[133] The Company had two masters, two wardens, and twenty associates. The first two masters were George Boldero and George Fysson, a clothier and a tailor, and the wardens chosen were the weaver Edward White and a clothier named Edmund Hynorde, both freemen.[134] In the borough charter, Baldero was named as one of twelve capital burgesses and described as a gentleman, and had also paid towards the costs of the 1606 charter.[135] Edward White was also elected as one of the twenty-four burgesses of the common council.[136] The new clothing Company was established by freemen who were part of the town's ruling body, possibly joining with other clothiers and clothworkers to create a new and powerful corporation.

The charter established wide-ranging powers for the Company. All who had served apprenticeships to these trades in Bury and its surrounding liberties were incorporated as 'one body Corporate' with the power to hold property, to sue and be sued, and to hold a common seal.[137] The government of the Company was to consist of representatives from each section of the trade. The twenty associates from these 'artes trades or Misteries' were appointed 'for the better governmente rule & direcc[i]ons' of the trade.[138] Such a large governing body suggests that this institution was intended to prevent any one subsection of the industry from dominating the internal politics of the Company. The new Company was given authority to regulate the cloth trade in both Bury and its extensive surrounding liberties.[139] It had the right to search and survey the work of everyone practising these trades, and to take fines and penalties from any producing deceitful wares.[140]

Annotations on the draft charter note that Coke had penned provisos onto a copy delivered to the Attorney General. This included the requirement that none be free of the Company unless they were free of the town corporation and that no additions be prejudicial to Bury's charter.[141] This was ultimately in line with what Barbara Malament has demonstrated was a continued desire by Coke to uphold frameworks of regulation despite his dislike of monopolies which infringed on subjects' liberties.[142] Clearly, the desire to prevent any clashes between the town and the Company overrode concerns that non-freemen might be excluded.

Crucially, the leaders of the Company also moved to petition Lord Chancellor Ellesmere, Sir Thomas Fleming, Chief Justice of King's Bench, and Coke, now Chief Justice of Common Pleas. On 28 August, they sent them seventy-two ordinances for the new Company.[143] Boldero, Fysson, Heinard, and White sought the judges' approval of the extensive ordinances designed for their 'better Rule & gov[er]m[en]t', citing an act of Henry VII's reign which required company ordinances to be reviewed by judges.[144] The ordinances were subsequently approved. Clearly, these men had moved to ensure that their new corporation had satisfied all necessary conditions to be recognised as a credible institution with approval from some of the realm's most important officials. The ordinances do suggest that the petitioners' desire to regulate trade was important to this corporate experiment. They included extensive rules to safeguard the interests of apprentices, wage-labouring weavers, and clothier employers, and to ensure that all cloth adhered to statutory regulations.

Alongside such regulations stood ordinances which allowed the Company more questionable powers. Among these was the power to tax all and every person using the trades of clothworking, weaving, and tailoring in the town and its liberties 'for any reasonable Cause or matter whatsoev[er]', including for any sums necessary for the service of the King or for the affairs of the Company.[145] This included the power to charge for the expenses incurred for obtaining this charter and the approval of the ordinances. The authority to assess subjects for these charges resided in the master, wardens, and associates. Even subjects who might not have wanted this charter could thus be forced to pay towards it. Further, in an ordinance similar to many monopolistic by-laws, it was ordered that no one should practise these trades until they had presented themselves before the master and wardens, and made proof of their apprenticeship.[146] Towards the end of their ordinances, the Company also established rules for punishing disobedient members, including any who sought to utter any 'Contemptuous or Contumelious wordes against his Ma[jes]t[ie]s Ch[art]re to them graunted'.[147]

The new Company had clearly expected that protest might be made against them. Beyond just protesting through mere 'wordes', some within the county moved to petition. Surviving in the Suffolk archives is an undated supplication addressed from subjects who claimed to be engaged in the trades of clothworking, weaving, and tailoring in the town and its liberties.[148] Whilst the document is unsigned, the petitioners articulated numerous complaints surrounding the effects of this incorporation on those practising the trade within the surrounding Hundreds, suggesting that it was cloth interests residing outside of the town who moved to protest the establishment of this new, monopolising body. Membership was restricted to freemen and this may have been a source of controversy for those without freeman status. It is also possible that disgruntled and excluded councillors in the town's government may have joined the campaign, moving against brethren such as Boldero.

The petitioners tried to undermine the legitimacy of the corporation by attacking the means through which it had been requested. They began their supplication by claiming

> That the said sute & Petic[i]on for the haveing of the said Corporac[i]on was preferred and prosecuted, and the Corporac[i]on aforesaid obteyned by some few men of those trades and they also of the meaner sort withowt the privety or Consent of the greater nombre of those which are of the Trades[.][149]

By presenting those who had sought this incorporation as the 'meaner sort', the petitioners questioned the legitimacy of this institution by painting its procurers as base men who had acted without the approval of those subjects practising the trade 'within the said Hundred[e]s'.[150] They failed to comment on the role played by gentlemen such as Baldero. Their petition requesting the incorporation was presented as lacking real legitimacy. Whilst it might have claimed to have been sent with the consent of clothworkers, weavers, and tailors throughout the county, this was but a falsehood. Instead, those who opposed the charter were by 'farr the greatest nomber of People vsing those Trades'.[151] It was thus a dubious body which had been granted under false pretences.

The petitioners proceeded to paint themselves as oppressed subjects, facing new restrictions and interferences in their trade. The corporation was not a legitimate body, but established by 'a very small Company' merely seeking their own gains.[152] As such, its governors sought to impose 'uniust Taxac[i]ons and Imposic[i]ons' on trade, taking money from the petitioners, the 'poorest sort' in the town and Hundreds.[153] This took the form of not only membership fees to join the Company (which stood at 3s. 4d.) but repeated exactions once subjects had joined, including fines if they refused to appear before the Company court at Bury when summoned. The ordinances attest to the wide-ranging powers of the Company to issue fines, including 12d. for the first failure to appear before the court and 2s. for the second.[154] Engaging with the language of slavery and bondage, the petitioners described this as a 'servitude', the like of which was not seen elsewhere in the realm.[155] Finally, the petitioners proceeded to paint this as a monopolistic institution. They claimed that the Company sought 'to suppresse others which will not submitt themself[e]s vnto their governement & to put them from vseing their honest Trades'.[156] They thus ended their appeal by stressing their desire to see this Company's charter revoked.

This petition offers but one example of the antagonisms and divisions which could be created by the establishment of new corporate bodies, especially those which could be painted as monopolistic institutions. Those protesting against the Company were successfully able to present it as a combination of a small number of men, seeking their own private gains. Attacking the legitimacy of their petition to request incorporation was one way in which the petitioners undermined the validity of this new body, using a tactic which we will see repeated throughout the period. Indeed, in this case, it appears that the petitioners were successful. No more is heard of this Company in Bury.[157] In an era where the granting of charters proliferated, weavers, clothiers, and tailors in the town, led by some notable town officials, embraced the opportunity to gain for themselves a form of monopoly over local industry, though their efforts failed in the face of determined petitioning opposition.

A similar set of events occurred in Ipswich. As we have seen, the Ipswich Tailors' and Clothworkers' Company had come under fire in the courts in 1615, yet it still appears to have remained in existence.[158] The Company had been incorporated in 1606, receiving a royal charter much like the Newbury weavers and the Bury clothworkers.[159] On 4 February 1620, two petitions were sent to the Council, one subscribed with the names of twenty-two merchants and another with the names of thirty-seven clothiers.[160] The merchants' petition expressed concern that the Company had detrimentally affected the quality of cloth dressing in the town, hindering their ability to sell it.[161] It was signed by merchants of the Eastland trade who exported cloths to Elbing. This included members of the prominent mercantile Cutler family. Roger Cutler, a merchant and burgess whose accounts survive for the years 1622–23, was one of the signers, as were his brothers and relations Robert, Samuel, and Benjamin.[162] The petition was signed by the Eastland merchant Robert Snelling, an MP in 1621, and Robert Knappe, an associate of Roger Cutler who exported 206 cloths to Elbing in 1623.[163] Other Eastland merchants such as Robert Gypps, Thomas Seely, and Matthew Brownrig also signed.[164]

In their petition, the merchants complained of the effects this Company had on the trade of cloth dressing, which had recently been 'soe much impayred and badly p[er]formed'.[165] The merchants' request was simple:

that the Council revoke the charter, leaving the government of the trade to the wider town. Here then was a clear case in which the issue of who governed trade, the Company or the wider town corporation, was at the centre of dispute.[166] Playing on the Council's fear of widespread unemployment in the cloth industry, the merchants suggested that they would only continue to purchase cloths if the charter was cancelled. They thus used their own importance to the trade as a bargaining tool to push for its revocation.

On the surface, this petition merely lamented the failure of the Tailors and Clothworkers' Company to regulate the dressing of cloth, rather than articulating any accusations of monopoly. However, when joined with the petition of the clothiers, this larger collective campaign questioned the legitimacy of the Company by focusing the attack on specific by-laws of the institution. Some of the petitioning clothiers can be identified. They included wealthy clothiers who regularly sold their cloth to Roger Cutler, including John Knappe, who appeared to have enough credit to sell cloths on promises of later repayment.[167] Other clothiers who signed, including George Acton, Thomas Hales, and George Raymond, would later turn against these very same merchants in an effort to break into the Eastland Company's monopoly privileges.[168] Their decision to join a petitioning campaign with them in 1620 shows the ways through which particular issues of industry could generate alliances and connections in trade which might be temporary, breaking and changing as circumstances altered. Alongside these wealthy clothiers stood those with less capital. This included clothiers at the other end of the wealth spectrum. Both George Parkhurst and Pedemanuel Allen, who signed the petition, had received loans from the town as part of a charity scheme to relieve clothiers.[169]

The clothiers' petition conjured a rose-tinted image of the past. They claimed that, in former times, clothiers had been free to dress cloths as they liked, either by themselves or by employing others. All workmanship had been performed 'in very good sort'.[170] However in recent years, the Company had imposed new ordinances 'for the restraint of the Clothier From that freedome of dressinge, w[hi]ch hee formerly enioyed'.[171] The Tailors and Clothworkers' Company appears to have monopolised the dressing of cloths, depriving clothiers of the ability to do this work themselves or to give it to non-members. By complaining of a specific ordinance pertaining to the dressing of cloths, the petitioners articulated similar concerns as addressed in *Davenant v. Hurdys*. The clothiers lamented the problems this had caused. Not only had the declining quality of cloths led the Drapers' Company in London to cease purchasing their products, but the very town of Ipswich was in a state of decay. Many clothiers in the countryside bypassed the town by dressing cloths themselves. The clothiers ended by using a strategy similar to the merchants. If the Company continued instituting vexatious ordinances, they would be forced to 'give ouer their Trades, to their vtter vndoeinge & the ouerthrow of many hundreths of poore people that live uppon them'.[172] They were simply too important a group of employers for the Council to ignore.

Perhaps most interesting in this dispute was the presentation of yet another petition to the Council, signed by forty-six clothworkers and tailors of the Company itself.[173] Some of those signing left their marks, suggesting that they were partially literate clothworkers, potentially weavers or shearmen rather than the large-scale clothier employers who had signed the other supplication. However, John Knappe was also listed as a signatory, suggesting some clothiers also signed, perhaps mobilising their employees. Fascinatingly, the petitioners adopted the very same tactic as that deployed by petitioners in Bury St Edmunds. To attack this corporation, they presented it as a combination intended only to enhance the private interests of a few members. They complained that the Company

> Should have bene beneficiall vnto them, but since that time they finde by experience, that the governem[en]t of their said company beinge managed by poore & unworthy p[er]sons, hath bene onely a meanes to raise mon[e]y by contynuall quarteridge & sundry Fines[.][174]

The Tailors and Clothworkers of Ipswich were here also accused of creating a corporation which issued excessive fines and used quarterage payments to serve their own interests. They were attacked as 'poore' men, much like the 'meaner sort' who allegedly requested the incorporation in Bury. The Company was presented as an institution which did not benefit its own members. Instead, they found themselves subject to the 'contynuall chardge and Fines which they susteine by reason of this governem[en]t'.[175] Clothworkers and tailors in the Company joined the town's merchants and clothiers to request that the trade be returned to the guiding hand of town authorities, attesting to the divides monopoly could generate within corporate bodies, and the ability for this issue to generate new alliances, in this case between tailors, clothworkers, and their employers.[176]

That the Company had been beset by internal divisions is attested to in a later report on the case produced by Sir Julius Caesar,Sir Thomas Edmondes, Treasurer of the Household and Sir Henry Hobart. They reported that the new Company had been 'full of suits amongst themselues since they were incorporate', and that some of the Company's ordinances had imposed unnecessary burdens on members.[177] By 1620, disgruntled tailors and clothworkers had clearly moved to petition against their brethren to higher authorities in a larger campaign involving the town's merchants, governors, and clothiers. This was a skilful way to add legitimacy to their complaints.

In response, the Council took decisive action. The petitions were presented by representatives of the town who attended the Council in person. They repeated the tailors and clothworkers' accusations that the Company's charter had been procured by 'some poore men of the Cloathworkers', who desired to usurp the authority of the town corporation.[178] To evoke the Council's concern, they stressed the 'disturbance and interruption' occasioned by this 'new errected Corporac[i]on'.[179] Constantly fearful of disorder, the Council referred the dispute to Caesar, Edmondes and Hobart for review. Town authorities used social status to undermine the legitimacy of this corporate body. In doing so, they articulated embryonic versions of arguments which played on fears of popularity and sedition, which would emerge as key to disputes surrounding corporate charters in the 1630s.[180]

By 26 February, the councillors had produced a final report on this dispute, ratified and confirmed by the Council on 3 March.[181] The report attests to the ways in which concerns and investigations with monopoly drew interest groups into active negotiations with government, which included not just towns and localities, but smaller interest groups and guilds.[182] Not only had representatives from the town appeared before them, but the Tailors and Clothworkers' Company had also been required to present their defence. Within the report, the very purpose of such corporate bodies received attention. The councillors expressed their opinion that 'theise under Corporac[i]ons in Townes and inferiour Citties are seldome of good vse', serving only to 'disturbe the gen[er]all goverment of such places'.[183] Implicit in this statement was the notion that such bodies might be more acceptable in larger cities like London. The report is also noteworthy for the light it can shine on why the town had only moved in 1620 to protest a Company which had been incorporated in 1606. Caesar, Edmondes, and Hobart noted that there was 'a suite in hande for errecting of another [corporation] of Mercers and Grocers in the same Towne', which they strongly urged be stayed.[184] The town, fearing the creation of yet another body which might infringe on its authority, had likely been persuaded to take the opportunity to articulate their objections with both. In a political and economic climate where corporatism was rife, mercers and grocers in the locality had been inspired to also petition for corporate privileges.

Despite their concerns, the councillors were reluctant to revoke the Tailor and Clothworkers' charter. In part, this was driven by an anxiety that this would undermine a royally bestowed charter, setting an evil example to others who might challenge prerogative rights. They also noted that the Company provided employment in the town.[185] However, the tenor of the report attests to their wariness that any monopoly of the cloth industry in Ipswich be avoided at all costs. They expressed their wish to avoid any scenario in which the clothmaking and dressing trade 'should passe thoroughe the Clothiers hande alone'.[186] Reforming the Company was the best means to preserve order in trade, ensuring good workmanship and preventing a situation in which clothiers dominated industry. They thus recommended that the Company wardens be joined with chosen town officers to act as searchers of cloth. This compromise would also ensure that the trade was not in the 'sole power' of the Company either.[187] Finally, their report recommended that the Company's ordinances be reviewed at the next Assize sessions and that a new ordinance be passed by the town to ensure all cloths were searched before being sold. A concern with ensuring regulation of industry and avoiding a slide into monopolisation by either the clothworkers, the clothiers, or town officials runs throughout this report.[188]

Both the cases of Bury and of Ipswich reveal the ways through which petitioning activity was generated by disputes surrounding monopoly and corporatism, reflective of a broader trend occurring throughout the realm. In the Bury case, it appears as if the petitioning protest was successful in securing the revocation of this new Company. In Ipswich, the Chief Justice of King's Bench Sir Henry Montagu and Assize judge Sir John Dodderidge offered their report on the Tailors and Clothworkers' ordinances, noting that many did 'abridg[e] the lawfull libertie' of subjects, including their excessive charges on members.[189] In this case however, the Company was not dissolved. New ordinances were approved by both the town and Company, the former given authority to appoint searchers to check all clothworkers' wares.[190] Throughout the dispute, the Tailors and Clothworkers' Company was actively involved in negotiations, with representatives physically appearing before councillors and judges to defend their interests and to prevent the revocation of their chartered privileges.[191]

## Protesting national patents

It was not only new corporate bodies which generated petitioning protest. Patents were issued to individuals for specific trades in local areas, generating backlash from affected subjects. Local courts received anti-monopoly complaints, and JPs acted as important mediators sending the concerns of subjects to central authorities. For example, a monopoly for the salting, drying, and packing of fish in Devon and Cornwall was granted in February 1592 by Elizabeth to the gentlemen Henry Warner for twenty-one years.[192] Petitions complaining of the patent were sent directly to Burghley in July 1592, in a campaign which involved Cornish justices.[193] Here, the justices noted that gentlemen, merchants, and fishermen had appeared 'in greate nombers' at the Assizes, delivering their 'greivous compleynt' against Warner and his patent.[194] Local officials clearly supported the plight of their merchants and fishermen, calling on the Council to take action to redress their grievances. They also proceeded to send two local representatives, a merchant named Henry Cloberie and a gentleman named William Treffrye, to articulate their concerns before the Council.[195] The patent does appear to have been temporarily stayed by letters from Burghley issued on 26 July, before renewed attempts were made to enforce the patent under the hands of Warner's deputy, Mr Richard Brown.[196] It appears that Warner had promised to increase the rent he paid Elizabeth from 20 marks to £20, convincing her that the patent was worth enforcing.[197]

In 1593, justices in Cornwall continued their petitioning campaign against the patent.[198] They presented this grant as nothing more than an attempt by Warner, alongside individuals he had selected to licence, to 'engrosse all these Comodities into their owne handes'.[199] In October, a set of twenty-four articles were produced by 'gentlemen, fisshermen & others' and sent to the justices of Cornwall. The petitioners articulated powerful arguments pertaining to their rights, describing themselves as 'free men' and the patent as occasioning 'amiserable servitude' akin to prohibiting them from gathering in their own corn at harvest time.[200] For them, the patent was a restraint on their ability to salt, pack, and dry fish necessary for their households. This grant triggered a local petitioning campaign which saw numerous aggrieved subjects united in their protest.[201] One petitioner thought good to remind Burghley that he had always been perceived as an 'enymy to thes[e] Monopolies', pushing him to cancel the same.[202] Petitioners were aware of which councillors to target, as news of their attitude to monopolies spread. A paper in Burghley's papers, dated 1597, repeated a familiar trope, claiming that opposition to Warner's grant had been driven by 'Dyvars (*sic*) Marchant[e]s and thar[e] assistant[e]s for thar[e] owne gaine', discrediting this opposition by presenting the merchants as the real cause of vexation in both counties.[203]

The repeated lamentations against the grant had their desired effect; by 1601 this would be one of many revoked by Elizabeth via proclamation.[204] However, the cancellation of a patent in one reign did not guarantee that relief from its clutches would be long-lasting. In 1619, the patent would be revived and awarded to the gentleman Henry Heron for thirty-one years at a rent of £20 per year, triggering further agitation in the form of petitioning and lobbying activity.[205]

Both Elizabeth and James also issued patents with a national scope to select courtiers. Petitions were sent from subjects in affected trades, whose objections showed an engagement with broader anti-monopoly discourses, including those which had been articulated in the legal sphere. This can be seen in the example of the expanding coal industry on the Tyne, controlled by the dominating Hostmen's Company. The Hostmen had established a monopoly over both the sale and production of coals in Newcastle, receiving an official royal charter in 1600.[206] This charter, like so many others, had generated petitioning protest to the Council of the North and to James in 1604.[207] The control of this industry by such a small and powerful body also occasioned continuous complaints from the city of London.[208] As William Cavert argues, this was driven in part by a strong association between coal and the necessities of the poor, leaving governors anxious to ensure its ready supply to prevent the outbreak of popular tumults triggered by rising prices and dearth.[209] However, these links between coal and poverty could also be exploited as a useful rhetorical strategy by vested interest groups seeking to dominate the trade.[210] The coal industry attests to the ways through which multiple monopolistic bodies could dominate one industry; whilst complaints about monopoly were frequently levied against the Hostmen as producers and sellers, the London-based Woodmongers' Company also dominated the transport and sale of coal within London, generating tension between, and against, both.

In James's reign, the Hostmen moved to protest a new patent, utilising the same discourses and criticisms which the Company had itself been subjected to. On 26 February 1616, James issued a patent for the office of surveyor of seal coals to Andrew Boyd, a client of the royal favourite, the Duke of Lennox.[211] This was justified as necessary given the constant mixing of coals with a host of unsavoury materials, rendering surveys to check quality essential. In return, shippers of coal were expected to pay new charges of 4d. per chaldron of coal for Boyd to conduct his surveys. This patent clearly allowed Boyd to benefit financially, but it was also rooted in a desire to regulate the industry and prevent abuses.

Unsurprisingly, the Hostmen protested a patent which they saw as creating an unnecessary officer, interfering in their trade for the pursuit of his own private profits.[212] On 6 March 1616, the Company court book recorded that members were to 'collect reasons' against the patent to deliver to two representatives of the city, who had been chosen to repair to London to handle this business.[213] It is likely that these 'reasons' would be gathered from company members and freemen in the city. These representatives were to inform the King and Council that this patent was both 'preiudiciall to the Comon Wealth' and grounded upon false pretences.[214] James referred the complaint for review to Sir Francis Bacon, Sir Henry Montague, and Sir Henry Yelverton on 30 April.[215] Both Boyd and representatives of the city were required to attend, attesting once again to the opportunities for participation rendered by these disputes.

By 21 June the Hostmen sent written reasons to the Council, presenting the patent as unnecessary for the commonwealth and as an illegal, impractical grant which would only serve to hinder trade.[216] John Nef suggests it was likely drawn up by the Company governor Sir Thomas Riddell.[217] As well as citing practical problems with ensuring that sacks of coal were not tampered with after Boyd's seals had been put on them, the Hostmen played on wider concerns with monopoly to present this new office not as a regulatory device, but as a scheme to dominate the industry. The Hostmen complained that this would lead to an increase in the prices of coals. Only those coal merchants who could afford to pay Boyd's fees would be able to remain in the trade, allowing them to have 'the sole and wholl[e] trade of coles', whilst all others would be debarred from the same.[218] Despite having monopolised coal selling in the city of Newcastle for decades, the Hostmen had no qualms utilising these very same arguments against an outsider who infringed on their trade. The Hostmen proceeded to draw heavily on ideas of legality, to present the 4d. fees charged by Boyd as nothing more than an illegal imposition, granted 'out of the smoake of ev[er]y mans chimney'.[219] Not only did this benefit one private man, but it was likely to generate a torrent of exclamations across the realm. Crucially, the Hostmen even directly cited the case of *Darcy v. Allen* to present the surveyor's fees as illegal. They referenced 'the printed case of Darcy and Alleyn reported by my lord cheife Justice [Coke] in his last booke of report[e]s fo. 84'.[220] Such a direct and specific reference was likely added by their legal counsel, but it served to add striking evidence for their claim that no patents could be issued that charged the subject without parliamentary consent. These issues were especially charged in James's reign, with the legality of impositions a source of much discussion in Parliament. By drawing on them, the Hostmen produced a list of objections which presented Boyd's office as creating an illegal monopoly.

In this instance, and despite the skill of their appeals, the Hostmen did not have immediate success. The case was heard in Star Chamber in May 1618 and numerous Hostmen were fined for their production of poor-quality coals.[221] In a letter calling for the continued enforcement of Boyd's patent, James referred directly to the petition from Newcastle, critical that the Hostmen had 'audaciously & obstynately' denied the need for a surveyor.[222] Much like the London Dyers, their petition had been seen as unacceptable, touching as it did on the royal prerogative. Despite this rebuke, this was not to be the end of the battle surrounding this grant, which continued to wage on throughout James's reign.[223] Such protest serves as a powerful example of the ways in which objections to monopoly could themselves be utilised by monopolistic bodies, as pre-existing institutions sought to defend their own privileges in the face of intrusions by courtier-patentees. Definitions and ideas of monopoly as articulated in law courts in London were also able to find their way into the supplications of petitioners in the provinces.

## Conclusion

This chapter has shown how the granting of patents of monopoly in various forms, be it to individuals or in the form of charters, generated tensions and conflicts in the late sixteenth and early seventeenth centuries. England's culture of corporation encouraged artisans to petition for new charters to organise trades, generating opposition and local 'conflicts of concessionary interest'. Ideas surrounding monopoly, order, and regulation underpinned the justification for these experiments in company organisation, but also saturated the language of protest. Notions of the commonwealth, public good, and private interest were part of a shared discourse, utilised in disputes as subjects sought to defend their trades. Some, like fishermen in Cornwall, were fighting to protect their livelihoods. Others, like the Hostmen, were instead moving to defend their own dominance. As Nef has argued, disputes in Newcastle were both political and economic, as groups opposed patents to protect and further their own interests.[224] Such disputes can be seen occurring throughout the realm, as the Crown's monopoly policy triggered subjects to protest to Assize Courts, the Privy Council, Parliament, and the Crown. Petitioning was integral to each case, serving as a device through which monopolistic bodies were proposed and challenged.

The prevalence of corporate bodies in economic life meant that many towns and cities had guilds and livery companies which could be accused of exercising monopolising powers. As some sought to have these powers confirmed or created through new charters, accusations of monopoly were rife even in local settings. This was especially pronounced in a period where patents and charters were issued so frequently. These contests were not simply the result of a growing tension between industrial and commercial capital, or a by-product of an attempt to channel trades into strict and increasingly unrealistic companies.[225] They must be recognised as especially pronounced in an age of monopoly, which created enhanced opportunities for bodies to gain charters and for privileges to be expanded. Patents providing individuals with the power to regulate trades and to establish deputies to search wares meant that agents of monopolists were physically present throughout the realm. Pre-existing bodies were affected by these new officers and institutions, entering contests to agitate against grants which threatened their own position in trade. Presenting corporate bodies as self-interested combinations, procured through dubious means or by 'inferior' subjects, was a means to undermine their legitimacy without launching a full-scale attack on the need for corporate bodies in society more generally: this was a tactic especially useful when corporations protested other corporate bodies.

England's 'era of incorporation' served not just to connect centre and locality in governance, or to inspire participation through humanist discourses. When combined with an age of monopoly, it triggered active negotiations, dialogues, and debates throughout the realm as subjects fought to protect their trades and grappled with prevalent ideas in economic discourse. In London, where livery companies were essential to the social, political, and economic makeup of the city, the Crown's monopoly policy was to have especially notable effects. It is to some of these cases of anti-monopoly protest that we must now turn.

## Notes

1 WSHC, G23/1/3, fo. 221v.
2 Withington identifies a similar order in Cambridge in 1615, see P. Withington, 'Company and Sociability in Early Modern England', *Social History*, 32:3 (2007), p. 298.
3 WSHC, G23/1/3, fos 224, 232v; G23/1/246–248.
4 WSHC, G23/1/3, fo. 223r.
5 *Ibid.*
6 WSHC, G23/1/248, p. 3.
7 Withington, *Politics*.
8 WSHC, G23/1/3, fo. 222r. It would later be ordered that all citizens be members of these companies, see fos 244, 246.
9 Butchers' Ordinances, WSHC, G23/1/248, p. 3.
10 Glovers' Ordinances, WSHC, G23/1/248, p. 2; Shoemakers' Ordinances, WSHC, G23/1/248, p. 15.
11 Withington, *Politics*, p. 18.
12 R. Tittler, *The Reformation and the Towns in England: Politics and Political Culture, c. 1540–1640* (Oxford, 1998), p. 188.
13 Withington, *Politics*, p. 38 and ch. 3 for ideas of civic participation.
14 *Ibid.*, pp. 17, 177. For a study of corporatism in political thought, see H. S. Turner, *The Corporate Commonwealth: Pluralism and Political Fictions in England, 1516–1651* (Chicago, 2016).
15 Patterson, *Urban Government*, p. 6; D. H. Sacks, *The Widening Gate: Bristol and the Atlantic Economy, 1450–1700* (Berkeley, 1991).
16 F. J. Fisher, 'Some Experiments in Company Organisation in the Early Seventeenth Century', *Economic History Review*, 4:2 (1933), pp. 177–94; D. Chan Smith, 'The Beginning of History for Corporate Law: Corporate Government, Social Purpose and The Case of Sutton's Hospital (1612)', *Seattle University Law Review*, 45:367 (2021), p. 368; Withington, 'Company', p. 298.
17 Ashton, 'Conflicts'.
18 Gadd and Wallis, 'National Regulation', p. 292.
19 Turner argues that anti-monopoly agitation targeted patents to individuals over corporate bodies, Turner, *Corporate Commonwealth*, p. 88.
20 S. Kramer, *The English Craft Gilds: Studies in Their Progress and Decline* (New York, 1927), ch. 2; Unwin, *Industrial Organization*.

21 B. Malament, 'The "Economic Liberalism" of Sir Edward Coke', *Yale Law Journal*, 76:7 (1967), pp. 1321–58; W. L. Letwin, 'The English Common Law Concerning Monopolies', *The University of Chicago Law Review*, 21:3 (1954), pp. 355–85.
22 Sacks, *Widening Gate*, ch. 6; Dean, 'Pressure Groups and Lobbies', pp. 139–52.
23 C. F. Patterson, 'Consensus, Division and Voting in Early Stuart Towns', in P. D. Halliday, E. Hubbard, and S. Sowerby (eds), *Revolutionising Politics: Culture and Conflict in England, 1620–60* (Manchester, 2021), pp. 145–63; Cust, 'Anti-Puritanism', pp. 23–4.
24 Patterson, *Urban Government*, pp. 151, 155–6.
25 Supple, *Crisis*.
26 Erikson, *Trade and Nation*, p. 5.
27 P. Withington, *Society in Early Modern England: The Vernacular Origins of Some Powerful Ideas* (Cambridge, 2010), pp. 136–7; Early Modern Research Group, 'Commonwealth: The Social, Cultural, and Conceptual Contexts of an Early Modern Keyword', *Historical Journal*, 54:3 (2011), pp. 659–63.
28 Withington, *Politics*, p. 68; 'Commonwealth', p. 664.
29 Holmes, 'Parliament, Liberty', pp. 148–9.
30 'Commonwealth', p. 669.
31 TLA, COL/CA/01/01/028, fo. 85v.
32 Holmes, 'Parliament, Liberty', p. 148.
33 T. E. Hartley (ed.), *Proceedings in the Parliaments of Elizabeth I* (3 vols, London, 1995), iii, pp. 375–6.
34 Withington, *Politics*, pp. 73–5.
35 Sgroi, 'Economic Debate', p. 184.
36 Mishra, *Business*; Sacks, 'Private Profit', pp. 121–42; M. Knights, *Trust and Distrust: Corruption in Office in Britain and Its Empire, 1600–1850* (Oxford, 2021), pp. 10–11.
37 Patterson, *Urban Government*, p. 40.
38 M. J. Braddick, *The Nerves of State: Taxation and the Financing of the English State, 1558–1714* (Manchester, 1996), p. 10.
39 *Ibid.*
40 R. Ashton, 'Revenue Farming under the Early Stuarts', *Economic History Review*, 8:3 (1956), pp. 310–22.
41 K. Wrightson, *Earthly Necessities: Economic Lives in Early Modern Britain*(New Haven, 2000), ch. 11; Supple, *Crisis*, p. 228.
42 Wrightson, *Earthly Necessities*, p. 251.
43 BL, Hargrave MS 321, fo. 73r.
44 P. J. Stern, *The Company-State: Corporate Sovereignty and the Early Modern Foundations of the British Empire in India* (Oxford, 2011), p. 7.
45 Gadd and Wallis, 'National Regulation', p. 292.
46 Withington, 'Sociability', p. 300.
47 Unwin, *Industrial Organization*, ch. 5; Gadd and Wallis, 'National Regulation', p. 293; E. Lipson, *The Economic History of England*, 6th edn (3 vols, London, 1956), iii, pp. 330–2.
48 Gadd and Wallis, 'National Regulation', p. 302.

49 Unwin, *Industrial Organization*, ch. 5.
50 *Ibid*.; Ashton, 'Conflicts'.
51 Mishra, *Business of State*, pp. 19–21.
52 Rabb argued that only regulated companies were attacked by gentry who favoured joint-stock enterprises, see T. K. Rabb, 'Sir Edwin Sandys and the Parliament of 1604', *American Historical Review*, 69:3 (1964), pp. 646–70. This was challenged by Ashton, see R. Ashton, 'The Parliamentary Agitation for Free Trade in the Opening Years of the Reign of James I', *Past and Present*, 38 (1967), pp. 48–9. For the later 17th century, see W. A. Pettigrew and T. Stein, 'The Public Rivalry between Regulated and Joint Stock Corporations and the Development of Seventeenth-Century Corporate Constitutions', *Historical Research*, 90:248 (2017), pp. 341–62.
53 Ashton, 'Free Trade', pp. 48–9.
54 Leng, *Fellowship*, ch. 5.
55 *Ibid*., p. 196.
56 Mishra, *Business*, p. 18.
57 *Ibid*., p. 9, ch. 1; P. J. Stern, 'Companies: Monopoly, Sovereignty, and the East Indies', in P. J. Stern and C. Wennerlind (eds), *Mercantilism Reimagined: Political Economy in Early Modern Britain and Its Empire* (Oxford, 2013), p. 178.
58 Stern, *Company-State*, p. 9.
59 *Ibid*., p. 7.
60 Mishra, *Business*, p. 31.
61 Unwin, *Industrial Organization*, p. 104.
62 PA, HL/PO/JO/10/1/15, fos 170r–186r; R. W. Hoyle, 'The Sheffield Cutlers and the earls of Shrewsbury: A New Interpretation', in R. W. Hoyle (ed.), *Histories of People and Landscape: Essays on the Sheffield Region in Memory of David Hey* (Hatfield, 2021), pp. 41–3.
63 PA, HL/PO/JO/10/1/15, fo. 171r.
64 *Ibid*., fos 170r–172r. This received a first reading in the Commons on 15 March 1621, *CJ*, I, p. 554.
65 PA, HL/PO/JO/10/1/15, fo. 177r.
66 *LJ*, iii, p. 400
67 Hoyle, 'Sheffield Cutlers', pp. 44–5.
68 *CJ*, I, p. 619; C. R. Kyle, 'Norwich', *HoP*, ii.
69 *LJ*, iii, pp. 151, 416.
70 L. A. Clarkson, 'The English Leather Industry in the Sixteenth and Seventeenth Centuries (1563–1700)' (unpublished PhD thesis, University of Nottingham, 1960), p. 232.
71 *LJ*, iii, p. 416.
72 G. Burgess, *The Politics of the Ancient Constitution: An Introduction to English Political Thought, 1603–1642* (Hampshire, 1992), pp. 5–6; Sommerville, *Royalists and Patriots*, ch. 3.
73 Burgess, *Ancient Constitution*, pp. 139–42.
74 Sacks, 'Private Profit', p. 131.
75 *Ibid*., pp. 126–32.

76 See P. Croft, 'Fresh Light on Bate's Case', *Historical Journal*, 30:3 (1987), pp. 523–39.
77 BL, Lans. MS 487, fo. 149v.
78 Sacks, 'Parliament, Liberty and the Commonweal', pp. 97–100.
79 N. Tyacke, 'The Puritan Paradigm of English Politics, 1558–1642', *Historical Journal*, 53:3 (2010), pp. 537–8; M. P. Winship, 'Freeborn (Puritan) Englishmen and Slavish Subjection: Popish Tyranny and Puritan Constitutionalism, c. 1570–1606', *English Historical Review*, 124:510 (2009), pp. 1050–74.
80 C. W. Brooks, *Law, Politics and Society in Early Modern England* (Cambridge, 2008), pp. 97–118; R. Giurato, 'The Language of Constitutionalism and the Royal Prerogative in the English Parliament of 1593: James Morice's Speech on the *Ex Officio* Proceedings and his Constitutional Thought', *Parliamentary History*, 37:3 (2018), pp. 327–49.
81 Brooks, *Law, Politics and Society*, p. 386.
82 Keller, *The Interlopers*, p. 32.
83 R. H. Tawney and E. Power (eds), *Tudor Economic Documents* (3 vols, London, 1924), ii, p. 254
84 Gadd and Wallis, 'National Regulation', p. 302.
85 TNA, SP 14/15, fo. 84v.
86 *Ibid.*
87 CP 112/63, fo. 63r.
88 *Ibid.*, fo. 64r.
89 Ashton, 'Free Trade'; P. Croft, 'Free Trade and the House of Commons, 1605–6', *Economic History Review*, 28:1 (1975), pp. 17–27; Rabb, 'Sir Edwin Sandys'; Pennington, '"Free Passage"'.
90 P. Croft, 'Parliamentary Preparations, September 1605: Robert Cecil, Earl of Salisbury on Free Trade and Monopolies', *Parliamentary History*, 6:1 (1987), p. 128. Croft also shows the self-interested motivations which led to agitation.
91 A. Friis, *Alderman Cockayne's Project and the Cloth Trade: The Commercial Policy of England in Its Main Aspects 1603–1625* (Copenhagen, 1927), p. 155.
92 Malament, '"Economic Liberalism"', pp. 1321–58.
93 BL, Add. MS 12,504, fo. 170r.
94 Chan Smith, 'Corporate Thought', p. 386.
95 J. Baker, *The Reinvention of Magna Carta 1216–1616* (Cambridge, 2017), p. 312.
96 *Ibid.*, p. 471.
97 *Ibid.*, p. 473.
98 *Ibid.*
99 *Ibid.*, p. 315
100 *Ibid.*, pp. 316–17; Sacks, 'Parliament, Liberty and the Commonweal', p. 95.
101 TNA, SP 12/286, fos 110r–122v.
102 J. H. Thomas and J. F. Fraser (eds), *The Reports of Sir Edward Coke, Knt. In Thirteen Parts* (6 vols, London, 1826), vi, pp. 159–66.
103 *Tudor Economic Documents*, ii, p. 251; TNA, SP 12/286, fos 118v, 120v.
104 TNA, SP 12/286, fo. 121r.
105 D. H. Sacks, 'Freedom to, Freedom from, Freedom of: Urban Life and Political Participation in Early Modern England', *Citizenship Studies*, 11:2 (2007), p. 139.

106 Malament, '"Economic Liberalism"', pp. 1336–7; *Reports of Sir Edward Coke*, vi, pp. 101–4.
107 *Reports of Sir Edward Coke*, vi, p. 103.
108 *Ibid.*
109 W. Money, 'The Guild or Fellowship of the Clothworkers of Newbury', *Journal of the British Archaeological Association, New Series*, 2 (1896), pp. 261–7.
110 'Norris v. Staps', in *The English Reports* (178 vols, 1900–32), LXXX, p. 357.
111 S. Bottomley, 'The Origins of Trade Secrecy Law in England, 1600–1851', *Legal History*, 38:3 (2017), p. 258
112 *English Reports*, 80, pp. 357–8.
113 *Ibid.*, p. 358.
114 Ewen, *Virginia Venture*, ch. 5.
115 *By the Queene. A proclamation for the reformation of many abuses and misdemeanours committed by patentees…* (London, 1601); Larkin and Hughes, I, pp. 504–5, 511–19.
116 Hartley, *Proceedings*, iii, pp. 249–51, 289–97.
117 *Her Maiesties most princelie answere, deliuered by her selfe at the court at White-hall…* (London, 1601).
118 C. R. Kyle and J. Peacey (eds), *Parliament at Work: Parliamentary Committees, Political Power and Public Access in Early Modern England* (Woodbridge, 2002).
119 *The Lord Coke his speech and charge with a discouerie of the abuses and corruption of officers* (London, 1607), fo. H1v.
120 Bellany and McRae, *Early Stuart Libels;* Pierce, *Unseemly Pictures*, ch. 3.
121 Unwin, *Industrial Organization*, p. 147.
122 D. C. Coleman, 'An Innovation and Its Diffusion: the "New Draperies"', *Economic History Review*, 22:3 (1969), pp. 417–29.
123 Fisher, 'Experiments', pp. 183–4.
124 J. M. Guilding (ed.), *Reading Records: Diary of the Corporation* (4 vols, London, 1892–1896), ii, p. 9.
125 George Unwin has offered the most comprehensive analysis of these companies, see G. Unwin, 'Industries', in W. Page (ed.), *The Victoria History of the County of Suffolk* (2 vols, London, 1907), ii, pp. 263–4. James Craig mentions this new Bury Company within footnotes in a larger discussion on the politics of the town, see J. Craig, *Reformation, Politics, and Polemics: The Growth of Protestantism in East Anglican Market Towns, 1500–1610* (Aldershot, 2001), p. 114.
126 Unwin, 'Industries' pp. 253–5.
127 M. Reed, 'Economic Structure and Change in Seventeenth-Century Ipswich', in P. Clark (ed.), *Country Towns in Pre-Industrial England* (Leicester, 1981), pp. 104, 107–8.
128 Craig, *Reformation*, pp. 126–32.
129 Unwin, 'Industries', p. 263; Craig, *Reformation*, pp. 129–30.
130 BRO, D9/1/1/A; C 66/1808, *CPR 7 Jas*, f. 36.
131 BRO, D9/1/1/A, p. 1.

132 Unwin, 'Industries', p. 263; Unwin, *Industrial Organization*, pp. 87–88, 96–7.
133 Craig, *Reformation*, p. 114. See *HMC Lincoln*, pp. 122–3.
134 BRO, D9/1/1/A, p. 4.
135 Craig finds links between Boldero and earlier, Puritan petitioning campaigns, Craig, *Reformation*, p. 127; *The Charter of Incorporation of the Burgh of Bury St Edmund'* (Bury, 1810), http://www.stedmundsburychronicle.co.uk/charter1606/chart1606.htm (accessed 18 March 2024).
136 *Charter of Incorporation*, pp. 15–16.
137 BRO, D9/1/1/A, pp. 1–2.
138 *Ibid.*, p. 6.
139 Unwin notes that this encompassed a third of Suffolk, Unwin, 'Industries', p. 263.
140 BRO, D9/1/1/A, pp. 11–12.
141 *Ibid.*, p. 14.
142 Malament, '"Economic Liberalism"', pp. 1352–4.
143 BRO, D9/1/1/B.
144 *Ibid.*, p. 1.
145 *Ibid.*, p. 22–3.
146 *Ibid.*, pp. 7–8.
147 *Ibid.*, p. 25.
148 BRO, D9/1/1/C.
149 *Ibid.*, p. 1.
150 *Ibid.*
151 *Ibid.*
152 *Ibid.*
153 *Ibid.*
154 BRO, D9/1/1/B, pp. 3–4
155 BRO, D9/1/1/C, p. 1.
156 *Ibid.*
157 Unwin, 'Industries', p. 264.
158 The Company attacked in 1620 appears to be the same Company incorporated in 1606, as this date is mentioned by Caesar and Edmondes in a report produced in 1620, see TNA, SP 14/112, fo. 190r. Reed argues that this was the same Company attacked in 1615, Reed, 'Economic Structure', p. 122.
159 F. Grace, 'c. 1550–1835', in D. Allen (ed.), *Ipswich Borough Archives 1255–1835: A Catalogue* (Woodbridge, 2000), p. xxxii.
160 TNA, SP 14/112, fo. 105; TNA, SP 14/112, fo. 106.
161 TNA, SP 14/112, fo. 105.
162 J. Webb, 'An Ipswich Merchant's Cloth Accounts, 1623–24', *Proceedings of the Suffolk Institute of Archaeology and History*, 37:2 (1990), pp. 124–34.
163 *Ibid.*, pp. 125, 127.
164 *Ibid.*, pp. 126–7.
165 TNA, SP 14/112, fo. 105r.
166 Unwin, 'Industries', p. 263; Patterson, *Urban Government*, pp. 152–3. This case has often been interpreted as an attempt by subjects to free themselves from oligarchic government, see J. P. Ferris, 'Ipswich: Borough', *HoP*, ii.

167 Webb, 'Accounts', p. 127. This was also signed by Anthony Gislingham, listed in 1622 as having unsold cloths on his hands, p. 129.
168 *Ibid.*, p. 126.
169 *Ibid.*, pp. 127, 129–30.
170 TNA, SP 14/112, fo. 106r.
171 *Ibid.*
172 *Ibid.*
173 TNA, SP 14/112, fo. 107.
174 *Ibid.*, fo. 107r.
175 *Ibid.*
176 This provides an earlier example of the type of attacks launched within livery companies by their members in what have been seen as democratic movements, see N. Carlin, 'Levelling the Liveries: Some Aspects of the Outlook of Craftsmen in the London Livery Companies of the Mid-Seventeenth Century', *Middlesex Polytechnic History Journal*, 1:4 (1984), pp. 3–25.
177 TNA, SP 14/112, fo. 190v.
178 TNA, PC 2/30, fos 408v–409r.
179 *Ibid.*
180 Cust, 'Anti-Puritanism'.
181 TNA, SP 14/112, fo. 190r; TNA, PC 2/30, fos 440–3; BL, Lans. 162, fo. 195.
182 Patterson argues this shows links between towns and central government, Patterson, *Urban Government*, p. 153.
183 TNA, SP 14/112, fo. 190r.
184 This was stayed until further notice, TNA, PC 2/30, fo. 442.
185 Patterson, *Urban Government*, p. 153.
186 TNA, SP 14/112, fo. 190r.
187 *Ibid.*
188 Reed argues that this decision left the Company under the control of merchants, Reed, 'Economic Structure', p. 122.
189 TNA, PC 2/30, fos 510–11.
190 *Ibid.*, fo. 510.
191 For later petitions by the Company, see TNA, SP 16/221, fo. 152; TNA, PC 2/39, fo. 551.
192 BL, Lans. MS 74/6, fos 12v–13v; N. Tyacke, 'Introduction: Locating the "English Revolution"', in N. Tyacke (ed.), *The English Revolution c. 1590–1720: Politics, Religion and Communities* (Manchester, 2007), p. 15.
193 See Lans. MS 74/1–9; TNA, SP 12/245, fo. 208.
194 BL, Lans. MS 74/4, f. 8r.
195 *Ibid.*
196 BL, Lans. MS 78/58, fo. 145. This is also described in BL, Lans. MS 74/1, fos 2r–3v.
197 BL, Lans. MS 74/9, fo. 18r.
198 BL, Lans. MS 74/1; BL, Lans. MS 74/3, fos 6v–7v.
199 BL, Lans. MS 74/3, fo. 7r.
200 BL, Lans. MS 74/8, fo. 16v.

201 BL, Lans. MS 74/5, fos 10r–11v.
202 *Ibid.*, fo. 11r.
203 BL, Lans. MS 86/9, fo. 19r.
204 *Proclamation for the reformation of many abuses.*
205 TNA, SP 14/187, fos 163r–164r; C 66/2205, *CPR 17 Jas*, fo. 198; TNA, SP 14/110, fo. 69; TNA SP 14/112, fo. 137; TNA, SP 14/112, fo. 138.
206 J. Hatcher, *The History of the British Coal Industry* (5 vols, Oxford, 1993), I, ch. 15; F. W. Dendy (ed.), *Extracts from the Records of the Company of Hostmen of Newcastle-upon-Tyne* (Edinburgh, 1901), pp. xxx–xxxi for this process, and pp. 10–17 for their charter.
207 For this petition to James and the Hostmen's reply, see Dendy, *Extracts*, pp. 20–5.
208 Hatcher describes this as an 'endless stream of complaints', Hatcher, *Coal*, pp. 508–9. For an example see Dendy, *Extracts*, pp. 2–9.
209 W. M. Cavert, *The Smoke of London: Energy and Environment in the Early Modern City* (Cambridge, 2016), ch. 7.
210 *Ibid.*, pp. 113–14.
211 TNA, SP 14/141, fo. 77r.
212 For protests from King's Lynn, see Patterson, *Urban Government*, p. 156.
213 Dendy, *Extracts*, p. 62.
214 *Ibid.*
215 TNA, PC 2/28, fo. 249r.
216 TNA, SP 14/87, fo. 133.
217 J. U. Nef, *The Rise of the British Coal Industry* (2 vols, London, 1932), ii, p. 242.
218 TNA, SP 14/87, fo. 133r.
219 *Ibid.*
220 *Ibid.*
221 TNA, SP 14/98, fo. 43; Nef, *Coal*, pp. 243–8.
222 TNA, SP 14/98, fo. 43r.
223 By 1620, a new patent for a surveyor for coals was proposed by the Duke of Lennox, see TNA, PC 2/30, fo. 536v; TNA, PC 2/30, fo. 575r. In August 1622, continued complaints concerning the quality of coals led the Council to appoint Boyd a commission to search and view coals in Newcastle, and by September 1623 a new patent would be issued to Sir Robert Sharpeigh and Alex Hartley, see TNA, SP 14/132, fo. 246r; TNA, SP 14/152, fos 74v–75r.
224 Nef, *Coal*, p. 240.
225 Unwin, *Industrial Organization*, ch. 2; Kramer, *English Craft Guilds*, p. 124.

# 2

# Petitioning the city and the Crown: the 1590s

On 11 March 1592, the Lord Mayor of London William Webb wrote to Lord Treasurer Burghley to inform him of an 'accident' which had occurred in his home that afternoon.[1] Webb dramatically described a physical altercation between the alderman Sir George Barne and the Queen's Groom of the Privy Chamber, Mr Edward Darcy.[2] Using both his 'tongue & hands', Darcy had contravened all expectations of correct politic behaviour in this civic space, striking Barne in the face.[3] What had been the cause of the altercation, and as described in a letter from the city aldermen, Darcy's 'furious & outragious beehavior'?[4] Darcy had been in Webb's home to discuss his recent receipt of a patent for the searching and sealing of leather. Barne and the city Remembrancer, Dr Giles Fletcher, had expressed their concern that the fees Darcy imposed on subjects were both 'hard and excessive', triggering a heated verbal exchange, before Darcy 'soodainly strake the sayed S[i]r George Barne w[i]th his fist on the face in most violent manner'.[5] The city's recounting of these affairs to Burghley was given added urgency, as the aldermen suggested that Darcy's very life was in danger if news of this outrage had spread amongst the apprentices dwelling nearby. After all, the very reason for Darcy's presence in Webb's house, his patent, was already causing rumblings amongst the city's populace. This was 'a thing not very gratefull to the comon sort of o[u]r Citizens nor to any other of hir Ma[jes]t[ie]s subiects as wee doe suppose'.[6]

Whilst the aldermen might have overstated the threat of disorder in their efforts to push the Council into action, their concerns with the unpopularity of Darcy's patent were far from exaggerated. Between 1592 and 1596, Darcy's patent for leather was the source of much agitation, causing city authorities to join with artisans, retailers, and livery companies to launch an extensive petitioning campaign.

Monopolies have hitherto been categorised as a feature of the 'second' reign of Elizabeth, or as part of the 'crisis' of the 1590s, a period of mounting socio-economic difficulties.[7] As explored in Chapter 1, scholars have linked the growth of concerns with monopolies in this period to Puritan interventions in politics and larger tensions surrounding the relationship between common law and royal prerogative. Underexamined is the way through which subjects other than MPs and religious radicals engaged with these issues outside of Parliament and the law courts, in such spaces as the Guildhall, company halls, and through supplications mediated by the pens of lawyers.[8] Rumours of monopolists and their activities buzzed around the metropolis as their actions fuelled discontent. A range of subjects in the city and the suburbs, including brewers, retailers, and illiterate leather dressers explored the issues raised by monopolies and corporatism through supplications, saturating their demands with powerful discourses of slavery, poverty, oppression, and liberty. The stakes in these disputes were high; leathersellers were imprisoned for their refusal to adhere to grants. The petitions produced by subjects reveal that the monopoly issue was a pressing point in which constitutional and economic grievances combined, as matters of constitutional import were discussed amongst a broader remit of subjects than has often been realised.

This chapter will focus on petitioning against monopolies in London in the 1590s, with a particular focus on the campaign directed against Darcy's grant. It will trace the role of the city authorities in the support of petitions and investigate the links between Court and city facilitated by the monopoly issue in the closing decade of Elizabeth's reign.[9] The city's desire to respond to the grievances of its citizens must be seen as part of its wider 'mediatorial' role.[10] It is clear that the creation of commissions and investigations of patents opened up new avenues for citizens to negotiate with authority, drawn into discussions surrounding prerogative and liberties by their knowledge of industries and concern with patent policy. Supplications were imbued with references to customs and liberties, a product of a widespread and popular knowledge of the law in society.[11] However, some petitions produced in the Darcy case also reveal the influence of legal counsel, namely, the Puritan firebrand Nicholas Fuller, suggesting that the employment of specific lawyers could itself be a strategy. As such, technical concerns with the effects of this patent on the industry were fused with broader reflections on political matters, as citizens attempted to protect their customs and livelihoods. Consequently, concerns with non-parliamentary taxation can be seen to have emerged as a charged issue by the closing years of Elizabeth's reign.

## The growth of monopolies and the protests in the city

Monopolies were one issue amongst many triggering discontent in the city in the 1590s, alongside such socio-economic pressures as plague, periodic

harvest failure, and declining real wages.[12] The extent to which these issues created a 'crisis' in authority in London has been frequently debated, though Ian Archer and John Walter have convincingly shown the existence of a *perception* of crisis amongst city authorities, tantamount to a 'crisis of authority'.[13] Both the city and Council were particularly sensitive to the potential for disorder, especially given the presence of wandering vagrants and soldiers in the capital. Their perception of crisis was shaped by their own anxiety, even if this was not a 'realistic' judgement of the actual level of danger they faced.[14] Archer has shown that this anxiety was important in ensuring that city authorities responded to grievances, thus helping to prevent unrest.[15] He also demonstrates the receptiveness of elites to popular concerns, and the avenues of participation available for subjects: all of which helped to maintain stability in the metropolis.

Protest against monopolies was vocal, and the aldermen's desire to protect the larger customs, rights, and liberties of the city also contributed to their willingness to respond to subjects' grievances.[16] The records of the Court of Aldermen attest to their desire to investigate and actively respond to the granting of a range of patents. On 28 September 1594, the aldermen appointed an internal committee to examine all patents granted by the Queen 'for searche or otherwise within this Cittye'.[17] This was a response to patents which provided holders with the power to search goods to ensure that they adhered to statutory regulations. Later in February 1595, they moved to charge their lawyers to examine a patent granted to the Queen's tanner, William Smith, for the searching of hides, and in June 1597, they appointed a committee to consider how to express their discontent with a patent for the searching of soap and butter.[18] Sir Walter Raleigh's patent for the selling of wine was also investigated by the city's learned counsel in conjunction with the Vintners' Company.[19] The range of goods subject to monopolisation was certainly impressive. Thus, the city moved to investigate the validity of a patent to the courtier Sir Henry Nowell for the sole making of brushes in 1594, and in July 1596, they examined a patent held by the Groom Porter Thomas Cornwallis to licence gaming houses and unlawful games, including dice.[20]

Even proposals for patents could cause the formation of new alliances and contests. The pursuit of patents generated tensions between companies, between companies and the wider city, and between the city, united with companies, against patentees.[21] In 1600, the Court of Aldermen were especially concerned with a patent granted to the Tallowchandlers' Company to search for oils, hops, vinegar, and butter.[22] By May they had collected £666 13s. 4d. from several livery companies to procure the patent for their own use, preferring that these rights resided with the broader city than with this one company alone.[23]

Companies could agitate for monopolies at the same time as they posited themselves as staunch defenders of trade against interfering patents. In 1591, members of the Skinners' Company expressed concerns that merchants were purchasing skins directly from gatherers, pedlars, and chapmen, thereby engrossing supplies and cutting out their traditional role of sorting skins to be dressed, sold, or exported.[24] In the same year, twelve handicraftsmen of the Company petitioned Elizabeth to complain that licences granted to merchants to export skins were causing these problems, interfering in the benefits they had enjoyed when the trade 'laie free and open'.[25] Despite their subtle invocation of the idea of a free trade, they attempted to secure their own patent and act to ensure that no one export or purchase skins or furs except these pass through the hands of freemen of the Company.[26] This attempt was resisted strongly by the Lord Mayor and aldermen and by merchants of the Eastland Company, as against the 'liberties' of the city and merchants.[27] This episode provides another example of the clashes which could be experienced by groups holding prerogative powers. The Skinners used the period of monopoly to advance their own interests: whilst they had frequently complained of the effect of licences for export, they also attempted to gain a monopoly on the export of coney skins.[28] The Eastland merchants, despite protesting these efforts, possessed a near monopoly on the export of skins to the Baltic, an irony which the Skinners were not afraid to point out.[29] The involvement of London's authorities in the dispute can similarly be explained through their economic interests. London's aldermen were heavily involved in overseas trades, and as merchants, were unlikely to accept a grant which favoured the interests of artisan skinners at the expense of mercantile freedom. By contrast, we will see that the city strongly supported the Skinners in their protest against Darcy. Alliances made between groups were transient and different patents could cause these very same interests to diverge.

Anti-monopoly protest could also manifest in disputes *between* different urban authorities, as cities and towns bemoaned any stranglehold of trade which affected their own interests. London's authorities invested much time and energy lamenting the state of the coal trade in Newcastle. This was in many ways driven by contextual issues of dearth and scarcity; as Cavert has argued, a perception of coal supplies as intimately linked to social stability pushed governors to ensure London had an adequate supply.[30] As the price of coal continued to rise, the aldermen expressed to the Council their concern with the monopolising activities of townsmen in Newcastle. The Hostmen were not yet incorporated, but some freemen had moved to secure full control of coal mines in the Tyne as partners in a Grand Lease.[31] Between October 1595 and July 1596 the Lord Mayor and aldermen complained of the enhanced price of coals and the continued mixing of good and bad coals together.[32] The co-partners were accused of erecting a 'plaine Monopoly' on the trade.[33] They articulated the dangers of letting so necessary a commodity reside in the hands of a few private individuals, whilst insisting that they were not attacking the wider privileges of Newcastle as a town, but only the engrossment of the trade by a few townsmen. Indeed, to attack the privileges of another urban centre would be to risk undermining the very principle that urban centres could possess such privileges and customs. Yet despite this insistence, the city still threatened authorities in Newcastle that they would have no qualms resorting to the next Parliament to fight this battle.[34] They were not the only subjects to express concern with the organisation of the industry: the Grand Lease had caused divisions amongst Newcastle's townsmen as some citizens resented the domination of the coal trade by their fellow brethren.[35]

The very process of granting and reviewing patents could be highly consultative, in processes which could last for years, and which saw pressures for the monopolisation of goods come from different quarters. Channels of communication were open between the city and Court, as suits for proposed grants were referred to the Lord Mayor and aldermen for review before they were passed. This attests to the wider awareness that knowledge on specific industrial matters was best gleaned from those directly involved in trade. However, it left both the city and the Council vulnerable to the machinations of interest groups.[36] As part of this process, petitions moved through different spaces and passed through the hands of numerous observers. Petitions for or against patents were copied and opinions on them were gathered. The consultative nature of economic policy therefore helped to foster a dialogic petitioning culture. For example, in June 1596 the Brewers' Company paid 3s. for a copy of a petition sent by Richard Skipwith, an employee in the Queen's stables, for a patent which they proceeded to challenge with the help of legal counsel, employing Fuller as their lawyer.[37] Meeting in their hall, the wardens conferred with lawyers and consulted all statutes concerning the brewing trade, before drawing a petition to Sir John Fortescue, Chancellor of the Exchequer.

The city's investigation of monopolies also generated new points of contact which allowed the opinions of citizens to be gathered and voiced. Often, the Council and Court of Aldermen were faced with a cacophony of demands and opinions which they needed to sift through, both before and after a patent had passed the seal. It has been recognised that the consultation of merchants was essential for the Crown's investigation of issues such as impositions, yet it is clear that the opinions of subjects below the level of leading city merchants were also readily sought.[38] In 1598, the Pewterers' Company petitioned the Council concerning their own long suit for all tin to be made into bars before export. They noted that their petition had triggered long deliberations and consultation with a variety of subjects, including tinners in Devon and Cornwall, merchants, and customs officials.[39] Despite numerous testimonies in favour of their grant, the Council had still decided to seek additional legal advice from the Attorney General. Likewise, in response to the city's complaints against Newcastle in 1595, the Bishop of Durham was appointed as a commissioner to investigate increases in coal prices, receiving reports and counter-rebuttals from authorities in both Newcastle and London.[40]

This process of consultation can be seen most notably in the barrage of protest surrounding a patent granted to the courtier Sir Richard Drake for the brewing of beer and ale to be used in the production of vinegar, aquavitae, and aquacomposita. Drake had insisted that such a patent was necessary to prevent the myriad abuses which had arisen in the brewing of beer and ale, which had increasingly been made from dregs of beer instead of from wholesome wine lees. This was said to have been fitter to be fed to hogs than consumed by humans.[41] The patent was thoroughly investigated before it was granted; Alderman Anthony Radcliffe wrote to Burghley on 19 November 1593 of his consultation with subjects involved in the making of vinegar and aquavitae.[42] He also received a report from the Brewers' Company who were given articles of the proposed patent to consider and answer.[43] Radcliffe's investigation led him to question a 'verye honest man of that trade', and even to stumble 'by chaunce' into the backyard of a vinegar maker of the city, where he witnessed the use of barrels of dregs.[44] Whilst Radcliffe expressed his concern that poor men would likely 'repine at anie newe graunt to restraine them', he supported the need for such a patent to reform what he had learned were indeed widespread abuses in the industry.[45] Even the process of granting patents could therefore involve the advice and input of city authorities, drawing on the knowledge of citizens.

Drake's patent was granted, providing him with extensive powers over the brewing trade. All producers of vinegar, aquavitae, and aquacomposita were to enter bonds promising to use only beer and ale provided by Drake, and only those licenced by Drake or his deputies could brew beer or ale for the making of these products.[46] Radcliffe's cautions concerning the potential opposition this might provoke proved to be correct. In the resulting protest which emerged, the city authorities became important mediators of the grievances of the Brewers' Company, who resented the increased cost of these materials and played on concerns that the grant would deplete grain supplies.[47] In April 1594, the aldermen ordered their legal counsel to confer with the wardens of the Company and all others who made aquavitae and aquacomposita, including tallow chandlers, to review and consider the patent and to meet with Drake.[48] The Brewers decided to meet in their hall to confer with Fuller to gather his opinion on how best to respond to the patent.[49] Their court books note payments of £3 to Fuller to draw a 'bill' in response, as well as payments for copies of Drake's patent and for articles written in support of it.[50] The Guildhall also emerged as an important space where legal minds and city authorities came to discuss Drake's patent; in December a meeting was held here to confer on the patent ahead of a hearing in Court.[51]

Company resources were incredibly useful when fighting vexatious grants, particularly given the charges involved in successful lobbying activity. The Brewers' records included a note that 40s. was to be repaid by 'vineger men and Aquavite' for charges due to Fuller for his legal counsel, suggesting that they had borrowed money from the wider Company to finance this collective suit.[52] In July, further payments were made to the clerk of the Brewers for drawing up supplications and two 'bookes' of articles against Drake's patent, and another £3 was paid to Fuller for helping to move the Lord Mayor and aldermen on the case.[53] By October 1594, payments were recorded to one Mr Wright for drawing a supplication to the Council.[54] Company clerks were vital for putting pen to paper and articulating members' grievances, whilst lawyers offered important legal advice.

The aldermen examined Drake's patent with much rigour in 1594, and despite their moves to support the Brewers in their protest to Queen and Council, Drake still attempted to persuade them to support his cause.[55] On 17 August, Drake wrote directly to the Court of Aldermen, alleging that the most part of the brewers, vinegar makers, and aquavitae men in the city saw his grant as necessary for the commonwealth.[56] The examination and consultations surrounding this grant triggered an important dialogic element at the level of the city, as both the Brewers and Drake constructed articles, petitions, and counter-rebuttals to defend their own interests before the aldermen, opportunistically deploying the language of commonwealth and liberty to advance their cause. As such, the aldermen were forced to sift through a torrent of rival 'truth claims'.[57] Drake complained that the Brewers' Company had written a set of 'vndiscrete vntrew and tedious' articles against him, which he had replied to, and to which he was eagerly awaiting a response.[58]

Drake proceeded to criticise his opponents by undermining their status as freemen and by questioning the agency of those alleged to have supported the protest. He claimed that the opposition against him was being stirred up by foreigners and strangers, requesting that any actual citizens who were grieved by his patent set down their names 'w[i]th theire owne hand[e]s'.[59] Later in 1596, Drake changed tactic, writing to the Council to accuse one named individual, 'Francis Oliver of London', as the inciter of this agitation. According to Drake, Oliver had travelled through numerous shires in the realm

> spreadinge abroade false Rumors, and withall informinge manye that himself and other his adherents had redie one thowsand pounde in a bagg to overthrowe the graunt, gatheringe the people together, p[er]swadinge and by giftes intysinge them to set theire hands to articles of his owne devisinge[.][60]

Voicing accusations similar to those launched by opponents to the corporation of Clothworkers in Bury St Edmunds, Drake attempted to undermine the petitioning opposition against him by presenting it as spearheaded by one malicious individual, who utilised false rumours, misinformation, and even bribery to persuade people to sign.

Drake's patent thus triggered the production of numerous petitions and articles of complaint, attesting to the dialogues and negotiations generated by the granting of monopolies. The year 1596 was a particular high point for petitioning by makers of aquavitae and aquacomposita from within and near the city.[61] In 1599, Drake's patent would once again be reviewed at law by Francis Bacon, the Attorney General Sir Edward Coke, and the Solicitor General Sir Thomas Fleming.[62] By 1601, it was one among many revoked by the Queen's proclamation.[63] As Archer argues, the Council adopted a 'mediatorial' role by referring petitions against monopolies to commissions for further review.[64] At the level of the city, the willingness of the aldermen to support the anti-monopoly campaigns of its citizens and to order reviews and consultations provided equally important opportunities through which subjects could articulate their demands. This support was perhaps no more noticeable than in the city's joining with the Leathersellers' Company in their vehement protest against Darcy.

## Darcy and the patent for leather

Leather was an exceptionally important commodity in early modern England. From the shoes sold in shops to the saddles used in horse riding, the leather industry helped to produce a variety of goods and set numerous subjects at work. The industry was divided into two main types: heavy leather crafts (including tanning and currying) and lighter leather crafts (including glove making and leather dressing with alum or train oil).[65] In the early seventeenth century, as many as three thousand glove makers and three thousand leather dressers resided in London and its suburbs.[66] The need for pits and access to water supplies meant that most tanners, glovers, and leather dressers resided in the suburbs, whilst leathersellers and cordwainers lived in the city.[67] Participants in the industry had a long history of lobbying Parliament to secure regulatory statutes.[68] The Leather Act of 1563 was one of the most important (albeit flawed) pieces of legislation passed for the industry in Elizabeth's reign, which provided regulations pertaining to the heavy leather crafts, although it left the lighter leather trades untouched.[69] This left one fruitful aspect of the industry ripe for monopolisation.

Within London, a variety of corporate bodies participated in the leather trade. Perhaps most important were the Leathersellers' Company, which specialised in the sale of leather within the city; they sold both finished leather goods and leather to craftsmen to work.[70] Under ordinances dating to 1398, the Company had rights to appoint two to four overseers to search for abuses in the trade and their first charter of 1444 extended this right to search nationally. Despite receiving a new, revised charter under Elizabeth, Attorney General Sir John Popham and Solicitor General Sir Thomas Egerton claimed in a report dated May 1592 that this right to search had lapsed via non-usage. This was seen as rendering Darcy's patent perfectly legal, though both recommended that the Leathersellers' privileges to search would need to be formally revoked at law.[71] Other companies also dealt with leather, including the Curriers', Cordwainers', and Skinners' Companies. The Skinners possessed chartered rights to regulate the qualities of skins and the expected size of fur linings. This included the right to search for deceitfully dressed skins within London and the suburbs.[72]

Like so many others, the leather industry was subject to divisions and tensions which would be given added intensity in the scandalous age of monopoly policy. The glovers were especially vexed with the ability of leathersellers to act as middlemen, supplying them with the materials they needed to produce their wares at excessive costs.[73] The Leathersellers' Company was a divided institution; its leadership was dominated by merchants and retailers and its generality by craftsmen. In 1498 the glovers and pursers had joined the Company, and by 1517 pouchmakers also entered the Company fold.[74] Tensions between craftsmen and merchant were present in this organisation, also manifesting in the physical landscape.[75] Whilst glovers and leather dressers free of the Company lived in the suburbs, the leathersellers tended to live and work in the city.

Darcy's patent was not the first to be issued over the industry. In July 1576 a patent was granted to the courtier Sir Edward Dyer, providing him with the authority to issue dispensations to subjects from the provisions of the Leather Act.[76] The Act was problematic and contained conflicting regulations which made it impossible for many tanners to abide by: so many needed dispensations that it proved to be an especially lucrative patent. Other proposals for patents over different aspects of the industry were penned. This included Smith's grant to search hides which was investigated by the city.[77] As noted, the lighter leather crafts were not subject to any statutory regulation. In this, Darcy skilfully spotted an opportunity. In 1588 he moved to request a patent to make and export skins and pelts from a variety of animals, including sheep, goats, deer, and horses. In a petition justifying the proposed grant to a reluctant Lord Burghley, Darcy offered his own definition of the differences between a legitimate patent and a monopoly.

> Where yo[u]r Lo: termed the sute a monypolye, I take that to be when a publique benefitte, is taken from many into one private mans handes, but this suite taketh benefit from none, and therfore yt can be no monypolye.[78]

Playing on distinctions between private and public interest and reflecting the ambiguous distinctions between legitimate grant and monopoly, Darcy represented the proposed grant as beneficial for the commonwealth. Despite his best efforts to persuade Burghley otherwise, Darcy's suit was rejected on the grounds that it would provide him with a monopoly control of the light leather dressing trade.[79]

Darcy was not perturbed by this setback. He turned to request a different type of patent a few years later, to establish an office to search and seal types of leather not covered by the 1563 statute for twenty-one years.[80] He claimed that the lack of regulation for the lighter leather crafts had led to the deceitful dressing of this kind of leather. By January 1592 the patent was granted, providing him and his deputies with the authority to search and attach his seal to leather which had not hitherto been subject to statutory restrictions.[81] This patent was far-reaching in its scope: as Leslie Clarkson notes, the absence of legislation dictating standards for the lighter leather crafts left Darcy free to impose his own ideas of what constituted acceptable quality for goods.[82] He also had authority to conduct searches at times and places he appointed, including at fairs, markets, and in cities. All who worked in leather were to enter bonds of £40 agreeing not to sell or work with unsealed leather, and any who violated these or refused to enter them could be imprisoned.[83] Consultation had once again been an important means through which Burghley attempted to ensure the grant would not prove too burdensome. In July 1591, Mr Peter Osborne, the Treasurers' Remembrancer in the Exchequer, wrote to Burghley to inform him that he had consulted with various leather workers in the city to ascertain acceptable prices for the seal.[84]

Despite these efforts, and as the incident in Webb's house made clear, Darcy's patent was to prove deeply unpopular, triggering a strong opposition campaign by the Leathersellers' Company and the city. However, the pre-existent fissures in the industry bubbled to the fore when the opportunity to break the Leathersellers' stronghold on the trade presented itself. Two surviving petitions show support for Darcy's grant from numerous glovers and leather dressers, a support which likely explained the decision to bestow his grant. Whilst both are calendared to 1593, it is likely that they were written prior to the passing of his patent to express support for the same and reviewed and collected by Burghley as he moved later to examine the validity of the patent.[85] Neither mentioned Darcy by name, rendering it unlikely that they were defences of his grant produced in 1593. Indeed, in his earlier petition of 1588, Darcy made reference to 'severall petic[i]ons' of workmen who supported his bid for a patent, providing him with added authority to claim that this was 'farre' from a monopoly, 'seing the workmen themselues do most desire yt'.[86] It is likely that Darcy again tried to rally the support of glovers and leather dressers for his patent for the search and seal of leather in 1592.

Glovers and leather dressers moved to produce suits independently of their Company brethren, calling for the erection of the very same office that Darcy would later receive. The first petition was from glovers to the Privy Council, who claimed to live within forty miles of the city.[87] It was likely written by glovers free of the Company who resided in the suburbs. A second petition was sent from leather dressers who claimed to reside in London, Surrey, and Middlesex.[88] The petitions had no signatures and no numbered demands, but both expressed strong concerns with the prevalent abuses hindering the industry. Whilst there is little information on the precise construction of these suits, they were likely written by disaffected artisans from within and outside of the Company ranks, who turned to attack the stronghold the Leathersellers' Company had over industry. The petition from the glovers read as a manifesto for reform, lamenting the 'misserable estate' of many thousands of glovers residing in and near London.[89] Their main point of contention was the alleged engrossment of leather supplies by the Leathersellers' Company, and their tendency to mix bad leather with good, causing a decline in the quality of leather which they could purchase for their crafts. The petitioners thus proposed numerous reforms for the industry, including a suggestion that all subjects be enforced to bring their leather to Leadenhall for sale, to ensure that all could purchase good leather and not be constrained to buy from the leathersellers.[90] The leather dressers also expressed their concern with the engrossment of leather supplies by leathersellers and their selling of poorly dressed leather.[91]

Both sets of petitioners articulated clear concerns with the industry. Their potential alliance with Darcy is evident in their main request. The glovers called for the appointment of an officer to search and seal leather in the realm, to ensure its quality and to maintain just prices.[92] They recognised the need to pay a small fee for this officer but argued that this was worth paying for the improvements in the trade which would ensue. Interestingly, they also requested that an office be granted to one man to ensure that only those licenced were able to export leather; as craftsmen reliant on leather supplies, it is not surprising that they would seek some means to regulate its export. In his proposal of 1588, Darcy had requested the power to export certain types of light leather. It is possible that Darcy's decision to move away from requesting rights of export in 1592 might have been a compromise designed to curry the glovers and leather dressers' favour. In their suit, the leather dressers also expressed their desire for a 'continewall v[i]ew and search' of leather, even offering to pay for the officer themselves.[93] They were at pains to stress that this request was not new, claiming that they had 'been alwayes of this minde that the onely meane of reforming the abuses aforesaid, might be had by sealing the good and the bad'.[94] However, they requested that this officer be elected from amongst leather artisans, rather than naming Darcy specifically. However, the similarities between this suit and that of the glovers suggest that it was part of a larger campaign, driven by an alliance between Darcy and these disaffected craftsmen. By harnessing their support and taking advantage of divisions in the industry, Darcy was able to present his grant as necessary for the commonwealth.

These petitions therefore offer an early example of the ways in which negotiations and deals for patents fostered connections between London and the Court, as courtiers proved willing to make alliances with craftsmen. Darcy of course stood to benefit financially from such an arrangement, whilst the backing of an important sector of the industry provided him with legitimacy when requesting his grant. Whilst the petitions of the glovers and leather dressers might be read as expressing a genuine desire for such an office to better regulate their industry, we might question why the glovers were willing to see this fall into the hands of a courtier, and why they and the leather dressers moved to support Darcy in 1593 once his patent had been granted.

As noted, the fissures within the Leathersellers' Company meant that many glovers and leather dressers felt alienated from company leaders. Between 1619 and 1621, they thus agitated for their own separate charter to form a new organisation.[95] Glovers and leather dressers residing in Westminster and within four miles sought an incorporation, dramatically likening themselves to 'Israelites desiring to be deliv[er]ed' from the 'red sea of theire troubles'.[96] A rhetoric of oppression saturated their demands, as they implored the Master of the Rolls, Sir Julius Caesar, not to 'send them backe to theire Egiptians', the Leathersellers' Company.[97] They described their constant efforts over the past seven years to secure their own charter. Later in the 1630s, they were even prepared to join with another courtier, Lady Killigrew, agreeing to allow her powers to appoint a searcher and to receive all fees in return for her support for their plight for separation.[98] By 1638 their struggle for incorporation would be achieved and the glovers moved to request that an officer to search and seal leather be appointed from amongst their own ranks.[99] As such, it is possible that the glovers and leather dressers moved to support Darcy in 1592 in the hope that this well-connected courtier might provide the necessary support for their own efforts to receive incorporation. Such an alliance also helps to explain how Darcy, an inexperienced courtier, had so much knowledge of the industry, knowing the defects in the Leather Act and which parts remained unregulated and ripe for monopolisation. As such, the petitions of the leather dressers and glovers were likely a product of this wider alliance. These artisans were not merely pawns in Darcy's proposals, but active agents able to enter alliances which also served their own interests. Corporatism facilitated clear links between the city and the Court.

The support shown for Darcy by the glovers and leather dressers was not representative of the broader mood of the city towards Darcy's patent. Almost immediately after its passing, the aldermen and the Leathersellers' Company united to oppose it. As early as January 1592, Webb informed the Council that Darcy's desire to have the terms of his patent published had caused disdain in Common Council.[100] Correspondence between Webb and the Privy Council between February and March showed the city's reluctance to adhere to Darcy's patent and a conference was scheduled to discuss its legality.[101] In April 1592, Common Council ordered that no composition or agreement was to be made with Darcy under any terms. Instead, it was strictly ordered that 'the Whole bodie of the said cittie, so farr as lawe & reason will p[er]mitt shall stande in Defence of the same', that is, in defence of the privileges and customs of the city.[102] In the face of such opposition, Darcy was forced to go to law to defend his grant. Most notably, the pre-existent rights of the Leathersellers to search leather proved a stumbling block for Darcy, who proceeded via a writ of *scire facias* to call for their repeal, citing non-usage.[103] Fighting the patent at law was a costly business. Between 1591 and 1592, the Leathersellers' account books recorded the payment of £20 7s. 6d. to oppose the grant.[104] This increased for the years 1592–93, as the Company recorded payments to lawyers, to the Recorder of London, for copies of legal proceedings, and travel costs to attend the courts.[105]

The city authorities proved especially important mobilisers of the various affected companies in this early petitioning opposition. On 5 February 1592, the Skinners' Company recorded their concern with Darcy's grant in their court book, alarmed by his powers to search and seal all tawed and dressed skins.[106] The aldermen were clearly instrumental in guiding them to join a collective campaign against the patent. Their account books for the summer of 1591 to June 1592 recorded payments of 10s. to pen a petition to the Council against the patent, upon commandment of the aldermen Slaney and Saltonstall.[107] Whilst this petition does not appear to have survived, references to it suggest that it was part of a forceful and targeted campaign.[108]

The Skinners thus noted that they would deliver to Burghley and to 'euery or most of the Counsaill' their supplication.[109] Payments were recorded for eight copies for this purpose.[110] Rather than presenting one copy to the Council as a whole, targeting councillors individually was clearly perceived as a means to try and curry favour for the suit. Their agitation also involved in-person lobbying. Payments were recorded for boat hire for the Master and the Wardens to attend the Council 'dyuers times' on Darcy's patent.[111] The charges to be paid by the members towards this campaign were to be decided according to assessments dictated by the Lord Mayor and aldermen. This stood in stark contrast to payments for the Skinners' simultaneous suit for their own monopoly, which was to be financed by the 'stock of the house', and thus, independently from the city authorities who so opposed it.[112]

By 1593, renewed protest began against the patent. On 25 February 1593, a large-scale petition was sent to the Council from the now Lord Mayor Sir William Rowe, on behalf of the 'Leathersellers & other poor Companies that trade w[i]thin this Citie'.[113] The sending of a supplication through city authorities added a degree of legitimacy to protests, and given their close involvement in the opposition against the patent in 1592, it is likely that Rowe and the aldermen were more involved than they cared to admit in this letter. According to Rowe, multitudes had planned to 'repair to the Court' to trouble Burghley in person, yet he had 'exhorted them to quietnes & obedience' by promising to acquaint the Council with their petition himself.[114] Rowe thus presented himself as a restraining force on petitioners who had planned to contravene accepted petitioning channels.

The petition was an impressive collective endeavour, addressed from thirteen groups of traders and artisans to the aldermen. This included not only the Leathersellers' and Skinners' Companies, but also sadlers, fellmongers, dyers, cutters, glovers, pursemakers, and even members of the Stationers' Company.[115] This attests to the ability of industrial issues to trigger collective petitioning campaigns which crossed company lines, involving a variety of affected craftsmen and artisans in need of leather supplies. Rowe noted his concern that the patent had proved troublesome for the 'porer sort' of these companies, who were concerned that it would overthrow their trades.[116] An extended copy of the petition in Burghley's papers was styled as a declaration and addressed to Burghley himself.[117] In this copy, the various groups of traders and artisans were again listed, yet the chief supplicants and organisers of the suit were identified as the 'Leathersellers of London', and an additional folio included an exhortation of the ancient privileges granted to the Leathersellers' and Skinners' Companies. The Leathersellers' accounts record the receipt of £5 from the Skinners towards opposing the patent at law, showing that they were engaged in a cross-company opposition campaign.[118] It is likely that both spearheaded this petition as Darcy finally moved to execute his patent, rallying others to join the suit and confident in the support of the city authorities.

The concerns expressed in the petition were manifold, as the petitioners deployed specific rhetorical strategies to convince authorities of the need to revoke the patent. Darcy's lack of skill and knowledge in the leather trade was cited by the petitioners, as well as their belief that Darcy had tricked Elizabeth into passing a grant which was harmful to the commonwealth. They focused on some of the practical problems caused by the patent, including the excessive rates imposed for the seal and the necessity for all leather workers to bring their goods to the city to receive it. Alongside their use of the rhetoric of commonwealth stood a strong appeal to the law, but more specifically, charter culture shaped the discourse and very form of this petition. The folio reciting the privileges conferred on both the Skinners and Leathersellers stood as a physical demonstration of their ancient rights. The petitioners recited the rights of the Skinners to search for deceitful skins and furs which had been bestowed as early as 1327 and confirmed by Henry VII.[119] The privileges of the Leathersellers to search for false leather dressing in the realm were also articulated. The petition, both in its demands and in its very form, was emblematic of the clashes between older privileges and new monopoly rights.

The supplicants in the copy of the 'Declaration' sent to the aldermen had also requested the appointment of 'grave and indifferent persons' to judge Darcy's patent and its negative effects on their industry.[120] In this request they were to have success. On 18 March the Council wrote to Lord Buckhurst, Sir John Fortescue, Sir John Wolley, Thomas Fanshawe, and two aldermen, Henry Billingsley and Nicholas Mosley, appointing them as commissioners to investigate the patent.[121] They noted the activity of 'divers leather dressers and leathersellers in the cittie of London', who they claimed had 'procured multitudes of people to complaine in clamorous sorte of the inconveniences' of Darcy's patent, to not only the Lords but also to Parliament.[122] This mention of 'clamour' was likely a direct reference to the 'Declaration', reflective of the Council's labelling of any petitioning activity which contravened conventional channels as 'clamorous'. In this case, the petitioners' plan to repair to the Court with a crowd rendered their activity dubious, despite their suit being sent through the mediation of Rowe. Even the mere *intention* to do so still proved an effective strategy which pushed the Council to listen to their demands and appoint a commission. Much like the investigations surrounding Drake's patent, this commission was intended to be consultative. Commissioners were given power to summon leather dressers and sellers in the capital and to examine all complaints exhibited against the grant. In the meantime, Darcy's patent appears to have been stayed pending investigation.[123]

The commission served as a new point of contact for those aggrieved by Darcy's monopoly. An undated petition titled as the 'humble petition of Artificers and Vendors of Leather' was addressed specifically to the commissioners Buckhurst, Wolley, and Fortescue, suggesting it was written after the appointment of the commission on 18 March, but before the 17 May, when Darcy responded to its contents with a point-by-point rebuttal.[124] The petitioners once again claimed to be from a wide variety of affected artificers, including those involved in the 'dressinge, Workinge, Makinge, vtteringe, and sellinge of leather'.[125] It is likely that some of the petitioners were members of the Leathersellers' Company, but unlike the Declaration, the petition did not claim to be chiefly from the wider Company.

The petition was a sophisticated document, stretching across two folios with a section detailing the 'some and efecte' of Darcy's patent, and a second section containing seven numbered grievances. This allowed the petitioners to reveal their knowledge of the patent, and to present their concerns as emanating from a detailed analysis of its provisions and effects. The petition was far from formulaic; it was crafted to articulate concerns about various aspects of the grant. This included complaints of the 'intollerable taxe' imposed for Darcy's seal, and the need for subjects to pay to enter bonds not to sell or use any unsealed leather, all of which had allowed the patentee to make excessive profits, to the 'vndoinge of manie Thousand[e]s Hir Ma[jes]t[ie]s poore and Duetifull Subiect[e]s'.[126] The petitioners also lamented the poverty the patent was causing in the city, a particular concern of authorities in the context of the 1590s. The number of subjects touched by Darcy's grant was, they claimed, akin to the number of parishes in the realm. Many subjects and their 'wives children servuant[e]s and families' were maintained by the trade.[127] To force them out by means of this patent was to further depress those who were 'already scarcelie able to lyve, by all their industries and indevors'.[128] Here was a clear allusion to the current presence of dearth, inflation, and scarcity throughout the realm. This was also a means to remind authorities of their own responsibility for tackling poverty, invoking the very same language used in proclamations and statutes to bemoan the idle beggars and vagrants proliferating in communities.[129] Here the petitioners presented themselves as wanting to work, reduced to this state of dependence by Darcy's patent alone.

The glovers and leather dressers who had supported Darcy's patent had also included a particular focus on poverty in their suits to the Council. For example, the glovers complained that they would soon be 'compelled to begg in the street[e]s', increasing the number of vagrants with which the realm was already 'pittifully pestered'.[130] The leather dressers similarly suggested that many households were soon to be 'eaten cleane out of dores' if leathersellers continued to employ unapprenticed individuals and dominate the trade.[131] Similarly in their opposition to Drake, brewers had expressed concern that aquavitae men and their servants would be forced to 'pester' the commonwealth through begging.[132] Drawing on the language of poverty was a useful strategy to try and capture the attention of authorities who were already concerned with their ability to control any eruptions of the many-headed monster.[133]

The Humble Petition also reveals the ways in which larger debates circulating in the high political and religious spheres imbued the petitioning protests of artisans. Much like the Declaration, the petitioners also used their supplications as a space to engage with the debates surrounding liberties, property, and servitude identified as so pertinent in the parliamentary sphere. These ideas trickled down into wider society. As such, the petitioners used the language of serfdom, expressing their concern with the 'bondage' faced by subjects who were forced to bring their wares to specific towns chosen by Darcy to receive his seal. They also expressed a concern with the bonds they were forced to enter. They were merely seeking to 'live by their lawfull trades and laboures', requesting the ability to live by the realm's laws, without being forced to pay or yield 'to anie suche bondage'.[134] Here, petitioners mirrored ideas that one's right to trade was akin to a form of property, and of the need for all to exercise their God-given labours.[135]

The petitioners also defended their rights to trade with strong references to liberties and concerns with arbitrary infringements. Their second grievance complained that the types of leather Darcy was allowed to search were not warranted to be viewed by any 'Acte of p[ar]liament nor Lawe', questioning how Darcy could attempt to exercise such an illegal grant, knowing that the Queen 'ruleth Hir Subiect[e]s onelie by the lawes of the Realme'.[136] Here was a strong appeal to the need for Parliament to scrutinise patents, reflecting too the belief that Parliament was a necessary body to regulate trade through statute. Crucially, the petitioners' fifth demand challenged the legality of the high rates imposed for the seal by presenting it as a form of non-parliamentary taxation. The merchants who had challenged the Skinners' attempts to monopolise the export trade in skins in 1592 had expressed a similar concern that any payments for licences for export would be 'equivolent to a newe Toall or Custome'.[137] Such complaints were more pronounced in the Humble Petition, which repeatedly described Darcy's seal as a 'tax', a revenue-raising device which had not received the consent of subjects. They questioned

> Whether the same taxe be meete, necessarie or Convenient to be laide uppon the people, not beinge graunted by p[ar]liament nor warrantable by Lawe[138]

Darcy's patent had no clear authority in pre-existing legislation (namely, the Leather Act). The petitioners also noted that this made the task of searching leather to ensure it adhered to prescribed regulations impossible. The Humble Petition offers a particularly early example of the articulation of arguments against taxation without consent, receiving expression in an anti-monopoly petition sent by artisans.

This strong rhetoric may make us question the precise involvement of legal counsel in this supplication. Many of the sentiments expressed in the petition mirrored the arguments on patents made by the Puritan Fuller.[139] The lawyer was a staunch defender of the common law and a protector of subjects' liberties against undue interference by the royal prerogative.[140] These sentiments made him an ideal lawyer for numerous companies in their campaigns against monopolies. In the Brewers' accounts, he was paid for writing two supplications to Lord Buckhurst and Robert Cecil, and to the Lord Mayor and aldermen concerning prices of ale and beer malts.[141] He was even recorded as holding a meeting in his house to discuss Drake's patent.[142] Later in 1604, tinners in Devon and Cornwall noted that 'Mr Fuller the Lawyer' was prominent in the campaigns of the Pewterers' Company as they sought to secure a suspension of a patent for the pre-emption of tin.[143] This is evidenced through a list of objections penned by the Pewterers in June 1603, which presented the monopoly as contrary to 'the lawes of god' and which expressed criticism of the patentees' use of oaths.[144] Fuller was also active in city government in the 1590s; he was employed as legal counsel and sent by the aldermen to Court to deliver numerous petitions on their behalf.[145] It is possible that his experience of being employed by the city to investigate specific monopolies strengthened his resolve against patents, all too aware of their infringement on pre-existing charters and rights.

The role of Fuller in providing counsel for these protests ensured that many petitions contained references to the common law and the prerogative. Sometimes it appears that he provided advice on suits, whilst at other times he penned the petitions. An undated set of articles by the Brewers against Drakes' patent, likely addressed to Parliament in 1597, noted that they had been 'informed' (likely by Fuller) that such a restraint of trade was 'contrary to the lawe and lib[er]tie of a free subiecte to be Compelled therevnto by any grante oth[er]wise then by acte of p[ar]liam[en]t', articulating similar arguments to those of the Humble Petition.[146] In January 1596, the Brewers' court books noted that a petition against the patent was 'Devised' by Fuller for the brewers and vinegar makers, before subjects signed it for delivery to the Lord Mayor.[147] However, this is not to say that members of the Company had no role to play in any of the petitions produced. Fuller offered advice on matters of the law, but the articles to Parliament combined appeals to liberty with more technical comments pertaining to the production of beer and ale, attesting to the Brewers' own involvement in the petition.

Further, it is likely that the choice to appoint Fuller was a deliberate one. The number of lawyers residing in London was especially high in Elizabeth's reign, yet multiple companies made use of his counsel.[148] Why make such a choice? News of his impassioned speeches in Parliament in defence of liberties had likely spread. His reputation as a staunch defender of liberties meant many perceived him as capable of offering sound legal advice on their rights to trade. Even the process of working with Fuller in campaigns meant that freemen were exposed to constitutional objections to grants. As legal counsel to the city who frequented Court, Fuller also provided an important connection to numerous channels of authority. Thus, in July 1594, the Brewers paid Fuller for his counsel in 'movinge my Lorde Maiore and courte of Alder[men]' on Drake's patent, and in October he was also paid 10s. for attending the Guildhall to discuss it.[149] For companies, even the choice of legal counsel could be deliberate, acting as another tactic deployed by subjects in the 'law-mindedness' of this period.[150]

Not until 1594 was Fuller officially employed by the Leathersellers' Company as their legal counsel. Specific payments or references to the production of the Humble Petition are not present in the Company account books. It is therefore possible that the lawyer used to advise on this supplication was funded by leather workers outside of the auspices of company organisation. It was common for communities to contribute to the collection of 'common purses' to fund legal suits and actions, and the process of going to law could be inexpensive.[151] Further, to cede to Fuller full responsibility for the legal sentiments employed in this petition and others where his involvement can be traced would be to undermine the sophistication of the leather workers' own views, in a period where the 'language of liberty' resonated widely.[152] London's freemen were acutely aware of their rights and customs, and those of the company in which they belonged.[153] In 1594, the Skinners recorded an objection made by one of their members, John Brickett, who was brought before their court for refusing work. Brickett claimed that 'althoughe he were a poore man...he doubted not but that he shoulde haue the Lawe of the Lande to defend hym'.[154] Awareness of the law and invocation of rights was widespread. As such, subjects could deploy this language in petitions as they fought to protect their trades and may have deliberately picked lawyers known to champion these rights to help them pen supplications which could articulate these sentiments more forcefully.

Another supplication produced during this campaign provides stronger evidence for Fuller's involvement. On 23 July, a petition was sent to Burghley by a group of leathersellers, titled as the 'reasons and resoluc[i]ons' for their refusal to yield to Darcy's patent, as requested by city authorities including the aldermen Sir Richard Martin and Sir John Harte.[155] The supplicants were identified by name as John Warde, Arthur Parkins, Anthony Quaplad, and Richard Ironside. Warde served as Warden of the Company from 1592–93 and Ironside was to serve as a Fourth Warden in 1602–03, elected to the Company's Court of assistants by 1604.[156] In 1587, he was described as a 'yeoman' employing four apprentices. In October 1595, the Privy Council ordered that Ironside, Quaplad, and one Richard Parkins shops be shut due to their continued disobedience, likely concerning the patent.[157] All were prominent freemen in the Company and householders with the means to employ apprentices, rather than poorer journeymen or apprentices. The petitioners called on authorities to consider whether their rejection of the grant rendered them worthy of imprisonment, suggesting a possibility that either all were imprisoned or facing the threat of incarceration as they continued to oppose the grant.

The Reasons and Resolutions was a highly technical supplication, heavy with religious rhetoric and shaped by debates surrounding the royal prerogative.[158] It is here that the influence of Fuller seems most apparent; the supplication went further than the Humble Petition in its discussion of the prerogative and common law. Company account books for August 1593 to August 1594 recorded payments to Fuller for writing a 'motio[n] to the court of Alderme[n] for the Releasing of o[u]r Brethern at that tyme in p[r]yson', possibly as a later payment for this suit, which was subsequently forwarded to Burghley and penned sometime between 1593 to 1594.[159] The Reasons and Resolutions celebrated the common law as

> the chieffeste inheritaunce ev[er]ye meane Subiecte is borne vnto, And the surest Anchare holde by w[hi]ch the greateste Subiecte in the Realme dothe enioye all he hath[.][160]

This veneration of the common law was used to express the petitioners' concern that neither their 'lives, libertyes, nor goodes, were worthie to be p[ro]tected' by law, given their condemnation for failing to adhere to this burdensome monopoly.[161] The petitioners argued that the prerogative was supposed to enshrine and protect their liberties. This was combined with an appeal to the city's pre-existent rights, framed with references to oaths and conscience. All freemen had taken a 'p[re]cyse oathe' to be upholders of the franchise and customs of the city, enjoyed by Londoners for over three hundred years.[162] The tensions triggered by conflicting sets of prerogative privileges were here referred to as a 'prioritie of graunt[e]s'. They stressed their concern that they might 'runne headlonge into the horrible sinne; of wilfull p[er]iurye' in adhering to Darcy's patent over the enshrined privileges of the city.[163] They thus ended their petition not with a standard plea for release, but by calling for the patent to be reviewed by Common Council, before they, the city, or members of the Council be made to 'defile o[u]r conscyenc[e]s, withe the Contagius venime therof', or injure their names with a 'p[er]petuall staine'.[164] Prominent and possibly imprisoned members of the Company made use of Fuller's skills to send a supplication which included specific appeals to the common law, conscience, and sin. Who better than this Puritan firebrand to articulate their demands in a powerful rhetoric? For these leathersellers, it is likely that their own perceptions of liberty, strongly rooted in charter culture and influenced by their own economic interests, fuelled their opposition. Aware that this contravened their rights, the Company deliberately employed a skilled lawyer known for his championing of the common law, to powerfully articulate these demands with references to prerogative, the sanctity of oaths, and sin.

The supplicants also appear to have shaped some aspects of the petition, suggestive that it was the product of a collaborative process between Fuller and company members. Their additions provide a sense of a lively atmosphere in the metropolis, where rumours of patentees and their actions proliferated. They thus embraced the opportunity to attack their economic rivals, the leather dressers, as 'the verye worste people', who like 'Idle drones seeke to feede uppon our industryes'.[165] They also included an interesting piece of rumour, arguing that one of Darcy's deputies was even 'lyinallye discended, from a witche, on the mother side'.[166] This aspect was likely added by the leathersellers as they sought to use an array of tactics to undermine the credibility of their opponents, even drawing on popular rumours which suggest a broader vilification of Darcy and monopolists was occurring within the confines of the city. Grasping deputies, they claimed, were 'never soe ryfe; as in this age'.[167]

In the face of petitioning protests, the commissioners continued to consult subjects from outside the Leathersellers' Company to test the validity of the claims made; accusations in petitions were scrutinised and investigated. Burghley's papers included a torrent of materials including reports and technical notes on the intricacies of the trade.[168] This process of investigating the patent facilitated the sending of petitions and counter-rebuttals, creating the conditions for a dialogic commission. For Darcy, the very fact that workmen had attested to the need for such an office, and that it was agreed that the charges should be paid by those who most benefited from the grant, challenged any notions that the rates for the seal were an unfair tax. Darcy also responded to the Humble Petition, refuting the petitioners' focus on the rule of law and the importance of Parliament by presenting himself as a staunch defender of the royal prerogative. For him, the prerogative was 'as stronge as a Lawe', and any patent granted to reform abuses was valid.[169] Darcy presented the petitioners as 'Rebells' whose desire to go to law was a means to 'try how far hir highnes prerogative stretcheth or extendeth'.[170] This was a skilful way for Darcy to invoke the anxiety of councillors by painting these petitioners as challenging the authority of the prerogative itself. The commission and the wider Council were forced to decide who posed the biggest threat to the leather trade: Darcy or the leathersellers.

To undermine the Leathersellers' Company further, Darcy also discredited the petitions of his opponents by framing them as the product of a dangerous petitioning campaign. This was something the Council were likely to be receptive to, given that they had already expressed their concern with untoward petitioning in their letter appointing the commissioners. One anonymous document in Burghley's papers attacked the 'deceit[e]s and abuses of the Lethersellers', reciting the problems in the leather industry and presenting Darcy's grant as the only means to protect it from the grasping greed of the leathersellers.[171] It is likely that this was produced by Darcy and his supporters. One section of the document slipped into the first person, claiming that workmen in London who were present 'at my howse' had affirmed that they would provide certain sums for the sealing of leather. Whilst the rest of the document described Darcy in the third person, this slip suggests he was its author.[172] Crucially, the document engaged directly with the concept of 'monopoly'. Darcy recognised that 'all monopolies are directly against the Comon Welth', but it was not he who was presented as the key monopoliser of the leather trade.[173] Instead, this accusation was turned on its head. Through a mixture of 'Collusion and Deceate', the Leathersellers' Company had engrossed all leather supplies to create their own 'Monopoli'.[174] They were described as 'Catterpillers in a Comon Welth' who extorted the realm's subjects.[175]

The document also included an attack on the processes through which the petitions written against Darcy had been organised to try and present this activity as illegitimate. The document mirrored objections which were later used by Drake in his attack against the Brewers. Darcy claimed that the leathersellers

> haue mutenously incited their seruaunt[e]s & such woorkemen to be onely vnder their Checque, as also gerdelers glov[er]s sadlers shomakers & such Like…to make a Tumoultious exclamation, as it wer[e] in manner of a Rebellion, against the aurthoretie of Hir Ma[jes]ti[e]s graunte, w[hi]ch is proued good in Lawe.[176]

By referencing the involvement of saddlers, girdlers, and glovers, this appears to have been a direct reference to the Declaration of February, which included all of these groups. Here this was presented not as a legitimate petition of grievances, but as a 'exclamation' amounting to a rebellion. Much like the allegations expressed against the new cloth companies in Bury and Ipswich, issues of social status were key to this dismissal: these subjects were merely 'servants' of workmen with little credibility or standing. The legitimacy of the petitioning campaign was called into question on the basis that these artisan leather workers had been duped into signing supplications, having been 'blynded w[i]th an Illusion of the Letherseller'.[177] Networks of trade, namely in terms of relations between masters and journeymen and apprentices, were credited with facilitating this protest as many had been 'incited' to sign. This served as a convenient way to explain the divisions which Darcy's patent had caused in the industry; those craftsmen who complained against the grant had merely been manipulated by their masters and their leatherselling brethren to engage in these 'vniust Clamors'.[178] The document thus ended with a warning: to cancel this lawful grant at the hands of popular pressure would be to persuade others that all patents might be revoked by 'popular & clamorous exclamacions'.[179] Such attacks on the legitimacy of petitioning campaigns would remain a key feature of disputes surrounding monopoly and corporatism, as a technique to undermine the authority of rival claims. Even the boundary between legitimate and clamorous petitioning was a contested one, explored in counter-replies and rebuttals.

The investigation of Darcy's patent continued into the summer of 1593, and commissions remained integral to this process. By July, a second commission was appointed to examine Darcy's patent. Three men were chosen as commissioners: Richard Young, Thomas Phillips, and Richard Carmarthen.[180] All were customs officials with knowledge of trade, but not all were impartial. In 1592 Young was granted a monopoly on starch making which the Council attempted to enforce in the face of staunch opposition from the Grocers' Company.[181] As a fellow monopolist, it is unlikely he would have felt much sympathy for the Leathersellers' plight. The commissioners were charged with investigating many of the issues raised by petitioners, attesting to the responsiveness of the Council and the ability for protesting subjects to shape the very direction of commissions' investigations. This included examinations of the rates imposed for the seal and the logistics of forcing leather producers to receive it at locations chosen by Darcy or his deputies.[182] Like its predecessor, the commission was also intended to be a consultative space; four leathersellers and four leather dressers were to act as representatives to it.

Perhaps unsurprisingly, the commissioners' final recommendations were sympathetic to Darcy's monopoly.[183] Consultation with leather dressers had revealed that there was an engrossment of supplies by the leathersellers, and the commissioners even suggested a proclamation be issued to inform subjects of the terms of Darcy's grant. However, they reported that they had also 'conferred' with a variety of subjects in the trade, many of whom had suggested that the rates Darcy imposed for the seal were too high.[184] Another document in Burghley's papers, potentially provided by the commissioners, noted that lowering the rates of seal for better sorts of leather might make the patent more palatable.[185] The document claimed that 'conference' with subjects who were not members of the Leathersellers' Company, but who 'haue had great dealing[e]s in Lether' had led them to affirm that the rates were excessive.[186] Another document dating from July included a set of rates which 'the letherdressers are agreed vnto'.[187] Crucially this was signed with the marks of numerous leather dressers, attesting to the involvement of even illiterate artisans in the deliberations surrounding the best means to reform the industry.

In 1593, petitioning against Darcy's patent had some effect. The Council had ordered two commissions to investigate the grant, creating additional opportunities for those on both sides of this industrial conflict to articulate their concerns to authority. The tensions produced were both specific, manifesting in debates about the rates for seals, and more general, feeding into broader concerns with the relative balance between royal prerogative and subjects' liberties. In the first stage of this petitioning protest, and despite being labelled as clamorous supplicants, the Leathersellers' Company and their supporters had secured some success; Darcy's fees were ordered to be lowered and, crucially, a revised patent containing these changes was issued in March 1594.[188] However, Darcy still had the power to make leathersellers and dressers enter bonds of £40, and to search for leather in all markets, ports, and shops. In the second stage of protest, Darcy's opponents were to experience a more resounding victory.

## The second stage of the petitioning campaign

Between 1594 and 1596, Darcy's revised monopoly would continue to occupy the time and attention of the city and Council. Burghley insisted that the city allow Darcy to exercise his patent, and yet another legal review of the patent was ordered.[189] Articulating similar ideas as those expressed in the 'Reasons and Resolutions', the Lord Mayor and Court of Aldermen insisted in September 1594 that they could not in good conscience abide by the revised patent, bound as they were by their oaths to maintain the 'good coustomes & priviledges of this Citie'.[190] Fuller was still employed by the city to help in their fight against grants which threatened their privileges. In December 1594, a payment was made to him and others to travel to Court and petition the Council against both Darcy and Drake's patents.[191] By January 1595, Fuller was even given a gift of £4 by the city for his frequent travel to Court on behalf of the Leathersellers.[192] Lawyers were important for advising and penning petitions, but also for physically representing corporate clients in the Court itself.

Petitions continued to be sent to challenge Darcy, and the support of the wider city remained an important means through which suits were sent to the Council. On 25 January 1595, the Lord Mayor Sir John Spencer forwarded a petition to the Council from prisoners, incarcerated for their failure to adhere to Darcy's patent.[193] Spencer and the city aldermen noted the 'murmurre' of the people throughout the realm, distressed by dearth and the ever-lingering threat of poverty.[194] They claimed that the 'violent' actions of patentees had oppressed subjects.[195] The poor were presented as ready to rise if further pressures were placed on them, as the threat of popular disorder was invoked to try to force the Council's hand.[196] Whilst the aldermen criticised the audacity of the prisoners for complaining that the city had neglected their duties to them by failing to inform the Queen of their grievances, this was excused as a product of their 'great grief & bitternes of hart'.[197] The aldermen's decision to support the complaints of the prisoners despite this indiscretion might have had an additional agenda, given the politics of Spencer's mayoralty. Spencer was particularly unpopular; rumours of his corruption and excessive wealth triggered much ill-feeling among citizens.[198] His harsh handling of apprenticeship riots in the summer left him open to further criticism, as libels and rumours buzzed in the metropolis, including claims that apprentices were planning to erect a gallows outside of his home.[199] In June, he wrote to the Council of the 'vniust and vntrue report[e]s' raised against him.[200] Spencer's decision to send the petition of the prisoners must be seen as a measure intended to court popularity, aware as he was of the importance of the 'politics of reputation'.[201] By contrast, whilst Lord Mayor Sir Stephen Slaney was later to note that the poor were 'pinched' by the increased prices of coal when complaining of the Grand Lease in Newcastle, he and the aldermen also stressed to the Bishop of Durham that they were 'able through Gods goodnes to bear ye brunt of this hard time'.[202] The situation seemed less urgent. Most likely this was because Newcastle's dominance of the coal trade, whilst a constant source of vexation, did not directly impugn the privileges of the city, in contrast to Darcy's grant.

The potential identity of the prisoners can be conjectured from other sources. By December 1595, the Council recorded the imprisonment in the Marshalsea of Ironside, Quaplad, and Richard Parkins, who had been incarcerated sometime before for their rejection of Darcy's patent. On 14 December, they were permitted to attend the Lords in person to relate the proceedings between their Company and Darcy.[203] As previously noted, in October 1595 all three had faced the censure of the Council for acting in 'Contemptuous sorte' and refusing to appear before them.[204] Ironside and Quaplad were also the petitioners in the Reasons and Resolutions, and Richard might have been a relation to its other named author, Arthur Parkins. Earlier in November, the new Lord Mayor Slaney also sent the Council a petition written by the wives of these imprisoned leathersellers which lamented the 'great extremit[e]s' caused by Darcy's grant.[205] Given their possible prior imprisonment in 1593 and their recorded imprisonment again later in the year, it is likely that the petitioners in January 1595 were these three prominent members of the Leathersellers' Company. On 30 January 1595, Fuller and other city notables were also sent to the Court on the business of the city and Leathersellers, perhaps to push this suit in person.[206]

A copy of an undated petition addressed directly to Elizabeth in the city records bears all the hallmarks of a supplication written by Fuller. The petition is not signed, however, the supplicants described themselves as entrusted with the 'government of this your Citie', suggesting that it was penned on behalf of the aldermen.[207] By 27 November, they would send a petition and set of grievances to the Privy Council which were similar in numerous points.[208] It is possible that this was an earlier draft, intended to articulate a wider defence of the city's continued rejection of Darcy's patent. The petition was similar to the Reasons and Resolutions in form; it contained no numbered grievances, demands, or articles, but was styled as a narrative of the 'great griefs' caused by Darcy's grant.[209] Fuller was certainly instrumental in the continued agitation against Darcy, suggesting his involvement. The Leathersellers' accounts listed payments in 1594 to both 'Mr Whyte and Mr Fuller for counsaile Aboute o[u]r pattent at three sondry tymes', for which they were paid £3.[210] By September 1594, Fuller was listed as one of the learned counsel of the Leathersellers' Company, employed to deal with any 'Cause betwene them or anye other p[er]son or p[er]sons'.[211] As such, it is likely that the city and affected leathersellers were provided with support from Fuller as the Company's official lawyer.

In its contents, the petition consisted of a strong appeal to the nature and authority of the prerogative. The petitioners noted their 'bouldnes' in directly addressing the Queen but presented it as their 'duetie' to inform her of their grievances.[212] The petitioners were presented not as opposers of the Queen's royal prerogative, but as its staunch defenders. Emblematic of the tension between old and newly granted privileges, they emphasised their desire to protect the liberties and rights bestowed on London through the prerogative, ancient rights which needed to be defended not only to protect the city, but the very royal powers which had bestowed them. They stressed that they had not intended to oppose the Queen's 'Princely prerogative', nor to 'provoke or call into question your sovereign authoritie'.[213] Instead, their protection of the city's rights was a means to defend the royal prerogative.

They celebrated the latter as a 'most holy & necessary thing', repeating ideas expressed in the Reasons and Resolutions that this was to work in tandem with the common law, to 'supply the defect[e]s of yo[u]r Highnes Lawes'.[214] They acknowledged that all of their rights, 'all yt wee have & all yt wee are', depended on the Queen's 'most royall scepter'.[215] Debates concerning the relationship between the prerogative and the common law therefore received expression in an economic petition designed to secure the cancellation of Darcy's monopoly.

The petitioners ended by recognising that some type of reform was needed in the leather trade; the findings of the commissioners in 1593 meant this was something they accepted. However, they requested that any searcher or sealer be appointed by the city and its companies, who would only desire the public good and introduce no fees amounting to a 'niew imposition'.[216] The petition concluded with a strong statement on the larger problems created by monopoly policy in recent years. They complained that the

> late griefs of yo[u]r poor people is exceeding great toutching this & other lyke Patents w[hi]ch beeing many at this present time are supposed by them to draw wholy from the Common wealth & privat[e] purse of yo[u]r poorer subiects the same not tending towards the relief of publique necessitie[.][217]

The petitioners presented the agitation against Darcy's grant as part of the larger discontent with monopolies pervading the realm.

That this draft petition was part of a larger city-directed campaign, aided by Fuller as legal counsel, is reflected in the aldermen's sending of both a letter and detailed set of objections against Darcy's patent to the Council by 27 November.[218] It appears as a more complete, albeit toned down, version of the above, with the aldermen clearly deciding that it would be best to approach the Council rather than petition the Queen directly. In an accompanying letter, seventeen leading city officials presented themselves as upholding the royal prerogative as a 'most sacred & necessary thing in hir Princly regiment'.[219] The petition consisted of fourteen articles, lamenting the practical problems caused by Darcy's grant and requesting permission to be allowed to test the validity of both Darcy and the cities' patents at law. The aldermen desired a 'iudiciall, & not arbitrary' trial to be held outside of the public eye to finally establish which patent had validity.[220] They also expressed criticism of Elizabeth's broader recourse to monopolies as a fiscal device. They directly referenced Drake's patent, alongside the grant for the searching of soap and butter, Nowell's patent for brushes, bottles, and stone pots, Sir Jerome Bowes's patent for playing cards, and a patent for searching and sealing cordage held by Henry Bellingham.[221] These they argued

> hath wrought a feare in the poor people that the like Patents maie bee graunted for all other comodities, w[hi]ch greif & feare in the popular sorte towtching that w[hi]ch concerneth their lyving & the whole mainteynance of their poor famylies maie worke Dangerous effect in the Common Wealth.[222]

The aldermen here utilised the Council's concern with tumults, noting that the 'Commons' of the city would only be satisfied if their governors took the patent to trial at law.

By December, Common Council also decided to petition the Queen to request the revocation of both Darcy's and Bellingham's patents. More boldly, they even called for the 'staye of all other letters patent[e]s graunted or to be graunted to perticuler persons preiudiciall to the lib[er]ties of this Citie or hurtefull to the Citizens and inhabitant[e]s thereof'.[223] In effect, they attempted to restrain future Crown policy to ensure that no privileges be granted which clashed with the city's rights. The process of penning these suits in Common Council is also revealed by a later order which noted that the petition, once written, was 'openly read' in Common Hall before councillors agreed that it should be delivered by the alderman Sir Richard Martin and others.[224] As such, even Common Council meetings served as an arena where councillors could approve and participate in the sending of supplications, showing their approval for the arguments within. This contributed to processes of politicisation, as those freemen present were exposed to some of the powerful legal and constitutional objections raised against monopolies. By the close of 1595, the city therefore sent petitions which included more generalised calls for the ending of monopolies as a fiscal device, alongside specific references to those patents which their citizens were vexed by.

This continued petitioning agitation had important effects, showing the real success anti-monopoly supplications could have. By late 1595, restrictions were imposed on Darcy's patent, responding to many of the problematic features of the grant complained of since 1592. The concern that Darcy could pick locations for leather to be sealed, as expressed in the Declaration and in the petition of the city, was rectified through a new proviso that any locations for the seal were to be chosen with the consent of the Leathersellers' Company.[225] Darcy's use of bonds, a source of such discontent in the Humble Petition, was also addressed. From now on, only those who contravened the patent were to enter them. The legality of the patent was ordered for yet another review. In the meantime, Darcy was only permitted to exercise his patent 'in the space of vij myles from the Citty of London'.[226]

A complete victory for the petitioners occurred by 24 January 1596: the patent was cancelled. Lord Mayor Slaney wrote directly to the Council to celebrate Elizabeth's 'good & gratious inclination to revoke hir Patent graunted to hir servant Mr Edward Darcey'.[227] In return, the city were ordered to pay a fine of £4,000. Trying their luck once more, they protested. After all, they and the Leathersellers should not need to pay any fine 'for redemption of that w[hi]ch [we] never yet forfeited'.[228] Slaney once again couched this protest in references to dearth and poverty, suggesting that the enforcement of this fine would have negative effects on the 'harts and myndes' of poor subjects.[229] The Leathersellers' Company also mobilised in protest. Their accounts list payments to Fuller for legal counsel for a petition concerning the 'Request to gyve Mr Darcy money'.[230] These records provide insight into the centrality of scribes and clerks to the petitioning process. Whilst certainly advising on protest, Fuller did not always pen petitions himself. Payments were thus recorded to 'Mr Fullers man for drawinge the petycion', and to an employee of the city Remembrancer, Giles Fletcher.[231] In this final act of protest, the city and the Leathersellers' Company emerged victorious: no records suggest that the fine was ever paid.

## The 1601 parliament – a sense of optimism?

The cancellation of Darcy's monopoly may have relieved the pressures on the leather trade, but the broader battle over patents did not cease. In the same month as Darcy's patent was cancelled, Common Council continued to draft their petition 'conteyninge sondrey greevances towchinge divers letters patent[e]s'.[232] The city continued to fight patents, whilst more widely throughout the realm, subjects in different trades found themselves vexed by the actions and demands of patentees.[233] Darcy was compensated for his loss of the leather patent with his new grant for the sole making and importing of playing cards.[234]

Discontent therefore erupted in Elizabeth's last two Parliaments. Monopolies had been raised as an issue in November 1597 and a motion was made for a bill on monopolies.[235] The Queen's subsequent promise to reform and investigate existing grants proved empty.[236] By 1601, a range of monopolies were attacked as MPs sought to represent the grievances of their constituents. In one particularly impassioned speech following a discussion on the range of goods monopolised, the MP and lawyer of Lincoln's Inn, William Hakewill, cried 'ys not bread ther?...For yf order be not taken for these, bread wilbe there before the next parleamente'.[237] Manuscript papers and lists of existent monopolies for such goods as steel, starch, glass, and paper circulated in the House.[238] Monopolies which had aggrieved the city also prompted complaints from the localities. Drake's patent was criticised by a burgess from Warwick, who complained of its effects on his own constituents.[239] A speech by Cecil showed the extent to which subjects throughout the realm were affected by patents in their everyday lives, as they came face-to-face with patentees and their letters of assistance from the Council. These were shown to 'some desolate widow, to some simple cottage, or poor ignorant people', who were often too poor to resort to London to challenge them.[240] Here was an acknowledgement that monopolies were a widespread grievance, reaching down to the bottom of society.

The charged issue of the prerogative received attention as MPs moved to debate whether proceeding against monopolies by bill would be hurtful to the prerogative.[241] Further, concerns with the potential outbreak of disorder, similar to those articulated by the aldermen, were expressed by the MP George Moore, who warned that patentees, as the hands of the body politic, were repressing the subjects, the foot. The danger, he claimed, was that the foot might soon rise against the head.[242]

It was not only MPs who ensured that the monopoly issue remained high on the parliamentary agenda. On 23 November, Sir Edward Hoby stumbled upon a group of subjects at the door of the Commons who styled themselves as 'commonwealthe's men'.[243] They complained that they had been 'spoyled, imprisoned and robbed by monopolists'.[244] These subjects actively presented themselves as spokespeople for the wider good of the commonwealth, attending the House in person to petition for relief. In this they appear to have found some sympathy; despite Cecil's outrage at their audacity to approach MPs in this way, he was to find himself without support from fellow members.

Such was the extent of pressure that Elizabeth was forced to respond. The impact of petitioning pressure on the Queen was made clear in a message delivered by the Speaker on her behalf on 25 November. Due to the advice of her councillors, as well as 'diverse peticions that have bene delivered unto her, both goeinge to the chapple and alsoe to walke abroad', Elizabeth had been made aware that many of her patents were hurtful to her subjects.[245] By 30 November, Elizabeth delivered her 'Golden Speech', blaming vexatious grants on the ill advice of courtiers.[246] On the same date, a proclamation was published throughout the realm revoking the most unpopular monopolies and leaving others for review at the common law.[247] Whilst this served to present Elizabeth as receptive to grievances, it also came with a clear warning on the widespread discussion of the prerogative. Reading this proclamation aloud in the company court later in February 1602, the Master of the Pewterers' Company warned members that none should seek to call into question the 'power or validitie' of the royal prerogative, or face the risk of imprisonment.[248]

News of MPs actions spread beyond the confines of Westminster, emboldening subjects to continue to petition and express their general disdain to these grants. In the House, Cecil complained that parliamentary matters had become 'ordinarye talke in the streetes'; from his coach he had heard subjects cry out to God to 'prosper those that further the overthrowe of these monopolies'.[249] He had even heard subjects demand that the prerogative 'touche nout our libertie', again suggestive that the interactions between economic rights and larger issues of prerogative and liberty was emerging as an issue intimately linked in the minds of subjects, discussed outside of the halls of Westminster.[250]

## Conclusion

The increased granting of monopolies throughout the 1590s triggered strong protest from affected citizens. In London, the Court of Aldermen and Common Council offered vital support in the campaigns of livery companies, motivated by a desire to protect the ancient privileges and customs of the city. The opposition directed against patents attests to the ways through which this fiscal device pushed subjects into negotiations and dialogues with authorities, at both the level of the city and even to the Council and Crown. The increased ease with which courtiers like Darcy and Drake could attain grants allowed pre-existing fissures within industries to coalesce around specific monopolies, whilst the readiness of the Crown to grant patents allowed interest groups a new weapon in their armoury of privilege-seeking tactics. As such, groups like the Skinners could gain patents to frustrate opponents and attempt to achieve primacy in their industries, whilst simultaneously drawing on anti-monopoly rhetoric to attack privileges held by their opponents. In the case of the leather industry, Darcy's desire to attain a patent allowed glovers and leather dressers to split from their brethren, prepared to ally with a courtier to achieve incorporation. Such courtier and city connections were represented through petitions which allowed those pushing for changes in their industry to endorse specific patents, whilst figures like Darcy gained added legitimacy for their requests.

The petitioning protest of the Leathersellers' and Skinners' Companies was triggered by their desire to protect their economic interests, emblematic of the tensions between old and new patents in an era of monopoly. This explains why both companies were prepared to dedicate resources to this campaign. However, the 'commonwealth's men' appearing before the Commons attest to the ability of subjects to organise protests outside of official company channels, their activism caused by their concern with the effect of grants on their livelihoods. These cases also demonstrate the importance of legal counsel in campaigns. Undoubtedly, Fuller helped to imbue these protests with languages prevalent in the political and religious sphere. However, this is not to take away from the active involvement of petitioners.

The choice of Fuller as legal counsel was deliberate; he was picked because his views were known, and because these matched with citizens' own perceptions of their economic rights. Continued interactions between lawyers and freemen only helped the language of liberty to spread further, providing many artisans and retailers with an important awareness of their rights. As such, these discourses would continue to saturate protests into the Jacobean period.

Even before patents were granted, investigative commissions served as an important point of contact between subjects and authority. They emerged as an essential aspect of economic policy, as Burghley sought the advice of merchants, artisans, and city authorities before recommending patents. This in turn provided courtiers and groups like the leather dressers and glovers with the opportunity to influence monopoly policy to further their own specific interests, aware of the strength recommendations in support of a patent might have. Commissions were also vital investigative spaces once patents were granted, triggered in the Darcy case by complaints, and offering another avenue for petitioning and consultation with subjects, including illiterate leather dressers.

Throughout the 1590s, the city authorities and the Council were receptive to petitioners' demands. Undoubtedly, the existence of a crisis of authority played a part here, whilst Lord Mayors like Spencer certainly played on the threat of disorder to push the Council into action.[251] The forwarding of petitions must also be seen as yet another avenue through which the city proved receptive to subjects' grievances in their efforts to maintain order, facilitating the connections between aggrieved citizens and central authorities.[252] It is within this context that we must also place the Council and Elizabeth's willingness to cancel Darcy's patent in its entirety. The city and the Leathersellers launched a relentless petitioning campaign, applying constant pressure for the revocation of the grant. However, achieving its full cancellation was no small feat. Elizabeth and her Council clearly perceived it as safer to cancel the monopoly then to face the wrath of vengeful artisans and retailers through the city, a threat which petitions had opened their eyes to. For city authorities, chief amongst their motivations was the challenge posed to their own privileges and customs, pushed into negotiations with the Council by the clashes generated by monopoly policy.

The sense of optimism generated by Elizabeth's 'Golden Speech' and proclamation might for many subjects have signalled a new beginning, an end to the infringements on their economic livelihoods which the increased use of monopolies had caused. In the courts, the case of *Darcy v. Allen* (with Fuller acting as legal defence) confirmed the ability of the common law to protect subjects's rights to trade, leading to the cancellation of Darcy's short-lived second grant. The accession of a new King in 1603 only added to this sense of hope. Yet it also provided new opportunities for pre-existing corporate bodies, courtiers, and syndicates to push for the extension of their own privileges. Nowhere was this more apparent than in the contests generated by the creation of new corporate bodies in the city. In many ways, the period of monopoly was only just beginning.

## Notes

1 BL, Lans. MS 69/26, fo. 66r.

2 For Darcy, see R. Virgoe, 'Darcy, Edward (1543–1612), of Dartford Place, Kent', in P. W. Hasler (ed.), *The History of Parliament: The House of Commons 1558–1603* (London, 1981), https://www.historyofparliamentonline.org/volume/1558-1603/member/darcy-edward-1543-1612 (accessed 11 December 2019).

3 BL, Lans. MS 69/26, fo. 66r; Withington, *Politics*, p. 174.

4 TLA, COL/RMD/PA/01/001, fo. 334r.

5 *Ibid.*, fo. 334r-v.

6 *Ibid.*, fos 334v–335r.

7 J. Guy, 'The 1590s: The Second Reign of Elizabeth I?', in J. Guy (ed.), *The Reign of Elizabeth I: Court and Culture in the Last Decade* (Cambridge, 1995), pp. 1–19; M. J. Power, 'London and the Control of the "Crisis" of the 1590s', *History*, 70:230 (1985), p. 384. For challenges to the idea of a 'crisis' in the 1590s, see Rappaport, *Worlds within Worlds*, ch. 9; Archer, *Pursuit*, pp. 5–14.

8 The main study of popular objections and lobbying against monopolies in the 1590s remains Archer, 'London Lobbies'.

9 For pre-existent analyses of Darcy, see Archer, 'Rhetorics of Metropolitan Incorporation', pp. 153–67; N. Tyacke, 'Locating the "English Revolution"', pp. 15–16.

10 Archer, *Pursuit*, ch. 2.

11 Brooks, *Law, Politics and Society*, p. 423.

12 J. Sharpe, 'Social Strain and Social Dislocation, 1585–1603', in Guy, *The Reign of Elizabeth I*, pp. 192–211.

13 J. Walter, '"A Foolish Commotion of Youth"? Crowds and the "Crisis of the 1590s" in London', *London Journal*, 44:1 (2019), pp. 17–36; Archer, *Pursuit*, p. 14.

14 Walter, '"A Foolish Commotion"', p. 28.

15 Archer, *Pursuit*, p. 8, ch. 2.

16 *Ibid.*, p. 37.

17 TLA, COL/CA/01/01/025, fo. 291r.

18 *Ibid.*, fo. 359r; TLA, COL/CA/01/01/026, fos 83v, 87v, 109v.

19 TLA, COL/CA/01/01/027, fo. 119r.

20 TLA, COL/CA/01/01/025, fos 217r, 560v, 570v.

21 Ashton, 'Conflicts'.

22 TLA, COL/CA/01/01/027, fos 24v, 39r, 62r, 85v.

23 *Ibid.*, fos 95r-v, 96r, 114r, 275r. For the Skinners' Company refusal to pay, see GL, CLC/L/SE/B/001/MS30708/002, fos 309v, 310v.
24 E. M. Veale, *The English Fur Trade in the Later Middle Ages* (London, 2003), *British History Online*, https://www-british-history-ac-uk.ezproxy-prd.bodleian.ox.ac.uk/london-record-soc/vol38 (accessed 22 January 2025), ch. 7; BL, Lans. MS 71/55, fos 119r–120r.
25 CP 167/30, fo. 37r. See also their petition to Burghley, CP 167/31, fo. 39r; GL, CLC/L/SE/B/001/MS30708/001, fos 54r–v, 56r; GL, CLC/L/SE/B/001/MS30708/002, fos 198v, 200v. They also moved in 1570 to petition against a licence for the export of rabbit skins, see GL, CLC/L/SE/B/001/MS30708/001, fos 15v–16v.
26 Veale, *Fur Trade*, ch. 7; BL, Lans. MS 71/54 fo. 117; BL, Lans. MS 73/16, fo. 53r. See the vast number of payments for this in GL, CLC/L/SE/D/007/MS30727/004; GL, CLC/L/SE/B/001/MS30708/002, fos 200v, 209v.
27 BL, Lans, MS 71/55, fo. 120r; BL, Lans. MS 71/54, fo. 117r; GL, CLC/L/SE/B/001/MS30708/001, fo. 57r; GL, CLC/L/SE/B/001/MS30708/002, fo. 212v.
28 Veale, *Fur Trade*, ch. 7; BL, Lans. MS 71/55, fos 119r–120r. By 1606 their bill in Parliament for the dressing of skins before export passed, see BL, Cotton Titus F IV, fos 303r–304v, 305r–307v.
29 BL, Lans. MS 71/55, fo. 120r.
30 Cavert, *Smoke of London*, ch. 7.
31 Hatcher, *Coal Industry*, I, pp. 514–15.
32 TLA, COL/RMD/PA/01/002, fos 53v–54r, 66v–71r; *APC*, 25, pp. 31–2.
33 TLA, COL/RMD/PA/01/002, fo. 67v.
34 *Ibid.*, fos 70r, 71r.
35 This would continue with disputes over their charter of 1600, see Hatcher, *Coal Industry*, I, pp. 514–16.
36 For economic interest groups influencing economic policy throughout Europe, see C. Tazzara, 'Managing Free Trade in Early Modern Europe: Institutions, Information, and the Free Port of Livorno', *Journal of Modern History*, 86:3 (2014), p. 527.
37 GL, CLC/L/BF/B/001/MS05445/009, n.f. (3 June 1596).
38 Brenner, *Merchants*, pp. 208–9. Keller claims there was little investigation before patents were granted, *Interlopers*, p. 49.
39 BL, Lans. MS 86/69, fo. 176; Archer, 'London Lobbies', p. 29.
40 TLA, COL/RMD/PA/01/002, fos 69v–71r, 77v, 78r; *APC*, 26, pp. 27–8.
41 BL, Lans. MS 74/10, fo. 21r. Drake noted that Burghley was reluctant to grant the patent, concerned that it might infringe on the liberties of subjects to make this in their houses, see CP 170/44, fo. 44r.
42 BL, Lans. MS 74/10, fos 20r–21v.
43 GL, CLC/L/BF/B/001/MS05445/009, n.f. (11 September 1593)
44 BL, Lans. MS 74/10, fo. 21r.
45 *Ibid.*, fo. 20r. For abuses in the industry, see TLA, COL/CA/01/01/025, fo. 75.
46 For details of the grant, see documents at the back of minutes, CLC/L/BF/B/001/MS05445/009.

47 Archer, 'London Lobbies', p. 33
48 GL, CLC/L/BF/B/001/MS05445/009, 11 April 1594; TLA, COL/CA/01/01/025, fos 201v–202r.
49 GL, CLC/L/BF/B/001/MS05445/009, 13 April 1594.
50 GL, CLC/L/BF/B/001/MS05445/009, 13 and 28 April 1594; TLA, COL/CA/01/01/025, fo. 218r.
51 TLA, COL/CA/01/01/25, fo. 332r.
52 GL, CLC/L/BF/B/001/MS05445/009, 23 July 1594.
53 *Ibid.*, 28 Jul. 1594; GL, CLC/L/BF/D/001/MS05442/005, n.f. (August 1593 to September 1594).
54 GL, CLC/L/BF/B/001/MS05445/009, 30/31 October 1594.
55 The aldermen wrote to the Council enclosing a petition written against Drake's patent on 14 December 1594, see TLA, COL/RMD/PA/01/002, fo. 36.
56 GL, CLC/L/BF/B/001/MS05445/009, 17 August 1594.
57 Braddick, *God's Fury*, p. 459.
58 GL, CLC/L/BF/B/001/MS05445/009, 'Drake's answer to the Brewers'.
59 GL, CLC/L/BF/B/001/MS05445/009, 17 August 1594.
60 BL, Lans. MS 81/22, fo. 57r. Interestingly, a Francis Oliver was named in the Spanish Company charter of 1605, see P. Croft, *The Spanish Company* (London, 1973), pp. 95–113.
61 TLA, COL/CA/01/01/025, fo. 526v; TLA, COL/RMD/PA/01/002, fo. 80r; BL, Lans. MS 81/21, fos 54r–56v; *APC*, 25, pp. 486–7.
62 *APC*, 30, pp. 132, 331–2.
63 *By the Queene. A proclamation for the reformation of abuses.*
64 Archer, *Pursuit*, p. 38.
65 For the best overview of the industry, see Clarkson, 'English Leather Industry'.
66 L. A. Clarkson, 'The Leather Crafts in Tudor and Stuart England', *The Agricultural History Review*, 14:1 (1966), p. 27.
67 Clarkson, 'English Leather Industry', p. 68.
68 L. A. Clarkson, 'English Economic Policy in the Sixteenth and Seventeenth Centuries: The Case of the Leather Industry', *Bulletin of the Institute of Historical Research*, 38:98 (1965), pp. 149–62; D. M. Dean, 'Public or Private? London, Leather and Legislation in Elizabethan England', *Historical Journal*, 31:3 (1988), pp. 525–48.
69 Clarkson, 'English Leather Industry', pp. 224, 251–4.
70 P. Hunting, *The Leathersellers' Company: A History* (London, 1994).
71 BL, Lans. MS 71/66, fo. 168r.
72 Veale, *Fur Trade*, ch. 3.
73 Clarkson, 'English Leather Industry', p. 215; R. W. Waggett, *A History of the Worshipful Company of Glovers of London*, 2nd edn (Chichester, 2008), ch. 3.
74 Clarkson, 'English Leather Industry', p. 226.
75 Unwin, *Industrial Organization*, p. 128.
76 For a blank dispensation, see BL, Lans. MS 20/7, fo. 19.

77 *CSPD*, 1591–4, pp. 569–70. For a later proposal to enforce regulations in the industry, see TNA, SP 15/41, fos 169–70.
78 BL, Lans. MS 56/68, fo. 212r.
79 BL, Lans. MS 65/47, fo. 141.
80 BL, Lans. MS 74/40, fos 114–15.
81 *CPR 34 Eliz*, no. 279, p. 45.
82 Clarkson, 'English Leather Industry', p. 269.
83 BL, Lans. 74/62, fo. 169r; *CPR 34 Eliz*, no. 279, p. 45.
84 BL, Lans. MS 67/84, fo. 206r.
85 BL, Lans. MS 74/50, fos 142–3; BL, Lans. MS 74/60, fos 164r–165v.
86 BL, Lans. MS 56/68, fo. 212r.
87 BL, Lans. MS 74/50, fo. 142r.
88 BL, Lans. MS 74/60, fo. 165v.
89 BL, Lans. MS 74/50, fo. 143r.
90 *Ibid.*
91 BL, Lans. MS 74/60, fo. 165v.
92 BL, Lans. MS 74/50, fo. 143r.
93 BL, Lans. MS 74/60, fo. 164r.
94 *Ibid.*
95 Clarkson, 'English Leather Industry', pp. 228–33. See agitation in BL, Add. MS 12,504, fos 156v, 157–8, 159–60, 161–2, 163–4.
96 BL, Add. MS 12,504, fo. 156v.
97 *Ibid.*
98 Waggett, *Glovers*, chs 4–5.
99 TNA, SP 16/383, fos 164–5. They would even reference Darcy's patent, arguing that their seals would be cheaper.
100 TLA, COL/RMD/PA/01/001, fo. 323v–324v.
101 *Ibid.*, fos 321v, 328v–329r, 329v–330r, 331v, 333r, 335r–v.
102 TLA, COL/CC/01/01/024, fo. 200r.
103 BL, Lans. MS 71/66, fo. 168r.
104 Leathersellers' Company Archive, Liber Curtes, Accounts and Inventories, ACC 1/2, fo. 45r.
105 *Ibid.*, fos 49v–50r.
106 GL, CLC/L/SE/B/001/MS30708/001, fo. 55v; GL, CLC/L/SE/B/001/MS30708/002, fo. 208v.
107 GL, CLC/L/SE/D/007/MS30727/004.
108 It seems unlikely that this was the later 'Declaration' sent by Rowe to the Council in February 1593 as this would suggest a gap of nearly a year before it was sent.
109 GL, CLC/L/SE/B/001/MS30708/001, fo. 55v; GL, CLC/L/SE/B/001/MS30708/002, fo. 208v.
110 GL, CLC/L/SE/D/007/MS30727/004, [1591–92 accounts].
111 *Ibid.*
112 GL, CLC/L/SE/B/001/MS30708/002, fo. 211r.
113 BL, Lans. MS 73/17, fo. 55r.

114 *Ibid.*
115 *Ibid.*, fo. 56r.
116 *Ibid.*, fo. 55r.
117 BL, Lans. MS 74/44, fos 124r–126v. Despite some differences in wording, both call for the patent to be suspended and reviewed, and it is likely that the petitioners first petitioned Rowe before writing an extended version for Burghley.
118 ACC 1/2, fo. 47v; GL, CLC/L/SE/D/007/MS30727/004, fo. CCCCXII [1592–93 accounts]
119 W. Herbert, *History of the Worshipful Company of Skinners of London, Principally Compiled From Their Own Record* (London, 1837), pp. 310–12.
120 BL, Lans. MS 73/17, fo. 56r.
121 *APC*, 24, p. 123.
122 *Ibid.*
123 The stay of the patent is described in BL, Lans. MS 74/47, fo. 135r.
124 BL, Lans. MS 74/48, fos 136v–137r.
125 *Ibid.*, fo. 137r.
126 *Ibid.*
127 *Ibid.*
128 *Ibid.*
129 Power, 'London', pp. 375–8.
130 BL, Lans. MS 74/50, fo. 143r.
131 BL, Lans. MS 74/60, fo. 164r.
132 GL, CLC/L/BF/B/001/MS05445/009, Reasons for revoking the patent
133 J. Walter, 'Crown and Crowd: Popular Culture and Popular Protest in Early Modern England', in J. Walter (ed.), *Crowds and Popular Politics in Early Modern England* (Manchester, 2006), p. 15.
134 BL, Lans. MS 74/48, fos 136v–137r.
135 See Chapter 1.
136 BL, Lans. MS 74/48, fo. 137r.
137 BL, Lans. MS 71/57, fo. 122r.
138 BL, Lans. MS 74/48, fo. 137r.
139 For his career, see S. Wright, 'Nicholas Fuller and the Liberties of the Subject', *Parliamentary History*, 25:2 (2006), pp. 176–213; R. G. Usher, 'Nicholas Fuller: A Forgotten Exponent of English Liberty', *The American Historical Review*, 12:4 (1907), pp. 743–60.
140 Tyacke, 'Puritan Paradigm', pp. 537–8.
141 GL, CLC/L/BF/B/001/MS05445/009, 26 July 1594.
142 *Ibid.*, 23 July 1594.
143 TNA, SP 14/6, fo. 155v.
144 TNA, SP 14/2, fo. 4.
145 TLA, COL/CA/01/01/025, fos 251, 291r; Archer, 'London Lobbies', pp. 33–4; TLA, COL/CA/01/01/027, fos 108r, 115v.
146 GL, CLC/L/BF/B/001/MS05445/009, Parliamentary petition [n.d.]
147 *Ibid.*, 27 January 1596.

148 C. W. Brooks, *Pettyfoggers and Vipers of the Commonwealth: The 'Lower Branch' of the Legal Profession in Early Modern England* (Cambridge, 1986), chs 4, 6.
149 GL, CLC/L/BF/B/001/MS05445/009, 28 July 1594 and 1 October 1594.
150 J. Walter, '"Law-Mindedness": Crowds, Courts and Popular Knowledge of the Law in Early Modern England', in M. Lobban and J. Begiato (eds), *Law, Lawyers and Litigants in Early Modern England: Essays in Memory of Christopher W. Brooks* (Cambridge, 2021), pp. 164–84.
151 *Ibid.*, pp. 169–70; Brooks, *Pettyfoggers*, p. 106.
152 Brooks, *Law, Politics and Society*, p. 423; See Peacey, *Madman and the Churchrobber*, p. 287 for ideas of the 'commoning' of the law.
153 Archer, 'Rhetorics', pp. 162–3.
154 GL, CLC/L/SE/B/001/MS30708/002, f. 204r.
155 BL, Lans. MS 74/42, fos 118r–119v.
156 I am grateful to former archivist of the Leathersellers' Company, Jerome Farrell, for providing me with information on these individuals. A Richard Ironside is also listed as a member of the re-chartered Spanish Company in 1605, see Croft, *Spanish Company*, pp. 95–113.
157 TNA, PC 2/21, fo. 22. Here his name is written as 'Waplade'.
158 For the most detailed analysis of its contents see Archer, 'Rhetorics', p. 165.
159 ACC 1/2, fo. 54v. It made frequent mention to a Council decree in February, possibly to a lost decree of 1594.
160 BL, Lans. MS 74/42, fo. 118r.
161 *Ibid.*
162 *Ibid.*, fo. 118v.
163 *Ibid.*
164 *Ibid.*
165 *Ibid.*, fo. 118r.
166 *Ibid.*
167 *Ibid.*
168 BL, Lans. MS 74/46, fos 129r–133v; Lans MS 74/55, fos 154r–155v; Lans MS 74/59, fo. 162; Lans MS 74/49, fo. 140.
169 BL, Lans. MS 74/51, fo. 146r. See also his second letter to Burghley Lans. MS 74/54, fo. 152r; Lans. MS 74/52 fos 148r–149v.
170 BL, Lans. MS 74/51, fo. 146r.
171 BL, Lans. MS 74/47, fo. 134r.
172 *Ibid.*, fo. 135r.
173 Ibid., fo. 134v.
174 *Ibid.*
175 *Ibid.*, fo. 135r.
176 *Ibid.*, fo. 134v
177 *Ibid.*
178 *Ibid.*, fo. 135r.
179 Ibid.
180 BL, Lans. MS 74/56, fos 156r–157v; Lans. MS 74/57, fos 158r–159v.
181 See Chapter 3.

182 BL, Lans. MS 74/56, fo. 156r.
183 BL, Lans. MS 74/57, fos 158r–159v.
184 *Ibid.*, fo. 158r.
185 BL, Lans. MS 74/49, fo. 141r. See also BL, Lans. MS. 74/46, fos 129r–133v.
186 BL, Lans. MS 74/49, fo. 141r.
187 BL, Lans. MS 74/41, fo. 117r.
188 *CPR 36 Eliz*, C66/1418, p. 120.
189 TLA, COL/RMD/PA/01/002, fos 8r, 32r, 63; TLA, COL/CA/01/01/025, fo. 299r.
190 TLA, COL/RMD/PA/01/002, fo. 32r.
191 TLA, COL/PA/01/01/025, fos 329v, 332r. See fo. 349v for an order to meet with the Recorder and others on the Leathersellers' business.
192 *Ibid.*, fo. 343v.
193 TLA, COL/RMD/PA/01/002, fo. 38r.
194 *Ibid.*, fo. 38v.
195 *Ibid.*
196 Archer, 'Rhetorics', pp. 163–4.
197 TLA, COL/RMD/PA/01/002, fo. 38r.
198 I. W. Archer, 'Spencer, Sir John (d. 1610)', *ODNB* (Oxford, 2004), https://ezproxy-prd.bodleian.ox.ac.uk:2095/10.1093/ref:odnb/26130 (accessed 18 February 2020).
199 Walter, '"A Foolish Commotion"', p. 25.
200 TLA, COL/RMD/PA/01/002, fo. 51r.
201 Walter, '"A Foolish Commotion"', pp. 21, 29.
202 TLA, COL/RMD/PA/01/002, fo. 69v.
203 *APC*, 25, pp. 106–7.
204 PC 2/21, fo. 22.
205 TLA, COL/RMD/PA/01/002, fo. 60.
206 TLA, COL/CA/01/01/025, fo. 346r.
207 TLA, COL/RMD/PA/01/002, fo. 39v. This is entered right after Spencer's letter on the prisoners' petition, so it is possible this was a copy of the suit, but it is very similar to the city's petition in the Cecil Papers from November.
208 CP 141/351, fo. 169.
209 TLA, COL/RMD/PA/01/002, fo. 39.
210 ACC 1/2, fo. 60r.
211 TLA, COL/CA/01/01/025, fo. 296v.
212 TLA, COL/RMD/PA/01/002, fo. 39r.
213 *Ibid.*
214 *Ibid.*
215 *Ibid.*
216 *Ibid.*, fo. 39v.
217 *Ibid.*
218 *Ibid.*, fos 40r–41v, 63r-v; CP 141/351, fo. 169r; CP 141/351, fo. 168r.
219 CP 141/351, fo. 169r.
220 *Ibid.*

221 *CSPD*, 1591–94, p. 557.
222 CP 141/351, fo. 168r.
223 TLA, COL/CC/01/01/025, fo. 82v.
224 *Ibid.*, fo. 83r.
225 TNA, SP 12/253, fo. 168r. The document is dated in calendars to September, but given the complaints articulated by the city in November, it likely dates to later. Fuller and others attended the court at Richmond in December on the Leathersellers' cause, perhaps pertaining to this, TLA, COL/CA/01/01/025, fo. 471r.
226 TNA, SP 12/253, fo. 168r.
227 TLA, COL/RMD/PA/01/002, fo. 73r.
228 *Ibid.*
229 *Ibid.*, fo. 73v.
230 ACC 1/2, fo. 65r.
231 *Ibid.*
232 TLA, COL/CC/01/01/025, fo. 83r.
233 For example, the city opposed a patent to John Spillman for the making of white paper, on the grounds that his licencing of the poor to collect rags and 'stuffs' for the process was causing begging and disorder. See TNA, SP 12/279, fo. 165r–166v; TNA, SP 12/279, fo. 164.
234 In 1598, Darcy also became involved in disputes between the city and Queen over the appointment of a new seacoalmeatre, writing a letter on their behalf, see TLA, COL/CC/01/01/025, fo. 342r.
235 J. E. Neale, *Elizabeth I and her Parliaments, 1584–1601* (London, 1957), pt. 5.
236 CP 87/70; TNA, SP 12/282, fo. 52.
237 Hartley, *Proceedings*, iii, p. 381; Neale, *Parliaments*, pt. 6.
238 Hartley, *Proceedings*, iii, pp. 382–4, 387–90.
239 *Ibid.*, p. 371
240 P. W. Hasler, 'Cecil, Robert (1563–1612), of the Savoy, London and Theobalds', in Hasler, *History of Parliament: 1558–1603*.
241 For example, see debates on 8 December, Hartley, *Proceedings*, iii, pp. 442–9.
242 *Ibid.*, p. 376.
243 *Ibid.*, p. 390.
244 *Ibid.*
245 *Ibid.*, p. 394.
246 *Ibid.*, pp. 411–15.
247 *A proclamation for the reformation of abuses*. See also a letter from Sir Francis Hastings to Cecil, on the popularity the cancellation of monopolies would render to him, CP 89/135, fo. 135. For the proclamation causing people to ignore grants, see CP 186/26.
248 C. Welch, *History of the Worshipful Company of Pewterers of the City of London: Based Upon Their Own Records* (2 vols, London, 1902), ii, p. 34.
249 Hartley, *Proceedings*, iii, p. 398.
250 *Ibid.*
251 Walter, '"Foolish Commotion"', p. 27–8.
252 Archer, *Pursuit*, ch. 2.

# 3

# Petitioning the new King: contesting corporations

Speaking on behalf of the city of London on 7 May 1603, the lawyer Richard Martin welcomed James VI and I to his new English kingdom at Stamford Hill. Martin addressed James as the 'bright starre of the North', who like a 'new Sunne rysing' had dispersed the clouds of fear overshadowing the realm.[1] Reflective of the didactic nature of early modern ceremonies, Martin's speech contained more than just oratory to flatter the new King. He also expressed the city's grievances, and in turn, their expectations for future policy, addressing James as a most 'skilfull and faithfull Phisition'.[2] Chief amongst their concerns was the desire to ensure that, from henceforth, no subject would have 'his marrow suckt with most odious and uniust Monopolies'.[3]

The city authorities were not the only subjects to use the accession as an opportunity to communicate their grievances and expectations to James. Nor was such stage-managed oratory the only mechanism through which ideas were expressed. Alongside ceremony and ritual stood the circulation of public petitions to influence the future direction of religious policy, alongside a torrent of suitors all seeking patronage from the new monarch.[4] Whilst Catholics and Puritans jostled to influence James's religious settlement, others were more concerned with the future direction of economic policy. In April 1603, a widely circulated and anonymous document which blurred the boundaries between petition and libel articulated fourteen numbered demands to James and the wider public. Titled the 'Poor Man's Petition', the text was worrying enough to warrant an investigation by Lord Treasurer Buckhurst.[5] Its seventh demand addressed the monopolies issue directly, calling on James to 'cutt off all the lycences, and all the monopolies' plaguing the realm, and cursing a 'fye vppon all those lyinge knaveries'.[6] Another anonymous manuscript penned in May offered a list of 'thinges grievous and offensive to the Comonwealth'.[7] Amongst its concerns were monopolies granted in the late Queen's reign, including Darcy's patent for 'sales of Leather'.[8]

Setting the agenda for the direction of economic policy was as central to James's immediate preoccupations as the need to solve the religious settlement. As early as 4 May, James appointed six commissioners to investigate all monopolies and grants which were 'offensive' to subjects, with a view to cancelling those which were particularly burdensome.[9] Commissioners were appointed to consider suits for bounty, and news of these developments was advertised to subjects by an 'open placard' on 30 May.[10] A few days later, James issued a proclamation which signalled a continuation of Elizabeth's monopoly policy as enshrined in her 'Golden Speech'. James called for the stay of all patents pending review by the Council, exempting only those granted to corporations.[11] Presenting himself as a poor man's King, willing and ready to hear grievances, James encouraged his subjects to approach the Council by petition if they were vexed by such grants in the future. Lest this inspire a torrent of burdensome petitioning complaints, the proclamation established some important caveats. Subjects were to supplicate without any 'numbers, without clamor, or any other kind of disorder', and were not to use the cloak of public causes to 'utter private malice'.[12] This encouragement of anti-monopoly petitioning was something subjects would be only too willing to embrace, yet the warning to avoid clamour and to cease the pursuit of private interests was one which various economic groups failed to heed.

In the early years of James's reign discussions of monopoly, corporatism, and free trade were rife. Almost immediately on the accession, conversations about trade were bound up in foreign policy considerations, as merchants and councillors debated the benefits and dangers of peace with Spain.[13] The topic of corporatism and monopoly remained especially charged in James's parliaments, and the creation and re-chartering of companies for overseas trade led to staunch debates on the merits of corporate organisation.[14] These debates were not only conducted at the Council table or on the floors of Parliament; Ashton has shown that they were essential to the interactions between the city and the Court.[15] They were also not confined to considerations of overseas trade. Increased opportunities for syndicates to control new and expanding domestic industries saw many merchants move away from traditional trading pursuits.[16] In this 'most scandalous phase' of monopoly policy, new charters were issued to a range of domestic companies.[17] As different interest groups sought to defend or further their causes, many turned to petition the Crown, Council, and Parliament for and against charters. A closer look at individual campaigns in the city early in James's reign reveals the ways through which the issue of corporatism and monopoly was debated, discussed, and considered through petitions, in taverns, company halls, and the bustling streets of the metropolis.

In particular, the case of the overlooked starch industry provides a window through which to observe the contests generated by corporatism in the early years of the new King's reign, reminding us that the organisation of domestic trade was just as contested as the organisation of overseas trading enterprises. The lingering and unclear boundary between monopoly and legitimate corporate body was a key feature of these campaigns. So too were the King's own proclamations on monopolies, spreading articulations against monopoly far and wide. The language and meaning of these public declarations were questioned and manipulated by petitioners as they presented their schemes as in line with the policy of their new King. At the same time, proposals for corporate enterprises revealed a sensitivity to avoid accusations of monopoly as groups, including craftsmen and artisans, used the opportunities of the accession to agitate for privileges.

## The pursuit of chartered privileges in the city

The drive for incorporation was keenly felt in London in the opening years of the seventeenth century. So often, this has been seen as resulting from contests between merchant leaders and artisan members in companies, whose conflicting economic interests led many of the latter to form their own splinter-group associations.[18] It is perhaps more useful to place these efforts in a broader context. James's public declaration in favour of corporate organisations emboldened subjects to seek incorporation.[19] These calls for corporatism coincided and clashed with equally loud calls for a loosening of trading restrictions. As Ashton argues, the opportunities opened by the peace with Spain in 1604, combined with a short period of time in which overseas trade was free, made it harder to justify the need for a strict regulation of trade, giving rise to growing demands for a 'free trade'.[20]

The circulation of rumours and mobilisation of resources by merchants towards profit-seeking enterprises began almost immediately on James's accession. On 20 May, the London merchant William Massam wrote to Cecil to inform him of rumours spreading on the Exchange concerning the farm of silk customs. These had been granted to Cecil by Elizabeth but surrendered into James's hands. Massam informed him that the previous under-farmers of the grant had attempted to obtain the grant 'wholy unto themselues'.[21] Since then, some merchants had 'preferred a Supplication to the Kings Ma[jes]tie' attempting to ensure that the farm be protected from these under-farmers, men who were 'very evill thought of'.[22] Massam expressed his hope that the farm would instead be awarded to more suitable merchants. Massam was heavily involved in fiscal projects throughout James's reign as a member of a powerful syndicate. Unsurprisingly, despite insisting that he wrote this letter only in 'Loue unto your Honour' and not in the hope of farming the customs himself, his syndicate would gain possession of this lucrative farm.[23] Powerful merchant syndicates rose in this period of peace, jostling to gain customs farms, licences, and patents, whilst using their court connections to influence economic policy.[24]

Alongside proposals and requests for licences and customs farms stood petitions for the granting of new charters. James granted these to a spate of overseas trading companies, including to the Spanish Company (1605), the Levant Company (1605), and the Virginia Company (1606).[25] It was also common for livery companies to seek confirmation of their royal charters on the accession of a monarch, a process which could be costly.[26] In the context of accession, even charters circulated as mobile documents. In 1605, the Drapers' Company paid for copies of the charters recently procured by the Ironmongers, Grocers, Haberdashers, and Barbersurgeons, hoping to imitate their example to ensure their own request for a renewed charter was successful.[27] They even spent 3s. 4d. on a copy of the Grocers' petition to James for their charter, attesting to the ease with which companies could procure copies of petitions, allowing them to mimic or refute their contents.[28] The discussion of their new charter involved conferences with lawyers, one of whom was even paid for counsel provided in the Company hall during a funeral dinner for a deceased member.[29]

A lingering anxiety surrounding monopoly protest in Elizabeth's reign informed councillors' approaches to re-chartering. As noted in Chapter 1, Lord Chief Justice Popham and Cecil, Earl of Salisbury (ennobled in May 1605), examined how to organise trade with France and the Levant without inciting opposition. Salisbury expressed concern with the number of merchants in the city who had set their hands to petitions demanding that these trades remain open.[30] This issue shaped the way interests couched their appeals for charter confirmations. In February 1604, one of the main founders of the original Turkey Company, Richard Staper, wrote to Cecil to appease his concerns that there be no 'Monopoli for the Turkey trade', offering a set of nine suggestions to ensure that a beneficial corporate body, rather than a monopoly, was re-erected to trade in the Levant.[31] Despite paying lip service to these ideas and allowing more prospective members to join for cheaper entrance fees, the Levant Company, like so many others, gained an extensive charter allowing them to monopolise trade in the Levant.[32] As such, petitioning protest still abounded: debates over the merits of the Spanish Company triggered a 'war of petitions'.[33]

Other groups tried their luck requesting charters for different domestic trades, playing on ideas of regulation and the commonwealth. In 1605, a collective of 'poore Cardmakers', claiming to be based throughout England, sent a supplication to Cecil lamenting the vexations they had faced when under the control of Darcy's patent for playing cards. This had allowed him to profit from the 'sweat of our browes', before it was cancelled by judges in *Darcy v. Allen* and James's proclamation.[34] They proceeded to ask him to intercede on their behalf to help further their suit to be made a corporation. Even artisans could explore the differences between legitimate and monopolistic bodies in supplications, as they made a distinction between 'Corporations thatt inable manie pore familes to Liue and Corporations of Monopolies thatt seeke the Ruyn of the Common Wealth'.[35] They presented their efforts as an attempt to establish an organisation to help their trade and to alleviate poverty, appealing to Cecil by stressing that it would produce subjects capable of paying the King all subsidies "fiftenes and all other dewties'.[36]

Projectors and courtiers also approached the King and Council with requests for the establishment of new offices, commissions, or profit-seeking enterprises. Much as in Elizabeth's reign, the consideration of proposed projects was time-consuming; figures including Sir Julius Caesar and Henry Howard, the Earl of Northampton, gathered petitions and economic advice papers to manage the economy.[37] Lamar Hill has demonstrated that Salisbury's first few months as Treasurer in 1608 involved extensive analysis of proposed projects and schemes.[38] In one particularly impassioned speech delivered before the King, Queen, and Prince in July 1608, Salisbury spoke against an attempt by the courtier Sir Thomas Bartlett to prohibit the import of foreign pins, a plan intended to encourage the domestic trade in concert with the realm's pinmakers.[39] He was recorded as 'rather wishing to die in the defence of this countries weale then suffer traffick to bee shaken or commerce interupted' by allowing such a measure to pass.[40] Clearly, discussions of proposed patents could incite powerful objections, voiced even before the royal family as they were considered at Court.

James was also personally involved in the examination of patents at the Council table. Earlier in his reign, the King took a particular interest in disputes surrounding a patent for the pre-emption of tin granted to Humphrey Wemes and Thomas Brigham by Elizabeth. This was opposed by some of the Pewterers' Company, who sought to dominate the buying and selling of tin supplies. James's proclamation had emboldened these subjects to resume their complaint against the patent, framing it as a 'plaine monopoly' to ensure its temporary suspension.[41] Given that the right to the pre-emption of tin anciently belonged to the Crown, and that the tin patentees had paid annual rents of £2,000 to the Exchequer, James's interest in the case is perhaps unsurprising. On 13 June 1603, James announced the suspension of the patent via proclamation.[42] He claimed that the patentees had been prepared to surrender their patent willingly, though a note of proceedings on the case suggests that he was more likely persuaded by the Pewterers' promise to pay the tinners outstanding money they were due.[43] Within the proclamation, James cited his previous anti-monopoly proclamation of May, in which he had made clear the required 'course' through which the complaints of aggrieved subjects should be voiced. The Pewterers' articulation of their grievances, followed by the Council's hearing of 'objections of either side', had led to the decision to offer the patentees a trial to maintain their patent.[44] They had, however, willingly surrendered it. The purpose of this proclamation appears to have been two-fold. Not only did it announce the suspension of the patent, but it also served to present to the public a neat narrative of the type of peaceful resolution of patent disputes which James expected all to mirror moving forward. As such, the proclamation reinforced the message delivered in James's earlier proclamation in May, as he here advertised the relief he could offer for subjects who challenged patents by 'duetifully and orderly appeale unto us'.[45]

The reality of the situation was rather different from the image of order so carefully crafted here. The dispute was not peacefully resolved, but heard in Star Chamber before James decided to resume the pre-emption into his own hands in 1604.[46] A new commission was appointed in October 1604 to investigate the case.[47] The episode caused clear fissures in the industry; tinners in Devon and Cornwall expressed their support for the patentees, whilst the Pewterers faced internal dissension as some in their fold were seen as opposing the patent for self-interested reasons, resenting the loss of their previous dominance in the selling of wrought pewter.[48] Petitions were integral to this dispute. The Pewterers petitioned the Council in October to complain of the recent renewal of the patent, lamenting that they had 'no sooner tasted the sweetnes of their form[er] libertie and freedome' before finding themselves vexed by the patentees once more.[49] Wemes and Brigham crafted a detailed reply on 14 October which articulated a different narrative of events than that proffered to the realm by the Pewterers and in the King's proclamation. The Pewterers had suggested that James, in his 'owne most royall p[er]son' had heard their complaints and decided that the patent was a grievance.[50] However, Wemes and Brigham complained that they had been deliberately kept out of the Council chamber through the machinations of the Pewterers, rendering James's decision ill-informed. The politics of access was crucial to the securing and maintenance of economic privileges.

Conflicting narratives of James's proclamations on tin lay at the heart of this petitioning dispute. For Wemes and Brigham, James had merely suspended the patent, not dissolved it. The case shows that the language of proclamations could be used by petitioners to bolster their cause. Wemes and Brigham noted that the proclamation had in fact stressed the need to proceed by 'ordin[er]ie Corse of iustice' to investigate the patent, rather than seeking any straight and hasty revocations.[51] They thus presented a rather different interpretation of the proclamation than the Pewterers as both sought to craft a specific narrative of the King's intentions and actions.

New patents to individuals were also the source of friction in the city, where authorities continued to investigate proposals for grants by consulting relevant interests.[52] As in the 1590s, the city authorities sent complaints against patents to the Council, continuing to shroud their objections in appeals to the law. In 1607 the Lord Mayor and Court of Aldermen forwarded a petition from tackle porters, protesting plans by one Peter John to create a new office to load and unload unfree merchants' goods at ports. This was rejected as nothing but a 'Monopoley to ingrosse the labours of theis men and take from them their meanes of liveinge'.[53] The Lord Mayor also acted as a check when courtiers falsely claimed widespread support for their proposed schemes. In December 1604, Lord Mayor Lowe forwarded Lord Chancellor Ellesmere a petition from the Bowyers' and Fletchers' Companies. They expressed concern that a petition had been sent on their behalf, without their knowledge or consent, in support of Sir Thomas Cornwallis's renewal of his patent for shooting, a patent which they complained had led to the proliferation of unlawful games in the city.[54] Clearly Cornwallis, like Darcy before him, was aware that citing the support of those involved in industries could mask appeals for monopoly as eagerly sought forms of regulation.

Companies could also hear rumours of proposed patents before they were passed, sometimes even before they were requested, moving to mobilise opposition. In 1608, the Skinners heard of a petition 'intended to be preferred' by three Gentlemen of the Chapel Royal for all coney skins to be tawed and dressed before export.[55] It is likely that this suit was instigated with the assistance of tawyers in the Company, who frequently fought with the artisan skinners on the prices and dressing of skins.[56] Later in April 1615, the Skinners received information that tawyers had escalated their tactics, petitioning James directly to request that all grey coney skins be tawed before export. Their court books reveal a frustration with their inability to procure a copy of this supplication.[57] In May, they requested a copy from the Lord Treasurer, presenting this as essential for them to reply.[58] The very process of sharing and circulating copies of petitions, even if amongst a limited number of affected subjects, facilitated the dialogic element of campaigns, allowing the production of counter-replies and rebuttals. However, blocking access to these suits was also a way to frustrate opponents and prevent them from articulating their objections.

James's willingness to grant new charters allowed many artisans seeking the advancement of their own interests, including the tawyers above, to turn to patents as a potential means to do so, sometimes with the help of well-connected courtier patrons. This generated tensions in the city as authorities were anxious to avoid the establishment of artisan-led companies which infringed on the privileges of pre-existing institutions. In August 1604 the city's feltmakers, craftsmen who specialised in the making of felt hats, successfully agitated for a charter.[59] They had traditionally been members of the Haberdashers' Company, yet the custom of London meant that many practising the trade were members of other companies. From 1577, feltmakers attempted to acquire their own charter, much to the chagrin of the Haberdashers, who jealously guarded their rights to regulate the trade.[60] James's willingness to grant charters meant that by 1604, the atmosphere was ripe for their efforts to finally bear fruit. However, their incorporation triggered a concerted campaign of opposition from the Haberdashers. In many ways, the text of their charter had anticipated the problems likely to arise by the simultaneous existence of two sets of charters governing the hat trade. It contained a proviso that nothing contained was to be to the 'hurte Losse hinderance or preiudice of the Maister Wardens and Fellowshipp of the Mistery of Haberdashers', their powers and privileges 'before the making of theis p[rese]nt[e]s' to remain in force.[61] Despite this proviso, the Lord Mayor and Court of Aldermen continued to resist calls for the Company to be recognised and petitions asking for members to be granted the freedom.[62] By contrast, they were willing to allow companies to petition for charters if they were sure their privileges would not be infringed, and if subjects followed correct procedures before petitioning the King. In March 1604 the Minstrels' and Turners' Companies sought and attained the aldermen's permission to seek charters from the new King.[63]

The feltmakers were not the only artisans whose pursuit of a corporate identity triggered city protests. On 18 January 1607, the Council wrote to the Lord Mayor Sir John Watts, describing the appearance before them of a delegation of aldermen and citizens, joined by the city's Recorder. This delegation presented a complaint concerning 'diu[er]s Pattent[e]s of late unduely procured…for certaine Companie[s] of the Cittie'.[64] The Council appeared sympathetic to the city's plight, showing a concern to establish which of these new patents were prejudicial to their rights, and who had begun such enterprises. This concern appears to have shaped their attitude towards the re-issuing of charters even to established companies. In February 1607, the Drapers noted that their renewed charter had been stayed by Ellesmere who wanted to ensure that nothing within was 'repugnant or p[re]uidicall to the auncient Customes of London'.[65] They even paid £3 to the Recorder to confirm that this was not the case.[66] In their reply to the Council, it was the efforts of members of three companies to secure charters which particularly vexed the city: the Feltmakers, the Cutlers, and the Skinners.[67] The bulk of their letter was spent describing the contests gripping the Skinners' Company, which in this case were not between the tawyers and skinners, but between artisan skinners in the Company fold and their leaders, many of whom were not active in the skinning trade.[68]

In 1606, forty-nine skinners petitioned James for a charter, seeking to use this device to secure for themselves greater representation in the government of the Company and to erect a new office for the packing of skins.[69] These attempts triggered protest from the larger city, whose complaints provide a lively insight into the processes through which, and the spaces where, such activism occurred. The city blamed this petition on two named skinners, John Warrand and Francis Gheast. Both sought legal counsel for advice on whether they could seek redress for their grievances against company leaders by acquiring a patent.[70] Their move to do this, as opposed to pursuing their grievances through the common law, reflects a shift in the forms of redress available for company members in this atmosphere of corporatism. Earlier in 1601, the city had expressed concern to the Council that subjects, including the cities' disorderly carmen, had utilised the common law to overthrow orders regulating their trade. They claimed that these actions had inspired 'some of the Companye of the Horners and others of the Companye of the Watermen of the river of Thames to Call there M[aste]rs and Overseers in question at the Common Lawe'.[71] By 1606 disaffected Skinners instead sought redress through the device of a patent.[72]

The city proceeded to document the processes by which Gheast and Warrand had gained support for their petition. Both men

> went to sev[er]all houses of diu[er]s Artezan Skinn[er]s and acquainted them w[i]th their purpose, and had their Consent[e]s afterward[e]s at a Taverne a meeting was had of diu[er]s Artezan Skinn[er]s where the matter was Concluded and resolued.[73]

Going to the houses of their fellow brethren and meeting publicly in a tavern, these skinners organised their campaign, discussing the issues of charters and corporate organisation in informal spaces throughout the city. Following this process of consultation with fellow skinners, they proceeded to have a petition drawn up to present to James. Indeed, the Skinners' court books attest to the importance of verbal exchanges to garner support for petitions. The Company noted their concern that one of their own Masters, Mr Dickenson, had even given permission for someone to sign his name to it, causing the Company to request that he absent himself from the Company court in February.[74]

The city corporation were anxious enough about these developments to petition the Council in person with a delegation, marking a difference from their intervention in the Leathersellers' case, where they had forwarded complaints with stern warnings of disorder. Their efforts were ultimately successful; later in February the patent was revoked.[75] The Council concluded that the Skinners' new charter 'doth rather tend to authorize the goverment of the inferior sorte then to anie necessarie or good p[ur]pose'.[76] Much like the attack on the clothworkers in Bury in 1609, issues of social status were key arguments deployed to undermine the credibility of new corporate bodies.

As the number of monopolies continued to grow, so too did the number of petitioners seeking patents or permission to embark on ambitious projects. In response, petitioning policy was adapted by James and his Council. Between 1607 and 1609, a Commission for Suits was established alongside the *Book of Bounty*, a printed text with instructions on the types of requests James was prepared to grant to suitors.[77] As Richard Hoyle notes, this was not only intended to tackle James's liberality, but also a device to help manage the sheer number of petitions for favour which were sent to authority.[78] The accompanying Commission was to meet at least once a week to consider petitions referred by the Master of Requests, including those for which expert advice was needed, such as requests for projects.[79] Amongst the suits forbidden to be proffered were those seeking monopolies, dispensing patents, or licences to export or import prohibited commodities.[80] Subjects petitioned this new Commission directly. In July 1609, the Skinners were vexed by efforts from some of their members to gain a licence to export untawed grey coney skins, moving to send a petition to the 'King[e]s Ma[jes]t[ie]s Comission[er]s assigned for suit[e]s of this nature', a likely reference to the Commission.[81] By approaching this body, they could draw attention to a request which contravened the regulations of the *Book of Bounty*, demonstrating a remarkable awareness of the spaces available for petitioning activity, and a broader knowledge of the recent proscriptions introduced on petitioning policy.

The Commission for Suits also sent petitions for proposed projects and new corporations to the Lord Mayor and Aldermen, seeking their advice on trading matters much as the Council had done in the Elizabethan period. In June 1611, the commissioners forwarded a petition of silkmen in the city who sought incorporation. Whilst the Council believed this might be a useful body, the city authorities warned that it would be detrimental to their government, serving to 'weaken and breake' other livery companies whose members might be forced to join.[82] Patents for trades based further afield were also sent to the aldermen. Earlier in May, a petition from Sir George Bruce for the sole making and selling of white salt in Boston, Lynn, and Kingston-upon-Hull was forwarded to them, as commissioners specifically requested that salters and salt retailers be made acquainted with its contents.[83] Consultation remained an integral feature of policy-making, whilst such actions served to spread the contents of individual petitions further than to just the intended recipient.

Later in June 1612, commissioners called on the city to consider a rather different patent proposed by one William Thomas for the sole collecting and dressing of heath to be made into brushes.[84] Despite believing the suit to be sound, the commissioners expressed their desire to consult tradesmen who might be affected by this. By July, Lord Mayor Sir James Pemberton informed the commissioners that he had consulted with Thomas, lawyers, brushmakers, and haberdashers, leading him to conclude that the proposed grant was a mere monopoly likely to hinder the 'open and free trade' of collecting heath present throughout the realm.[85] The Commission for Suits emerged as an important space bringing subjects into considerations of proposed patents through the city authorities. This was undoubtedly a consequence of James's acceptance of the need for counsel when making decisions on economic policies, and of his councillors' consultation of documents like petitions to inform on matters of trade.[86] Yet it also allowed discussions of economic policy to extend further down the social scale, beyond councillors, projectors, and local elites alone.

## Agitation in James's first parliament

As petitions proliferated in the metropolis, Parliament remained an essential recipient of anti-monopoly petitions. James's first parliament (1603–10) witnessed the outbreak of intense discussions surrounding the use of monopolies, impositions, and the Crown's rights of purveyance.[87] On 23 March 1604, the monopoly issue was first moved by the MP Sir Robert Wroth in the Commons, and all those with anti-monopoly grievances were later invited to bring in their complaints in writing.[88] MPs debated the distinction between monopoly and corporatism as they considered how to organise overseas trade. In the first session, a bill for free trade into foreign countries was passed in the Commons, though failed to pass the Lords before adjournment. In the session of 1605–06, an Act for free trade to France, Spain, and Portugal successfully passed into law.[89] Thomas Leng has shown that the initial free trade bill introduced in April 1604 was intended primarily as an attack on the Adventurers, driven both by outports hostile to London domination and by interlopers hoping to break into the profitable cloth trade.[90] Concern was also expressed with the new charter of the Spanish Company. In March 1605, Thomas Wilford had warned Salisbury that many would oppose its re-incorporation, and that if a new charter were granted, it would be 'browght in questyon every parlament'.[91] His predictions were correct. The Spanish Company's charter was hotly contested, especially in the second session. Outport jealousy, combined with individual gentry interests, contributed to these protests. Pauline Croft has shown that MPs from the West Country were particularly concerned with the effects corporatism might have on their own ability to engage in the fishing and corn export trades.[92]

Even when approaching a Commons so hostile to monopoly privileges, pressure groups vied to safeguard their interests. During discussions on the bill for free trade to Spain, France, and Portugal on 27 February 1606, both Bristol's Merchant Venturers' Company and Exeter's merchants sought an exemption for their pre-existing privileges to trade overseas.[93] Regardless of the questionable motivations of some, powerful arguments pertaining to liberties to trade were articulated in these debates, and appeals were made to the changed atmosphere generated by the introduction of peace.[94]

The nature and organisation of petitioning campaigns were also a source of discussion, mirroring techniques deployed outside of Parliament to label petitioning campaigns as seditious. In 1606, accusations were voiced that the West Country MP Sir George Somers had invested resources to overthrow the Spanish Company through a inter-county campaign. MPs investigated claims that Somers had

> sent messengers, vp and downe all the West Country to collect money and procure hand[e]s to overthrowe ye corporac[i]on as by a coppy of his l[ett]re will appeare, And there vpon (as is informed) the hand[e]s of Tapsters, Dyers, Tuckers, Weavers, and of diuers Mecanycall fellowes were procured to ye petic[i]ons.[95]

An attack on the social composition of petitioners, groups who were left out of a corporate body reserved for 'mere merchants', was here intended to undermine the suit's legitimacy. Such 'Mecanycall fellowes' were enticed by money alone, and the widespread resentment in the outports to the new Company was explained as resulting from this co-ordinated campaign. Despite the obvious attempts here to discredit the supplication, it reflects an awareness amongst contemporaries that concerns with corporatism could generate discontent in the provinces and that subjects could be mobilised to participate in larger campaigns of protest.

Beyond the sending of petitions, an array of subjects were brought into negotiations on the organisation of trade through parliamentary committees. The Commons' Journals recorded the presence of a 'great Concourse of Clothiers and Merchants of all Parts of the Realm, and especially of London' to offer their advice on the free trade bill in May 1604.[96] Crucially, it was not only overseas trade which was debated and discussed. Other corporate bodies lobbied Parliament on domestic trade. In 1604 the Clothworkers'

Company delivered a printed petition to the Commons, combining their concerns with licences to merchants for the export of undressed cloths with complaints concerning the use of devices known as gig-mills to row cloth in Stroud in Gloucestershire.[97] This provides a remarkable example of the early use of print to petition Parliament by a Company intending to inform MPs of their plight, a practice which would become common by the 1640s.[98]

Patents for domestic trades were also a source of complaint. In 1606, a bill was introduced in the Commons to restrain both monopolies and grants for the execution of penal statutes.[99] By 9 April, the Commons aired their complaints with the Earl of Nottingham's patent to sell wines, a patent to Sir Roger Aston for fees and fines in the Duchy of Lancaster, and with the patents for the pre-emption of tin and for the importation of logwood.[100] The cloth trade also aroused concern. The Scottish courtier Ludovick Stewart, the Duke of Lennox, had been granted a contentious patent as alnager of woollen cloths in 1605, triggering complaints by MPs.[101] It was even moved that committees copy testimonies delivered against Lennox for him to peruse.[102] This motion appears to have been rejected, but attests to the continued desire to allow patentees to answer complaints against them, fostering a culture of replies and rebuttals. A patent to Sir Edward Hoby for the buying and selling of wools, granted in 1602, was also a source of complaint, with clothiers and spinners sending certificates to communicate their concerns to the House.[103]

These grievances were presented to James on 14 May 1606.[104] In response, James seemed to cast doubt on their legitimacy, asking MPs 'whether the Countryes from whence we came did possesse us with these Grievances, or that the Same were suggested here in London'.[105] James thus hinted that this discontent might have been stirred by city interests. Perhaps the attacks on the self-interested machinations of London's merchants during the free trade debates had instilled in him some caution in trusting the true nature of grievances presented. Regardless, when Parliament reconvened in November, James announced that he had taken action to review the legality of many of the monopolies which had been complained of in the previous session.[106] This was to prove an empty promise. In July 1610 the Commons were still complaining about Nottingham and Lennox's patents in a petition to the King, the latter of which was seen as much abused and 'stretched' throughout the realm by Lennox's deputies.[107]

Concerns were also voiced in the Commons with the underhand dealings which lay behind so many monopoly schemes. Despite the strength of anti-monopoly fervour, companies and syndicates used Parliament in their efforts to secure new patents.[108] The feltmakers approached the Commons in their drive to secure incorporation. On 5 May 1604, a bill for the making of hats and felts was reported by Nicholas Fuller from the committee.[109] Harry Duckworth, John Bowler, and Stephen Freeth have argued that it was necessary for the feltmakers to introduce this bill to secure the repeal of an earlier statute which imbued the Haberdashers with authority to govern the trade in the city.[110] The processes by which this had been introduced triggered some controversy. Fuller announced that one William Typper had been paid £100 for 'following and procuring' the bill in the House, entering into a bond to secure the procurement of a charter in return for this sum.[111] In response, Typper admitted that he had taken £100 from feltmakers, but only to cover the 'Charges' accrued for the passing of their charter under the Great Seal.[112] It was common for even the most established companies to pay individuals including clerks and even doormen for renewed charters.[113] Typper was even recorded in the Grocers' Company court books as helping to procure their new charter.[114] However in the feltmakers' case, this payment was presented as dubious. As an employee of the city which so opposed the Feltmakers' incorporation, it is perhaps no surprise to find Fuller framing this as an example of corruption. Despite the concerns raised, the bill was successful, serving as a necessary precursor to the granting of their charter later in the year. As we will see, Parliament was also used in the efforts of a far more powerful, and merchant-dominated syndicate to monopolise a rather different commodity: starch.

## A new corporate enterprise: the Starchmakers' Company

The battle to control starch provides a particularly lively example of the contests caused by clashes between old and new privileges, and the use of the accusation of monopoly by groups seeking to protect their own restrictive trading privileges. Starch was primarily used as a stiffening agent for linen and for the large ruffs worn on the necks of many courtiers.[115] Whilst it had previously been imported from the Low Countries, it was produced in England from the 1560s.[116] Its production was time-consuming but needed little specialised equipment beyond barrels and access to water.[117] As such, the starching of linen emerged as an important source of female employment, especially in London's suburbs.[118] The product was made using wheat; the use of food supplies emerged as a focal point of contention utilised by projectors and petitioners when battling for control of the commodity before the King and Council.[119]

Starch had been at the centre of profit-seeking enterprises in Elizabeth's reign. In 1588 and in 1594 patents for the production, sale, and import of starch were granted to the Middlesex JP Richard Young and to the courtier Sir John Pakington respectively.[120] These developments triggered opposition from one company in particular: the Grocers. The Grocers were one of the Great Twelve livery companies, specialising in the retail of luxury goods including spices, currants, and tobacco.[121] The Company consisted both of wholesalers who imported and purchased commodities in bulk, and smaller retailers who sold products in their shops for private consumption.

The Grocers fought the starch monopolies throughout the 1590s, using a mixture of active resistance and petitioning protest. As retailers, their main objections to the monopolies rested on the restrictions imposed on their ability to sell starch and the requirement that they purchase it from licenced makers. The patents were a source of much rumour and speculation within the wider city. In 1594, the Council heard reports of an attempt by apprentices to steal a cartload of starch, and their assault of individuals working alongside a starch deputy named James Anton.[122] These were quelled by Lord Mayor Spencer: there had merely been a verbal altercation as Anton's deputies attempted to search the goods of a carman.[123] Despite the exaggerated reports of the outrage, this incident reveals the ways through which the presence of the deputies of monopolists caused tension in the metropolis. Such antagonism spread further afield. In May 1596 an alderman from Exeter, William Martin, was investigated by the Council for uttering 'undutifull and seditious wordes' against Pakington's patent in 'open place and in assemblie'.[124] Again, monopolies became an issue discussed and lamented in rather public spaces.

The starch monopoly was revoked by Elizabeth's proclamation in November 1601. However, the ease with which groups like artisan skinners and feltmakers were receiving charters meant that the city's starchmakers requested a patent in the first year of James's reign.[125] Indicative of the enduring belief in the need for centralised regulation of industries, they also sought the appointment of commissioners to establish and enforce orders to reform abuses. To entice James, they offered to provide a yearly rent of 10s. upon each hundred weight of starch they produced. Much like the feltmakers, the starchmakers also appealed to Parliament to achieve their goals. On 17 May 1604, an act was introduced in the Commons to redress abuses in starch making.[126] It appears as if the starchmakers had been advised that this act was a necessary foundation for the lawful establishment of their desired corporation.[127] Despite receiving a second reading, it was put to rest until the next session.[128]

A surviving summary of undated proposals for a new corporate body suggests that the starchmakers continued in their efforts to secure a charter. Sometime in 1606–07, they petitioned Salisbury to be made a 'Corporation as other Trades be', with powers to establish laws for the 'good gov[er]nment' of their trade.[129] This was justified not only by recourse to familiar arguments pertaining to the links between corporate organisation and regulation, but by hinting at the other corporations recently confirmed by the new King. Other anonymous documents written to justify the proposals for the new company attest to some of the opposition it faced, and the intense lobbying and petitioning activity involved in ensuring it came to fruition. It is likely that these were written sometime in 1607, at the height of efforts to incorporate a new company. They reveal that the use of wheat in the production of starch became a powerful tool to stress the dangers of the unregulated trade which had grown since 1601. The starchmakers complained of the vast consumption and 'dayly waste' of wheat in starch making.[130] In addition to requesting permission to be made a 'Guilde or fraternitie' with the power to elect a governor, issue oaths, and write a constitution, the starchmakers also requested a proclamation to prohibit the making of starch from any materials bar bran or pollard, to prevent the waste of food supplies.[131] Whilst this body was envisaged as being national in scope, such a restriction would serve to render the trade a London-based industry, as it was claimed that only the city and its suburbs had the supplies of bran necessary to make starch.[132] However, the starchmakers took care to engage with distinctions between monopoly bodies and legitimate corporations to present their proposal as beneficial for the entire realm. Whilst they hoped that James would prohibit the import of foreign starch, they claimed that this would not render their proposals monopolistic. After all, this prohibition would be an 'equall & absolute restraynt to all'.[133]

Despite the strength of these proposals, they faced opposition. The Lord Chief Baron Lawrence Tanfield questioned whether such a 'base' trade was fit to be made into a corporate body, raising interesting questions as to whether a trade which had so recently been brought into general use could be drawn into a corporation.[134] Clearly, concerns surrounding infringements on liberties were a key part of considerations of new corporate enterprises, as judges attempted to prevent the creation of monopoly bodies. Perhaps one of the main objections articulated against these plans, however, was against the voluntary contribution of 5s. on each hundredweight of starch which the starchmakers now offered to pay James. This was justified as a means to recompense James for loss of customs from starch imports, which would be prohibited to allow the domestic trade to flourish.[135] Tanfield expressed a concern that such a sum could not be imposed on subjects.[136] In response, the starchmakers suggested that this fee would only be exacted on Company members, and that as a voluntary payment, it could be 'assuredly levyed'.[137] This issue was central to deliberations on the validity of the new corporate enterprise, dominating many of the documents produced to lobby for the corporation. In another set of proposals, the authors tackled the issue head-on, arguing that the proposed payment was 'no imposic[i]on by his Ma[jes]tie vpon the subiect', but merely a 'Voluntarie p[re]sentm[en]t'.[138]

This reflected the lingering anxiety caused by the recent storm surrounding the use of unparliamentary impositions. Similarly, one of the main concerns raised against Lennox's alnage of cloths was his levying of fines for seals which the Commons criticised as 'Excessive...in the nature of Subsidies heretofore granted by Parliament'.[139] Debates surrounding the legality of unparliamentary revenue-raising devices became a feature of debates surrounding domestic corporate enterprises.

Following the example of so many others, the starchmakers allied with a courtier to achieve their aims. This was Lord Harrington, guardian of Princess Elizabeth and a keen investor in numerous fiscal schemes.[140] A lobbying document penned by a self-proclaimed 'Counselle' of Harrington noted that the starchmakers had joined with him in the hope that 'by his mediac[i]on to the Lord[e]s...his Ma[jes]tie might be moued' to grant their petition.[141] Harrington, petitioning James directly, noted that this was necessary as they did not possess the 'Charg[e]s requisite to the p[er]fectinge and orderinge of this busines'.[142] In return, Harrington too stood to benefit. For furthering the suit in Court, he requested the grant of new impositions on starch for twenty-one years, paying an annual rent to the King.[143]

Harrington was not the only courtier interested in this lucrative commodity. Starch garnered the attention of two prominent merchants: Lionel Cranfield and Arthur Ingram. Both were joined in a syndicate involved in a variety of money-making schemes, working alongside prominent city merchants including Thomas Dalby, William Massam, and William Angell.[144] Cranfield was a member of the Adventurers' Company and would later serve as Lord Treasurer.[145] Ingram was a merchant with myriad court connections, becoming Cofferer of the Household and later, Secretary of the Council of the North.[146] The courtier associated to their syndicate was the Earl of Northampton. Theirs was involved in a plethora of schemes, including the monopolisation of logwood.[147] A letter penned by Cranfield to Ingram in August 1607 reveals their craftiness in ensuring that their schemes be masked as necessary enterprises to avoid the censure of monopoly. Writing on the logwood issue, Cranfield urged Ingram to assure Salisbury that 'yt shalbe no monopoly', and that it would not trigger any 'generall Clamor' from subjects, being 'no more skandall' than schemes for the imposition of wines or currants.[148] Profit was at the centre of these plans. Indeed, Cranfield ended his letter by expressing his hope that the two would continue to 'Ioyne together faithfully to rayse owr fortunes', never working to enrich one at the expense of the other.[149]

Earlier in Parliament in 1607, the Cranfield-Ingram syndicate had been ready to put their plans to control the starch industry into motion. As in 1604, efforts were made to restrict starch making.[150] On 23 February, a bill was introduced in the Commons to 'avoid the wasting of Wheat, and other Grain, by Making it into Starch'.[151] The bill had the support of both Sir Edward Greville, heavily involved in Cranfield and Ingram's business ventures (and later, Ingram's father-in-law) and Cranfield's own attorney, Richard Martin, despite his oration against monopolies in 1603.[152] Their plans at this point were unsuccessful; by 29 May the bill was rejected.[153]

This did not dampen the syndicate's resolve to control starch making. Instead, they moved to reach their own agreement with the city's starchmakers, undermining Harrington in the process and using rather dubious means to learn the details of their agreements with the courtier. Cranfield's associate, Dalby, had been entrusted to gather information on their deal with Harrington through a starchmaker named Daniel Balgay, by pretending to desire a share in the agreement himself.[154] Balgay was presented as the figurehead for the starchmakers' interests. Through this deception, Dalby learned that Harrington had entered bonds to pay starchmakers 30s. for each hundredweight of starch they could make, and in return, they were to pay 5s. per hundredweight for licence to make the product.[155] Cranfield proceeded to offer advice to Ingram on the best means to wrestle the trade from Harrington. He should persuade the starchmakers that the industry would be better regulated via commissioners. This was a tactical strategy designed to appeal to the starchmakers' own aims, being something they themselves had expressed their desire for in their earliest petition to James. Cranfield also suggested that the undertakers reserve a third of the profits for themselves. Plots and underhand negotiations were an essential aspect of London's commercial world.

Cranfield's letter and Harrington's petition to the King might make it appear that the starchmakers lacked agency in these negotiations, pawns to the wider machinations of merchants and courtiers. However, it seems that the starchmakers were able to dictate their own terms in these alliances. Cranfield suggested that they had even 'abused' Harrington in their deal as 'Kinges', proposing a scheme which saw Harrington provide them with a 'greate price' for starch, as they moved to produce the product quickly, tricking him into believing it could be retailed at a higher price than its current market value.[156] Further, through their broader plans for a corporate enterprise, the starchmakers were able to shape the proposals for the form of the new body to ensure that they would benefit from its establishment. The lobbying documents for a corporation were likely penned with the assistance of Cranfield's syndicate, but these suggest that something of a compromise was reached, offering benefits to both investors and poorer members. They proposed that poorer starchmakers, with no stock to set up their industries near cities and towns, be employed in starch houses. Not only would this provide employment, but it would also allow any 'Willing to put in stock' to make profits.[157] Remarkably, it was even suggested that the profits be shared 'p[ro]portionally as the parties themselues makeing starch in the saide houses shall haue', almost like a joint-stock enterprise.[158] The proposal even suggested safeguards to ensure the Company was not ruled by an oligarchic elite. Whilst its provost or governor would be elected for life, upon their death it was hoped that a new officer would be elected according to a majority vote, by the 'most voyces' of the fraternity.[159] This is especially notable given that other artisans, including the city's watermen, skinners, and goldsmiths, were agitating for enhanced rights in the election of their leaders.[160] Thus, whilst the courtiers and merchants involved in these plans clearly sought to enhance their own profits through a joint-stock form of organisation, starchmakers attempted to shape proposals to ensure that they too received some of the benefits associated with corporate governance, in a scheme which also offered relief for poorer starchmakers.

The Cranfield/Ingram syndicate succeeded in their endeavours. On 23 August 1607, a proclamation was issued to introduce a new licensing system for starch.[161] The degree of the syndicate's influence is revealed by a draft version of this proclamation dated July 1607, which ordered the full prohibition of starch making, citing the waste of corn and noisome smells caused by its production.[162] However, in the proclamation of August, James changed his mind. He acknowledged that he had intended to prohibit the trade, yet upon the 'humble suit' of his loving subjects, he had been convinced of the necessity of allowing it to continue in a restricted form.[163] In a later proclamation, James again acknowledged that a petition from 'the better sort of the Starchemakers themselues' had persuaded him of this scheme.[164] James announced a new system for the regulation of starch making. A commission was to be appointed to licence all who used the trade in England and Wales, ensuring that starch was made from bran only. Commissioners had the power to view and survey all houses in the kingdom where starch was made. This was envisaged as a devolved form of policy, with local JPs and mayors assisting the commissioners with enforcement. All who wished to continue the trade were to appear before the commissioners at Founders' Hall in London to receive their licences, or to send the commissioners their names, alongside a certificate from local officials, presumably attesting to the goodness of their trade. These requirements might therefore exclude those starchmakers without the resources to come to the city or to acquire these certificates.

Given that the draft proclamation aimed to prohibit trade, it is likely that Cranfield and Ingram made use of their connections to Northampton to change James's mind, possibly spurring the starchmakers to send this supplication. Their efforts paid off; by 3 September the commissioners were appointed.[165] James's proclamation had explicitly noted that commissioners were of 'good qualitie and credite', further playing into distinctions made between legitimate schemes driven by the 'best' sort and dubious commissions and corporations consisting of inferior subjects.[166] Cranfield, Ingram, Massam, and Greville were all appointed. On the same day, a new imposition of 10s. on each hundredweight of imported starch was also introduced, a move designed to encourage its domestic production, whilst allowing James and any subsequent farmers to reap substantial profits.[167]

The final move employed by the syndicate to control the starch industry was the successful incorporation of a new body; by 8 November 1607, the Starchmakers' Company was incorporated.[168] Unsurprisingly, Cranfield and Ingram were members, and the Company's first master was Balgay.[169] As in their petitions to the King, they promised to ensure all starch was made from bran, paying James 5s. on each hundredweight of starch produced, and 10s. for each hundredweight of imported starch. The Company was able to dominate the industry, with powers to search and seize illegal starch in warehouses.[170] Meanwhile, only those licenced by commissioners could make the product. The connections between the syndicate and Northampton are attested to by the granting in March 1608 of the farm of the duties on both domestic and imported starch to Northampton, which he later sublet to Cranfield, Ingram, Dalby, and other syndicate members.[171] Ingram was also named as a collector of the impositions on starch by April 1608.[172] The incorporation of the Company, alongside the licencing system, served to create a new monopoly on the industry. Whilst in the 1590s, the starch monopolies had granted control of the trade to one courtier and his deputies, the trade was now regulated through a commission and a new corporate institution. It appears as if the starchmakers, whilst playing a role in negotiations, had not managed to secure a corporate institution free from the influence of powerful merchants. Balgay at least had protected his own interests. In his proclamation in August, James was able to distance this enterprise from the earlier monopolistic schemes for starch which had characterised the Elizabethan period, veiling this in a discourse of paternalism, as a body to protect precious food supplies. In reality, the scheme shows the ways through which commissions, corporate bodies, and even impositions could be used as devices by courtiers and merchants as they moved to monopolise industry and trade for their own profits.

## Conflict and protest: the Grocers' Company

In response to these developments, the Grocers' Company emerged as active petitioners. Much like the Leathersellers in their pursuit against Darcy, the Grocers had the vital support of the Lord Mayor and Court of Aldermen.

On 5 February, Lord Mayor Henry Rowe wrote to the Council to enclose their petition of protest, exhorting them to consider their complaint, touching so closely on the liberties and customs of the city.[173] The petition can be dated to around January–February 1608 on account of this letter. It was a large document, consisting of a folio of text with an impressive 106 names collected into seven columns, likely added in by a scribe.[174] The petition was addressed from the 'retailinge Grocers within ye Cittie of London', who were 'members all' of the Grocers' Company.[175] The Company's court records suggest that the initiative to launch this suit came from retailing grocers within its ranks. In January, the court noted that a letter from the Council on the starch business had triggered a complaint by retailing grocers of the various 'wrong[e]s & greivaunces by them susteyned in theire restraynt (by the Pattentees in this behalfe) from the buyeinge' of starch.[176] The Company thus gave permission for these retailing grocers to petition the Lord Mayor and aldermen for their aid in bringing their concerns before the King and Council. Clearly, the grocers in the Company fold were following acceptable petitioning channels. Unlike the artisan skinners in 1606, they sought the permission of their leaders before sending complaints through the city authorities, a move which undoubtedly added legitimacy to their complaints.

However, court records show that anxieties were high within the Company, as suspicions spread that some members might have had a hand in the starch business. At this meeting, a renter warden of the Company, Mr Robert Harvey, was suspected of being involved. In reply Harvey promised on his 'Credytt' that he had no dealings in the same.[177] If Harvey had supported such an enterprise, as had Mr Dickenson in the Skinners' Company, he would have been tainted with the stain of acting against his fellow brethren and the good of the larger Company.

Written in a neat, secretary hand, the petition was likely drawn up by the Company clerk, although the court order described above does suggest that the retailing grocers were given room to articulate their own complaints. There had been earlier instances in which retailing grocers had played a role in financing the Company's fight against patents, much like the leathersellers in the Humble Petition. In March 1602, the Grocers' court books noted an agreement that money that had been delivered to their past warden Mr Thomas Box by members for use in matters of starch should be used by the leadership as they thought fit.[178] By August, Boxe had paid £9 from a total of £14 10s. 6d. he had received during his wardenship from 'divers brothers of this Companye' towards revoking the starch patent.[179] Seven of the twenty-nine individuals listed as providing money were also named in a collection of thirty-eight testimonies gathered in 1601 which listed various abuses grocers had faced at the hands of the patentees.[180] It is therefore likely that these grocers had provided sums towards opposing the monopoly, and that this statement of grievances was part of a larger, member-funded campaign of protest. No explicit payments for legal counsel to produce the petition against the Starchmakers in 1608 is present in the Company account books, in contrast to the myriad payments recorded for counsel to help in their battles against the separation of the Apothecaries in their fold.[181] It is therefore likely that the Company's usual clerk helped aggrieved members to pen their petition.

Throughout the supplication, the Grocers lamented the effects of the new provisions for starch making, presenting the new company not as a legitimate organisation, but as a burdensome monopoly which restricted the trade into a few hands and enhanced the price of the commodity.[182] This was not an entirely false claim; accounts in Cranfield's ledgers suggest that by 1609, the price of some parcels of starch had increased to as much as 35s. per hundredweight.[183] The Grocers repeated many accusations which they had voiced against starch monopolies in the 1590s. They complained of the restrictions on imports and attempted to appeal to the Council's concerns with dearth as reflected in James's proclamation. They suggested that the domestic production of starch be prohibited and that all starch should be imported. This would advance customs whilst preserving wheat supplies. In reality, it would allow wholesalers in the Company to import and sell starch in bulk, to control the commodity. The support of the city for the Grocers on this point is shown by a letter sent from Rowe to Salisbury later in June. Discussing the problems with corn supplies, Rowe suggested that it would be best if starch was imported.[184] Rowe asserted that there was too much wheat used in starch making despite 'what shewe soever hath ben made to the Contrary', a likely allusion to the claims of the Starchmakers' Company.[185] These sentiments were driven not only by a concern with dearth and maintaining order, but by the city's attempts to protect the Grocers' interests.

The Grocers' petition was tactical and rhetorically rich, shaped to appeal to the perceived policy agendas of the King. The Grocers included a reference to James's proclamation of May 1603 to present the Company as an affront on James's publicly stated monopoly policy, which had served to 'signefye vnto all his lovinge subiectes his princly care in the suppresinge of the same'.[186] The Grocers also used the blurred boundaries between corporation and monopoly to present the Starchmakers as a monopolistic institution, referring to them throughout the petition not as a Company, but as 'patentees'.[187] The clash of corporate privileges central to such protests was given expression by the Grocers' lamentations that such a system was contrary to their own liberties, and the rights of freemen in the city to buy, sell, and trade in any commodity. The Grocers therefore drew on charter culture and expressed their belief in the economic rights bestowed on citizens by the freedom. They argued that

> by ye lawes of this Realme and ye Charters graunted to ye Maior and cominaltie & Cittizens of London, by ye Kings most excellent Ma[jes]tie & his noble Progintors, every freeman may by & sell, and vse every honest arte & means apperteyninge to his trade; yt he can devise, to gaine his livinge w[i]thout any imprisonment[.][188]

As freemen, the Grocers had gained their rights by 'longe seruice'; to be restrained of the liberty belonging to the trade 'for w[hi]ch they serued' was an affront to the rights integral to corporate citizenship.[189] The retailing grocers deployed the languages of citizenship and the freedom as a negotiating strategy in this economic dispute, as they sought to protect their own specific interests. As with the petitions explored in the agitation against Darcy, we should not dismiss these inclusions as added by lawyers alone given the widespread articulation of the language of freedom in city circles.

Further, James's proclamation announcing the commissioning system in August had itself made use of similar languages and ideas to criticise the Elizabethan starch monopolies. James noted that these patents had served to prejudice the liberties of subjects 'by reducing that into few mens power, which in the Common libertie of the Subject was free to all'.[190] His decision not to completely restrict starch making was presented as a means to provide subjects with 'the libertie and free use of their needfull Trades'.[191] This rhetoric was spread throughout the realm through such proclamations, emboldening petitioners to use the same arguments to fight the new regulations.

The dialogic nature of economic disputes is demonstrated by the decision of the Starchmakers' Company to offer their own articles in response by 17 February.[192] Their reply was unsigned, but it is likely that Cranfield and Ingram were involved in its construction. In form they mirrored many other replies offered by patentees, providing a point-by-point summary of the main contents of the Grocers' suit, followed by a detailed rebuttal. The patentees for the pre-emption of tin, Wymes and Brigham, had similarly used this form when challenging the Pewterers' complaints against them. They had included a list of objections to the main accusations of the petitioners, as they sought to respond to the 'articles conteyned in the said Petic[i]on'.[193] That patentees could reply in such a way shows that manuscript petitions moved *across* city interests; they were shared and circulated amongst those touched by the questions they raised, allowing groups to respond to their specific contents.

The Starchmakers challenged many of the accusations against them, denying that they had required bonds from those purchasing starch and insisting that they only seized imported starch if custom duties had not been paid. However, their main focus was on their existence as a legitimate corporate body. They presented themselves as an open and compassionate company, repeating ideas expressed in their early petitions for incorporation.[194] In their tenth point they claimed that the 'pretence of a Monopolie imagined to ensue by anie thing done by vs ys vainelie surmized'.[195] In reality, none of their actions could 'fall w[i]thin the Compas of that imputac[i]on'.[196] The contested definition of monopoly provided an opportunity for such accusations to be skilfully challenged by those so labelled. For the Starchmakers, the best means to challenge this was to present themselves as a large institution which would continue to consist of many members. All could profit from its enterprises, as 'every p[er]son hath may or shall haue interest in all the p[ro]ffytt[e]s of the companies bargayneing & dealing[e]s'.[197] Of course, this was likely to be true for those members of the syndicate who had secured financial benefits from its creation and for those with shares in the body.

The Starchmakers claimed that the only issue affecting their members was the refusal of grocers to purchase supplies from licenced starchmakers. This had forced the Company to levy a stock to help their poorer brethren, acting as a compassionate body intending to aid its members. The Starchmakers also challenged the accusation of monopoly by suggesting that all who made starch prior to the introduction of the licensing system could continue to do so, provided they make this in suitable locations and take it to the King's Beam to be searched. As such, the Starchmakers presented themselves not as creating a stranglehold on trade, but as requisite for its regulation. For the Cranfield/Ingram syndicate, pursuing their control of the industry through corporate organisation provided them with the ability to disguise their scheme amidst the broader acceptance of the need for regulation in economic thought.

The Starchmakers mirrored the tactics of the Grocers by also positioning themselves as loyal followers of James's policies, drawing on his proclamation of 1607, rather than that of 1603, to legitimise their existence. They noted that this had seen James publicly credit a petition with persuading him to allow the domestic trade to continue. This suit, they claimed, had been collectively penned by grocers, brownbakers, and starchmakers. As such, the Grocers' call for the commodity to be imported was a sudden change of agenda, a self-interested move to try and gain profits. This was given added strength by the Starchmakers' claim that there was no law or charter which even invested the right to buy and sell starch with the Grocers' Company.

Perhaps most striking was the Starchmakers' attempts to discredit the legitimacy of the Grocers' petition, repeating the tactic used by so many petitioners. The Grocers' respected position as one of the Great Twelve meant the Starchmakers had to undermine its legitimacy by presenting it as a product of the clamorous designs of a few malicious individuals, rather than the wider Company. They thus presented it as the work of a few 'warehowse men'.[198] This was likely wholesalers who benefited from starch imports: a later document penned in 1621 in the midst of trade depression commented on the wealth of 'the Warehousemen in London'.[199] Throughout their response, the starchmakers made attacks on their engrossing and forestalling activities, blaming them for hiking up the prices of grocery wares and as contravening expected norms of economic behaviour. Through their influence, retailing grocers had been persuaded to sign this 'vntrue and Claymorous petic[i]on'.[200] They were presented as nothing more than 'contemn[er]s of his Ma[jes]t[ie]s lawfull p[ro]ceedeing[e]s', proving that 'their owne gayne not the good of the Comon wealth ys the mark they ayme at'.[201]

This response, combined with the involvement of such a well-connected syndicate in the enterprise, hindered the Grocers' efforts to have the patent revoked at this stage. This was an even harder task given the extent to which the syndicate personally benefitted from the arrangement. Linda Levy Peck has estimated that Northampton made as much as £15,750 from the starch monopolies and from a pension granted to him on their eventual cancellation.[202] This was in stark contrast to the meagre revenues which the Crown obtained; in 1619 it was estimated that James never received more than £166 13s. 4d. in rents from the starch monopoly.[203] Greville faced spiralling debts.[204] By 5 July 1608, continued pressures on grain supplies saw James move to criticise 'bad and ill disposed persons' who set up starch houses without a licence, ordering that only those authorised by the Council make starch using musty and spoiled supplies.[205] In addition, commissioners were appointed to search all wheat and bran before it was made into starch. Commissioners included the Lieutenant of the Tower Sir William Waad, Ingram, and Balgay.[206]

Only in the face of continued grain shortages was the Company finally dissolved. In January 1610, a full prohibition on starch making was ordered via proclamation, and all supplies were to be imported.[207] The widespread nature of the trade made these restrictions hard to impose, whilst others jostled to reap financial benefits from this prohibition. One individual wrote to Caesar to request that a patent be granted for him to oversee the proclamation against starch making, to ensure that the houses of all offenders be searched and their goods seized.[208] In another document, possibly penned by the same individual, it was noted that discussion with JPs in Surrey had led the author to realise that it would be best not to meddle in this business during a parliament time, given that this might arouse opposition amongst MPs and peers. He informed Caesar that starch makers had 'gone out in speech: That they will still contynue & vse their Trade', preparing to 'fortifye their houses' to oppose interference, whilst more broadly, disdain was expressed that these restraints on trade were contrary to both 'Lawe & the good of the comon welth'.[209] Starchmakers uttered their resistance to regulation through the language of liberty and commonwealth, whilst deputies and appointed officials intruded into their homes as they claimed to be working to ensure profits for the King.[210]

The Grocers' self-interested motivations for opposing the grant were also revealed through their later complaints that imported starch was 'ill dryed & seldome or neuer well made'.[211] In another proclamation issued in August 1610, James attacked grocers throughout the realm for their continued purchasing of starch from 'needy and meane persons', as they sought only to enhance their 'great gaine' by facilitating its domestic production.[212] The Company's calls for importation in 1608 had clearly been opportunistic. The potentials of the growing trade meant that it remained the focus of attempts to devise fiscal projects. In May 1620, James complained that many men 'of wealth and ability' had been investing in the starch trade 'secretly', providing stocks of money to set people at work.[213] His concerns led to the introduction of another licensing system to ensure that starch was made from inedible materials. This was to emerge as one of many such schemes attacked in Parliament in 1621.[214] By 1622, another Starchmakers' Company was established.[215] This reflected the continued importance and use of both commissions and corporate bodies as important tools for the regulation of expanding industries. Multiple attempts were made to establish corporations for the same industry, despite earlier failures. Its charter was remarkably similar to that of 1607, though the Company farmed the impositions on starch in return for an annual rent of £2,000 to the King.[216] Its success was also short-lived: by 1637 the Company was recorded as 'lyeth sleepinge' for failing to pay its rents to the Crown.[217]

## Conclusion

Starch captured the attention of projectors, syndicates, and retailing grocers, yet it also saw the rise of a new interest group, starchmakers, who like the artisan skinners and the feltmakers, utilised the opportunities of this Jacobean era of incorporation. The mechanisms and underhand dealings of courtiers and merchants were integral to the Jacobean starch monopolies, yet it is also clear that the starchmakers played an active role in these negotiations, seeking corporate organisation to protect their own involvement in what was emerging as an especially lucrative industry. Similarly, artisan skinners sought a charter to secure redress from their corporate leaders, whilst tawyers in the Company fold attempted to gain patents with courtier-backing to ensure for themselves a steady supply of work. In this age of incorporation, the pursuit of patents and charters became an important tool through which collectives protected their own interests.

The protest levied against the Starchmakers', Feltmakers', and Skinners' Companies attests to the tensions generated by the establishment of new institutions in a city littered with holders of charters, grants, and patents. James's propensity to issue patents generated new economic tensions, such as that between the Grocers and Starchmakers, but it also added fire to pre-existing disputes.[218] For feltmakers, it enabled them to finally secure a separation from their larger Haberdasher brethren. The conflicts generated by the chartering of overseas companies have long received attention, yet it is equally important to recognise the ways through which the topic of corporate organisation and regulation of trade was discussed in company halls and taverns, encompassing expanding industries and older trades. As well as noting the making of these alliances and conflicts, an analysis of the language in which protests were articulated allows us to observe the power and widespread nature of the language of the city freedom and liberties, which became essential to the political action of myriad subjects.

Both those seeking charters and their opponents utilised discourses surrounding corporatism and the commonwealth to shroud their demands in wider understandings of how the economy should be regulated and governed. However, the precise definition of what constituted a monopoly remained contested. The vague boundaries between monopoly and corporate body were a useful tool as interest groups sought to negotiate for their own privileges, presenting themselves as driving attempts to regulate commerce, protect the King's customs, and prevent scarcity. By contrast, their opponents were merely self-seeking monopolists. As such, the Grocers and Starchmakers could utilise similar language whilst presenting radically different interpretations of the type of bodies both institutions were. At the same time, the status of those seeking corporate bodies crept into these disputes. The city had expressed concern that the Skinners' efforts to procure a new patent were driven by the inferior sort, and that this might encourage others to follow suit. Similarly, when protesting a new patent procured by the Cooks' Company in 1614, the city suggested this would prove a dangerous example for other victuallers and alehousekeepers, who might 'receaue encouragement and attempt the like'.[219] The attempt by the glovers and leatherdressers to separate from the Leathersellers in 1619 similarly triggered concerns that this would set a dangerous precedent for all 'the Mechanick trades about London'.[220] The social standing of those seeking corporations became a key means by which the legitimacy of their efforts could be questioned. This was linked to concerns with social order and stability, as these petitioners were often presented as clamorous in their actions and as posing a threat to the established government. For the starchmakers, their ability to present themselves as a compassionate body consisting of both poorer members and investors meant this was not an accusation which could be easily articulated against them.

Petitions and the charters which provoked them were mobile. The appearance of counter-replies and rebuttals in many of these cases reminds us that, even prior to the advent of print, petitions were circulated amongst interest groups. Copies were obtained as groups sought to respond to their contents, allowing counter-replies to be constructed which could offer point-by-point rebuttals of accusations. Clerks were central to this process, penning copies of charters and petitions to foster this dialogic culture.

James's propensity to issue proclamations provided a new means through which petitioners could justify their demands. Starting in May 1603, James's decision to renounce monopolies, whilst leaving corporate institutions untouched, strengthened understandings that companies were different from monopoly patents, whilst feeding into an emerging language of criticism against monopolists and projectors. James used proclamations to enforce new devices to regulate trade and to announce monopoly projects. Stirrings against this began to be voiced in Parliament in 1607. On 27 April, the MP Edward Alford reminisced that in Henry VII's reign, no man had been touched 'in his Life, Goods, Liberty, or Member, by any Proclamation'.[221] By 1610 the Commons would cite James's use of proclamations, including for the starch patents, as one of their chief grievances, fearing that they were a step towards the establishment of arbitrary government.[222] Proclamations were an integral device for spreading news in the realm, informing subjects of changes in economic policy.[223] Equally important were the ways in which they could be actively used by subjects in their petitions, as another avenue in which the language of the state was 'manipulated' by subjects to negotiate with authorities.[224]

As James's reign progressed, his granting of patents and monopolies only continued. Those 'clouds' of fear described by Martin in his oration to the King had not dispersed; they now took the form of ever-darkening storm clouds caused by the looming presence of monopolies. By the Parliament of 1621, these clouds would burst, leading to an outpouring of petitioning complaints in a particularly fractious Parliament. One group of artisans eagerly embraced the opportunity to seek redress through Parliament: glassmakers.

## Notes

1 R. Martin, *A Speach Deliuered, to the Kings Most Excellent Maiestie in the Name of the Sheriffes of London and Middlesex...* (London, 1603), sig. A4r.

2 *Ibid.*, fo. A4v. For the importance of royal entries for communicating ideas, see I. Archer, 'Royal Entries, the City of London, and the Politics of Stuart Successions', in P. Kewes and A. McRae (eds), *Stuart Succession Literature: Moments and Transformations* (Oxford, 2019), p. 258.
3 Martin, *A Speach Deliuered*, sig. B1r.
4 S. Doran, '1603: A Jagged Succession', *Historical Research*, 93:261 (2020), pp. 452–3, 459–61.
5 TNA, SP 14/1, fo. 64r; TNA, SP 14/1, fo. 65r; G. Heaton, '"The Poor Man's Petition": Anthony Atkinson and the Politics of Libel', *Huntington Library Quarterly*, 69:1 (2006), pp. 105–20.
6 TNA, SP 14/1, fo. 64r.
7 TNA, SP 14/1, fo. 127.
8 *Ibid.*
9 *APC*, 32, p. 497.
10 TNA, SP 15/35, fos 29r–32v; *APC*, 32, p. 499; R. W. Hoyle, 'The Master of Requests and the Small Change of Jacobean Patronage', *English Historical Review*, 126:520 (2011), p. 559.
11 Larkin and Hughes, I, pp. 11–14.
12 *Ibid.*, pp. 13–14.
13 Gajda, 'War, Peace and Commerce', pp. 459–72.
14 Ashton, 'Free Trade'; Croft, 'Free Trade'; Rabb, 'Sir Edwin Sandys'; Pennington, '"Free Passage"'.
15 Ashton, 'Conflicts'.
16 *Ibid.*, p. 116.
17 Ashton, *City*, pp. 70–8; Thirsk, *Policy and Projects*, ch. 4.
18 Unwin, *Industrial Organization*, pp. 126–7. Archer has shown that the extent of differences in companies could vary, see Archer, *Pursuit*, p. 101.
19 Thirsk, *Policy and Projects*, pp. 99–100.
20 Ashton, 'Free Trade', p. 45.
21 CP 100/25, fo. 25r.
22 *Ibid.*
23 *HMC Sackville*, pp. 58–9; R. H. Tawney, *Business and Politics under James I: Lionel Cranfield as Merchant and Minister* (Cambridge, 1958), pp. 96, 101–2. Tawney also notes the number of these farms and how many were let out in James's reign, see p. 96.
24 Tawney, *Business and Politics*, p. 85.
25 Croft, *Spanish Company*. See also plans for a fishing company, J. Cramsie 'Commercial Projects and the Fiscal Policy of James VI and I', *Historical Journal*, 43:2 (2000), p. 354; T. K. Rabb, *Enterprise and Empire: Merchant and Gentry Investment in the Expansion of England, 1575–1630* (Cambridge, 1967), ch. 1.
26 DA, Court Minute Book 1604–40, fos 6r, 28r, 29r, 43r.
27 DA, WA6/3, fos 44, 48–51. See also charges in WA6/4, fos 43–6.
28 DA, WA6/3, fo. 49.
29 *Ibid.*, fo. 48.
30 TNA, SP 14/15, fo. 84v.

31 TNA, SP 14/6, fo. 134r; TNA, SP 14/6, fos 136–7; TNA, SP 14/6, fo. 138.
32 Ashton, *City*, pp. 87, 91. This charter did not allow them the sole trade in currants, however.
33 Croft, *Spanish Company*.
34 CP 189/80, fo. 153r.
35 *Ibid.*
36 *Ibid.*
37 L. L. Peck, *Northampton: Patronage and Policy at the Court of James I* (London, 1982), ch. 5; N. Millstone, 'Sir Robert Cotton, Manuscript Pamphleteering, and the Making of Jacobean Kingship during the Short Peace, ca. 1609–1613', *Journal of British Studies*, 62 (2023), p. 139.
38 L. M. Hill, 'Sir Julius Caesar's Journal of Salisbury's First Two Months and Twenty Days as Lord Treasurer: 1608', *Historical Research*, 45:112 (1972), p. 313.
39 Ashton, *City*, pp. 79–81.
40 Hill, 'Caesar's Journal', p. 323.
41 TNA, SP 14/2, fo. 5r; TNA, SP 14/23 fo. 112v.
42 Welch, *Pewterers*, ii, pp. 37, 42–3; Larkin and Hughes, I, pp. 28–9. The Pewterers had earlier launched their own efforts to gain a patent for all tin to be exported in bars or as made wares, joining with Henry Jackman, see Welch, *Pewterers*, ii, pp. 21–2.
43 TNA, SP 14/2, fos 6r–7v; *APC*, 32, pp. 499–500.
44 Larkin and Hughes, I, p. 29.
45 *Ibid.*
46 TNA, SP 14/23, fos 113r-v; Welch, *Pewterers*, ii, pp. 37–8; Larkin and Hughes, I, p. 29.
47 Welch, *Pewterers*, ii, p. 45.
48 TNA, SP 14/6, fos 155r–156v.
49 TNA, SP 14/9A, fos 201–2.
50 *Ibid.*, fo. 201r.
51 *Ibid.*
52 See for example TLA, COL/RMD/PA/01/002, fo. 139.
53 *Ibid.*, fo. 136v–137r.
54 *Ibid.*, fo. 122v.
55 GL, CLC/L/SE/B/001/MS30708/001, fo. 100v. These men were likely Richard Plumley, Leonard or James Davies, and John Amery, all of whom were Gentlemen of the Chapel Royal. I am grateful to Oscar Patton for information on these men.
56 See for example, GL, CLC/L/SE/B/001/MS30708/001, fos 137–8, 142r.
57 *Ibid.*, fo. 144r.
58 *Ibid.*, fo. 144v. This was obtained by June, see fo. 146r.
59 See I. W. Archer, *The History of the Haberdashers' Company*, 2nd edn (Bognor Regis, 2017), ch. 5; H. Duckworth, J. Bowler and S. Freeth, 'The Feltmakers' Wool Adventure 1610–24' (London, Worshipful Company of Feltmakers, 2015), chs 2–3; C 66/1640, *CPR 1 & 2 Jas*, fo. 121v.

60 Archer, *Haberdashers*, p. 80; H. Duckworth, J. Bowler, and S. Freeth, 'The Early History of Feltmaking in London 1250–1604' (London, Worshipful Company of Feltmakers, 2013), pp. 27–31.
61 TLA, COL/CC/01/01/031, fo. 346r for a copy of the charter collected in 1618.
62 See for example TLA, COL/RMD/PA/01/003, fos 82–3; COL/CA/01/01/030, fos 7r, 62r, 72r; COL/CC/01/01/028, fo. 144v.
63 TLA, COL/CA/01/01/029, fo. 301r. The Curriers also asked permission to petition for a charter in January 1605, see fo. 506v.
64 GL, CLC/L/SE/B/001/MS30708/001, fo. 87r.
65 DA, Court Minute Book 1604–40, fo. 45r.
66 DA, WA6/3, fo. 48.
67 For Cutlers, see TLA, COL/RMD/PA/01/002, fo. 131.
68 Ashton, *City*, p. 54.
69 For their demands, see GL, CLC/L/SE/B/001/MS30708/001, fos 88r–v.
70 *Ibid.*, fo. 87r.
71 GL, COL/RMD/PA/01/002, fo. 107r.
72 By the 1640s, they would petition the Long Parliament. See Carlin, 'Levelling the Liveries', pp. 3–25.
73 GL, CLC/L/SE/B/001/MS30708/001, fo. 87r.
74 GL, CLC/L/SE/B/001/MS30708/002, fo. 385v.
75 GL, CLC/L/SE/B/001/MS30708/001, fos 87v, 90v.
76 *Ibid.*, fo. 87v.
77 TNA, SP 14/37, fos 148r–154r; TNA, SP 14/37, fos 164r–165r.
78 Hoyle, 'Masters of Requests', p. 560; Cramsie, *Kingship*, p. 91.
79 Hoyle, 'Masters of Requests', pp. 561, 573–6.
80 TNA, SP 14/37, fo. 152r.
81 GL, CLC/L/SE/B/001/MS30708/002, fo. 405v.
82 TLA, COL/RMD/PA/01/003, fos 17–19.
83 *Ibid.*, fo. 11–12r. For Bruce's petition and the city's certificate, see fos 12r–13r, 14r.
84 *Ibid.*, fo. 52r.
85 *Ibid.*, fo. 57r.
86 Cramsie, *Kingship*, pp. 51, 60.
87 *CJ*, p. 278. For purveyance see P. Croft, 'Parliament, Purveyance and the City of London 1589–1608', *Parliamentary History*, 4:1 (1985), pp. 9–34.
88 *CJ*, pp. 151, 153. For processes of petitioning parliament, see Chapter 4.
89 Friis, *Alderman Cockayne*, ch. 3; *CJ*, pp. 176, 215, 256, 264; TNA, SP 14/19, fos 175r–177v.
90 Leng places this in the context of the internal controversies generated in the Company by the Imperial Mandate controversy, see *Fellowship*, pp. 196–7; TNA, SP 15/36, fos 54–5.
91 CP 104/59, fo. 59r.
92 Croft, 'Free Trade'.
93 *CJ*, p. 275. For Bristol, see Sacks, *Widening Gate*, ch. 6.

94 This will be explored by Dr Alexandra Gajda and I in a forthcoming essay, 'Prosperity, Petitions, and Parliament: Peace and Economic Debate in Early Jacobean England, c. 1604–1607'.
95 TNA, SP 14/19, fo. 178v.
96 *CJ*, pp. 216–21.
97 TNA, SP 14/6, fo. 207r.
98 Peacey, *Public Politics*.
99 Friis, *Alderman Cockayne*, p. 148.
100 *CJ*, p. 295. For bills against logwood, see pp. 351, 386. For a more detailed account of proceedings, see D. H. Willson (ed.), *The Parliamentary Diary of Robert Bowyer 1606–1607* (Minneapolis, 1931), pp. 109–42.
101 *CJ*, pp. 295–6, 299.
102 *Ibid*., p. 296.
103 *Ibid*., p. 299; *Diary of Bowyer*, pp. 131, 142.
104 *Diary of Bowyer*, pp. 160, 165.
105 *Ibid*., p. 166.
106 *CJ*, pp. 316–18.
107 E. R. Foster (ed.), *Proceedings in Parliament, 1610* (2 vols, New Haven, 1966) ii, pp. 268–71.
108 See *CJ*, p. 264 for a bill by the Pinmakers.
109 *Ibid*. p. 199. This had been sent by Robert Sadler, later assistant of the Company, see Duckworth, Bowler and Freeth, 'Feltmakers' Wool Adventure', p. 14.
110 Duckworth, Bowler, and Freeth, 'Feltmakers' Wool Adventure', pp. 3–4.
111 *CJ*, p. 199.
112 *Ibid*., p. 200.
113 DA, WA6/3, fos 44, 46–51.
114 GL, CLC/L/GH/B/001/MS11588/002, p. 398.
115 Thirsk, *Policy and Projects*, pp. 84–6.
116 *Ibid*., p. 85.
117 *Ibid*., p. 84.
118 See N. Korda, *Labors Lost: Women's Work and the Early Modern English Stage* (Philadelphia, 2011), ch. 3.
119 Tawney, *Business and Politics*, p. 103.
120 C 66/1312, *CPR 30 Eliz*, no. 560; C 66/1417, *CPR 36 Eliz*, no. 769. It appears as if Buckhurst and Cecil became involved in the enterprise in 1598, see R. Zim, 'Sackville, Thomas, first Baron Buckhurst and first earl of Dorset', *ODNB*, https://doi-org.ezproxy-prd.bodleian.ox.ac.uk/10.1093/ref:odnb/24450 (accessed 16 May 2025). For more details of these early patents and opposition to them by the Grocers, see E. Paterson, 'Bloodsuckers of the Commonwealth: Anti-Monopoly Petitioning in Late Elizabethan and Jacobean England, c. 1590–1625' (unpublished DPhil, University of Oxford, 2023), ch. 2.
121 J. Stobart, *Sugar and Spice: Grocers and Groceries in Provincial England, 1650–1830* (Oxford, 2013).
122 *APC*, 25, p. 16.
123 TLA, COL/RMD/PA/01/002, fo. 56v.
124 *APC*, 25, pp. 374–5. The Council noted that there was concern these allegations had been made by his enemies. For resistance from outside of London, see pp. 49, 197, 258, 412–13.

125 BL, Cotton Titus B/V, fo. 260r.
126 *CJ*, p. 212.
127 BL, Cotton Titus B/V, fo. 260v.
128 *CJ*, pp. 243, 252.
129 CP Petitions 2108.
130 CP 141/348, fo. 165r. This has been misdated in calendars to 1592 but refers to 'his majesty' throughout.
131 *Ibid.*, fo. 165r-v.
132 BL, Cotton Titus B/IV, fo. 297v.
133 *Ibid.*, 298r.
134 CP Petitions 2108.
135 CP 141/348, fo. 165v
136 CP Petitions 2108.
137 *Ibid.*
138 BL, Cotton Titus B/IV, fo. 297r.
139 *Diary of Bowyer*, p. 112.
140 J. Broadway, 'Harrington, John, First Baron Harington of Exton (1539/40–1613)', *ODNB*, https://doi.org/10.1093/ref:odnb/12327 (accessed 1 December 2020); Duckworth, Bowler, and Freeth, 'Feltmakers' Wool Adventure', pp. 18–19.
141 BL, Cotton Titus B/V, fos 260r–v.
142 CP Petitions 1007.
143 *Ibid.*
144 Tawney, *Business and Politics*, p. 87.
145 For his career, see Tawney, *Business and Politics.*
146 A. F. Upton, *Sir Arthur Ingram c. 1565–1642: A Study of the Origins of an English Landed Family* (Oxford, 1961).
147 Tawney, *Business and Politics*, pp. 68–9, 85–6, 103–5; *HMC Sackville*, p. xxi.
148 WYA, WYL100/PO/6/XI/I, fo. xi (b).
149 *Ibid.*, fo. xi (c).
150 BL, Cotton Titus B/V, fo. 260v.
151 *CJ*, pp. 339, 342.
152 For Greville, see *HMC Sackville*, p. xxvi.
153 *CJ*, p. 376.
154 WYA, WYL100/PO/6/XI/I, fo. xi (a).
155 *Ibid.*
156 *Ibid.*
157 CP 141/348, fo. 165r.
158 *Ibid.*
159 *Ibid.*, fo. 165v.
160 For trouble in the Goldsmiths' elections, see TLA, COL/CA/01/01/029, f. 396r.
161 Larkin and Hughes, I, pp. 163–6; TLA, COL/CC/01/01/028, fos 141v–142r.
162 TNA, SP 14/28, fos 36r–38r.
163 Larkin and Hughes, I, p. 164.
164 TLA, COL/CC/01/01/028, fo. 258v.
165 C66/1744, *CPR 3–5 Jas*, fo. 338r.

166 Larkin and Hughes, I, p. 164.
167 *HMC Sackville*, pp. 154–5.
168 C66/1740, *CPR 3–5 Jas*, fo. 332v.
169 C. T. Carr, *Select Charters of Trading Companies: A.D. 1530–1707* (2 vols, London, 1913), I, p. 120. Carr compares the charter of 1607 to a later one granted in 1622, the text of the latter is included here.
170 *Ibid.*, p. 121.
171 Peck, *Northampton*, p. 68; Upton, *Ingram*, pp. 19–20; C66/1726, *CPR 3–5 Jas*, fo. 311r; C66/1749, *CPR 3–5 Jas*, fo. 343v; TNA, SP 14/32, fo. 84; CP 129/18.
172 *HMC Sackville*, p. 155. There was also a commission in June 1608 to search ships to ensure impositions were paid, C66/1772, *CPR 6 Jas*, fo. 45.
173 CP 120/59, fo. 59; TLA, COL/CA/01/01/031, fo. 155r.
174 CP Petitions 2110.
175 *Ibid.*
176 GL, CLC/L/GH/B/001/MS11588/002, p. 485.
177 *Ibid.*
178 *Ibid.*, p. 274; GL, CLC/L/GH/D/001/MS11571/009, p. 44.
179 GL, CLC/L/GH/B/001/MS11588/002, p. 283.
180 These men were Fabian Fitche/Fryth, Henry Marshe, John Wiseman, John Nevill, Nicholas Scott, Nicholas Andrews, John Adshead, see TNA, SP 12/282, fos 54r–55r.
181 See GL, CLC/L/GH/B/001/MS11588/002, pp. 851, 898, 902–3, 918; GL, CLC/L/GH/B/001/MS11588/003, pp. 31, 55.
182 For more details, see E. Paterson, 'The Politics of Starch: Guilds, Monopolies, and Petitioning in Late Elizabethan and Early Stuart England', *London Journal*, 48:1 (2022), pp. 30–46.
183 *HMC Sackville*, p. 157.
184 TLA, COL/RMD/PA/01/002, fo. 151v.
185 *Ibid.*
186 CP Petitions 2110.
187 *Ibid.*
188 *Ibid.*
189 *Ibid.*
190 Larkin and Hughes, I, p. 163.
191 *Ibid.*, p. 164.
192 CP 142/127, fo. 141; Oxford, Bodl., MS. North A. 2, fos 67v–68r.
193 TNA, SP 14/9A, fo. 201r.
194 Pennington notes that similar methods were used to justify the company for fish busses, see Pennington, '"Free Passage"', p. 294.
195 CP 142/127, fo. 141.
196 *Ibid.*
197 *Ibid.*
198 *Ibid.*

199 Oxford, Bodl. MS North A.2, fo. 242r.
200 CP 142/127, fo. 140v.
201 *Ibid.*
202 Peck, *Northampton*, p. 69.
203 TNA, SP 15/41, fo. 243r.
204 *HMC Sackville*, p. 156.
205 Larkin and Hughes, I, pp. 189–92.
206 C66/1771, *CPR 6 Jas*, fo. 44. By August 1609 they were awarded another commission to execute the proclamation, TNA, SP 14/141, fo. 37r; C66/1820, *CPR 7 Jas*, fo. 44; *CD 1621*, vii, p. 440.
207 Larkin and Hughes, I, pp. 237–41.
208 BL, Lans. MS. 152, fos 117r, 121r–122v, 123r–124v. It is possible that this was Zachary Jones, a previous starch commissioner, as one of the documents is signed from Jones.
209 *Ibid.*, fo. 123r.
210 One Richard Brown wrote an undated letter discussing the failure of the starchmakers to bring profits to the Crown and their imposition of new duties on makers, which seems to refer to the Company, see BL, Cotton Faustina C II, fo. 127r.
211 BL, Lans. MS 152, fo. 123r.
212 Larkin and Hughes, I, p. 252.
213 Larkin and Hughes, I, p. 474.
214 *CD 1621*, VII, pp. 511–15. For a bill introduced by the Grocers against this and other monopolies, see GL, CLC/L/GH/B/001/MS11588/003, pp. 165–6, 292.
215 Larkin and Hughes, I, pp. 537–40. The issue of incorporation was also addressed in 1612, see BL, Lans. MS. 152, fos 127r–128v.
216 Carr, *Select Charters*, pp. 117–22.
217 TNA, SP 16/377, fo. 82r.
218 Ashton, 'Conflicts'.
219 TLA, COL/RMD/PA/01/003, fos 163–65.
220 BL, Add. MS 12,504, fo. 158r.
221 *CJ*, [27 April second scribe]. For more on Alford, see Chapter 4.
222 R. W. Heinze, 'Proclamations and Parliamentary Protest, 1539–1610', in D. J. Guth and J. W. McKenna (eds), *Tudor Rule and Revolution: Essays for G. R. Elton from his American Friends* (Cambridge, 1982), pp. 237–60; *Proceedings, 1610*, pp. 22, 257–61.
223 C. R. Kyle, 'Monarch and Marketplace: Proclamations as News in Early Modern England', *Huntington Library Quarterly*, 78:4 (2015), pp. 771–87.
224 Braddick and Walter, 'Grids of Power', in Braddick and Walter (eds), *Negotiating Power*, p. 16.

# 4

# Petitioning Parliament

> The 26th of March to be kept holly by gen[er]all Sermons ov[er] England to declare the King[e]s honor and Justice and the deliu[er]ance of the Subject fro[m] the oppression of Mompessons and his agent[e]s.
>
> Two Statues of brasse to be erected to the King and Prince as monum[en]ts of their hono[ra]ble Justice.[1]

In March 1621, the House of Lords pronounced sentence on one of the most notorious monopolists of the Jacobean age, Sir Giles Mompesson. Associated to the Duke of Buckingham's half-brother, Sir Edward Villiers, Mompesson had emerged as the recipient of numerous revenue-raising projects from 1616. This included serving as a commissioner to licence inns and alehouses, to confiscate concealed lands, and to enforce restrictions on the manufacture of gold and silver thread.[2] As part of a larger revival of their judicial authority, the Lords impeached Mompesson, depriving him of all titles and prohibiting him from coming within twelve miles of James or Prince Charles's courts.[3] The day of his judgement was to be marked by thanksgiving sermons which, alongside two new brass statues, would serve as perpetual reminders of the King's justice. Yet it was not through James alone that this notorious official had been brought to heel. Both the Lords and the Commons had played a pivotal role in investigating the patents for the licensing of inns and the production of gold and silver thread, collecting depositions, examining witnesses, and receiving petitions of grievances. These were not the only individuals and patents examined by Parliament, nor were the petitions of alehousekeepers and silkmen the only ones in which cries of injustice were proclaimed to MPs and peers.

The calling of Parliament in 1621 and 1624 offered subjects yet another opportunity to articulate their economic grievances and to lobby for the furtherance or protection of their corporate privileges. James's final two Parliaments have been celebrated as pivotal in the fight against monopolies, and whilst older perceptions that these sessions witnessed constitutional conflict between Parliament and Crown have been revised, it is still recognised that the monopolies issue was a central grievance, a 'point of contact' where the concerns of James and his subjects could coalesce.[4] Historians have argued that religion and foreign policy were drivers of political discussion in the early 1620s, spurred by debates on Prince Charles's Spanish Match and affairs in the Palatinate.[5] Of equal importance were economic concerns, which not only pushed subjects to engage with Parliament, but caused MPs to collect petitions and lobbying documents as they devoted time and attention to the scrutiny of industrial issues.

The 1620s have also been identified as a liminal moment in Parliament's history, witnessing important institutional developments. Developing processes and procedures in the Commons and Lords for the examination of grievances, including the use of standing committees, facilitated the presentation of petitions and the punishment of odious patentees. As Chris Kyle and Andrew Thrush have demonstrated, petitioning emerged in this context as an essential feature of early Stuart Parliaments, overtaking bills as the main way through which many sought redress.[6] James Hart has also traced a revival in the Lord's judicial authority beginning in this period, giving rise to private petitioning as subjects approached Parliament as a court of justice.[7] This, combined with the increased accessibility of Parliament both physically as a space and through the volume of news emanating from its chambers, allowed it to emerge as a pre-eminent institution in the public sphere.[8]

The centrality of Parliament in the fight against monopolies, combined with these developments, renders it essential to our narrative of anti-monopoly petitioning agitation. As seen in Chapter 3, free trade and corporatism were essential features of James's first Parliament. Kyle has shown that members of corporate bodies proved adept at using the different avenues open to them to express their anti-monopoly demands, embracing the calling of Parliament in 1621 as an opportunity to articulate their grievances to a new body of authority.[9] This was not necessarily because they saw the Council as failing to offer any chance of redress against patents which were so often connected to Court intermediaries; the case of Darcy shows petitioning both the city and the Council could bring results.[10] However, it is clear that many subjects, from female apprentices to tobacco pipe-makers, saw Parliament as likely to support their monopoly concerns.

Whilst it has been recognised that institutional developments facilitated this petitioning activity, it is also necessary to consider the ways in which these changes were responded to, and actively engaged with, in ways beyond subjects' ability to approach both Houses with greater ease. In turning to Parliament, subjects adapted their rhetoric to appeal to MPs and peers, and crafted narratives surrounding past parliamentary decisions. In so doing, they contributed to processes which saw the wider historisation of

Parliament as an institution in the early seventeenth century.[11] Peal Seaward has explored the ways through which diaries and record-keeping contributed to this crafting of institutional memory.[12] Memory was crucial to Parliament, yet unexplored are the ways in which subjects actively shaped narratives of parliamentary decisions through petitions, thereby contributing to this process of historicising Parliament's role. History could be used to 'political effect', and petitioners, struggling to protect their trades, deployed it as a tool in their disputes. Further, their reflection on the roles and values of Parliament provides an important insight into their 'political imaginaries', as petitioners frequently compared the relief Parliament could offer them with the failure of other institutions to redress their plight.[13] The actions of past Parliaments were referred to and expected to act as a guide for future MPs and peers: as subjects called for them to be considered, MPs collected notes of these past proceedings and decisions, further contributing to the crafting of institutional identity through record-keeping practices.

One group of subjects eagerly embraced the calling of Parliament to articulate their concerns with monopoly: the realm's glassmakers and glaziers. Objections to a glass monopoly held by Sir Robert Mansell took up the time and attention of the Council, Crown, and the Commons in 1614, 1621, and 1624.[14] This well-documented case, which includes a host of overlooked materials in local archives, provides insights into the ways through which petitioning rhetoric was adapted and crafted as different institutions were addressed. First, however, it is necessary to examine the links between monopoly and the Villiers' faction emerging in the 1610s, which provide the necessary context for Parliament's investigation of patents in the 1620s. The developing procedures facilitating petitioning activity in Parliament will be traced before we turn to consider how the disputes over the glass monopoly were transformed as they moved to parliamentary forums. We have already seen how the issues of monopoly and corporatism generated battles and contests fought in the city and before the Council. Now, we must consider how these same issues facilitated greater interactions between subjects and Westminster.

## Monopolies and the Villiers' clan

Despite the constant protest levied against patents in James's opening years, the King did not stop relying on monopolies and projects as a central tenant of financial policy. Following the death of Salisbury in 1612, a treasury commission headed by figures including Northampton and Caesar continued to scrutinise projects to rectify the deficit in crown finances.[15] Despite James's re-appointment of the Commission for Suits in 1618, subjects continued to petition for new monopolies.[16] Once again, the hearing of testimony from experts was an integral process of the workings of the Commission. This was even more essential as James complained that many had worked to 'hinder the examining and distinction of mens suites' by preparing warrants for grants before petitions for them had even been examined.[17]

The rise of George Villiers, the Duke of Buckingham, as a powerhouse in James's Court ushered in a new, more exploitative phase in monopoly policy as patents were granted to his clients and kin.[18] Perhaps most odious of all were commissions to enforce the patents for the manufacture of gold and silver thread and for the licensing of inns. In 1611, a patent for the sole making of gold and silver thread was granted to Mathias Fowle, Richard Dike, and their associates for twenty years.[19] By March 1618, James decided to take the patent into his own hands, maintaining commissioners, including the unpopular Francis Michell, to licence subjects to make the product and prohibiting imports.[20] In October 1618, Mompesson was appointed as one of these commissioners and Sir Edward Villiers also had an interest in the business as an investor from 1616.[21] By October 1619, another proclamation was issued to express concern that silkmen were purchasing illegal gold and silver thread to produce goods including lace and buttons, and that gold refiners and wiredrawers were producing the commodity without licence.[22] Later, the commissioners were accused of forcing subjects to enter bonds promising not to work in their trades and of using violence and illegal detainments on the pretence of searching for tools in private houses. The introduction of a 'quota' system saw the commissioners force wiredrawers to enter bonds to produce certain amounts of gold and silver thread, and to pay fees to recieve an official seal on goods. These infringements sparked protest from city authorities and from the Goldsmiths' Company who felt that the patent infringed on their ancient trade of wiredrawing.[23]

Equally contentious was a patent for the licencing of alehouses granted to Mompesson on 3 March 1617. The patent allowed Mompesson to issue excessive fees for licences, including from the holders of inns which had previously been shut down for disorderly conduct.[24] The Stuart 'era of incorporation' also continued as new dubious corporations were erected with links to the Villiers' clan, including a Company of Goldbeaters and, by 1623, a Company of Gold and Silver wiredrawers.[25]

Court and city connections continued to be facilitated through courtier-artisan alliances, designed to provide grants with a veneer of legitimacy, whilst providing artisans with patronage networks necessary to further their interests. In June 1618, Secretary Sir Robert Naunton wrote to Thomas Wilson of an attempt by artisan skinners to join with Buckingham's brother,

Christopher Villiers, to promote a suit in Court. Naunton was determined to ensure that this would be successful, the grant intended by James to be 'for ye use of Mr C. Villiers'.[26] Whilst the details of the suit were not stated, it is possible that this was another attempt to monopolise the export of skins. Naunton noticed that the discussion of this issue sparked debate, reflecting the divisions and fissures present at the Council table as different groups sought to further their agendas. Many in the Council opposed the grant, which had previously been in the hands of their 'Clyents', merchants who were sure to resent any new patent.[27] Monopolies and patents were clearly bound up in the complexities of court politics. Indeed, Naunton's decision to lobby for Christopher's interests so wholeheartedly was a product of the already dubious arrangements made between the two men; Christopher had been named as Naunton's heir in return for his receiving of the office of secretary.[28]

The granting of patents caused protests in London, whilst city authorities continued to scrutinise proposed grants, sometimes coming under pressure from the Court to pass them. In December 1618, a petition was sent from a client of Buckingham, Captain Henry Bell to James, requesting an office for the searching of English lead for thirty-one years. This does not seem to be an industry with which Bell, a military officer, had much experience. He had no qualms informing James that he had spent the past three years 'solicitinge and seekinge after suits', before finally he had 'hit vpon one' which seemed profitable.[29] Bell claimed that James had promised him that he could be granted 'any reasonable suite hee should bee able to fynde out': clearly James was not opposed to issuing blanket promises for patents. In his efforts, Bell had the support of some members of the Plumbers' Company, as well as a powerful patron in the form of Buckingham, who wrote directly to the city to express his support for the proposal.[30] However, it was strongly opposed by merchants, and the Commission for Suits struggled to find any degree of consensus when investigating it. Instead, they found 'marchant against marchant, and plum[m]er against plummer, one affirmeinge one thinge and another denyinge the same, and affirmeinge the contrary'.[31] Even proposed patents could cause clashes of interest within industries. Continued pressure from Bell and Buckingham saw the patent granted by September 1619 before further protest led to its cancellation in 1620.[32] Petitioning the Lords in 1624, Bell even requested compensation for the losses he had incurred in the enterprise. Bell complained that these were so great that he had been imprisoned for his debts and 'fedd w[i]th the bread of afflicc[i]on'.[33] Interestingly, despite the anti-monopoly stance of this Parliament, Bell evidently believed that the Lords might prove a sympathetic body to the plight of patentees.

## The glass patents

The looming threat of monopolisation continued to cast its shadow over a range of goods and industries. In the interim between Parliaments, subjects affected by patents sought redress through the city, Crown, and Council as explored in previous chapters. However, in one industry in particular, the glassmaking trade, a new institution was established to hear complex disputes caused by the existence of multiple, overlapping patents. Much like the commissions appointed in the city, commissioners launched an active investigation into the glass monopoly, bringing glassmakers and glaziers into their orbit. Meanwhile, the industry itself was divided over the utility of these grants; transient alliances were made, and fissures within the Glaziers' Company opened in the 1610s. In the Parliaments of 1621 and 1624, these events were narrated by petitioners as they protested and supported a monopoly of another Buckingham client, Sir Robert Mansell.

Under Mary I and Elizabeth, patents had been issued to foreign artisans to make glass and to settle in the realm to teach Englishmen the trade.[34] By James's reign, glassmakers, glass sellers, and glaziers all participated in the industry, the latter working in the selling, cutting, and repairing of glass. In London, the Glaziers' Company was an unchartered body, only gaining their royal charter in 1638.[35] They would emerge as essential in the parliamentary investigation of the glass monopoly. Also important were the realm's glassmakers, many of whom were descendants of earlier medieval glassmaking families based in Suffolk and the Weald. This included members of the Hensey, Tysack, and Bungard families.[36]

James's accession witnessed a scramble to gain patents for this lucrative commodity, both from previous holders of monopolies and from new courtiers. The bestowal of multiple patents for the industry triggered contests not between pre-existing companies and patentees as seen in so many of our cases, but between different patentees and groups of syndicates hoping to profit from these enterprises. From 1606 to 1608, at least four different patents for the making of crystal glass and drinking glasses in England and Ireland were issued to courtiers and syndicates.[37] Technological developments, combined with prevailing concerns over wood scarcity, soon enabled courtiers to push for new patents to cover inventions and newly found processes for making glass. In particular, the use of coal instead of wood to fire furnaces led to the granting of a patent in March 1611 to make window glass using only sea or pit coal for fuel for twenty-one years. This was awarded to the King's glazier, Thomas Mefflyn, the inventor Thomas Percival, and two courtiers, Bevis Thelwall and Sir Edward Zouch.[38] The simultaneous existence of multiple patents for this industry made it a crowded one; disputes between patentees were heard before the Council table and by the

Attorney General and Solicitor General.[39] By March 1614, the patent was expanded in scope to redress these problems. All other glass patents were revoked, and subjects were prohibited from making glass using timber supplies.[40] As this was the primary method for making glass, many glassmakers were deprived of their trades, deliberately evading the patent's conditions by importing glass or making it with their wood-fuelled furnaces.[41] In the Addled Parliament of 1614, glassmakers united with the Glaziers' Company to petition against this patent.[42]

By 19 January 1615, yet another patent was issued for glassmaking. Alongside the previous patentees were added a range of courtiers, including Sir Thomas Howard (also a recipient of fees for the patent for gold and silver thread), the Earl of Montgomery, and Mansell.[43] As Treasurer of the Navy and a Gentleman of the Privy Chamber, Mansell had risen to prominence in the wake of the Cadiz expedition.[44] He was no stranger to corruption; he was found guilty of embezzling £1,000 in wages whilst in the Navy. His connection to Buckingham likely explains his ability to still cling to power, and indeed, his involvement in this lucrative patent. Despite emerging as a vocal opponent of monopolies in debates in Parliament in 1614, Mansell was happy to become a partner in what was an even more restrictive grant by 1615.[45] The patent provided these men with the sole rights to make glass with coal. By 23 May, James issued a proclamation prohibiting the use of any wood in the glassmaking process, and prohibiting all glass imports, thus officially confining the trade to the patentees.[46] Any wishing to make glass needed a licence and employment in official glass houses, or had to enter contracts with Mansell to operate their furnaces.[47] Many glassmakers were forced to enter bonds promising to give up their wood-fired furnaces. Mansell later bought out his fellow patentees; in 1618, he was recorded as paying rents of £1,000 per annum to James for the patent and £1,800 to the previous patentees.[48] Both Mansell and his wife, Lady Elizabeth Roper, were especially active as they sought to channel the glassmaking trade through their newly erected glasshouses in Broad Street, London and later, in Newcastle.[49]

Glassmakers and glaziers moved to oppose this with zeal. Especially important to this and to the later opposition in Parliament were four men: Isaac Bungard, Paul Vinion, Lionel Bennett, and John Dines.[50] Bungard was a descendant of French glassmakers who had settled in Wisborough Green in Sussex, a figure who was able to dominate London markets with his window glass.[51] Vinion described himself in a petition to the Council as a glassmaker based in Wisborough Green, whose family had long practised the trade.[52] These glassmakers resented the effects of the monopoly, which had deprived them of their rights to produce glass without receiving licence or employment directly from Mansell. Some glaziers in the city, concerned with the quality of the glass Mansell produced, also opposed the patent. Lionel Bennett had been an assistant of the Glaziers' Company in 1612 and would emerge as a staunch opponent of Mansell.[53] Dines too was a London glazier who, despite working in Mansell's employ as an agent, seems to have moved to oppose him by 1620.[54] In April 1617, the Glaziers' Company petitioned the Council to express their concern that Mansell's patent, alongside the prohibition on imports, had led to a scarcity of glass.[55] That there were problems with Mansell's ability to supply adequate stores is attested to by the Council's willingness to grant temporary licences to Bungard and others to continue producing glass to prevent further scarcity.[56]

In the interim between the Addled Parliament and the session of 1621, glassmakers and glaziers followed many other petitioners in directing their complaints against the monopoly to the Council and Crown. Yet in this case, their continued petitioning gave spur to an important institutional development, leading to the erection of a Commission for Glass, an example of the capacity for petitioners to impact processes of state formation.[57] In part, this Commission was intended to streamline the torrent of complaints the Council received. However, the Commission was also the product of the jurisdictional clashes created by the existence of two simultaneous glass monopolies, leading James to erect an entirely new institution to handle disputes. In December 1610, James issued the courtier Sir George Hay with a patent to make glass in Scotland for thirty-one years.[58] The simultaneous existence of two monopolies was utilised by subjects in their efforts to undermine Mansell. Opponents in England began to claim that Hay's glassworks produced superior glass, requesting permission to import it into England. They also used covert dealings to persuade Mansell's employees to leave his glassworks and find better conditions and pay at Hay's glasshouses.[59] In November 1619, disputes between the patentees were heard before the Council.[60] By 10 January 1620, James decided to appoint four commissioners to examine these conflicts.[61] Two Scottish and two English officials were appointed: the Duke of Lennox, James Hamilton, Gentlemen of the Bedchamber, William Herbert, the Earl of Pembroke and Lord Chamberlain of the Household, and Thomas Howard, the Earl of Arundel.[62]

The commissioners had the power to examine all subjects upon oath and to punish any who contravened the patents or the King's proclamations.[63] It emerged as not only a space to enforce the patents, but as a consultative body, serving as another point of contact facilitating petitioning activity. In a proclamation on glass imports issued in February 1620, the erection of the Commission was publicly announced, informing subjects that this body would hear any grievances which might arise between the patentees and subjects.[64] The commissioners proceeded to examine petitions complaining of the quality of Mansell's glass and requesting permission to import supplies.[65] The personnel in charge of the Commission were far from impartial figures. Lennox, as cloth Alnager, was unlikely to allow the authority of a prerogative patent to be challenged. Hamilton likely owed his appointment to his patron, Buckingham.[66] A document in Sir Robert Phelips' papers questioned Herbert's impartiality as a 'neere kinsman' to a previous glass patentee, the Earl of Montgomery, whilst his brother was also an assignee to a previous patentee.[67] Perhaps only Arundel had a real knowledge of the industry, maintaining a strong interest in architecture and sitting on a range of commissions, including that for buildings in 1619.[68]

Despite this potential bias, the commissioners responded to a 'Petition exhibited' to launch an investigation into the quality of Mansell's glass in March 1620.[69] Much like the temporary commissions formed in the city to investigate proposed patents, subjects with an interest in the trade, members of the Glaziers' Company, were invited to offer testimonies on the quality and quantity of Mansell's glass. Depositions were collected from the assistants and wardens. Lionel Bennett, Abicok Kirby (a warden), Richard Spearman (assistant in 1612), and John Inman (assistant) produced a report at the 'direcc[i]on' and 'appoinetem[en]t' of the commissioners.[70] They were rather lukewarm in their findings, reporting that whilst some of the glass delivered from Mansell's glasshouses was fit for service, other parcels had been mixed with poor glass.[71] A self-proclaimed, albeit anonymous, assistant of the Company also declared in a more negative report that the glass found was 'vnserviceable and for no vse'.[72]

The quality of Mansell's glass was a divisive issue. Whilst glaziers in the city thus produced rather mixed reports, Inigo Jones and Thomas Baldwin, the Surveyor and Comptroller of the King's Works, were much more critical. Their search of Mansell's storehouse had revealed that many of his cases were mingled with good and bad glass, with much 'very thyn'.[73] It is perhaps not surprising that these royal officials should be so critical of Mansell's product. A set of depositions collected by commissioners in February suggested that Mansell and his assignee, William Robson, had even refused to provide suitable glass for the King's use. One set of deponents claimed that Robson had purposefully sent eight to nine cases of unfit glass to the London-based glazier John Dines, who supplied and cut glass for the King's glazier, Thomas Baggley.[74] On being asked why he had done so, Robson had allegedly claimed that 'he did itt the rather in Respect thatt both the kinges glasier and dynes did find fault w[i]th glase, and spoke against his m[aste]r S[i]r Robertt Maunsell'.[75] Dines even testified that another of Mansell's deputies, Lancelot Hobson, referred to Baggley as a 'scurvey palterey knaue, for all he was the king[e]s glasiar'.[76]

Mansell's monopoly had caused real fissures within the glass industry, the source of antagonisms and verbal insults. Within London, the Glaziers'

Company expressed their concern with the effect of the glass monopolies in both 1614 and again in 1617, whilst some members also criticised Mansell's glass before the Commission for Glass in 1620. This Commission acted as a new point of contact, allowing glaziers and glassmakers to express their opinions on the grant as part of a broader investigation into the merits of Mansell and Hay's glassworks. It also offered another space through which subjects, including merchants, glaziers, and glassmakers could enter dialogues with authority, even if this was for the purpose of requesting permission to land their illegal glass imports. By 1621 these complex alliances appear to have shifted and solidified as glassmakers and glaziers readied themselves to fight before Parliament.

## Battling in the Parliaments of 1621 and 1624: a participatory culture

Developments in Parliament allowed both Houses to investigate the monopoly issue more rigorously than they had in Elizabeth's final Parliament. The development of standing committees and the volume of materials emanating from its chambers rendered Parliament a more accessible institution in the 1620s.[77] These institutional changes, combined with widespread frustrations with monopoly, contributed to the formation of a more participatory, political culture in Parliament. A range of subjects from across the realm approached Parliament, driven by their economic concerns, predating the engagement of the public with both Houses so often identified as a unique feature of the 1640s.[78] As Kyle notes, Parliament was 'an open house'.[79] Invited inside were subjects touched by monopoly in the metropolis and the provinces.

From the onset, economic issues were key to both Parliaments, meeting as they did in the context of a European-wide depression.[80] As MPs arrived armed with the complaints of their constituents, a drive to free trade from the shackles of monopoly manifested in vocal debates on the floors of both Houses. Bills were introduced to take advantage of these sentiments, aiming to remove restrictions on the trade in Welsh cloths, the fishing industry, and the wool and coal trades.[81] Corporate bodies including the Adventurers and the East India Company faced scrutiny, and Alastair Bellany and Thomas Cogswell estimate that as many as 100 patents were examined in 1621 alone.[82] Those associated to the Villiers' faction were the first to be attacked as the Lords revived their ancient powers of impeachment.[83] They established three committees to investigate the most scandalous of these patents: a committee for the patent for inns (chaired by the Lord Chamberlain), for gold and silver thread (chaired by the Earl of Arundel), and for concealed lands (chaired by the Earl of Southampton).[84] Their findings of extensive misconduct led James to issue a proclamation in March cancelling the patents for inns, alehouses, and gold and silver thread.[85] The impeachment of Mompesson and Michell led to the production of broadsides and libels, further informing subjects of parliamentary developments whilst fuelling anti-monopoly sentiments.[86] During the summer recess in July 1621, another proclamation cancelled a range of monopolies complained of in both Houses and left others for review at the common law.[87] In addition to investigating the actions of particularly unpopular patentees, the Lords also examined the former Attorney General Sir Henry Yelverton and Lord Chancellor Bacon for their roles as referees for patents and for their imprisonment of subjects who resisted them.[88]

The development of standing committees facilitated petitioning.[89] The Commons' standing committees allowed subjects to petition cheaply and efficiently. In 1621, the committees for grievances and for trade acted as vital spaces investigating the abuses of patentees and the realm's economic condition.[90] Their chairmen did not appear to charge for introducing petitions, in contrast to the fees of £5 to the Speaker and £2 to the clerk necessary to introduce bills, and this was a quicker means to gain redress than initiating bills.[91] As such, the number of petitioners to Parliament increased. Kyle calculates that by 12 March 1621, the Commons' committee for grievances had been presented with eighty petitions, some of which were printed to facilitate 'discreet' petitioning efforts to persuade MPs of their causes.[92] To manage the number of petitioners, the Commons appointed a subcommittee of six members to vet all petitions, an important procedural development which was repeated in 1624.[93]

The Lords also established a standing committee for petitions in both 1621 and 1624, chaired by the Earl of Bridgewater.[94] Hart calculates that the number of petitions sent to the Lords increased fourfold between the sessions of 1621 and 1624.[95] Much like committees appointed by the Council, the committee for petitions circulated supplications which it was investigating amongst parties involved, allowing witnesses to be informed of their contents and facilitating the penning of counter-petitions.[96] Corporate bodies and interest groups could also push their agendas in the Lords by introducing private bills. The examination of these at committee stage offered ample opportunities for counter-petitions and briefs to be sent, and for affected subjects to be consulted.[97]

These developments led subjects to not only petition, but to physically appear before both Houses. In the Commons', Elizabeth Read Foster has shown that witnesses were summoned and depositions collected as part of committee investigations into monopolies.[98] This allowed a range of subjects to be brought into physical contact with Parliament as an institution.[99] When at Westminster, they were further exposed to the news, printed and scribal, circulating in its lobbies, including printed petitions and lists of committee members.[100] Exposure to these materials contributed to processes of politicisation.

The expansion of scribal and printed news from Parliament coalesced with this intense scrutiny of economic issues. Consequently, material circulating in both Houses was not only focused on the Spanish Match or concern with popery but also centred on quite specific economic disputes. The personal collections of MPs including Sir Robert Phelips, Edward Alford, and Sir Thomas Jervoise contain a wealth of such material. Phelips served as a representative for Bath and was active in the investigation of abuses including legal corruption and the actions of patentees.[101] Alford, MP for Colchester, was a staunch opponent of monopolies and any undue extensions of the royal prerogative.[102] Jervoise represented Whitchurch and, whilst certainly less active than Phelips and Alford in debates on the floor of the House, he collected a substantial body of materials, many of which included petitions on local trading issues.[103] They were just three of many MPs gathering separates, petitions, drafts of acts, and newsletters on parliamentary affairs.[104] The Southampton merchant Thomas Squibbs sent two bills and a petition to the Recorder of Salisbury and the MP for Southampton, Henry Sherfield in 1624 concerning customs on cloth and the illegal activities of trucksters selling goods in the realm.[105] Squibbs made clear that these matters were 'not the least' amongst the range of 'waightie affayres' being dealt with by Sherfield in this Parliament.[106] Lobbying subjects recognised that economic issues were high on the agenda of MPs, and for many, it was these concerns which pushed them to approach this institution.

For some corporations, the opportunity to continue long-standing disputes and to infuse these with new accusations of monopoly was eagerly embraced. Kyle has shown that London's livery companies adopted a 'two-pronged strategy', introducing petitions *and* bills to advance their causes.[107] The Woodmongers and Wharfingers' Companies both petitioned to accuse each other of monopoly, continuing their long-standing dispute over the issue of carting in the metropolis.[108] Others capitalised on the anxiety created by this attack on monopolies to pursue their own agendas. In a dispatch of April 1621, the Venetian ambassador Girolamo Lando bragged that he had encouraged grocers in the city to petition Parliament against the Levant Company's trade in raisins. He noted that this was the best way to put pressure on the merchants to loosen their hold on the import trade, 'since they well know that there are many in the assembly who intend to destroy all the companies, the roots of a thousand disorders, and to make trade free'.[109]

The anti-monopoly atmosphere and anticipation for change surrounding both Parliaments did not prevent others from petitioning for corporate privileges, sometimes repeating calls already articulated before the King and Council. Unclear definitions of monopoly continued to be at the centre of these disputes. The glovers and leather dressers of Westminster renewed their efforts to be separated from the Leathersellers' Company.[110] Playing on the narratives of order and regulation so essential to corporatism, they presented this as necessary to prevent the suburbs from remaining as a 'vast Repceptacle of a disorddred multitude of Imp[er]fect Workemen & misgov[er]ned people'.[111] Perhaps unsurprisingly, the Leathersellers offered a rebuttal, presenting this bill as nothing but an attempt to 'build a Monopolie' through the passing of restrictive ordinances.[112] This was enough to ensure that the glovers' efforts to secure a charter were unsuccessful.[113]

Similarly, the Grocers petitioned the Commons in 1621 against the recent incorporation of the Apothecaries' Company. In December 1620 they had discussed rumours in their court that the Apothecaries would seek parliamentary confirmation of their charter, deciding to consult with legal counsel to frustrate these efforts.[114] In their petition, they presented the Apothecaries as a dubious institution rather than a legitimate corporate body, obtained 'against the will of many able auncyent and skilfull Apothecaries'.[115] The new Company was presented as a threat to the government of the city, requiring all using the trade to leave their current companies, a violation of the custom of London. Much as in the cases of leather and starch, issues of social status were mixed with these claims, as the Grocers expressed their concern that this would set a precedent amongst the 'least men of other Companies' to seek similar separations.[116] Interestingly, the Grocers also attacked Lord Chancellor Bacon for confirming the charter, contrasting this to the late Chancellor Ellesmere's reluctance to see it passed, tactically tapping into concerns with Bacon's corruption which would lead to his censure in this Parliament. Ahead of the next Parliament in 1624, the Grocers requested that the clerks of both Houses inform them of any more bills or petitions entered by the Apothecaries.[117] They were finally to secure success as the charter was adjudged a grievance by the committee for grievances on 6 April.[118]

In a similar vein to the Apothecaries, other corporate bodies attempted to secure statutory confirmation of their chartered privileges. The Gardeners' Company of London, incorporated in 1605, introduced an act for confirmation of their charter.[119] The Company had been accused by the city of engaging in 'disorderly' conduct, leading to an investigation into the actions of their wardens and assistants in 1606.[120] Complaints had also been issued against them by inhabitants of Fulham for extracting high taxes. This unpopular body failed to rouse the support of MPs who were so suspicious of monopolistic enterprises; their bill was rejected.

Outside of official company channels, subjects engaged in collective petitioning efforts to complain against monopolies and charters. In July 1619 James issued a charter to the Company of Tobacco Pipe Makers of Westminster.[121] A proclamation in May 1620 announced that this charter confined the trade of making tobacco pipes to members of the new Company, criticising those who had 'fortified themselves in their houses with weapons' to resist arrest by JPs for harbouring illegal tobacco pipe-makers on their premises.[122] Seven named tobacco pipe-makers petitioned the Lords in 1621 to complain of this corporate body.[123] As Misha Ewen notes, the petitioners weaved a narrative heavily saturated with a rhetoric of violence and appeals to paternalism to criticise the patentees.[124] According to the petitioners, members of the Company had broken into homes and seized subjects' tools. Indeed, the proclamation of May had given the Company authority to search the houses of all suspects and by August, this was extended to authorise them to break into homes to arrest offenders.[125] It is evident that these powers had been abused. Such was the extent of the Company's aggression that the petitioners claimed that some of their wives had even miscarried from the stress.[126]

Similar complaints had roused the Lords in their investigation of the gold and silver thread patent, and it is possible that the decision to include these accusations was designed to curry their sympathy. Claims of assaults on pregnant women had also been included in the Grocers' list of testimonies against Pakington in 1601; the inclusion of such shocking narratives was intended to persuade readers of the unnatural and excessive violence utilised by patentees whilst simultaneously invoking rights to property.[127] The petitioners ended by requesting permission to attend the House in person to deliver further proof of their oppressions, demonstrating not only their willingness to offer depositions but also their awareness of the processes by which committees investigated monopoly complaints.

It was not only official patents which were the source of parliamentary investigation. A particularly interesting petition from Southampton provides insight into the presence of frauds and deceptions in the realm, as subjects took advantage of the presence of overlapping monopolies, deputies, and commissions to trick others. On 21 April 1621, fifteen shopkeepers from Southampton petitioned Parliament to complain of two men, John Carpenter and Nicholas Baylie, who had 'by coullor of a pretended deputation vnto them' demanded fines and yearly rents for the alnage on cloth.[128] Whilst this was a very real patent in the hands of Lennox, these men had falsely claimed to be his deputies, threatening to confiscate shopkeepers's wares if payments were not made.[129] Included with their petition were eight receipts signed by Baylie and Carpenter for payments collected from these shopkeepers in 1619 and 1620.[130] The petitioners, aware of their rights, likened these sums to a 'new imposition laid vpon vs, and not knowne or heard off amongst us at any time heeretofore'.[131] Annotations, possibly made by Jervoise, made clear that they had paid over £9 in rents and fines in the space of a year. The age of monopoly provided opportunities for such tricksters to operate, though the calling of Parliament could generate anxiety amongst them; no rents were collected by the fake deputies in 1621 and it was noted that this was because they were aware that Parliament was in session, posing a threat to their dubious enterprise.

Even legitimate patentees were anxious as Parliament investigated grants. Surviving in Phelips' papers is a petition by Sir Francis Blundell, the holder of a patent for the licensing of pedlars. Blundell noted that this was a 'hatefull Patent', claiming he had been drawn into involvement with it whilst away in Ireland, falsely believing it would be a 'good, and an honest busines'.[132] Blundell actually called on Parliament to cancel the patent, suggesting that he had already been punished enough by being called 'hither as an offendor against his Countrey', the 'heaviest affliction that ever fell vpon him in his life'.[133]

As noted, petitioners and witnesses were invited to offer testimony before the Commons. Surviving depositions in the Parliamentary Archives provide evidence of how these processes also worked in the Lords as they investigated the patent for gold and silver thread. Subjects were summoned to attend the Lords in person to take an oath before giving their testimonies against monopolists.[134] Cross-house collaboration appears to have been integral to these proceedings: subjects sent petitions to the Commons, only to be brought before the Lords to offer their testimony under oath. For example, a petition was sent in 1621 to the Commons by four female spinners, Elizabeth Cockren/Cockerill, Mary Fitch, Jane Newe/Ewe, and Anne Mitchell (Cockren's daughter), all of whom resided in Cripplegate.[135] Fitch was described in her deposition as the wife of a Goldsmith of the city, whilst Newe, aged twenty, was her apprentice.[136] The petitioners lamented their incarceration in Finsbury prison for six days at the hands of the commissioners for gold and silver thread. The petition was signed with the marks of Cockren and Fitch and was most likely drawn up with the help of a clerk.[137] Later, these same women gave depositions to the Lords, taking their oaths in the House on 16 March.[138] It is likely that the petitioners were sent up to the Lords after sending their petition, upon recommendation from the Commons.[139]

In addition to hearing the testimony of these spinners, the Lords collected testimony from Cockren's daughter, Ann Mitchell, aged just fifteen years old, as well as from other spinners and their servants.[140] Female apprentices and spinners from the city were drawn to the Lords to describe the effects of this particularly contentious monopoly on their livelihoods. Similarly, seven

London-based merchants who petitioned the Commons to complain of the confiscation of their imported gold and silver provided testimony to the Lords.[141] These depositions would be central to the case against the patentees; they were even read out directly to Michell on the floor of the House.[142]

Many of these petitioners described their efforts to petition other bodies for redress before Parliament was called. The merchant William Parker claimed to have shown Mompesson a petition he intended to send to the Treasury Commission, inciting Mompesson to threaten him that he 'shold be layed by the heeles yf he did deliver up the same'.[143] A silkman named Samuel Buckley noted that he had stood in attendance at the Court of Aldermen 'from morning till night, intreating theire aide' for fourteen days to recover his confiscated goods, providing a fascinating insight into the processes by which individual petitioners sought to solicit the aid of city authorities.[144] For many of these petitioners, Parliament offered an opportunity to articulate complaints to a body of authority which might prove more sympathetic to their individual appeals for compensation, as peers and MPs moved to investigate a grant closely connected to the royal favourite. As we shall see, for glassmakers this expectation and hope was central to the very way they framed their appeal as they sought to historicise the institutions' role, providing relief against patentees.

## Glassmakers, glaziers, and parliamentary memory

The monopoly protests of the glassmakers and glaziers represent merely the tip of the iceberg of a mass of petitions and complaints heard before Parliament in 1621 and 1624. Having fought against the glass monopolies since 1614, glassmakers approached the Commons with their complaints. However, MPs were met with a plethora of documents presenting conflicting arguments on the utility of the patent, as some city glaziers articulated a new support for Mansell. Overlooked petitions and lobbying materials on the dispute in Phelips's papers show that both groups participated in Parliament's burgeoning print and scribal culture. Like other corporate groups, they produced broadsides and manuscript breviates for circulation amongst MPs as they attempted to advance their causes in the Commons. This was even more impressive given that the glassmakers were not an incorporated body; instead, they joined with disgruntled members of the Glaziers' Company to launch this campaign. Other members of the Glaziers' Company supported Mansell, even producing a detailed and comprehensive character assessment for circulation amongst MPs to undermine the petitions against him. These documents offer a unique opportunity to examine the ways these petitioners engaged with the issue of institutional memory in their appeals. It was not only parliamentary note-takers and diarists who were able to construct narratives of events, as petitioners themselves fuelled the growing presentation of Parliament as receptive to the realm's grievances.[145]

A petition against Mansell's monopoly was first presented to the Commons by sixty-nine glassmakers, glaziers, merchants, and bugle makers.[146] They included a short summary of their concerns alongside an annexed set of twenty grievances.[147] Both survive in copies in Phelips and Alford's papers with only slight differences in their content: articles four and five are swapped in order in both and the copy in Phelips's papers contains additional detail in its final article on the Commission for Glass. Heading the list of petitioners were five named glassmakers and glaziers: Bungard, John Worrall, Paul and Peter Vinion, and Abraham Lisco. All had been prominent and active opposers of Mansell's patent: Bungard had even been imprisoned as recently as February 1621 for uttering 'disgracefull speeches' against Mansell.[148] Other signatories included members of ancient glassmaking families, including the Strudwick family who were based in Kirdford in the Weald.[149] London glaziers including John Dines and the King's Glazier, Thomas Baggley, also subscribed. So too did members of the Glaziers' Company who had signed the lukewarm report on Mansell's glass the year before, including the assistants Bennett, Robert Parsons, Richard Sadler, and John Markes, who had served as Master in the Company in 1620 as the sitting master was not trained in the glazing trade.[150]

The petitioners crafted a narrative of past parliamentary decisions to appeal to the institutional memory of Parliament. In 1614 MPs had denounced Zouch's glass monopoly; Nicholas Fuller had even compared it to Darcy's patent for playing cards.[151] This previous condemnation would emerge as a focal point of the glassmakers' complaints in 1621. In their petition, they noted that at the 'late Assembly for the last p[ar]liament', the glass patent had been adjudged a monopoly upon 'full hearing and mature deliberac[i]on', a decision which remained in the records of the clerk of the Commons.[152] The petitioners presented Mansell's patent as a direct infringement on the authority of Parliament. 'In contempt of the Judgement of that greate Counsell vpon vntrue suggestion to his Ma[jes]tie a new Patent hath bene procured', which was merely a 'Monopoly of like Nature'.[153] The petitioners thus called on the Commons to survey their previous judgement, alongside their articles of grievances, to offer relief for themselves, their wives, and children. The petitioners appealed to both the collective memory of the House and the desire for MPs to safeguard Parliament's decisions and authority. They even noted that some of the agents in the patent had been 'violent opposers' to the glass monopoly in 1614, a likely allusion to Mansell himself.[154] Their appeal to MPs to peruse the records of the Commons appears to have been successful. Surviving in Phelips' papers is a copy of the order of the Commons in 1614, combined with a list of those burgesses in the current Parliament with ties to the patent.[155] The collecting of documents of past orders as part of the investigation of the monopoly contributed to the enhanced record-keeping procedures of Parliament emerging at this time.

In their annexed articles, the petitioners not only criticised the effects of Mansell's patent on their trade, but also reflected on the institutions available to them to petition. In their final article, they presented their recourse to the Commons as a necessity, given that the

> Lord[e]s Comissioners apoynted by his Ma[jes]tie for examinac[i]on of all greevances and iniuries comitted by this Patent, having refused to deale with any thing that may question the validitye of the same.[156]

As such, Parliament was upheld as the only institution capable of examining the patent. This provides insight into their own perception of the Commission for Glass. Despite numerous glassmakers and glaziers offering testimony and supplications to this body, the Commission's failure to pass judgement against Mansell left them with little hope that it would ever offer them their end goal: the cancellation of the patent. By contrast, the petitioners' demands suggested they held the Commission for Suits in a higher regard, but that they were concerned that the procedures in place to examine petitions for patents were being contravened. They expressed outrage that Mansell's request for his patent had not been referred to the 'Comissioners for Suites' to ascertain its fitness, a clear disregard of the procedures established to hear petitions for bounty.[157] This meant that there was no space for 'hearing the reasons and obiecc[i]ons which might iustly have bene made against it'.[158] As we have seen, this was something James himself complained of when re-appointing the Commission in 1618. In criticising both the failure of the Commission for Glass to rectify their grievances and the disregard for correct petitioning procedures shown by Mansell, the petitioners presented Parliament as the last remaining beacon of hope in their long-standing struggle. Their reflection on the merits and problems of various institutions also demonstrated their knowledge of the structures in place to secure redress, and their willingness to offer opinions on them. Similarly, in their petition against the Apothecaries, the Grocers complained that James's proclamation announcing their charter had commanded 'that none presume to petic[i]on his Ma[jes]tie for alterac[i]on of the aforesayd order'.[159] In a more subtle way, they also presented Parliament as their only hope for redress.

Whilst precise details on the construction of the glassmakers' suit are lacking, its contents suggest this petition was penned as part of a collective enterprise, combining the concerns of glassmakers, glaziers, merchants, and bugle makers. It is likely that the petition was spearheaded by Bungard and Bennett. On 7 May, Bungard offered testimony before the committee for grievances.[160] However the petitioners do seem to have consulted with other disgruntled subjects as they collected names and prepared the articles. Thus, their nineteenth demand lamented the specific problems caused by prohibitions on the import of coloured glass for bugle makers. The concerns of glaziers were included in the thirteenth article, which complained that Mansell's glass was often sent from his houses 'already cutt', causing the undoing of the 'poore Glasiers, a maine p[art]e of whose gaine was the cutting of such Glasse'.[161] The seventeenth article complained of the enhanced prices of scientific equipment used for distillation. It is likely that this was included to communicate grievances held by apothecaries in London, who would even petition the grievances committee on this point directly.[162] This extensive petition therefore placed specific concerns on the effects of the patent within a broader narrative designed to present the Commons as protectors of the glass industry and Mansell as a contemner of the House's dutiful proceedings.

The petition triggered a staunch investigation into Mansell's monopoly by the Commons' committee for grievances.[163] Mansell's absence abroad on naval business meant that his wife Elizabeth was summoned to attend the Commons; a breviate of the case commended her for 'redely' attending.[164] Glaziers did not maintain a united front in opposing the patent. It is at this point that some of the Company moved to shift their alliances, launching a three-pronged campaign as they petitioned the Commons, the Privy Council, and the Commission for Glass to testify to their wholehearted support for Mansell's monopoly.[165] As we have seen, the Glaziers' Company had expressed concern with a scarcity of glass earlier in 1617, and their report on Mansell's glass in 1620 had been mixed. By 1621, Mansell's monopoly caused a fracture in the Company. In opposition to members such as Markes and Bennett who petitioned firmly against Mansell, others now signed petitions to support him.

The reason for this switch in allegiances was suggested in a later petition penned by the glassmakers in 1624. They claimed that those glaziers who supported Mansell were those who 'receiue a benefit of this Patent, because Glasse being onely to be had in the City of London, they buy it of Sir Robert Mansel', selling the same to country glaziers at their own prices.[166] It has been suggested that these glaziers might have entered into a deal with the courtier to be supplied with the best glass, or received exclusive rights to buy and sell his glass to others in the city.[167] Such underhand dealings were also suggested in another petition produced by glaziers who opposed Mansell, who alleged that some of his undertakers, including Launcelot Hobson and even John Dines, had monopolised the best glass for themselves and their acquaintances.[168] To these motives might be added an additional agenda: the desire to recieve a charter. In 1616, the Glaziers' Company had petitioned the Court of Aldermen and Common Council to complain that freemen outside of their organisation were engaging in the glazing trade, requesting that they be translated to their Company.[169] By October they secured a Common Council Act imposing their ordinances on any freemen practising the trade.[170] It is possible that Mansell reached an agreement with some of the Glaziers' Company by 1621, promising to use his patronage to secure them the charter necessary to strengthen their authority in return for their support for his patent.[171]

A petition was sent from the 'glasiers of the City of London' to the Commons, who presented themselves as the authoritative voice on the industry, being those that 'use most glass'.[172] Their petition was subscribed with the names of forty-two glaziers, including the warden John Bargeman and two assistants, John Inman and Abicok Kirby, both of whom had signed the report on Mansell's glass in 1620 alongside Bennett and Spearman. Signatories also included Lancelot Hobson, Mansell's agent. It is likely that the Commons' committee for grievances, in its investigation of Mansell's grant, fostered the dialogic element in this case, providing the petitioners with a copy of the glassmakers's supplication to enable them to produce this petition. The glaziers thus directly responded to four of the articles offered by the glassmakers.[173]

Crucially, the glaziers recognised that their sudden decision to vehemently support Mansell might raise some eyebrows. To address this, they too moved to paint a particular story of the events in Parliament in 1614, albeit in a rather different way from the glassmakers, as both battled to control the narrative. For these glaziers, it could not be denied that they had opposed Zouch's glass patent in the Addled Parliament, leading to its condemnation. However, they argued that both they and MPs had been given false information on the effects of the patent, their own testimonies shaped by the machinations of Bungard, Bennett, and Dines. They admitted that they had been

> suters to that hono[ra]ble assembly for the prevenc[i]on of som[e] Inconveniences that weare to be Feared would ensue to this Common wealth by the execution of a pattent graunted to S[i]r Edward Zouch.[174]

However, their complaints had been misguided, being persuaded by Bungard and Bennett that if the 'pattenties should p[re]vaile in theire designe that then wee should bee tirannized over to our vtter Ruine'.[175] It was these fears which had led them to complain of the glass monopoly. Since this time, they had found themselves 'misled in our said Course of Complaint', finding that they enjoyed a 'Constant Course' and benefit under the 'Comfortable protection' of Mansell's patent.[176]

The glaziers painted Bennett, Bungard, and Dines as the real monopolisers of their industry and as the 'principall petic[i]oners against the pattent', acting as the 'setters on and p[ro]curers of such others as have subscribed to the said petic[i]on'.[177] Much as they themselves had been tricked in 1614, all who had signed the glassmakers' recent petition had been duped into joining by the self-interested machinations of these scheming tyrants. The glaziers also thought it necessary to excuse their earlier petitions against Mansell to the Council in 1617, where they had requested that Bungard and other glassmakers be licenced to operate their furnaces. They claimed to have been falsely persuaded by them that this would allow the market to be filled with sufficient glass supplies. In reality, Bungard had created an artificial dearth to raise prices. In many ways, the glaziers' presentation of the machinations and duplicitous dealings of the Bungard–Bennett–Dines faction was similar to the allegations deployed by counter-petitioners in the cases of starch, leather, and tin. In the Parliament of 1621, many other petitioners would adopt similar languages and rhetoric shaped by prevailing concerns with corruption, faction, and conspiracy.[178] These petitions saw subjects show a system of thought in line with what Noah Millstone has coined as 'politic reasoning' – interpreting events as caused by the moral qualities of political actors, resorting to deception and dissimulation to achieve self-interested agendas.[179] The petitioners combined this narrative of dissimulation with a powerful rhetoric of bondage and slavery, arguing

> many haue bin the devises practises and attemptes both secrett and open whereby they have endevoured to Ruine and overthrow the same which malice of theires wee are well assured tendeth but theire owne end[e]s and to opresse and bring vs vnder theire bondage and Slavery in which they have held vs Longe before the tyme of the pattent.[180]

The glaziers demonstrated their ability to utilise languages and tropes especially pertinent in 1621 to explain their sudden reversal in alliances, suggesting that it was members of their own industry, rather than Mansell, who had terrorised them. These fissures would physically play out in the physical space of the committee for grievances; on 14 May, Bungard fought with a glazier before the committee over the prices and quality of glass.[181]

The glaziers proceeded to answer the articles pertaining to glazing. In their thirteenth article, the glassmakers had complained that many towns had a scarcity of broad glass, depriving glaziers of work in cutting glass. The glaziers responded by skilfully engaging with concerns surrounding London's domination of trade as articulated in James's first Parliament. Previously, they claimed, many parts of the kingdom had recourse to London for their cut glass, the metropolis acting as a 'stoarehouse' for the realm.[182] Now, Mansell's building of glasshouses throughout the realm acted as a check on London's domination, allowing the trade to be dispersed in a range of convenient locations, so that 'the Citty of London is prevented of that benefit of trading as Formerly it hath hadd'.[183] The glaziers presented themselves as representing the case of the 'Cuntry glasiers', suggesting that the glassmakers and glaziers who opposed Mansell only did so to retain their dominant hold on trade. As a London company that had most likely made a deal with Mansell, the glaziers's deployment of these arguments must be seen as purely rhetorical, designed to appease those MPs who feared that the monopolisation of trade in the city had caused the decline of the outports. The glassmakers themselves had appealed to this rhetoric of free trade, claiming that Mansell's monopoly had caused 'the overthrowing of the free trading which ought to be in the kingdome'.[184] Here, the glaziers turned this accusation on its head to present the glassmakers as attempting to enforce a London-based domination, and Mansell as furthering the economic wellbeing of the entire realm. The glaziers also challenged the ninth, eleventh, and eighteenth articles of the glassmakers, arguing that Mansell's glass was no more expensive than before the patent and that it was of a fit and sufficient quality to use.

The glaziers ended their appeal by making two requests. Firstly, they expressed their concern that they 'not fall vnder the Scottish pattent', presenting this as the ultimate goal of glassmakers, many of whom were alleged to have interests in Hay's glasshouses.[185] Again, the simultaneous existence of two monopolies for the trade triggered tensions within the industry. Perhaps most notably, they made a direct reference to the Commission for Glass, albeit their presentation of the utility of the body was markedly different from that of the glassmakers. Whereas the latter had suggested the Commission had failed to heed their concerns, the glaziers crafted a more positive image of the institution, asking that it be 'Continewed to heare and Releeve our Complaintes in Case of necessitie'.[186] This was perhaps unsurprising given that the Commission had so far worked to uphold Mansell's patent. They concluded by expressing their desire to remain 'vnder the pattent then danger of a Combinac[i]on by som[e] of our owne Fraternitie'.[187]

The move of some members of the Glaziers' Company to support Mansell did not escape the attention of parliamentary diarists, who recorded debates in the grievances committee which show that the patent generated fissures in the industry. John Pym observed that rising glass prices seemed to have affected London less than areas such as Gloucestershire, though he suggested this might be because glaziers in the city were closer to the Court to complain.[188] Another diarist suggested that London glaziers were supplied with cheap glass, whilst subjects elsewhere faced excessive prices.[189] Despite the glaziers' attempts to present Mansell's grant as preventing London's dominance in the industry, it seems as if Mansell's glassworks in Broad Street supplied those in the capital with a steady supply of cheap glass, whilst subjects elsewhere faced excessive prices.[190] In reality, this discrepancy was a product of the alliance between Mansell and these members of the Glaziers' Company.

The glaziers also participated in Parliament's vibrant manuscript culture. Phelips collected numerous documents on the glass case. Some appear to have originated from the Mansell-camp, including a breviate titled 'A breife of the Lady Mansells cawse touchinge the Pattent of glasse', and a list of reasons to prove the validity of the glass patents.[191] A copy of the latter was also sent to Caesar in December 1621.[192] These lobbying documents were an important way through which appeals were made to MPs.[193] Once again, social status was used to undermine opponents. The brief contrasted the lowly status of the glassmakers with the certificates of fifty glaziers of the 'better sorte' who could speak to the patent's benefits.[194] The separate list of reasons in favour of the patent revealed the benefits that the support of the glaziers brought for Mansell. Its author (possibly Elizabeth) stated that 'I will approue by the glaisers of London which haue vsed the most glasse that there was never better nor larger glasse made by Bunger or anie other'.[195]

The attack on status was continued in a detailed character assessment of the chief petitioners against Mansell. It appears to have been written in response to their collective petition, consisting of three sections to question the motivations and designs of the glassmakers, glaziers, merchants, and bugle makers named in the collective petition.[196] That it was the work of Lady Mansell and her glazier supporters is apparent in its contents, which repeated the narrative that Bungard, Bennett, and Dines were master manipulators, whilst presenting Mansell as a hapless victim to their schemes. The statement presented Mansell as tirelessly working to employ glassmakers in his glasshouses. Even Bungard was said to have received 'enterteynement' at Mansell's table, yet he had still boasted to others that he had £1,000 to overthrow the patent. Bungard had allegedly encouraged glassmakers to breach their contracts with Mansell or to destroy and spoil his furnaces. Whilst Mansell had tried to employ them (thereby doing the opposite of a monopoliser who restrained trade), Bungard had broken all the behaviours expected of civil society, accepting Mansell's gracious hospitality whilst plotting his downfall.

The statement repeated accusations that Bungard had orchestrated a seditious petitioning campaign. He had

> travailed & searched out all the sedicious, malicious, discontented, irreguler p[er]sons, that are to be found in any p[ar]te of the kingdome, to clamour to the Lord[e]s, and the former p[ar]liam[en]t, and in the like maner are his p[ro]ceeding[e]s at this p[re]sent to this ho[nora]ble Assembly.[197]

Lest MPs were not persuaded by this presentation of a seditious campaign, they proceeded to present an image of the glass trade as highly interconnected through kinship ties. Most of the glassmakers in the kingdom, it was claimed, were Bungard's 'kindred and haue dependency on him', explaining why so many had complained of the patent.[198] It was this which had emboldened Bungard to 'Crosse and destroy the purposes of the king, and State in this kinde' by defying a royally bestowed patent.[199] It was not only Bungard who was attacked in this document. The glassmaker John Worrell was also cast as a schemer who had dissuaded any who fell within 'the compasse of his tongue' to buy Mansell's glass.[200] He had even threatened Lady Mansell, informing her that 'he wanted clothes but would make none new, vntill he had a peece of the pattent to make a measure for his Tailor'.[201]

Alongside such dramatic anecdotes stood accusations which suggested extensive, albeit flawed, research had gone into producing the assessment. For example, the glassmaker Abraham Liscourt was accused of plotting to kill any who taught English subjects how to make glass. The breviate claimed that he was following in the example of his father who had murdered one Balthazar Henzey in Lorraine. Whilst Henzey had indeed been murdered in 1579, this was by one Christopher de Thysac.[202] The statement continued to attack other glaziers, including Bennett and Dines, whilst the Glaziers' Master, John Markes, was attacked for investing £50 in the Scottish glassworks despite his initial support for Mansell's patent.[203] The document also ended by suggesting that one of the bugle makers who signed the supplication, 'Maddoun Casar', had imported great stores of glass without paying customs.[204]

The documents collected by Phelips on the glass case attest to the powerful and intense lobbying used to protect Mansell's monopoly. Whilst opponents of the patent could refer to past parliamentary decisions and utilise the general anti-monopoly sentiments of the Commons to advance their cause, Lady Mansell and her glazier supporters turned to focus on the status and character of petitioners, mirroring techniques seen in many counter-petitioning campaigns. The glassmakers were not prepared to give up this battle, sending another petition to answer allegations that they refused to teach native subjects the trade.[205] The petitions were enough to ensure that the glass patent received considerable attention in the committee for grievances.[206] Sir Edwin Sandys spoke for the patent, expressing concern that Scotland would dominate glass making if it were revoked, but the glassmakers appear to have successfully garnered the support of the influential Coke and the MP for Tregony, Thomas Malet.[207]

Opinions on the glass patent were collected from beyond the metropolis. Glaziers in Gloucestershire lamented that the price of glass had increased from 16s. to 24s., whilst glaziers in Lancaster complained that they were 'much oppressed by the excessive Prices of Broad Glasses, by Means of the Patentees'.[208] Glassmakers in Staffordshire alleged that they had been forced to give up their glass houses and been imprisoned in London.[209] Some complaints were presented as written petitions; glaziers in Wiltshire and Southampton petitioned against the patent.[210] Meanwhile, testimonies were provided and witnesses were called from Herefordshire, London, and Newcastle.[211] The hand of the Venetian ambassador may well have been at work here. In his dispatch of April, he reported that he had 'tactfully encouraged' subjects to push for the cancellation of Mansell's glass monopoly to re-secure the import trade from Venice.[212] By contrast, spectacle makers in the city petitioned in favour of the grant.[213] Such was the strength of agitation that Mansell's patent was declared a grievance in the Commons on 16 May.[214]

Despite this judgement, James decided to protect Mansell's monopoly by referring it to the Council for further review.[215] The Council thus let it remain in force due to Mansell's absence abroad, arguing that this made it difficult for him to defend his grant.[216] Glassmakers, emboldened by the Commons' investigation, erected new furnaces, imported foreign glass, and refused to pay rents to Mansell, convinced that Parliament's pronouncement had freed them from the shackles of monopoly.[217]

News of Parliament's condemnation of other monopolies quickly spread far and wide. In June, Secretary Calvert wrote to the Lord Mayor, Sir Francis Jones, of his concern that officers at London's ports had stopped collecting money due to the patentees for lighthouses at Wintertonness and Dungeness, both of which had been criticised in the Parliament.[218] Calvert was alarmed that this had been ordered 'by colour of an order supposed to bee made to that purpose by the Comons howse of Parliam[en]te'.[219] In response, Jones insisted that he had been visited by three burgesses (who all conveniently failed to provide him with their names) who showed him two copies of orders made by the Commons, attesting to the ways in which news of proceedings, even if inaccurate, spread during the summer recess.[220]

By 19 December, the Commons wrote to Cranfield, seeking his support to persuade James to stay the glass patent in light of their previous judgement.[221] Despite James and the Council's support for Mansell, the glassmakers' protests had not been in vain. In June, Hay was given permission to export Scottish glass into England.[222] As compensation, Mansell's obligation to pay an annual rent of £2,800 for his patent was cancelled. This was not enough to appease him. In October 1622, he agitated for a new patent on the grounds that he had no means to sue for money owed to him by subjects who evaded his grant. Strikingly, Mansell expressed his desire to see the Commission for Glass act as an arm of his patent, requesting that it be deployed to 'recover such summes of money as now are or shalbe hereafter become due unto him'.[223] In this, Mansell attempted to transform the body from a commission intended to hear grievances to an institution designed to help enforce his patent, similar to the commission for gold and silver thread.

Mansell was to secure a new patent to make glass for fifteen years by 22 May 1623.[224] Crucially, the memory of the Parliament of 1621 was integral to the way in which this grant was justified and presented, showing the sophisticated ways through which parliamentary condemnation of grants could be flipped by patentees and their supporters. The Council were aware that the patent had been declared a grievance, and it was this which was used to explain the necessity of passing a new one. References to the 'petic[i]ons and certificates' sent by London's glaziers, glass sellers, and spectacle makers in the last Parliament were included in the text of the patent, to present it as something which was desired within the industry.[225] Resistance continued as the battle over glass continued to wage on. In the interim between 1621 and 1624, Bungard and Worrell petitioned the Council, even requesting to be recipients of the patent for glass instead of Mansell.[226] By the Parliament of 1624, the stage was set for yet another confrontation between them.

## Moving to print: lobbying in 1624

In the Parliament of 1624, the glass monopoly continued to be investigated, albeit Mansell's return from naval business allowed him to fight in person. For Bungard and the glassmakers, Parliament's condemnation of his patent in both 1614 and 1621 likely filled them with a sense of optimism that his newly granted monopoly would face similar censure. Parliament for them was not an event, but an institution, allowing them to transfer their suits back to the body given the recent history of its interaction with them.[227] Similarly, Mansell's tactics as a patentee went beyond invoking ideas of the commonwealth or pointing to the revenues his enterprise generated for the Crown. Instead, he was forced to respond to the glassmakers' presentation of Parliament as a protector of their trade by shaping a rather different interpretation of past events as he also turned to print to present his case.

Mansell's deployment of a printed broadside saw him respond to the larger changes affecting parliamentary petitioning and lobbying culture, as part of 'discreet' lobbying efforts designed to appeal to MPs.[228] Mansell produced an exhaustive narrative of the history of his patent and of his tireless efforts to perfect the process of making glass with coal.[229] It was framed as a direct response to a petition presented to the Commons by the glassmakers and ended by requesting that Parliament would 'ratifie' his grant, freeing him from the 'heauy imputation of contempt' imposed on him by the petitioners.[230] The document represents the sometimes blurred lines between petitioning and lobbying; it focused on a particular grievance, but it also included substantial evidence to try and influence the policy of Parliament, especially as Mansell was striving to get his patent exempt from the Statute of Monopolies.[231] It might therefore be classed as a counter-petition which also aimed to lobby on monopoly policy.

The document primarily rehearsed Mansell's continuous efforts to work for the public good, contrasting this with the schemes and plots of Bungard. Many of the accusations in the character assessment of 1621 were repeated, including the allegation that Bungard had shown 'a bagge of money' to Mansell's workmen to entice them away.[232] This was remarkably similar to Richard Drake's complaint in 1596 that Francis Oliver had shown bags of money to subjects to overthrow his patent for the brewing of beer and ale for aquavitae and aquacomposita.[233]

Mansell presented the Common's decision in 1621 as unfair, playing on his own absence abroad to suggest that the House was not adequately armed with the requisite facts to reach an appropriate judgement on the case. Somewhat unfairly to Elizabeth, who had led such a strong campaign in his absence, Mansell presented her as woefully unprepared to defend the grant, without his 'speciall papers and writings'.[234] As such, James's decision to allow his patent to stand despite the Common's order was presented as just. Mansell's new patent was defended as legitimate. It had been bestowed, he claimed, after all proper courses of examination had occurred, receiving scrutiny at committee before it passed. In emphasising this, Mansell was preventing glassmakers from repeating accusations they had made in 1621 that his patent had been granted without proper examination by the Commission for Suits. Mansell asserted that the new patent was actually intended to respect Parliament's condemnation of his previous grant. It was no monopoly, but a rightful patent for a new invention.

The glassmakers also responded by using print, revealing the capacity for unincorporated collectives of subjects to escalate their lobbying tactics in line with broader developments in parliamentary culture. They produced both a printed list of reasons against Mansell's monopoly and a set of answers to Mansell's breviate.[235] Whilst their response was anonymous, it is likely that Bungard and Bennett were instrumental in its construction, working with legal counsel to produce a document which included specific allegations of Mansell's abuses alongside references to the law. They moved their appeals beyond describing the last condemnations in 1614 and 1621 to raise questions as to where the authority to regulate this industry ultimately lay: with Parliament or with the Crown. This was based around the issue of wood scarcity which had justified the need for the patent. In their seventh demand, the petitioners suggested that scarcity was better redressed through statute than through patent or proclamation. They argued that when 'inconueniences haue appeared to ensue vnto the Common-wealth, the ysuall redresse hath alwayes been by Act of Parliament'.[236] As such, a 'Patent to restraine men of their lawfull trade because of the consumption of wood, was neuer seen before this Patent granted'.[237] By including these arguments, the glassmakers tapped into previous concerns raised in 1610 with the use of proclamations to enforce policies, including the starch monopolies.[238] It allowed them to appeal to parliamentary authority in a new way given that the patent of 1623 had not yet been condemned by Parliament, leaving them with less room to present it as a deliberate violation of the Common's judgement. Subjects were thus able to link their concerns with the glass trade to wider frameworks and debates surrounding economic regulation and the relative balance between statute and prerogative authority in a document seemingly focused on a rather specific industry.

By the close of this Parliament, the Statute of Monopolies was engrossed as law. Yet it was far from watertight. As Conrad Russell argues, it was still not clear what constituted a 'monopoly', and the blurred boundaries between monopoly and corporatism remained.[239] MPs and peers debated whether charters to corporations were monopolies, deciding that they would only be deemed as such if they granted the sole production or sale of a product to one body.[240] Corporations were thus made exempt, as were a handful of monopoly patents. Following parliamentary proceedings closely, two petitioners named Thomas and John Browne petitioned the Commons to complain of a proviso attached to the bill, exempting a patent for the sole casting of iron ordnance held by Sackville Crow. They called on the Commons to consider their 'petic[i]on reasons, and certificates', already sent to the House, before allowing this to pass.[241] These petitioners were evidently watching events unfold as they awaited a response to their complaint. Another contentious proviso was that for Mansell's monopoly. On 7 April, Mansell requested that his patent be exempted, touching as it did upon his 'whole fortune'.[242] By 1 May, Coke reported that his request had been granted, not for any love for the patent, but to ensure that the bill successfully passed both Houses; Mansell's influence was too powerful to overcome.[243] Whilst Coke promised that Mansell's patent would not be renewed on its expiry, the glass patent would continue to vex subjects into Charles's reign.[244] By 1638, the Glaziers' Company would re-unite and emerge as Mansell's staunch opponents, demonstrating the temporary nature of their alliance in James's reign.[245] Yet this co-ordinated opposition did not bring them a greater degree of success: only the turmoil of the Civil Wars would see Mansell's glassworks finally close their doors.

## Conclusion

Glassmakers, glaziers, merchants, spinners, and glovers were just some of the myriad subjects who utilised Parliament in 1621 and 1624 as a point of contract through which to send their anti-monopoly complaints, making their voices heard in the chambers of Westminster. Subjects were clearly adept at using whichever avenues were open to them to launch their campaigns, transferring suits from one arena to another when required. This amounted to a process of what Jason Peacey and Brodie Waddell have termed as 'forum shopping'.[246] As such, disputes were raised in multiple institutions and in different parliamentary sessions. For the realm's glassmakers at least, their decision to approach the Commons was presented as a necessity, incapable as they were of finding redress through other institutions. The strength of free trade debates in James's first Parliament served to foster an idea amongst subjects that Parliament was a protector of their economic liberties. Parliament's continued attack on vexatious patents and corporate bodies in 1621 and 1624 only strengthened this perception, fostering a widespread belief in its role as a protector from corruption that would endure into the Long Parliament.

Glassmakers engaged in sophisticated processes of narration as they crafted their petitions, presenting past parliamentary decisions as proof that the Commons had always been on their side. In so doing, they contributed to Parliament's perception of itself as a centre for the redress of grievances, already growing in light of the institutional changes allowing petitions to be presented with greater ease. Their petitions suggested that MPs were respecting the decisions of their predecessors by condemning the glass patents and protecting the rights of glassmakers throughout the realm. This suggested a perception of continuity between Parliaments; whilst years could pass between sittings, the decisions and precedents of both Houses needed to be respected and upheld. Peacey has used the issue of parliamentary protections to trace Parliament's increased concern with its own reputation as a responsive body in the seventeenth century, as it answered petitions sent by individuals.[247] Subjects also contributed to this development of Parliament's identity as a space for justice through the image they crafted of Parliament in petitioning appeals.

The skilful supplications of the glassmakers and glaziers were in some ways tactical; appeals to free trade seem to have been a strategic attempt to rouse the sympathy of MPs. However, their suits still provide some insights into their own perceptions of Parliament: not all of this was rhetorical. The Common's support for the glassmakers likely generated some genuine faith in the institution's ability to offer redress, especially compared to the Commission for Glass. When approaching the Council, petitioners had sometimes received a hostile reaction; in 1623, the glassmakers John Worrall and Robert Lambert were warned not to attend with any more suits on the glass business or face imprisonment, and Bungard had been imprisoned for his speeches against Mansell earlier in February 1621.[248] In a later surviving breviate of the case dating to 1626, glassmakers complained of the lack of redress offered by the new king Charles: 'after followeing his Ma[jes]tie to preferr their petic[i]on for releife some of them were Imprisoned'.[249] It is possible that they felt safer sending appeals to Parliament, noting here that the Commons could offer them and other suitors protection from subpoenas as Mansell launched legal action against them.[250] Indeed, glassmakers continued to fight Mansell's patent in the Long Parliament, repeatedly insisting that their case be transferred from examination in the Lords to the Commons.[251] It is hard not to conclude that the memory of its decisions against Mansell in the 1620s was partly to explain for their insistence that the Commons hear their dispute, perceiving of MPs as long-standing allies in their battle.

The increased accessibility of Parliament and the torrent of news flowing from Westminster was a crucial development in the 1620s. So too were the number of materials entering it. Petitioning and lobbying brought subjects into contact with the institution, as they responded to developments by experimenting with the use of print by 1624. The glassmakers' own foray into the printed word also reminds us that subjects, acting outside of official company channels, could utilise these mediums. The investigation into monopolies brought subjects physically into Parliament's remit, offering depositions to both the Lords and the Commons, repeating processes seen with the commissions appointed in the city and Court to investigate trade. Institutional developments were clearly key for facilitating petitioning activity in the 1620s, but no less important is understanding the ways through which subjects perceived Parliament as a body, and how they shaped their rhetoric accordingly. Aware of the anti-monopoly sentiments of both Houses, subjects proved adept at using accusations of monopoly to bolster their cause. For others, frameworks of corruption and conspiracy were an important means through which patentees or new corporate bodies were attacked. For some, these discourses were rhetorical tools. But for others, like the female spinners imprisoned for refusing to enter bonds, they reflected a very real concern with the forces of corruption littering the political landscape. For so many of these subjects, their engagement with Parliament was not driven by their concern with the Spanish Match, nor by the factional politics surrounding Buckingham. Rather, their economic concerns pushed them to offer petitions and depositions to the Commons and the Lords as they attempted to gain redress. Undoubtedly, these processes contributed to politicisation, exposing them to languages and issues pertaining to prerogative, liberty, and free trade.

James's final two Parliaments met during a period of economic depression, heightening the desire of MPs and peers to investigate problems in trade. For another corporate body, the calling of Parliament created not a sense of hope, but anxiety. In the face of intense pressures on the cloth trade, the Merchant Adventurers faced attacks both in and outside of Parliament. In the interim between them, yet another commission would emerge as a point of contact for petitioning activism: the Commission for Trade.

## Notes

1 PA, HL/PO/JO/10/13/7, fo. 49v.

2 S. Lee and S. Kelsey, 'Mompesson, Sir Giles (1583/4–1651/63)', *ODNB* (2004), https://doi.org/10.1093/ref:odnb/18932 (accessed 29 July 2024).

3 J. S. Hart, *Justice Upon Petition: The House of Lords and the Reformation of Justice 1621–1675* (London, 1991).

4 W. Notestein, *The Winning of the Initiative by the House of Commons* (London, 1924); Zaller, *Parliament of 1621*; Russell, *Parliaments*, pp. 87–8 and chs 2–3; G. Yerby, *The Economic Causes of the English Civil War: Freedom of Trade and The English Revolution* (New York, 2020), p. 154; S. D. White, *Sir Edward Coke and the 'Grievances of the Commonwealth', 1621–1628* (Manchester, 1979), ch. 4.

5 T. Cogswell, *The Blessed Revolution: English Politics and the Coming of War, 1621–1624* (Cambridge, 1989); Lake and Pincus, 'Public Sphere', p. 279. Millstone also notes that most pamphlets in 1624 dealt with the Spanish Match, Buckingham, and war, see N. Millstone, *Manuscript Circulation and the Invention of Politics in Early Stuart England* (Cambridge, 2016), pp. 114–15.

6 Kyle, *Theater*, ch. 5–6; Thrush, 'Legislation and Petitions', *HoP*, i.

7 Hart, *Justice*.

8 Kyle, *Theater*, p. 1 and ch. 4; C. R. Kyle and J. Peacey, '"Under cover of so much coming and going": Public Access to Parliament and the Political Process in Early Modern England', in Kyle and Peacey, *Parliament at Work*, pp. 1–23; Dean, 'Pressure Groups and Lobbies'.

9 Kyle, *Theater*, chs 5–6; Kyle, 'Carting'.

10 This has been argued by Foster, 'Procedure', p. 77.

11 P. Cavill and A. Gajda, 'Introduction', in P. Cavill and A. Gajda (eds), *Writing the History of Parliament in Tudor and Early Stuart England* (Manchester, 2018), pp. 2, 23.

12 P. Seaward, 'Institutional Memory and Contemporary History in the House of Commons, 1547–1640', in Cavill and Gajda (eds), *Writing the History of Parliament*, pp. 212–13.
13 Peacey, 'Parliament, Printed Petitions', pp. 350–63.
14 For the best narrative of the patent, see E. S. Godfrey, *The Development of English Glassmaking 1560–1640* (Oxford, 1975), chs 3–4; J. W. Gough, *The Rise of the Entrepreneur* (London, 1969), ch. 10.
15 Cramsie, *Kingship*, pp. 128–30. Suffolk was also Treasurer from 1614 to July 1618.
16 TNA, SP 14/97, fos 31r–32r; TNA, SP 14/97, fo. 33r–37r; BL, Add. MS 10038, fo. 2; TNA, SP 14/97, fos 40r–46v.
17 TNA, SP 14/97, fo. 33v. For the Commission referring suits, see TNA, SP 14/116, fo. 155r; TNA, SP 14/117, fo. 7r
18 Cramsie, *Kingship*, p. 164. See also R. Lockyer, *Buckingham: The Life and Political Career of George Villiers, First Duke of Buckingham 1592–1628* (London, 1981), ch. 4.
19 S. R. Gardiner, 'On Four Letters from Lord Bacon to Christian IV King of Denmark, with Observations on the Part Taken by Him in the Grants of Monopolies Made by James I', *Archaeologia*, XLI (London, 1867), pp. 219–69.
20 Larkin and Hughes, I, pp. 384–9. Commissioners were appointed on 22 April 1618, see Gardiner, 'Four Letters', pp. 251–3.
21 M. A. Abrams, 'English Gold and Silver Thread Monopolies, 1611–1621', *Journal of Economic and Business History*, 3:3 (1931), pp. 385–94; *CD 1621*, vii, p. 365; Gardiner, 'Four Letters', p. 258.
22 Larkin and Hughes, I, pp. 441–6.
23 Gardiner, 'Four Letters', pp. 241–44; A. H. Siegler, 'Royal Prerogative and the Regulation of Industry: Regulation of the Gold and Silver Thread Trade under James I and Charles I' (unpublished PhD thesis, University of Chicago, 1980), ch. 3.
24 *CD 1621*, vii, pp. 379–86.
25 A. Bellany and T. Cogswell, *The Murder of King James I* (New Haven, 2015), pp. 117–18; C 66/2206, *CPR 17 Jas*, fos 209–10.
26 TNA, SP 14/97, fo. 257r.
27 *Ibid.*
28 A. F. Pollard and S. Kelsey, 'Villiers, Christopher, first earl of Anglesey (d. 1630)', *ODNB* (2004), https://doi-org.ezproxy-prd.bodleian.ox.ac.uk/10.1093/ref:odnb/28287 (accessed 29 July 2024).
29 Ashton, *City*, pp. 117–18; TLA, COL/RMD/PA/01/005, fos 6r–7r.
30 TLA, COL/RMD/PA/01/005, fos 8, 18.
31 *Ibid.*, fos 24–25, 37–38.
32 *Ibid.*, fos 22–23; *CD 1621*, vii, pp. 391–3.
33 PA, HL/PO/JO/10/1/27, fo. 95.
34 Godfrey, *Glassmaking*, chs 1–2.
35 For the Company's history, see C. H. Ashdown, *History of the Worshipful Company of Glaziers of the City of London, Otherwise the Company of Glaziers and Painters of Glass* (London, 1919).

36 G. H. Kenyon, *The Glass Industry of the Weald* (Leicester, 1967), ch. 8.
37 Godfrey, *Glassmaking*, ch. 3. For the grants, see C 66/1711, *CPR 3–5 Jas*, fo. 287v–288r; C 66/1727, *3–5 Jas*, fo. 313r; C 66/1744, *CPR 3–5 Jas*, fo. 337v; C 66/1751, *CPR 6 Jas*, fo. 219; *APC*, 33, pp. 162–3.
38 C 66/1926, *CPR 9 Jas*, fo. 184
39 *APC*, 33, pp. 162–3, 173, 192–3, 250, 269.
40 C 66/1993, *CPR 10–11 Jas*, fo. 261.
41 *APC*, 33, pp. 376–7, 545–6, 634–5, 643, 668–71. Previous patentees also demand compensation, see pp. 497–8, 659–60; *APC*, 34, pp. 15–16, 95–6.
42 See Paterson, 'Bloodsuckers', pp. 153–6.
43 C 66/2019, *CPR 12 Jas*, fo. 98. This appears to have been Sir Thomas Howard, second son of Thomas Howard, Earl of Suffolk and MP for Cricklade in 1621. He was identified as involved in the patent in SRO, DD/PH/222/99, fo. 176r; H. Lancaster and B. Coates, 'HOWARD, Sir Thomas (1587–1669), of Charlton Park, Charlton, Wilts', *HoP*, iv.
44 A. Thrush, 'Mansell, Sir Robert (1570/1–1652), Naval Officer and Administrator', *ODNB* (2008), https://doi-org.ezproxy-prd.bodleian.ox.ac.uk/10.1093/ref:odnb/17992 (accessed 19 November 2020).
45 M. Jansson, *Proceedings in Parliament 1614 (House of Commons)* (Philadelphia, 1988), p. 430.
46 Larkin and Hughes, I, pp. 342–3.
47 For a later dispute with Sir William Clavell on these contracts, see *APC*, 37, p. 343; *APC*, 38, p. 8; *APC*, 39, pp. 11, 57–8.
48 *APC*, 36, p. 329.
49 For Elizabeth's active role, see TNA, SP 14/105, fo. 28r; TNA, SP 14/148, fo. 65r.
50 Godfrey, *Glassmaking*, ch. 4. Interpretations of Mansell's patent have been polarised: Godfrey regards the Zouch and Mansell patents as essential for the development of the industry. Hartshorne described Bungard as a 'vindictive, untruthful, and unscrupulous knave', see A. Hartshorne, *Old English Glasses: An Account of Glass Drinking Vessels in England, From Early Times to the End of the Eighteenth Century* (London, 1987), p. 198. By contrast, Price describes the glass monopolies as 'parasitic', Price, *English Patents*, p. 80.
51 Godfrey, *Glassmaking*, pp. 34, 55–7.
52 TNA, SP 14/105, fo. 27r.
53 Ashdown, *Glaziers*, p. 57.
54 Godfrey, *Glassmaking*, pp. 89–90.
55 *APC*, 35, pp. 232–3. Godfrey notes that the glaziers sent a petition to the Council at this time, arguing they complained of Bunger and Bennett, but proceeds to cite the text of their later petition to parliament in 1621. The petition of 1617 as recorded in the *APC* was against Mansell's monopoly, see Godfrey, *Glassmaking*, p. 87.
56 *APC*, 34, pp. 469–70; *APC*, 35, pp. 290–1; *APC*, 36, pp. 329–30.
57 Waddell and Peacey, 'Introduction', p. 18.
58 J. Turnbull, *The Scottish Glass Industry 1610–1750: 'To Serve the Whole Nation With Glass'* (Edinburgh, 2001), ch. 4. This was one of many patents granted in Scotland, see Cramsie, *Kingship*, p. 72.

59 TNA, SP 14/112, fo. 46; TNA, SP 14/112, fo. 48; TNA, SP 14/112, fo. 49.
60 BL, Lans. MS. 162, fos 65r–66v.
61 Smedmore MSS, B2/2, in *HMC Smedmore*, pp. 154–6.
62 R. Macpherson, 'Stuart [Stewart], Ludovick, Second Duke of Lennox and Duke of Richmond (1574–1624)', *ODNB* (2004), https://doi.org/10.1093/ref:odnb/26724 (accessed 6 June 2022); D. Stevenson, 'Hamilton, James, Second Marquess of Hamilton (1589–1625)', *ODNB* (2015), https://doi.org/10.1093/ref:odnb/12085 (accessed 6 June 2022); V. Stater, 'Herbert, William, Third Earl of Pembroke (1580–1630)', *ODNB* (January, 2008), https://doi.org/10.1093/ref:odnb/13058 (accessed 15 July 2022); R. M. Smuts, 'Howard, Thomas, Fourteenth Earl of Arundel, Fourth Earl of Surrey, and First Earl of Norfolk (1585–1646)', *ODNB* (2015), https://doi.org/10.1093/ref:odnb/13943 (accessed 15 July 2022).
63 Smedmore MSS, B2/2, p. 155.
64 *Ibid.*; Larkin and Hughes, I, pp. 464–6.
65 *APC*, 37, pp. 154–5. For an analysis of these petitions, see Paterson, 'Bloodsuckers', pp. 164–5.
66 Stevenson, 'Hamilton'.
67 SRO, DD/PH/222/99, fo. 176r.
68 Smuts, 'Howard, Thomas'.
69 TNA, SP 14/113, fo. 101r.
70 TNA, SP 14/113, fo. 100r; Ashdown, *Glaziers' Company*, p. 57.
71 TNA, SP 14/113, fo. 100r.
72 TNA, SP 14/113, fo. 101r.
73 TNA, SP 14/113, fo. 102r.
74 TNA, SP 14/112, fo. 109r. For details on Robson and Dines, see Godfrey, *Glassmaking*, pp. 88–90, 96.
75 TNA, SP 14/112, fo. 109r.
76 TNA, SP 14/112, fo. 110r.
77 Kyle and Peacey, 'Public Access'; Kyle, *Theater*, p. 120.
78 K. Lindley, *Popular Politics and Religion in Civil War London* (Aldershot, 1997).
79 Kyle, *Theater*, p. 9.
80 For an overview, see Russell, *Parliaments*, chs 2–3.
81 *LJ*, iii, pp. 82, 134–6; PA, HL/PO/JO/10/2/2B; HL/PO/JO/10/1/22; HL/PO/JO/10/1/14, fos 119r–123r.
82 Bellany and Cogswell, *Murder of King James*, p. 117.
83 Russell, *Parliaments*, pp. 105–6.
84 *LJ*, iii, pp. 46–7. For the patent for concealed lands, see *CD 1621*, vii, p. 346.
85 Larkin and Hughes, I, pp. 504–505. A proclamation for the apprehension of Mompesson was issued, see HL/PO/JO/10/1/14, fo. 26.
86 Pierce, *Unseemly Pictures*, pp. 70–81.
87 Larkin and Hughes, I, pp. 511–19.
88 *LJ*, iii, pp. 77, 121. Phelips kept notes on the investigation, see SRO, DD/PH/221/67.

89 Thrush, 'Legislation and Petitions'.
90 C. R. Kyle, 'Attendance, Apathy and Order? Parliamentary Committees in Early Stuart England', in Kyle and Peacey, *Parliament at Work*, p. 47.
91 Thrush, 'Legislation and Petitions'; Kyle, *Theater*, p. 141.
92 Kyle, *Theater*, p. 142, ch. 6; Peacey, *Public Politics*, ch. 8.
93 Thrush, 'Legislation and Petitions'.
94 For instructions on petitions, see PA, HL/PO/JO/10/1/19, fos 12r–13r. For a catalogue of petitions, see fos 130r–131v. For an order appointing a committee to discuss grievances with the Commons, see PA, HL/PO/JO/10/13/7, f. 37.
95 Hart, *Justice*, p. 16.
96 *Ibid.*, p. 38.
97 Often private acts were introduced via petitions, see E. R. Foster, *The House of Lords, 1603–1649: Structure, Procedure, and the Nature of Its Business* (London, 1983), pp. 191, 193. For an example, see bills and petitions on the lighthouses at Wintertonness, *CD 1621*, vii, Appendix A, pp. 6–15. For a brief by George Morgan on alum, see HRO, 44M69/L39/4.
98 Foster, 'Procedure', pp. 67–72.
99 Kyle, *Theater*.
100 Kyle and Peacey, 'Public Access', pp. 1–23.
101 A. Davidson, J. P. Ferris, and S. Healy, 'Phelips, Sir Robert (1585/6–1638)', *HoP*, v.
102 A. Thrush, 'Alford, Edward (c. 1565/6–1631)', *HoP*, iii.
103 V. C. D. Moseley and R. Sgroi, 'Jervoise, Sir Thomas (1587–1654)', *HoP*, iv.
104 Kyle, *Theater*, p. 88.
105 HRO, 44M69/L39/113/1–3.
106 HRO, 44M69/L39/113/3. The topic of these bills has heretofore remained unidentified, but these letters reveal their focus on matters of the economy. See P. Hunneyball, 'Sherfield (Shervill), Henry (1572–1634), of Lincoln's Inn, London and Salisbury, Wilts', *HoP*, vi.
107 Kyle, *Theater*, pp. 142, 180.
108 Kyle, 'Carting'.
109 A. B. Hinds (ed.), *Calendar of State Papers Relating to English Affairs in the Archives of Venice* [hereafter *CSP Venice*] (37 vols, London, 1864–1947), xvii, no. 26.
110 PA, HL/PO/JO/10/1/14, f. 98; HL/PO/JO/10/1/15, fos 96r–110r, 111r–112v; *LJ*, iii, p. 151.
111 PA, HL/PO/JO/1/1/15, fo. 102r.
112 *Ibid.*, fo. 112r.
113 *LJ*, iii, p. 416.
114 GL, CLC/L/GH/B/001/MS11588/003, pp. 159, 172, 179.
115 PA, HL/PO/JO/10/1/21, fo. 65r.
116 *Ibid.*, fo. 67r.
117 GL, CLC/L/GH/B/001/MS11588/003, p. 270.
118 *Ibid.*, pp. 271, 273–4. For printed petition to parliament, see BL, Harl. 1996, fos 255v–256r.

119 PA, HL/PO/JO/10/13/7, fos 32–6; *CD 1621*, v, p. 280; C 66/1685, *CPR 3–5 Jas.*, fo. 49v; TLA, COL/CC/01/01/028, fos 13r–14r.
120 *CD 1621*, vii, pp. 361–2; TLA, COL/CA/01/01/030, f. 106v for their initial investigation of the patent. They were also investigated in Parliament in 1624 and forced to attend the Commons awaiting a hearing, see BL, Harl. 6803, fo. 114r.
121 *CSPD*, 1619–1623, p. 67.
122 Larkin and Hughes, I, p. 479.
123 PA, HL/PO/JO/10/13/9, fo. 99r. The tobacco-pipe patent was cancelled in July 1621, dating this to this session.
124 Ewen, *Virginia Venture*, p. 129.
125 Larkin and Hughes, I, p. 480; *CSPD*, 1619–23, p. 175.
126 PA, HL/PO/JO/10/13/9, fo. 99r.
127 See Chapter 2.
128 HRO, 44M69/G2/524/1.
129 For the alnage and abuse in Yorkshire, see H. Heaton, *The Yorkshire Woollen and Worsted Industries: From the Earliest Times up to the Industrial Revolution*, 2nd edn (Oxford, 1965), pp. 177–84.
130 HRO, 44M69/G2/524/2–12.
131 HRO, 44M69/G2/524/1.
132 SRO, DD/PH/216/5, fo. 9. For the grant, see *CD 1621*, vii, pp. 418–19.
133 SRO, DD/PH/216/5, fo. 9.
134 *LJ*, iii, p. 46.
135 PA, HL/PO/JO/10/1/21, fo. 15.
136 PA, HL/PO/JO/10/1/15, fo. 28.
137 PA, HL/PO/JO/10/1/21, fo. 15.
138 PA, HL/PO/JO/10/1/15, fos 28–29; *LJ*, iii, pp. 48–9.
139 See *LJ*, iii, p. 88 for an order in April that petitions could only be received if exhibited by the party complaining or if 'commended' from the Commons.
140 PA, HL/PO/JO/10/1/15, fos 29–32.
141 PA, HL/PO/JO/10/1/21, n.f.; HL/PO/JO/10/1/15, fos 33–9; *LJ*, iii, pp. 48–9.
142 *LJ*, iii, p. 89.
143 PA, HL/PO/JO/10/1/15, fos 36–7.
144 *Ibid.*, fo. 45.
145 Seaward, 'Institutional Memory', p. 213.
146 *CD 1621*, vii, pp. 540–1; SRO, DD/PH/222/100, fo. 177r. Is likely that this petition dates to 1621 as opposed to 1624. It mentions only one past parliamentary condemnation of monopolies, whereas in printed petitions of 1624, the events of 1614 and 1621 were mentioned. Equally, the petition notes that the patent required Mansell to pay a rent, something which was removed in his patent of 1623.
147 *CD 1621*, vii, pp. 541–5; SRO, DD/PH/222/101,102, fos 178r–179r.
148 *APC*, 37, p. 343.
149 Kenyon, *Glass Industry*, pp. 14–15.
150 Markes was named as Master by opponents, see SRO, DD/PH/222/103, fo. 181r. See also TNA, SP 14/113, fo. 101r.

151 Jansson, *Proceedings*, p. 111.
152 SRO, DD/PH/222/100, fo. 177r.
153 *Ibid.*
154 SRO, DD/PH/222/101,102, fo. 178r.
155 SRO, DD/PH/222/99, fo. 176r.
156 SRO, DD/PH/222/101,102, fo. 179r.
157 *Ibid.*, fo. 178r.
158 *Ibid.*
159 PA, HL/PO/JO/10/1/21, fo. 66.
160 *CD 1621*, iii, p. 196.
161 SRO, DD/PH/222/101, 102, fo. 179r.
162 *CD 1621*, iii, p. 196.
163 *Ibid.*, pp. 255–8.
164 SRO, DD/PH/222/106, fo. 184r.
165 For their petitions to the Commission, see TNA, SP 14/120, fo. 132r; TNA, SP 14/120, fo. 108r.
166 TNA, SP 14/162, fo. 111r.
167 C. Ross, 'The Development of the Glass Industry on the Rivers Tyne and Wear, 1700–1900' (unpublished PhD thesis, University of Newcastle, 1982), pp. 38–9.
168 TNA, SP 14/113, fo. 96r. This has been calendared to 1620, but Godfrey suggests a date of 1618 is more likely, as Dines moved against Mansell by 1620 and was no longer his undertaker, Godfrey, *English Glassmaking*, pp. 88–9. Mansell's answers however may date to 1638, as they articulate similar claims as repeated in a Council order of January 1638 pertaining to the effects of the plague in Newcastle and Mansell's use of materials like ashes and sapphire. See TNA, SP 16/378, fos 163r–164v; TNA, SP 14/113, fo. 98.
169 TLA, COL/CA/01/01/036, fo. 259v.
170 TLA, COL/CC/01/01/031, fos 44r, 132r–133r, 339r.
171 They petitioned for a charter in 1636, see Oxford, Bodl. MS Bankes 12, fos 40r–41v.
172 SRO, DD/PH/222/104, 105, fo. 182r; *CD 1621*, iii, p. 256.
173 In their petition to the Commission they had noted their desire to respond to these four articles, see *CD 1621*, vii, p. 549.
174 SRO, DD/PH/222/104, 105, fo. 182r.
175 *Ibid.*
176 *Ibid.*
177 *Ibid.*
178 E. Paterson, 'Corruption, Conspiracy and Collusion: Anti-Monopoly Petitioning in the Parliament of 1621', *Parliamentary History*, 42:3 (2023), pp. 289–308.
179 Millstone, *Manuscript Circulation*, pp. 146–7.
180 SRO, DD/PH/222/104, 105, fo. 182r.
181 CD 1621, iii, p. 256.
182 SRO, DD/PH/222/104,105, fo. 183r.

183 *Ibid.*
184 SRO, DD/PH/222/101,102, fo. 179r.
185 SRO, DD/PH/222/104,105, fo. 183r.
186 *Ibid.*
187 *Ibid.*
188 *CD 1621*, iv, p. 353.
189 *CD 1621*, v, p. 122.
190 Godfrey, *Glassmaking*, p. 111.
191 SRO, DD/PH/222/106, fo. 184; SRO, DD/PH/222/107, fo. 186.
192 BL, Add. MS. 12,496, fos 165r–166v. This might suggest it was written in response to a Commons' letter on 19 December calling for the patent to be revoked, see TNA, SP 14/124, fo. 117r.
193 Peacey, *Public Politics*, ch. 10.
194 SRO, DD/PH/222/106, fo. 184r.
195 SRO, DD/PH/222/107, fo. 186v.
196 SRO, DD/PH/222/103, fos 180r–181v.
197 *Ibid.*, fo. 180r.
198 *Ibid.*, fo. 180v.
199 *Ibid.*
200 *Ibid.*
201 *Ibid.*
202 Kenyon, *Glass Industry*, p. 129.
203 SRO, DD/PH/222/103, fo. 181r.
204 *Ibid.*, fo. 181v.
205 SRO, DD/PH/222/108, fo. 187r; *CD 1621*, vii, pp. 539–40.
206 This challenges Godfrey's suggestion that it received less attention than other grants, see Godfrey, *Glassmaking*, p. 105.
207 *CD 1621*, v, pp. 166, 170; *CD 1621*, iv, p. 355.
208 *Proceedings and Debates of the House of Commons in 1620 and 1621* (2 vols, Oxford, 1766), I, *Eighteenth Century Collections Online* (accessed 9 July 2020), pp. 360–1.
209 *Ibid.*, p. 361.
210 *Ibid.*
211 *Ibid.*, pp. 361–2.
212 *CSP Venice*, xvii, no. 26.
213 *CD 1621*, iii, p. 256.
214 Godfrey, *Glassmaking*, pp. 113–14.
215 TNA, SP 14/121, fo. 108r; SRO, DD/PH/222/98, fo. 174v.
216 TNA, SP 14/121, fo. 216r; *APC*, 38, p. 17.
217 *APC*, 38, p. 8.
218 TLA, COL/RMD/PA/01/005, fo. 129r. For the patent, see *CD 1621*, vii, pp. 396–402.
219 TLA, COL/RMD/PA/01/005, fo. 129r.
220 *Ibid.*, fo. 130r.
221 TNA, SP 14/124, fo. 117r.

222 *APC*, 37, pp. 400–1.
223 *APC*, 38, pp. 329–30.
224 *Ibid.*, pp. 406–7. For the text of the patent, see Hartshorne, *Old English Glasses*, pp. 416–23. For a Council letter of assistance, see *APC*, 39, pp. 57–8.
225 Hartshorne, *Old English Glasses*, pp. 418–19.
226 TNA, SP 14/124, fo. 227r; TNA, SP 14/124, fo. 228r.
227 C. Russell, 'The Nature of a Parliament in Early Stuart England', in H. Tomlinson (ed.), *Before the English Civil War: Essays on Early Stuart Politics and Government* (Basingstoke, 1983), pp. 124–5.
228 Peacey, *Public Politics*, pp. 275–6, 307.
229 TNA, SP 14/162, fos 108–109.
230 *Ibid.*, fo. 108. For glassmakers, see BL, Harleian 6803, fo. 5r.
231 For distinctions, see Peacey, *Public Politics*, pp. 269, 300.
232 TNA, SP 14/162, fo. 109r.
233 See Chapter 2.
234 TNA, SP 14/162, fo. 109r.
235 TNA, SP 14/162, fos 110–11v.
236 *Ibid.*, fo. 111r.
237 *Ibid.*
238 See Chapter 3.
239 Russell, *Parliaments*, p. 191; C. Dent, '"Generally Inconvenient": The 1624 *Statute of Monopolies* as Political Compromise', *Melbourne University Law Review*, 33:2 (2009), pp. 415–53.
240 Russell, *Parliaments*, p. 191.
241 BL, Harl. 6803, fo. 121r.
242 '7 Apr. 1624', *PP 1624*.
243 '1 May 1624', *PP 1624*.
244 HRO, 44M69/G2/31, fo. 39.
245 TNA, SP 16/378, fo. 163r. Bungard also became a member, see Ashdown, *Glaziers*, p. 35.
246 Waddell and Peacey, 'Introduction', 14.
247 Peacey, 'Petitions, privileges and the place of Parliament', pp. 83–114.
248 *APC*, 38, p. 465.
249 HRO, 44M69/G2/31, fo. 39.
250 *Ibid.*
251 PA, HL/PO/JO/10/1/57, fos 105–6; HL/PO/JO/10/1/62, fo. 16; HL/PO/JO/10/1/67, fo. 24; HL/PO/JO/10/1/68, fos 175–6; HL/PO/JO/10/1/120, fo. 88; E. Paterson, 'Approaching the "great Court of Justice now sitting": Petitioning and Parliamentary Memory in the Long Parliament (1640–1642) (unpublished paper, delivered 11 March 2025, Parliament, Politics, and People Seminar, IHR London).

# 5

# Petitioning commissions: economic crisis and the making of trade policy

> Doe require & chardge them that they & ev[er]ie of them faile not as they will answear their Contempte therin at their p[er]ills & to be p[er]sonallie before vs at the Crowne in Sudbury upon Satterday next being the 23th day of this instant moneth of February by eight of the Clock in the Morneing ther to doe & p[er]forme such p[ar]ticuler servic[e]s as by force of the said l[ett]res We are to require of them[.][1]

On 19 February 1622, JPs in Suffolk sent instructions to the High Constables of the Hundred of Babergh, to be shared with the Mayor of Sudbury. The constables were ordered to attend a meeting at a local institution, the Crown in Sudbury, in four days' time alongside all who exercised 'the Trade & Misterie of Cloath makeing'.[2] In the meantime, the Constables were to acquaint themselves with all those with unsold cloth supplies lying on their hands, preparing a list of their names and the towns in which they resided to present to JPs. Why did JPs desire a public meeting with the counties' resident clothiers?

Earlier, on 9 February, the Privy Council had written to officials in ten counties, targeting those which were centres of the cloth trade.[3] The Council had expressed their concern that instability and disorder were looming on the horizon on account of the 'great distresse' of spinners, weavers, and fullers.[4] Between 1615 and 1624, England was in the midst of an economic depression. The cloth trade suffered: fluctuating markets and currency manipulations abroad had seen cloth priced out of foreign markets.[5] Traditionally, undressed and white broadcloths had been exported by the Merchant Adventurers' Company to their mart towns in Germany and the Low Countries and by the Eastland Company to the Baltic. Yet exports had declined. Struggling to sell their goods, merchants ceased purchasing cloth, leaving many clothiers with unsold stocks. As many clothiers employed weavers, spinners, and fullers on a putting-out system, this drop in sales had a knock-on effect for many subjects who found themselves out of work as looms were put down throughout the realm. Within their letter, the Council noted that they had received reports of distress from many unemployed subjects, instructing JPs to ensure that clothiers be commanded not to dismiss their employees. Meanwhile, they required merchants to purchase remaining stocks from clothiers and took action to ensure that wool was sold at reasonable prices. It was this letter which prompted JPs in Suffolk to organise a meeting with the counties' clothiers as they sought to communicate these instructions in person.

The meeting which occurred was not, however, merely an occasion for local authorities to articulate demands to subjects in a top–down fashion. JPs acted as mouthpieces for these clothiers, sending information on the state of the industry back to the Council. By 23 March, they reported that across twenty of their towns, 4,453 broadcloths remained unsold.[6] The JPs had taken the opportunity to solicit the clothiers' opinions, asking them 'what they did thinke should occasion this alteration & deadnes of their trade'.[7] The meeting at the Crown provided these clothiers with a chance to offer their own report on the condition of their industry, ideas and opinions which were subsequently sent to the Council. Clothiers in Suffolk were not the only subjects to communicate their opinions to authorities. Those in Oxfordshire and Gloucestershire also produced written reports and petitions, forwarded by JPs to the Council for review.[8] These contained not only cries of distress, but saw clothiers actively engage with the issues of corporatism and monopoly as they promptly laid the blame at the hands of the Adventurers' Company.

The depression of the 1620s has been extensively studied by scholars seeking to ascertain the causes, chronology, and consequences of this economic upheaval.[9] The proliferation of pamphlet literature flowing from the pens of such economic theorists as Thomas Mun, Edward Misselden, and Gerard de Malynes has been a focus of study, whilst historians including Joyce Appleby and Lars Magnusson have traced contemporary developments in economic thought and the rise of political economy.[10] No less important were the ways in which a wider remit of subjects, including the clothiers, spinners, and weavers so personally affected by these changes, conceptualised the depression. As noted in Chapter 4, historians have recognised that discussion of the economy took up the attention of Parliament in 1621 and 1624, as petitioners and MPs expressed their opinions on the cause of the realm's economic woes. Calls for free trade were an important rallying cry heard both in and outside of Parliament, as subjects proved adept at using this discourse to push for the opening of trade restrictions, sometimes tactically.[11] Yet in the interim between these Parliaments, the Crown and Council turned once again to the use of commissions as a mechanism to gather opinions and bring subjects into the remit of economic policy-making. Commissions to survey the decline in bullion, discuss the cause of economic depression with the outports, and to analyse exchange markets were appointed in 1621 and 1622.[12] By April 1622, the Council would appoint a temporary Commission for Trade as it sought to gather opinions from clothiers. Much attention has been focused on a report produced by the commissioners, described by Barry Supple as a 'résumé of contemporary opinion'.[13] Such was the success of the Commissions' work that, by October, a permanent Commission for Trade was established.

As Paul Slack has argued, the formation of this permanent commission marked an important development in Jacobean economic policy, moving towards a more participatory system designed to draw subjects into the formation of policy.[14] Carlos Suprinyak has also recognised the importance of the various commissions appointed to examine the economy in the 1620s as spaces where the management of trade was debated and discussed.[15] He argues for the need for historians to move away from analysing economic thought through printed pamphlets and to turn attention towards the discussion of these issues in public spaces including Parliament and Council committees.[16] Answering such calls, this chapter will analyse the ways through which the temporary and permanent Commissions for Trade acted as new points of contact, drawing subjects into the compass of their work to discuss the issues of corporatism and monopoly. In the process, we can gain insights into their views of the roles and responsibilities of these commissions and of their own beliefs in the value of their voices to offer advice on economic policy. Whilst not espousing theories of mercantilism or the balance of trade, clothiers still engaged in important processes of economic *thinking*, making their voices heard as they attended committee meetings. By re-conceptualising these commissions as points of contact between subjects and authority, they can be seen as facilitating politicisation, allowing the fostering of networks as clothiers from multiple counties were brought to the metropolis to discuss and dispute the issue of monopoly. As Corey Tazzara has argued, spaces including guild halls and customs houses were sites for the discussion of economic ideas throughout Europe.[17] Commissions, halls, and even the houses of JPs served a similar purpose in England.

Whilst David Pennington has recently noted the role played by the Commission and MPs in reducing the privileges of the Adventurers' Company by 1624, the range of petitions sent to both commissions have often been overlooked, despite these influencing the stance and opinion of the commissioners towards trade organisation.[18] Equally in a period of economic tension, it was not only clothiers who attempted to use these commissions to negotiate on policy. Conflicts of interest between corporate bodies were only enhanced in this period, the depression infusing industrial battles with a new sense of urgency, as companies were able to present the fulfilment of their aims as necessary to remedy the depression. As such, institutions including the Grocers', Staplers', and Drapers' Companies used both Commissions to further their own interests. In this atmosphere, temporary alliances of the type explored throughout this book continued to be made, as clothiers moved to ally not only with each other but with the Staplers. By centring the petitions penned at the centre of analysis, this chapter will consider the ways through which subjects from across the realm were drawn into economic debates, motivated by concerns with monopoly.

## England's cloth trade

Corporate institutions were key to the organisation of England's cloth trade. From the fourteenth century, overseas trade had been dominated by two regulated companies: the Staplers and the Merchant Adventurers. Prior to the development of the domestic cloth industry, wool was one of the realm's most important commodities, exported by the Staplers to their staple port at Calais.[19] They faced a decline in their fortunes as cloth came to replace the wool-export trade in the fifteenth century. In turn, the Staplers found themselves eclipsed in importance by the Adventurers, who specialised in the export of cloth and were formally created as a united body in 1486.[20] As the Staplers lost their influence in the export trade, many turned their attentions to the domestic wool trade, acting as middlemen to purchase wool from producers and supply it to clothiers in the localities.[21] As such, the Adventurers were to note in 1621 that the 'moderne Staplers are not as those of that Company were 40 yeares past'.[22] Despite the general disdain and statutory prohibitions for the activities of middlemen, the Staplers were given permission to sell 'refuse' wools which they could not export abroad in domestic markets.[23]

The Staplers' fortunes were to decline in James's reign. In 1614, James issued a proclamation prohibiting the export of English wools abroad, putting an end to this struggling aspect of their trade.[24] Their role as middlemen also came under increased pressure, as informers prosecuted staplers for buying and selling wools. In the Addled Parliament, the Staplers tried and failed to secure an act allowing them permission to engage in this trade.[25] Like so many others, they were willing to strike a deal with courtiers to reverse their fortunes. The privy councillor and Scottish favourite of the King, Thomas Erskine, Viscount Fenton, was awarded a patent in 1615 alongside his associates Roger Gwynn, John Gwynn, Matthew Gwynn, and Christopher Nicholl to collect fines from illegal wool middlemen.[26] As the patentees vigorously enforced their grant, many staplers found themselves facing prosecution for their activities as wool broggers. A compromise was struck in June 1616. The Council gave leave to the Staplers to act as middlemen in the wool trade for one year, as an experiment designed to assess the impact their activities would have on the realm's trade.[27] By March 1617, the Staplers made a deal with the patentees.[28] They attempted to bring all wool dealers into their fold for high entrance fees of £100. Any who dealt in wool outside of the Company were fined by the patentees, and in exchange for upholding their monopoly, the Staplers provided Fenton and his associates with the revenue generated from these entrance fees.[29] Unsurprisingly, their carefully forged alliance came under attack by MPs in 1621 who expressed concerns that such ancient corporations had 'turned presently into Conspiracies'.[30]

Despite growing in influence in city government and dominating exports of the realm's most crucial commodity, the Merchant Adventurers also faced threats in this period of monopoly. As seen in previous chapters, this included frequent calls for greater freedom of trade by clothiers and outport rivals. The growth of the new draperies led to discussions surrounding how best to regulate the production of this new commodity, whilst James's continuous drive to seek revenues led him to take a 'gigantic gamble' on the cloth trade.[31] In 1615, James's interest was piqued by a scheme led by the Eastland Company merchant Sir William Cockayne, in collaboration with the London Clothworkers' Company, to replace the export of white, undressed broadcloths with more profitable dyed and dressed equivalents.[32] Persuaded by their promises, James incorporated a new body, the King's Merchant Adventurers, to establish this trade, revoking the charter of the Adventurers' Company. The new Company failed to establish a domestic dyeing and dressing trade, and the threat of unrest in the clothing industry forced James to restore the old Adventurers in 1617, providing them with a charter which was expanded in scope. It gave them increased powers to act against interlopers and the sole authority to export new draperies.[33] In order to recompense them for the sums necessary to acquire it, they moved to introduce a new imposition on cloth, an issue which would place their new charter at the heart of protests.

Inter-company tensions were a marked feature of the cloth industry. The Staplers, not content with trying to dominate the wool trade, frequently attempted to break into the Adventurers' monopoly, claiming for themselves the right to transport cloth as a 'staple' commodity.[34] In 1621 they introduced a bill calling for permission to enter the cloth export trade, appealing to the importance of corporatism despite facing criticism for their monopolising control of the wool trade in this Parliament.[35] Naming it an act for 'restoring the free Trade of the Marchant[e]s of the Staple' was a skilful way to deploy the language of free trade to present their own push for powers as akin to the efforts of subjects to protect their liberties in the face of monopoly encroachments. In the text of the bill, they noted the necessity that the cloth trade remain under 'a forme of governement' whilst expressing the desire to prevent the 'appropriatinge of the said Trade into few mens hand[e]s which is p[er]nicious to the Comon Wealth'.[36] This was not enough to persuade MPs of its merits; Sir Thomas Roe noted that the bill would 'overthrow the Merchant adventurers', and despite being sent to the Lords, it failed to pass before the adjournment.[37] The Adventurers responded to it by highlighting that the existence of two corporate bodies governing the same trade would create a 'Confusion of the gouernement of the trade', it being impossible that two companies could co-exist without one being subordinate to the other.[38]

It was not only merchant organisations who had a viable interest in the industry. In London, the Clothworkers', Drapers', and Dyers' Companies were important bodies. The Clothworkers were responsible for the finishing of cloths and were long aggrieved by the export of undressed and unfinished cloth by the Adventurers. They maintained that the establishment of a finishing and dyeing industry would provide employment for subjects, and the Company continuously lobbied and petitioned for a greater number of cloths to be finished in the realm.[39] Their interests were often tied with the Dyers' Company. In the context of depression, the age-old antagonism between these bodies and the Adventurers would rear its head. On 29 March 1617, Secretary Winwood wrote to Sir Thomas Lake of rumours he had heard touching a 'pestilent practice' planned by clothworkers and dyers against the newly re-chartered Adventurers, and against their prominent leaders William Towerson and Lionel Cranfield.[40] The information he had received, he claimed, 'speake[s] noe mylder language then the cutting of all their throates'.[41] The new charter and the restored Company generated profound tensions, receiving expression in a rhetoric saturated with violence.

The Drapers' Company sold cloth via retail and wholesale.[42] They had traditionally held the right to conduct searches to check the quality of cloths taken to Blackwell Hall, a key centre for the sale of cloth, as well as in fairs throughout the city. Their new charter of 1607, the intense lobbying for which was described in Chapter 3, confirmed their rights to search the houses and shops of cloth sellers to inspect their goods.[43] Despite possessing these rights and attempting to uphold them, the Drapers appear to have ceased conducting searches at Blackwell Hall.[44] Indeed, by James's reign, many of the freemen of the Company practised different trades altogether. The Drapers had found that their trade was increasingly practised by freemen from other companies and by foreigners and strangers in the city.[45]

Beyond the metropolis, clothiers, weavers, fullers, and spinners were employed in the trade. As seen in previous chapters, clothiers and clothworkers were especially active petitioners, both in their efforts to secure corporate organisation in the localities and in their lamentations of the effect of monopolies on their industries. In areas like the West Country and Gloucestershire, clothiers often purchased wool from growers and supplied this to local spinners, weavers, and carders to work, before taking their cloths to Blackwell Hall in London or other regional markets to be sold to merchants.[46] However in other counties, such as Yorkshire, clothiers took a more active role in cloth working.[47] Farmers and households could also engage in weaving as a by-employment, something which was common in counties with pastoral economies.[48] In London, Blackwell Hall, situated close to the Guildhall, stood at the centre of the cloth trade. At weekly markets held on Thursdays, Fridays, and Saturdays, cloth was displayed in chambers and sold to merchants for export.[49]

As Keirn argues, the cloth trade was divided between 'a plethora of often competing sectional interests'.[50] However, the connected nature of the industry and the mobility of many clothiers allowed these subjects to engage in co-ordinated political action. As highlighted by John Walter, the very nature of the cloth trade, pulling together localities and cities such as London, produced a set of dialogues and connections which allowed those in the trade to engage in collective action.[51] He describes the 'umbilical cord woven of wool' which allowed important connections between centre and locality to be fostered by the industry.[52] David Rollison has argued for the development of a 'national' consciousness in the cloth industry between 1549 and 1622, triggered by industrialisation and the spread of the industry across the realm.[53] Spaces like Blackwell Hall must be seen as important for facilitating co-ordinated action. Those clothiers who travelled to the capital to sell their wares were brought into close contact, and able to hear and spread news. In turn, this provided a space where collective action across county lines could be co-ordinated and planned, and petitions penned. Thus, despite lacking the institutional organisation of a national corporation, the nature of the cloth trade allowed clothiers to foster a sense of occupational identity.[54] Authorities were certainly aware of this ability for co-ordinated action, which often translated into a fear of a general uprising of clothworkers during periods of trade depression.[55]

Insights into the processes by which local clothiers came together in the locality, whilst so often hidden, can be gleaned from early petitions produced by subjects as trade began to struggle in the early 1620s. Between 1618 and 1622, the total volume of cloth exported from London declined by a quarter and reports and petitions complaining of distress were sent to the Council from Gloucester, Southampton, Winchester, and Wiltshire.[56] In 1620 spinners, fullers, and weavers in Wiltshire petitioned their JPs at Quarter Sessions to lament their distress.[57] Local JPs engaged in active dialogues with these subjects, informing the Council that they had had conferences with clothworkers and their clothier employers to ascertain the cause of these problems. Wiltshire's JPs collected evidence from clothiers at a local space called Temple Hall on 11 May, hearing personal testimonies on how many looms were out of service in their county.[58] It appears that clothiers were not afraid to inform JPs of the actions of fellow clothiers; John Gale of Chippenham, a keeper of six to seven looms, noted that his neighbour Edward Stafford intended to put half of his looms down.[59] The testimonies reveal a real awareness of local trading conditions as clothiers in the county informed authorities of the extent of their enterprises, all gathered in this public hall to discuss problems in trade. Through these reports, JPs were able to inform the Council that around 132 looms had been put down in Wiltshire, causing the unemployment of as many as 2,640 subjects.[60] JPs thus acted as conveyors of the concerns of local clothiers to central authority, in many ways mirroring the processes by which city authorities helped forward the complaints of disgruntled freemen to the Council. This provoked an active response from the Council, who called for the clothiers to appear before them personally to inform them why they were putting down their looms, again drawing them into processes of active consultation whilst they were in the city.[61]

However, those clothworkers who had petitioned at Quarter Sessions also showed their willingness to 'escalate' petitioning tactics when required, albeit by changing the recipient of their complaint rather than going to print.[62] In May, weavers in Bromham, Chippenham, and Calne petitioned the Council directly.[63] They noted their previous complaint to JPs of their 'pittyfull & wretched estate', but complained of their continued lack of work, 'w[i]th hungry meales & weepinge eyes', as they called on the Council for relief.[64] It is likely that this petition was penned with the help of a scribe as many of the petitioners left marks to subscribe. Their utilisation of a strong rhetoric of poverty triggered a response; by 19 May, the Council hauled the Adventurers before them to answer to the complaints of a stand of sales at Blackwell Hall.[65] Interestingly, the Company would embrace the opportunity to blame these problems on the restraints they themselves were facing from the patents for gold and silver thread, glass, and the Levant Company.

Like the glassmakers, clothiers in Wiltshire were also prepared to embrace the opening of Parliament in 1621 to complain of problems facing their trade as the Commons' committee for trade investigated the depression. On 7 May, the Commons received a petition from clothiers in Wiltshire which was referred to committee.[66] It is likely that this is a reference to a undated petition surviving in the papers of the MP Sir Thomas Jervoise.[67] It is possible that the petition was penned in such a space as Temple Hall by clothiers who worked closely together in the locality, showing their ability to petition outside of company organisation. The petitioners complained that the decline in the sale of their broad cloths had reduced the employment of weavers, spinners, and tuckers in their locality. They identified three reasons for these problems: the Staplers', Adventurers', and East India Companies. They criticised the Staplers' actions as middlemen, providing further proof for MPs that their monopolisation of the industry had caused them to drive up prices and engross wool supplies. They also attacked the Adventurers' new charter, complaining that the impositions they placed on cloth had hindered its sale. Other, precise policies of the Adventurers were attacked, including their use of the stint (limits on how much cloth each member could export based on seniority) and their set departure times for ships twice a year. They questioned how a Company consisting of 'Verrie fewe' men could hope to carry 'all the trade of soe much Cloath under theire girdle'.[68] The clothiers ended their suit by warning that trade would soon be undone if no action was taken to ensure that 'any man may bie', hinting at the need to loosen trading restrictions.[69]

Despite the strength of these complaints, the Adventurers found themselves protected by James in this Parliament. On 3 May, James called on the Commons not to meddle with the Company or its charter.[70] However, they were not to leave this session totally unscathed. By the summer, it was agreed that the outports were to have liberty to export new draperies to the Adventurers' mart towns in Germany and the Low Countries.[71] This was not seen by the outports as a significant concession. As representatives of Southampton would later complain, there was little market for the new draperies here, being light commodities which were 'unfitt and unapte for those Climats'.[72] This also failed to still the cries of distress heard from clothing counties, which were to be articulated with a new intensity by 1622.

## Responding to crisis: early petitions and reports

It was in response to growing tensions that the Council wrote to JPs in ten clothing counties in February 1622, occasioning the reports and petitions sent from JPs in Suffolk, Oxfordshire, and Gloucestershire. In all three counties, JPs informed the Council of the opinions of subjects on the causes of the crisis. In Suffolk, JPs presented themselves as having taken the initiative to solicit the opinions of clothiers, gathering their thoughts on the trade at their meeting in Sudbury. It is likely that this was similar to the meeting between clothiers and JPs at Wiltshire in Temple Hall in 1620.

More extant evidence from the petitions and reports sent from Oxfordshire and Gloucestershire provides further insight into the processes behind the construction of these complaints, suggesting that the initiative to petition came directly from clothiers. In Oxfordshire, the justices were careful to stress that complaints had come from poor weavers, spinners, and fullers and not from 'the clamors of any Turbulent dispositions'.[73] They noted that the 'Cheifeste Clothiers' in their county had decided to deliver them 'in wryting certen reasons vnder their hands' for the depression, which they forwarded to the Council to peruse.[74] The report, signed by six clothiers, was not self-styled as a petition but as a list of reasons, yet it blurred the boundaries between both by including humble language and ending with a clear request to JPs.[75] In Gloucestershire, the mayor and justices noted that clothiers, having been called before them, had requested time to prepare 'their reasons & greeifes in writinge vnder their hand[e]s'.[76] The JPs noted that they proceeded to present a petition alongside their 'Workefolck[e]s' to the Justices of Assize at the next Sessions, signed and subscribed by thirty-four clothworkers.[77] In Oxfordshire and Gloucestershire therefore, clothiers used the opportunity provided by these meetings to articulate their opinions to local authorities. By doing so, they ensured that their suits were sent to the Council via officials who could add legitimacy to their complaints. For example, JPs in Gloucestershire described the petition as 'of speciall weight and consequence', given that so many of the poor in their county 'doe already steale, and are like to starve or doe worse'.[78] They expressed their concern that clothiers had stressed to them with 'greate Vehemencye' that they would be forced to utterly abandon their trade within fourteen days if their cloths remained unsold.[79] They therefore forwarded a copy of the petition of the clothiers with a further letter from the Justices of Assize.[80] The judges Sir Humphrey Winch and Sir William Jones noted that they had consulted with justices in both Oxfordshire and Gloucestershire and implored clothiers in both counties to continue to employ their poor workfolk.

Petitioners in all three counties identified similar reasons for the decay of trade. They expressed concern with the illegal exportation of wool and fuller's earth, increases in cloth-making by foreign competitors, and the various charges laid on cloths at home and abroad. Interestingly, these clothiers also expressed their concerns with the monopoly of the Adventurers' Company, articulating similar complaints as sent by Wiltshire's clothiers to Parliament. Clothiers in Oxfordshire complained that, whereas the Adventurers were previously a 'greate Company of worthy Merchants', they were now but a 'small Company' made up of 'younge men' who were 'not able to Carry the Trade'.[81] They expressed concern with the monopolistic control of the trade by an ever-decreasing number of merchants, identifying this as a key reason for their inability to sell their cloths: fewer merchants meant fewer buyers. They complained that many of them now carried their cloths from market to market, unable to sell 'in any sorte'.[82]

A similar complaint was levied in Suffolk, albeit with a more specific attack on corporate governance.[83] JPs noted that the clothiers had complained that

> The Marchant[e]s being Incorporated and settled into companyes, doe by Constitutions amonge them selves so crosse the aunciente & accustomed course of their trade, concerning the free selling & buying of their Cloth (limitinge it to certaine times, persons & nombers & at what prices the members of their companyes shall buye & sell againe aswell here as beyond the Seas[.][84]

The clothiers expressed concern with the ordinances of merchant companies, targeting the use of the stint and limited shipments abroad.

By attacking companies more broadly, they also hinted at their displeasure with the Eastland Company. In 1622 the Company's export of cloths had declined by one-half to two-thirds of former levels.[85] In a separate collective petition sent in May, clothiers in Suffolk and Essex complained to the Council that the Eastland Company had failed to purchase cloths.[86] This had decisive effects; the Council gave permission to customs officers to allow clothiers free liberty to export cloth if the Company failed to do so.[87] Meanwhile, merchants in Ipswich (including Matthew Brownrig and Roger Cutler, whom we met in Chapter 1) complained that local clothiers were refusing to sell them their cloths, with the aim of travelling down to London to secure a warrant for permission to export it themselves.[88] Clearly, not all clothiers were as distressed as their reports suggested, some embracing this opportunity to break into the lucrative export trade. Crucially, two of the clothiers complained of had previously joined with these same merchants to protest the Tailors and Clothworkers' Company, George Acton and Thomas Hales. Alliances were transient and shifting; by 1622 merchants and clothiers in Ipswich were now in dispute as they battled over the Eastland Company's monopoly.

The articulation of anti-Adventurer sentiments was even more pronounced in the petition sent to Assize judges in Gloucestershire. In total, it included eleven demands, eight of which dealt explicitly with the Adventurers. They argued that

> Ye Merchant[e]s Adventurers are not sufficient to take off ye bulk of Cloth made within ye kingdome because many of them have left off trading, & therfore [they] doe humblie praie that more buyers may be admitted therevnto w[hi]ch will enlarge ye trade, improve ye Comoditie, advance Manufactures, increase ye number of Merchants, Navigac[i]ons, & his Ma[jes]t[ie]s Customes, prevent privat[e] combinac[i]ons & practizes & tend to the wealth & Honor of their King & his Subiect[e]s.[89]

The petitioners expressed their belief that restrictions on trade needed to be lifted, allowing the involvement of a greater number of merchants to trigger production. This was an appeal to the perceived aims of the King and Council – it would improve shipping, customs, and the kingdom's wealth. The clothiers requested that the entrance fines of the Adventurers be reduced, and like clothiers in Suffolk, targeted specific corporate policies such as the stint. Finally, the petitioners expressed their concern with the changes wrought on the industry in the wake of the Cockayne project. Since the Adventurers' restoration, they complained, all strangers had been forced to pay double customs to export cloth and new 'unreasonable imposic[i]ons' had been placed on the product.[90] The clothiers showed that they were not ignorant of the reason for these new charges, which had been justified by the Adventurers in order to repay the 'great somes of money payed by them to procure newe priviledges & restraints, as by their owne Charter & confessions will appeare'.[91] Clothiers in all three counties expressed their grievances with the Adventurers' monopoly, holding the company's restrictive membership and new charter responsible for the decay in trade.

The similarity in these grievances raises interesting questions as to how, and why, clothiers from different counties were able to articulate similar concerns. As noted, the interconnected nature of the trade facilitated cross-county communication, allowing clothiers to lament similar issues as they travelled to local markets or to Blackwell Hall. In their letter to the Council, JPs in Suffolk noted that many of their clothiers were absent from home.[92] It is likely that they were present at markets, allowing them to converse and discuss their trade. Collective supplications which crossed county lines were often sent by clothiers; in March 1622, makers of new draperies in Essex, Norfolk, and Suffolk petitioned the Council to complain of the influx of unskilled and unapprenticed workers in their industry.[93] Similarly, the Justices of Assize, Winch, and Jones, noted that they had consulted with JPs and clothiers in Oxfordshire and Gloucestershire, perhaps bringing them together to hear their opinions before each produced petitions with similar complaints.[94]

The extensive discussion of the cloth trade in Parliament in 1621 also likely played a part, generating processes of feedback between parliamentary discussions and petitioners' concerns. Clothiers present in the capital to petition against the Adventurers likely heard news of discussions in the chambers, further cementing the impression amongst the industry that it was the Adventurers who were to blame for the crisis. This, combined with the long-standing concern of clothiers with the Company's policies, likely triggered those in different counties to articulate similar anti-Adventurer sentiments. In these reports we might therefore trace the formation of a sense of industrial consciousness amongst the clothiers, as they moved to see their plight as connected to that of clothiers throughout the realm, united in their fight against the mighty Adventurers.

An alternative, more sinister, explanation for the similarity in these complaints was suggested by the Adventurers, who moved to respond by penning a specific answer to the Gloucestershire clothiers and a larger 'Answere and declarac[i]on' on 9 April, the latter of which seems to have been ordered by the Council.[95] The Adventurers included a list of eleven articles to respond to the eleven grievances raised by the Gloucestershire clothiers, demonstrating once more the dialogic nature of economic petitions. Within their response, the Adventurers claimed that problems in cloth sales were not the result of the number of their members or their impositions; rather they were caused by difficulties in foreign markets. Responding to the clothiers' eighth article, which had complained that the merchants refused to sell cloths to Englishmen living beyond the seas, the Adventurers suggested that this did not appear to be the 'Clothiers owne obiection'.[96] Instead this complaint had been 'borrowed' from interlopers who sought to break into the Company's monopoly.[97] They proceeded to complain that many of their articles had been 'raked together', consisting of 'stale stuffe of the Interlopers, Staplers, and like adversaries of the Marchants Adventurers'.[98] The Adventurers, like so many other monopoly bodies, used accusations of collusion and conspiracy to challenge petitioning campaigns against them.

The Company likewise explained the similarity between reports sent from clothiers from various counties in their larger 'Answer' by presenting this as an orchestrated, cross-county petitioning campaign. They alleged that

> One County calleth to another: and all the Clothiers ioyning with the Woollgrowers, Staplers and Interlopers stirre vp the Justices of Assisse to strengthen their Complaints: though there be little cause on their parts, and lesse falt on ours.[99]

The clothiers were presented as colluding with the Staplers, interlopers, and woolgrowers as the Adventurers even referenced the support shown by the judges Winch and Jones to clothiers in Gloucestershire and Oxfordshire. They claimed that the only cloths remaining at Blackwell Hall were faulty. The Adventurers were rather dramatic in their description of this conspiracy, presenting themselves as 'wearied & discouraged by the resteles Complaints of the Clothiers and Woollgrowers'.[100] They dramatically declared that they would rather 'abandon their trade...then thus to remayne vnder the incessant torture & vexation of soe many & soe importunate clamors'.[101] In reality, this seemed like a rather convenient means to question the legitimacy of petitions and reports against them; as Leng has argued, the Company frequently blamed problems on interlopers.[102] However it did show an awareness that clothiers were tapped into larger networks of trade, rendering such alliances possible.

It is also likely that some Staplers may have been involved in this agitation. In their report, clothiers in Oxfordshire had requested that all wools be weighed by men 'sworne to deale truly betweene the buyer & the seller', in effect requesting the creation of authorised middlemen.[103] This inclusion might hint at a potential alliance between Staplers and clothiers in the area, as a request designed to revive the Staplers' position as wool middlemen. Following the cancellation of their scheme with Fenton, the Staplers may well have been pushing for renewed involvement in the domestic wool trade, and their voices may be identified as lurking amongst the clothiers' demands.

The Adventurers' response suggests that the Council had asked them to respond to two key accusations: that their impositions were a burden and that more merchants should be admitted into the Company. The Adventurers noted that the Council had asked them to suspend their impositions on cloth until Allhallowtide next (1 November) and to allow non-members to export new draperies from London to the mart towns.[104] Whilst the latter was not something explicitly requested by the clothiers, parliamentary pressure in 1621 had already led to the concession that the outports could freely export new draperies. As this type of cloth had only recently come under the auspices of the Company's monopoly, it is likely that the Council saw it as a good section of the industry through which to experiment with a freedom of trade.

Unsurprisingly, the Adventurers were obstinate in their response. On the issue of their impositions, they reminded the King and Council that the only 'ground and cause of that charge was the some of money w[hi]ch we paid vnto the Kings Ma[jes]tie vpon our restaurac[i]on'.[105] The implication was clear: this charge would not have been introduced if the Cockayne project had not forced them to pay for a new charter. They complained that they had been forced to borrow money from merchants to finance this. As such, if the impositions designed to recuperate this sum were cancelled, this money would be called in, and their credit overthrown. On the new draperies, the Adventurers claimed that they would only consider opening the trade if they were not made to cancel these impositions. However, if they were forced to, then they dramatically claimed that they would 'not be able to subsist any longer in any part of the trade, but must humbly surrender our Charter to his Ma[jes]tie'.[106] However, if they could levy the sum, they reluctantly accepted the request to allow 'interlopers' to export new draperies from London, provided that they refrain from exporting broadcloths and that they paid all required fees.

The Company ended their Answer in a particularly dramatic fashion, concluding that

> If therefore your Highnes and Lo[rdshi]pps be not satisfied with o[u]r former remonstrances of the inconveniences of the admission of the Interlop[er]s

> & with o[u]r iustificac[i]ons against their and the Clothiers & Staplers asp[er]sions: if we be not now found good subiect[e]s & necessary members in this Comon Wealth: if there be noe other course to content the Clothiers and their adherents, but by buying vp the Cloth by assessement soe long as they complaine: we shalbe contented...to leaue all and to be vtterly excluded from returning to the trade in the better tymes[.][107]

Interlopers, clothiers, and staplers were presented as attacking this faithful corporate institution, when the real causes of the realm's woes were problems in cloth making and the long-standing impacts of the Cockayne scheme.

The Adventurers' responses, whilst likely exaggerated in the depiction of a co-ordinated conspiracy, do provide insights into the processes through which clothiers from different counties were brought together. Worsening conditions in trade created opportunities for clothiers to appear directly before the Council in London. The Adventurers noted that many, including subscribers of the Gloucestershire petition, had recently been before the Lords, where they had 'professed a contrary opinion' to their current complaint that more merchants would strengthen trade.[108] They claimed that clothiers had also petitioned the Council against rising wool prices. Clothiers were thus presented as keeping well abreast of developments in the Crown's policy towards trade. The Adventurers' claimed that rumours of an intended proclamation to order the wearing of cloth at home had already caused wool growers to increase prices.[109] In their more general set of answers, they also expressed their frustration that rumours that they would cancel their impositions had been 'talked of by Clothiers'.[110] As Walter has argued, the cloth trade was so dependent on government regulation that many of its participants were forced to keep informed of recent proclamations, statutes, and patents.[111] In a period of depression, this was only intensified as clothiers were periodically brought before the Council, local authorities, and Parliament to testify to problems in their trade. This, combined with the buzz of rumours and news on the industry, seems to have allowed cross-county collaborations to occur. In turn, clothiers could create networks with others in their trade, seeing themselves as united against a common corporate enemy.

## Petitioning the temporary Commission

On 10 April 1622, the Council wrote again to JPs in twenty-five clothing counties, announcing James's intention to 'graunt forth a Comission to certaine Gentlemen to treate and conferr aswell w[i]th the Marchant

Adventurers of London, as also w[i]th the most discreete and sufficient Clothiers of every Sheire'.[112] Presented with a multitude of petitions and reports, they were persuaded to appoint a commission to examine the causes of the decay of trade. This was not unusual: in 1621, a similar commission had consulted with the outports, and between 1621 and 1624 commissions were appointed to investigate the scarcity of coin and foreign exchanges.[113] Problems in trade rendered commissions an important facet of economic policy, and this was part and parcel of what Millstone has coined the 'state knowledge economy', with councillors heavily reliant on advice to manage the realm.[114] This reflected trends in Europe more broadly, where merchants were increasingly consulted on matters of trade.[115] However, the temporary Commission for Trade in April was to collect information from not only merchants but also from clothiers from every clothing shire, continuing processes whereby non-elite subjects were drawn into the remit of government business through economic commissions.

The Council's letter called for chosen clothiers to appear before the commission in London by 2 May, and the Adventurers were also ordered to appoint representatives to appear at their 'severall Meeteing[e]s' as required.[116] Evidence shows that these letters were circulated amongst local officials to ensure that clothiers were picked to attend, through processes which in themselves were participatory. The Council's letter had been circulated by the High Sheriff William Powlett to JPs in Wiltshire.[117] By 30 April, the JPs informed the Council of their choice of two clothiers, Edward Carpenter and William Webb, to attend the commissioners, joining this information with an impassioned plea of the worsening poverty in their county.[118] Meanwhile in Hampshire, the sheriff George Philpott sent a letter to JPs in Southampton on 16 April, attaching the Council's letters alongside a note requiring them to ensure that clothiers attend the village of Winton, 'at Rob[er]t Collmas howse upon Monday the 22th of this instant Month'.[119] Clothiers were to attend to ensure the 'p[er]fect accomplishm[en]t' of the Council's instructions.[120] This meeting seems to have been intended to inform clothiers of the Council's letters and to facilitate the selection of two clothiers. Here, a private house was to serve as a space where clothiers from Southampton could meet with JPs to discuss trading issues, participating in the choice of representatives to attend commissioners.

By 23 April, letters had been sent from the King to the twelve officials and merchants chosen as commissioners.[121] Those appointed all had strong links to government or to the city.[122] They included Solicitor General Sir Robert Heath, Attorney General Thomas Coventry, and the Master of Requests Sir John Suckling. Also appointed was Sir Paul Pindar, a merchant and diplomat with extensive experience in Venice and Constantinople.[123] The economic theorist Thomas Mun, a director of the East India Company, was also chosen.[124] Other appointees included Sir Richard Sutton, the Auditor of the Imprests in the Exchequer, Heneage Finch, Recorder of London, and Abraham Dawes, a customs farmer and Surveyor of the Outposts.[125] A merchant named William Turner was also appointed; it is possible that this was the same Turner who had sublet an earlier glass patent.[126] The Commission consisted of active merchants and government officials with trading and legal expertise to allow them to offer informed advice on the depression. The chance to sit on a commission was likely welcomed by these men, offering an opportunity for those like Mun to protect their respective corporate interests.

The letter appointing the commissioners made clear that they were expected to consider 'all particular greevances and obiections w[hi]ch the said Clothiers can make'.[127] In the context of this period, this call for the active consultation of subjects is even more interesting. The outbreak of popular discussion on such topics as the Spanish Match had led James to issue proclamations in 1620 and 1621 prohibiting discussion of matters of state amongst subjects.[128] In a letter sent to judges in several circuits in March 1622, the Council expressed concern with the widespread 'licentious' and 'undutifull speech touchinge the secrets of state or gover[n]ment'.[129] Conversely in April, the King and Council actively solicited subjects to advise on the economy. They seemed less worried that a wider discussion of the realm's economic woes might lead to criticism of the King, despite the Crown's monopoly policy.

The temporary Commission served as a new point of contact for petitioning activity. In addition to attending in person, clothiers also presented written supplications. A manuscript petition by an anonymous group of clothiers, penned sometime between April and May 1622, was directed to the newly appointed Commission.[130] Another copy of the petition gives some clue to its geographical origins, providing a list of figures of the number of unsold cloths in Kent, Suffolk, Essex, and Somerset.[131] It is likely that the petition was a collective endeavour produced by clothiers from these counties. In form, the petition contained numbered remedies for the stand in cloths, before including a humble supplication lamenting specific grievances. The petition evidences a real engagement with debates surrounding corporate regulation. As noted by J. D. Gould and John Cooper, clothiers here articulated forceful calls for the cloth trade to be made free to all subjects, expressing concern with the strict monopolistic control of the Adventurers' Company.[132] The clothiers requested that

> there may be liberty of trade granted to all his Majesty's loving subjects to buy and vent any woollen cloth into any foreign parts beyond the seas, or that the ancient and hereditary right of shipping cloth may be restored unto the

> merchants of the Staple, and that it may be lawful for any man to come into their company upon such rates as have been anciently allowed.[133]

The clothiers articulated their desire for an opening of the trade in a rhetoric saturated with the language of liberty and customary rights. Their request that the Staplers be allowed to participate in the trade likely reflected their awareness that some degree of corporate regulation was still necessary for the industry. This inclusion, like the request from clothiers in Oxfordshire earlier in February, suggests that some alliance had been made between clothiers and the Staplers, similar to the connections between Court and city generated by monopoly disputes. However, in this case, connections were fostered between clothiers in the *locality* and city merchants.

The bill introduced by the Staplers to Parliament in 1621 gives a sense of why clothiers might have found it necessary to make common cause with them. The Staplers noted that many clothiers were forced to travel distances of over one hundred miles to sell their cloths at Blackwell Hall. They claimed that, unlike the Adventurers, the Staplers were 'dispersed into most partes of the launde', and thus if they were to become cloth exporters, clothiers would have more merchants to sell to at local markets.[134] Not only would this provide clothiers with a greater choice of buyers, but they would also be spared the arduous journey to London. It is quite possible that clothiers were persuaded by such arguments, aware that they could be better served by fostering alliances with this established corporate institution. The clothiers also proceeded to attack other patents and restraints on the trade which were targeted in the Parliament of 1621, suggestive again of a process of feedback between parliamentary debates and petitioning demands. They criticised various patents for dyes whilst also mirroring concerns of MPs that the East India Company were exporting bullion.

The second half of the clothiers' report consisted of a traditional petitionary appeal, playing skilfully on the threat of unrest. They called on the commissioners to remember that they did 'employ a great number of poor people', urging them to consider how difficult it would be to contain the same 'from mutiny and rebellion'.[135] The poor in their counties had already been forced to commit robberies of corn; it is possible that clothiers from Wiltshire included this concern, JPs having described such conditions when writing to the Council on 30 April.[136] The clothiers ended with a stern warning, noting that further disorders would be 'out of the compass of our power to prevent' without decisive action by the Commission.[137]

The text of the petition gives some insight into the processes through which this document may have been constructed. The clothiers noted their reluctance to return home in these present conditions, unless their grievances received some 'sudden reformation'.[138] Clearly, these supplicating clothiers were absent from their home counties. It is likely that they were in London, to attend the Commission. These clothiers were consequently able to prepare and present their joint supplication to the Commission, as well as informing commissioners of their plight verbally. Not only did the Commission serve as a new point of contact for petitioning activity, but it also emerged as an institution facilitating contacts *between* clothiers. By drawing clothiers from different counties to one space, conditions were created which allowed subjects to come together to discuss trade and to arrive at some consensus on the factors to blame for the problems in the industry, alongside remedies to benefit them all. Indeed, it is even possible that members of the Staplers' Company, also appearing before the Commission, were able to make the most of the presence of these clothiers to convince them that it was they who were best able to remedy the stand in cloth sales. That these clothiers were invited to offer their opinions verbally only served to embolden them to prepare written supplications, seeing themselves as active participants in the commissioners' work.

Other clothiers followed suit. Clothiers from fourteen counties noted that they had been commanded by the Council and their JPs to attend the Commission, causing them with a 'generall & vnanimous consent' to present their grievances as a collective petition.[139] Once again, their physical presence in the city to attend the Commission facilitated this action. These clothiers noted that 'vppon mature deliberation serious advise & consultation each w[i]th other', they had decided to prepare their petition.[140] In their demands, they lamented the 'bottomles pitt of remediles destruction' which they found themselves in, blaming this on the 'contraction & extenuation of owr trade by reson of charters graunted to particuler companies'.[141] Despite describing their plight as 'remediles', they targeted specific issues which needed to be resolved. They complained of the charges

> as are Imposed by ye companies themselues for the susteyning of theyr monopoly and they are eyther ordinary for ye mayntenanc[e] of theyr govermnent & politie or extraordinarie for ye payment of theyr debts.[142]

The clothiers openly attacked these corporations as 'monopolies', rather than legitimate institutions necessary for the good order of trade. By referring to the extraordinary charges introduced to repay debts, the clothiers hinted that they were aggrieved by the impositions of the Adventurers. Later, they even suggested the need to dissolve the East India Company for its export of bullion. The clothiers also included a precise list of the various charges imposed on cloth, both foreign and domestic, which had been 'proved' in the last Parliament.[143] These clothiers had been exposed to the volume of information emanating from Westminster, receiving news of proceedings which in turn was utilised to add empirical evidence to their supplication.

The temporary Commission also emerged as a space for corporate petitioning activity, as two companies, the Staplers and the Drapers, moved to advance their interests through it. The Drapers sent commissioners a brief alongside a more detailed supplication in May, mirroring parliamentary petitioning techniques.[144] Whilst they claimed that their petition was from the 'Drapers of England', they noted that it was 'preferred by the Drapers of London', claiming to be speaking for drapers throughout the realm.[145] The Drapers took the initiative to approach the Commission; they began their suit by expressing discontent that commissioners had failed to request their presence at their meetings.[146] In all likelihood, this reflected their lack of political activity in recent years and the reality that many of the freemen in their fold had ceased to engage in the cloth retail trade. Tom Girtin has found that of 528 freemen in the Company paying quarterage in 1624, only 25 were labelled as active drapers, although many were prominent in the Adventurers' trade.[147] Nonetheless, the Drapers assured the commissioners that their grievances were 'no less worthie hearing and redresse then any of the rest' as they pushed to have a voice in this investigation.[148] To do so, they undermined the utility of the opinions of the clothiers and Adventurers who could only speak to the specific types of cloth they produced or exported. By contrast, they as Drapers dealt with all types of woollen commodities.

A hitherto unnoticed document was also sent to the Commission by the Staplers. In contrast to the Drapers, their report had been prepared following a command from the commissioner Sir John Suckling.[149] They presented their grievances in the form of a neutral report detailing the 'probable Reasons of the decay of trade of Cloth', yet the document they sent was a masterpiece in corporate lobbying, using the guise of impartiality to issue requests designed to further their interests.[150]

Both the Drapers and the Staplers framed their appeals around the issues of corporatism and monopoly as they staked their claim to be the authoritative voice on the industry. Their responses show that appeals to corporatism were just as powerful as the adoption of a rhetoric of free trade when pushing for the expansion of privileges in the charged atmosphere of the 1620s. The Drapers constructed a sophisticated narrative of the problems facing the industry, culminating in the presentation of themselves as the corporate body best suited to rectify problems. They identified a range of factors for the depression, some of which had been mentioned in the previous reports and petitions of clothiers. This included the illegal exportation of wool, the meddlesome actions of wool middlemen, the reduced wearing of cloth, and even losses caused by pirates seizing goods at sea. They also referenced the 'Overballancing of trade' and issues in exchange rates, reflective of their knowledge of, and active engagement with, the discussions on the depression occurring in Parliament.[151]

However, the main reason identified by the Drapers was abuse in cloth making, damaging its reputation and reducing sales abroad. The Drapers identified numerous causes of this, chief of which was the proliferation of unskilled and unapprenticed subjects who littered the industry. By including such complaints, the Drapers supported the Adventurers' assertions that their inability to sell was the fault of the clothiers who produced shoddy work. As many drapers were involved in the export of cloths, it is possible that they agreed with the Adventurers on these points. The Drapers suggested that the current system by which abuses were checked was tainted by corruption. They referenced Lennox's patent, citing the 'remisnes and Coruption of the Alinger', who frequently sealed 'defectiue' wares.[152] The Drapers noted that statutory provisions dictated that the alnager should face imprisonment and removal from office, a clear call for the punishment of Lennox and his deputies.

The Drapers proceeded to highlight the failures of current statutory regulations for the trade, presenting an image of an overcrowded industry lacking proper regulation. Many clothiers were practising the trade despite failing to serve seven-year apprenticeships as required by the Statute of Artificers. In turn, they produced false cloths which were purchased by forestallers and sold outside of drapers' shops, in locations including alehouses. Factors in the city sold cloth to strangers in private houses or at the Exchange, 'allewring them from the drap[er]s shopps' and from Blackwell Hall.[153]

Indeed, this was an issue which had been brought before Common Council via petition. In December 1619, freemen who purchased cloths complained of the actions of factors, clothworkers, and strangers.[154] Later in October 1620, Common Council investigated concerns that subjects, including nonfreemen, were selling cloth in private houses and contravening the custom of foreign bought and foreign sold. They moved to instigate new orders to ensure all cloths sold in the city were taken either to Blackwell Hall or to newly appointed rooms at Leadenhall.[155] The Drapers similarly painted a picture of a chaotic and disordered industry, made worse by a mass of unapprenticed workers. Redemptioners had made use of 'great mens letters' to purchase their freedoms in cities and corporate towns, trespassing into the trade and opening it to 'the Commons'.[156] This had caused the overthrow of gentlemen's sons, who no longer found any benefits from the trade after completing their apprenticeships. The Drapers also engaged with broader contextual concerns with competition generated by an influx of foreigners in the city, which a newly appointed Commission for Aliens was investigating in May 1622.[157] Aliens could purchase their freedoms, whilst stranger merchants were also free from the burdens imposed on native subjects, able to export their cloths at any time they wished. To rectify the retail of deceitful cloths, the Drapers requested that from henceforth, cloth be sold in public markets alone. This would prevent those who did not belong to corporations from selling defective cloths, which was causing the 'great abusing of the drap[er]s of Corporations and such as haue no other trade but the sale of Cloath to live by'.[158] The Drapers complained that the individual making and selling false wares was both impeaching the laws of the kingdom and a 'destroyer of this Trade of Citties and Corporations'.[159] They were presented as ungoverned and unruly subjects, free to commit all manner of abuses.

The Drapers contrasted this picture of a disordered and crowded trade with the benefits they brought to it as a central corporation in the clothing industry. As Herbert Heaton has argued, this brought their demands in line with so many other groups who articulated the need for economic organisation in James and Charles's reigns.[160] After all, their trade was the 'principall piller of woollen Manifactures', as they set on work all clothworkers and dyers.[161] The Drapers were jostling for prestige and influence, using the opportunity to present themselves as 'the true Merchant of the Staple, more woollen Comodities lying contynewally in drap[er]s hand[e]s then in any Company of Marchant[e]s, or woll in the Staplers'.[162] They asserted that all cloths should be bought and sold either by merchants to export or by drapers through wholesale or retail. Having spelt out the necessity of corporatism and regulation, the Drapers took the opportunity to push for the expansion of their privileges. They requested that the 'whole government of Blackwell Hall' be left 'at the disposing of the M[aste]r and wardens of the society of the drap[er]s'.[163] As noted, the Drapers had previously held searches of cloths at Blackwell Hall and been given the right to nominate the Keeper here, although evidence suggests that they no longer conducted these searches.[164] Their petition was a plea to regain this lost power, whilst they simultaneously attempted to monopolise the retailing of cloth in the city.[165] The Drapers were thus able to use the city's concern with evasions by foreigners and abuses at Blackwell Hall to call not only for the necessity of public markets, but for their own government of this crucial space.

Concluding their petition, the Drapers engaged directly with the clothiers' complaints to the Commission of the small number of merchants exporting cloths. They noted that

> Lastly wheras Clothiers Complaine they lacke sale, and suggest that yf all were buyers it would be better, We Conceaue thay are mightely mistaken, and could not want Markett[e]s to Carry away there Cloath yf the lett[e]s and hindrances menc[i]oned were remoued by your Honowrable wisdoms.[166]

Both the Drapers and the clothiers articulated different views as to the best means to regulate the trade. Whilst the clothiers desired an opening of trade and the loosening of corporate privileges, the Drapers articulated the rather different view that problems had been occasioned by the 'misteries' of cloth-making being made open to all. The real problem lay in too many subjects making and selling deceitful cloths. The Drapers, with their corporate structure, organisation, and apprenticeship system, offered the best chance of remedy. They thus appealed to the notions of order and regulation which underpinned the corporate system.

Similar arguments were articulated by the Drapers in their communications with the Council at this time. In May 1622, they sent councillors a 'humble Answer'.[167] Whilst evidence surrounding its construction is scant, the Drapers answered objections made by the Clothworkers' Company that they were attempting to monopolise the retail trade. It is possible that the Clothworkers had received news of the Drapers' petition to the Commission, triggering concerns that they were reaching for further powers for the searching and selling of cloth. Even here, the Drapers articulated their views on the necessity of corporate governance. They mocked the Clothworkers' desire for the trade to be made open to all, claiming that if all trades were for 'every mans vse', then 'every one might be a groser and a Fishmonger'.[168] Corporatism and regulation were necessary to prevent chaos.

Unsurprisingly, the reasons articulated by the Staplers in their report were rather different, as they embraced the opportunity to continue their campaign to export cloths. For them, the accusation of monopoly proved a useful term of criticism to throw at opponents. In their very first point, the Staplers identified the 'ingrossing and monopolizing of the cheifest trades of the kingdome' as the key cause of the decay in trade, citing not only the cloth trade, but also the trades of the Muscovy and Greenland Companies.[169] The Staplers proceeded to focus their attacks on the Adventurers, criticising the enhancement of their powers in their new charter. In a damning criticism of the Company, they claimed that

> The Merchant[e]s adventurers haue monopolized and ingrossed much more trade into their hand[e]s by Culler of their last l[ett]res patent[e]s then euer heretofore, for they haue taken to themselues the sole power of Exporting all white Clothes, Cullored Clothes, Kersies, bayes, sayes, serges, p[er]petuanoes and all other new draperies...w[i]th power to punish the persons and Confiscate the good[e]s of any other Englishe merchant[e]s that shall vse any part of that trade.[170]

They complained of the exclusion of strangers from the export trade and the Adventurers' monopolisation of the new draperies. The Staplers claimed that these enhanced powers had robbed them of their ancient rights to export cloth, presenting their own narrative of the King's intentions in bestowing this new charter. The proclamation restoring the Adventurers had, they claimed, abused the intention of James's letters patent, which had contained a proviso that nothing within should be prejudicial to the Staplers' rights.[171] There was some historical precedent for their claims; the Adventurers' charter of 1564 had been sent by Burghley to the Staplers with the insistence that it did not infringe on their liberties.[172] The tensions created by conflicting charters were reflected in the Staplers' complaints. The Adventurers had 'vsurped power and authority' from them, despite being an 'ancient' company first chartered in the reign of Edward I.[173] Appealing to charter culture, they noted that their rights and privileges had been confirmed in around forty grants issued by the King's predecessors. A trade which had thus formerly been distributed amongst many was now left in the hands of the 'Merchant adventurer only'.[174]

In an attached list of reasons, produced in response to further questions posed by the commissioners, the Staplers sought to prove that they were exempt from the proclamation announcing the restoration of the Adventurers' privileges. Like the Starchmakers, the meaning of this proclamation was heavily contested by the Staplers as they claimed it was not intended to bar them from the cloth trade. They argued that it had ordered the trade to be governed according to the Adventurers' charters and previous privileges, and thus, the proviso protecting their rights allowed them to export cloths.[175] The Staplers therefore offered their own interpretation of the changes of 1617 to suggest that neither James's proclamation nor the Adventurers' new patent were intended to restrain their rights.

The Adventurers' control of trade was presented as even more questionable in the face of the current trade crisis – how could a small company manage this crucial trade during a time of such trouble? Like the clothiers and the Drapers, the Staplers took note of the false making of cloth. Yet rather than blame this on Lennox or unapprenticed workers, they blamed this on the Adventurers, who simply were too small to properly regulate the industry. This, they claimed, encouraged clothiers to make false wares. The Staplers proceeded to express concern with the Adventurers' use of the stint, impositions, and limited departures of ships.[176] They presented their concerns with the latter policy in a way designed to appeal to authorities, noting that this caused the decay of shipping and navigation. Like the Drapers, they too commented on issues surrounding exchange rates and the export of coin.

Crucially, the Staplers also engaged with debates surrounding corporate regulation and free trade, replicating the language of protest present in

Parliament in 1621. They articulated a view more in line with the outports, criticising the dominance of Londoners. They argued that

> Limiting trade to one Company, and so by consequence to so small a number residing for the most part at one port as at London is a generall preiudice to the whole Kingdome for it inforceth needeles and chargeable carriage and recarriage of duiers Comodities.[177]

This created burdens for clothiers living in 'remote part[e]s of the land', who were forced to sell their wares via London, whilst contributing to outport decline, as ports were left 'allmost desolate & forsaken'.[178] By contrast in foreign countries, where 'more freedome of trade is allowed', trades were improved, native manufactures advanced, and navies augmented.[179] This articulation of free trade sentiments by the Staplers must be read as part of their broader campaign to regain their own lost authority. Their attempt to control the wool brogging trade had shown that the Staplers had no problems with monopoly when it suited their interests. They ended their petition by requesting permission to join the cloth export trade, calling for all merchant companies to accept members upon reasonable entry fines.[180] Again, they unsurprisingly made no mention to their use of incredibly high entrance fines of £100 in their earlier wool brogging scheme. In their attached list of reasons, the Staplers aimed to persuade commissioners that, if allowed to export cloths, they would be a large and open corporate body, mirroring tactics used by the Starchmakers in 1608.[181]

The Staplers and the Drapers engaged with debates surrounding corporate institutions and the benefits of free trade to push their agendas. By appropriating this language and the ideas circulating in Parliament and within the Commission, both offered differing views on the problems in the industry, turning the Commission into another space in the city for the hearing of trading conflicts. Indeed, other subjects appear to have similarly embraced the chance to use the depression to advance their interests. Earlier in December 1620, when expressing concern to the ward of Aldgate with the numbers of strangers and foreigners purchasing cloths outside of Blackwell Hall, the Lord Mayor had noted that some had even attempted to procure a patent 'pretendinge thereby the reformac[i]on of these greate abuses', complaints having been articulated to the Court of Aldermen by merchants, mercers, and drapers 'much lamentinge the decay of Trade'.[182] The widespread selling of cloth outside of public markets was recognised as a pertinent problem in the industry, yet it was also seen by some, possibly the Drapers here, as an opportunity to reach for patents.

In the counties, clothiers also approached this new point of contact to articulate their grievances against the Adventurers, possibly working in alliance with the Staplers in London. In doing so, they too engaged with the debates surrounding economic regulation and monopolies which were so prevalent in the early 1620s. Their calls for a free trade appear as more genuine, triggered by a belief that more merchants would lead to more cloth sales. As these issues became increasingly paramount in the context of depression, clothiers were emboldened to rearticulate their desire for a free trade. Indeed, by actively encouraging clothiers to attend the Commission, the Council and King inadvertently contributed to their further politicisation.

## The commissioners' report and the permanent Commission for Trade

The temporary Commission for Trade thus emerged as an important space for the presentation of supplications and reports. The net effect of these activities was the production of a final report by commissioners on 22 June.[183] Comparison between the petitions sent to the Commission and the report attests to the influence supplications had on the opinions of commissioners. They embraced that their report had been produced after 'manie Conferenc[e]s' with merchants, companies, drapers, dyers, gentlemen, and clothiers.[184] This contrasted markedly with James's attitude to the discussion of matters of state and religion by uninformed subjects.

In total, the report offered eight causes for the decay in the cloth trade, alongside detailed remedies to help solve both these problems and the decline of bullion supplies. The causes included many which had been articulated in petitions, including the illegal export of wool, the false making of cloth, the decline of cloth wearing, and the number of charges imposed on cloth, including the pretermitted customs, imposed by the Crown.[185] The commissioners also engaged with the grievances surrounding corporate regulation. In their fifth reason, they noted the concern with

> the pollicyes of the Merchant Adventurers, Which drawe vpon them suspition of Combinac[i]on in tradinge; and the Smalenes of their Nomber w[hi]ch nowe doe vsuallie buye and vent Clothe; and the Like pollicyes of other Merchant[e]s, whoe are not able or willinge to extend themselues in this tyme of extremitye to take of the Clothe from the hande of the Clothier.[186]

The commissioners acknowledged complaints pertaining to the small number of merchants in the Company, proceeding to urge that merchants be allowed to join for entrance fees of five marks, whilst agreeing with the clothiers and Staplers that their new impositions on cloth should be removed.

However, whilst they acknowledged that companies were 'spoken against by many', they still recognised the need for the order which regulated companies could provide, showing a belief that corporatism and a greater freedom of trade could co-exist. Company ordinances pertaining to the government of trade needed to remain in force, but any allowing 'Combinac[i]on either in buyinge at home or sellinge abroad' should be prohibited.[187] This was reflected in the commissioners' recommendation of a scheme to create clothing corporations in different shires; clearly, memory of the protest towards corporations of clothworkers in Ipswich and Bury was not enough to deter proposals in this age of corporatism. Heavily influenced by a project first set on foot by the projector Walter Morrell, the commissioners proposed that each county be given commissions or patents establishing them as corporations to regulate the new draperies.[188] By contrast, the commissioners expressed the view that joint-stock companies were a hindrance to the commonwealth (exempting only the East India Company) expressing similar sentiments as MPs in 1604. Whilst regulated companies allowed members to trade on their own accounts, joint-stock organisations created limited opportunities to trade, with set voyages and directors. As such, in a joint stock, 'it is as if one man alone were the Adventurer and Buyer'.[189] Whilst acknowledging that corporate regulation was a necessity, the commissioners recommended a particularly significant change for the supervision of mercantile companies. They proposed that, from henceforth, their ordinances and constitutions should be approved by a committee, to ensure that nothing be issued which furthered private interests over the public good.[190] In addition, no merchant company was to impose charges on its members which might endanger the export of cloth without government approval.[191]

Ultimately, the commissioners had proven receptive to subjects' concerns and the reality that some corporations might seek private benefits at the expense of the commonwealth. Commissioners had not shied away from discussing the issue of corporate governance, and whilst not articulating calls for an entirely free trade, they did propose reforms designed to reduce the Adventurers' monopoly. Keith Wrightson has argued that economic thought surrounding corporations shifted throughout the seventeenth century, moving away from the unquestioned assumption that trade needed to be regulated to the idea that such regulations needed to be justified.[192] In the petitions and reports of the temporary Commission, we see the beginnings of reflections on the values of corporations occurring before the end of the century, as commissioners were aware of the need to distinguish between, and in turn justify, those institutions which were useful and those which were damaging to trade and industry.

The report produced by the commissioners did not fall on deaf ears; James listened to its recommendations. By 28 July, a proclamation was issued prohibiting the export of wool, fuller's earth, and yarn and ordering that woollen cloth be worn at funerals to stimulate domestic demand.[193] It also prohibited the use of false dyeing materials, allowing the Dyers authority to search and seize logwood. Crucially, James also informed subjects that these measures were the work of the temporary Commission, who had had 'conference' with gentlemen, merchants, and clothiers to produce their report.[194] This public acknowledgment of its work informed subjects of its existence, whilst signalling James's willingness to allow clothiers and merchants to participate in the making of economic policy.

This willingness to hear opinions would only be enhanced by the creation in October of a permanent Commission for Trade, the letters of appointment drafted on 28 September.[195] The need for this institution had been suggested by the temporary commissioners to offload the burdens on the Council and to hear all future disputes arising between wool growers, clothiers, and merchants.[196] In this sense, the recommendations for its creation were similar to the reasons articulated in the formation of the Commission for Glass. In his proclamation of July, James announced his intention to appoint this Commission, thereby spreading news of this new point of contact.[197] The permanent Commission consisted of the same twelve individuals who had served on the temporary Commission, alongside an additional thirty-nine officials. It was to be headed by Henry Montagu, Lord President of the Council, and crown officials including Sir Julius Caesar and Ralph Freeman. Montagu had previously served as Recorder of London and, by 1620, he had investments in five different joint-stock enterprises.[198] His mercantile experience and strong links to the city account for his employment. Both the President of the Council of the North, Emanuel Scrope, and the President of the Council of Wales, William Compton, were appointed. The antiquarian Sir Robert Cotton was a commissioner, presumably for his skills in researching precedents for financial affairs.[199] Sir George Paule, a commissioner for starch, was also appointed and may well have owed this to his patron Buckingham.[200] Individuals with a keen interest and involvement in trade were selected, including the East India and Virginia Company merchant Sir Dudley Digges and the Virginia and Somerset Island Company member Sir Edward Sackville.[201] London's merchant community was again well-represented. Alongside the re-appointment of the temporary commissioners Pindar, Robson, and Dawes came the appointment of the farmer of the customs Henry Garway, later to emerge as a warden of the Drapers' Company by 1623.[202] One of the city's wealthiest merchants, Sir John Wolstenholme, was elected, as were the merchants Anthony Abdy and Clement Harby.[203]

The chance to serve on the Commission was likely eagerly embraced. Whilst their examinations would undoubtedly take up much time, being a member of a commission offered opportunities to issue patronage. An anonymous set of 'principles' for the new Commission also suggested that if the current customs farmers should relinquish their offices, the customs farm was to be managed by the commissioners.[204] It is possible that, if such a situation did occur, this position could be used to secure concessions for themselves and their clients.

The instructions sent to the commissioners made clear that this new institution was intended to advise on policy as conditions altered. James noted that trading conditions were always fluctuating. They were 'various, & must be directed & governed as times & occasions doe varye'.[205] The King admitted that it would therefore be impossible to establish 'constant Rules for trade'.[206] As such, the commissioners were expected to sit as a constant arm for the making of economic policy, consulting with subjects and hearing grievances, whilst informing the King and Council of developments. The letter of appointment made clear that this was to 'be a standing Comission', to continue until the King decided to dissolve it.[207] In many ways, its appointment was a natural progression from the range of temporary commissions appointed to investigate industrial conflicts and to peruse proposals for patents.

This permanent institution was also designed to receive petitions. Commissioners were thus instructed to hear any complaints presented to them and to mediate between parties. Crucially, it was expected that some of these grievances might be in the form of anti-monopoly complaints. The instructions sent to commissioners referred directly to the 'suspitio[n]… raised vppo[n] the societyes & company of ye Marchaunt[e]s adventurers & oth[er] march[an]ts' in recent years.[208] To assist them in investigating allegations that corporations had instituted ordinances to further their own private interests, the commissioners were given the power to view and search ordinance books. If any were found which were 'unfitt', tending to the private gain of a few individuals, they were to be revoked.[209] Later, the commissioners were also granted authority to review the ordinances of handicraft companies.[210] These were already required to be approved by law officers according to a statute of 1503.[211] However, the granting of authority to peruse the orders of mercantile companies, which had not previously been required to be approved, marked an important change which rendered merchant companies more firmly subject to government supervision.

The Commission was charged with myriad responsibilities, from investigating the effects of dyeing patents and joint-stock companies to considering how best to ensure a balance of trade. Amongst its tasks was the consideration of calls for the introduction of a freer trade. This was presented as a direct consequence of recent complaints made that trade was 'imprisoned'.[212] The anti-Adventurer petitions sent to the Council and the temporary Commission, combined with the extent of free trade debates in

Parliament in 1621, had clearly persuaded James that some form of free trade might be necessary. If so, commissioners were to advise on how this was to be achieved. However, the general desire to preserve order and regulation was advanced in James's insistence that any such reforms ensure that 'goverment & order in trade may be p[re]serued & confusion avoyded'.[213] One cannot escape the impression that James designed this body not only to relieve him and the Council from the torrent of anti-monopoly suits they had received in recent years, but to put in the work necessary to devise policies for trade which the King could proceed to implement with little personal effort.

The permanent Commission marked an important turning point in the message it conveyed to subjects. Not only did its powers to survey ordinances signal that this body was designed to scrutinise corporate bodies, but its ability to hear complaints made clear that subjects could continue to make their voices heard in the sphere of economic policy. It was even suggested by the commissioners that copies of the letters appointing them be sent into the counties, so that 'all men taking notice of them may come up' and consult them.[214] As such, even the 'comon people' could 'reioyce' at James's love for his subjects, and acting as 'good patriots', contribute to their vital work.[215] Whilst this public announcement did not occur, Slack has argued that it would have amounted to a broad appeal for public participation.[216] However, the King's earlier proclamation of July had announced his intention to appoint it, ensuring that news of the body spread. That its existence was known and even embraced is attested to by the range of petitions sent to it.

## Petitions, the Commission for Trade, and the reduction of the Adventurers' monopoly

The active work of the permanent Commission for Trade has often been overlooked. Scholars have acknowledged the role commissioners played investigating the monopoly of the Adventurers' Company alongside the Commons in 1624, but the petitions sent to the Commission prior to Parliament have often been excluded from the narrative of these events.[217] Notes and supplications in Caesar's papers reveal that the Commission actively investigated problems in the cloth trade, consulting with interested parties to form policy. The commissioners agreed to meet every Tuesday during the legal term and on Tuesdays and Fridays during the vacation at Haberdashers' Hall.[218] A clerk was to be appointed to register the proceedings of meetings, and the commissioners decided to first assess the wool trade.[219] By June 1623 commissioners informed the Council of new regulations they had established for the cloth trade in Norwich after consultation with the mayor and aldermen, and in a report penned sometime between 1623 and 1625 the commissioners noted that they had sought the advice of mayors and officers in other towns including Colchester, Canterbury, and Sandwich.[220] They also investigated issues including the importation of wool from Ireland and Scotland, the establishment of corn magazines, cloth factors in the city, and interestingly, plans for the establishment of clothing corporations in each county, as suggested by the temporary Commission.[221] In one report, they suggested that those given oversight of trades in the localities consist both of 'persons of skill and experience and some others of worth and quality'.[222] Whilst wanting to ensure experienced opinion was sought, we can read here a sense of a continued wariness to avoid any commissions or corporations being dominated by workmen alone, similar to Caesar's concern with 'under corporations' as voiced in his report on the Ipswich Tailors' and Clothworkers' Company in 1620. Commissioners also considered the possibility of granting patents or 'Commissions into all County[e]s, City[e]s & Towns corporate in the nature of Incorporations', to give JPs authority to appoint officers to enforce regulations for the cloth trade.[223] This ultimately speaks to the continued belief in the need for corporate structures in this age of corporatism, even if the Commission remained wary of the policies and ordinances of pre-existing institutions. It also suggests that the experience of commissioners encroaching on subjects' lives, including those for gold and silver thread, had not tainted the idea of using commissions to regulate industries.

Similarly, in Reading, efforts were made by the corporation to instigate new means of regulation, suggesting that similar proposals were attempted in local settings. In October 1623, clothiers were ordered to attend the Guildhall where it was agreed that two clothiers be appointed as overseers in each parish, to work with churchwardens and overseers of the poor to set spinners and carders on work.[224] These 'Clothiers overseers' were to meet every Monday morning at the Town Hall, to hear complaints of lack of work, and news of their appointment was to be declared at local churches the next Sabbath day.[225] Rather remarkably, local clothiers were here chosen to examine petitions and to provide work in the context of economic crisis.

As intended, the Commission for Trade emerged as a new institutional space for the presentation of petitions at a central level, especially by those subjects seeking redress for continuing problems in the cloth trade. Individual and collective suits were sent to commissioners. For example, on 6 December 1622, Richard Cutter from Kent petitioned to complain about the illegal exportation of fuller's earth and wood ashes in the county.[226] Later in March 1623, a collective petition was sent from subjects involved in the making and weaving of new draperies in Norfolk, Suffolk, and Essex and by the Norwich worsted weavers.[227] Its collective authorship once again attests to the capacity for subjects to cross county lines. These subjects called on the commissioners' aid to ensure that no one engage in the trade unless they had served seven-year apprenticeships and that all statutes pertaining to trade be enforced. They also sought a greater degree of regulation, requesting that each town elect wardens annually to ensure that only those who had served apprenticeships practise the trade. This reflects the continued desire for regulation even amongst the calls for free trade heard in this period.

In their petition, the clothworkers provided a narrative of their attempts to secure redress through different institutions. They noted that they had petitioned Parliament in 1621, but its dissolution forced them to petition James in January 1622. Evidence reveals that their suit had subsequently been referred to Justices in all three counties to review.[228] JPs had testified to the validity of their complaint but left it to the Council to decide on the best means to reform abuses.[229] Their suit was then referred to the Commission for Trade on 20 December 1622. Notes in Caesar's papers show that the Commission proceeded to launch investigations into the new drapery trade in these three counties.[230] Approaching the Commissioners in March 1623, the petitioners narrated their long and tireless pursuit for redress, repeating their demands.[231] This suggests that the Council did indeed expect commissioners to help them respond to economic grievances, referring petitions even if supplicants did not directly approach the Commission.

Much as with the temporary Commission, this new permanent Commission was also utilised by corporations.[232] In some cases, this was made possible by the commissioners's propensity to consult and ascertain opinions as part of its investigations. The Staplers were approached by the Commission as they investigated the domestic wool trade. Unsurprisingly, they embraced the opportunity to gain a foothold in the cloth export trade. On 6 December 1622, the Mayor of the Staple was brought before the Commission and asked how surplus wool in Scotland and Ireland might be brought to England.[233] He proceeded to suggest that this might cause a glut of wool supplies unless James issued licences for the export of overplus wool, a request intended to restore the Company's role as exporters of refuse wools. A further surviving list of answers presented by the Company to commissioners on 13 December 1622 shows that their opinion has been sought on the reasons for the decline in wool prices and its illegal exportation.[234] The Staplers' response once again demonstrated their willingness to use any opportunity possible to attack the Adventurers. Utilising a question-and-answer format, they presented their case. The enlargement of the cloth export trade was essential, they claimed, to make sure that 'trade…run as swifte as a streame in the Channell'.[235] The Adventurers' monopolisation of trade had made 'the Co[m]en wealth sicke of a Plurisy'.[236] More merchants exporting cloth would increase demand, providing work for clothiers, and consequently, a greater demand for wools, preventing its illegal exportation. When the 'damme or bancke' restricting trade was removed, more cloth would be made and demand for wools increase, drawing wool growers to places where cloth was made 'as the Fish followes the water'.[237] The support shown by clothiers and woolgrowers for the enlargement of trade in the previous Parliament and via petitions was also directly cited as proof of a consensus in the industry that the Adventurers' monopolisation of trade was a hindrance. The pressure they brought to bear on the commissioners had some success; by 17 December, Caesar recorded that the Adventurers, made to answer the Staplers' accusations, had agreed to accept more members into their fold if they paid relevant Company charges.[238]

The permanent commission also emerged as a new point of contact for domestic livery companies. On 7 March 1623, retailing members of the Grocers' Company approached their Court of Assistants, desiring permission to send a petition 'to the Lords Commissioners appoynted by his Ma[jes]ties p[ro]clamac[i]on for the releife of Greevanc[e]s'.[239] It is likely that the Grocers were hoping to send their complaint to Buckingham and other councillors, who had been appointed by James in February 1623 to hear petitions.[240] Instead, the Grocers' lawyers penned a petition asking the city authorities to commend their suit to 'his Ma[jes]ties Commissioners for Trades'.[241] The wider Company was clearly aware of the appointment of this permanent Commission, seeing this as a better avenue through which to channel complaints 'touchinge Trades & Comerce'.[242] The city authorities agreed; by June they wrote to commissioners, noting that the Grocers' complaints were well within 'ye Compasse of that hon[ora]ble Comission for trade'.[243] Thus, whilst the proclamation announcing the appointment of the Commission was never issued, this did not prevent news of its existence from spreading within the city.

The source of the Grocers' complaint was, perhaps unsurprisingly, the charter of the Apothecaries. The Commission for Trade was perceived as a body which might well prove receptive to inter-corporate disputes, likely because the commissioners had powers to investigate the ordinances of both mercantile and handicraft organisations. Clashes between patents were investigated by the Commission, as the Lord Mayor called on commissioners to ensure that both the Apothecaries and Grocers could be content 'without encroaching vpon the others rights'.[244] The commissioners do appear to have investigated the case. By 7 July, they ordered the Grocers to deliver their full complaints within fourteen days, and by October, the Company were invited to send representatives before them.[245]

The processes through which the Grocers' petitioned the Commission also allow us a further window into the mechanics of corporate petitioning. Much as in the case of starch, the initiative to launch this suit came from retailing grocers, who sought the permission of the wider Company before sending their complaint. This support was beneficial; not only did it add legitimacy to the petition, but Company leaders also agreed to pay for the suit from the Grocers' coffers.[246] Despite the involvement of lawyers in the drafting of the suit, retailing members were afforded a role in its construction. The Wardens were instructed to call before them two persons from each subsection of the trade affected by the Apothecaries' charter, who were to 'sett downe in wrightinge their p[ar]ticuler grievances'.[247] These in turn were used to inform the petition sent to the city and later, to commissioners.

The Commission acted to review the powers and authority of one key corporation: the Adventurers. In the Parliament of 1624, the Company faced a fresh onslaught of attacks as MPs continued to discuss the trade depression. The Staplers once again reared their heads, placing further pressure on the Commons for permission to export cloth.[248] Petitions were also presented by disaffected clothiers and merchants, complaining of the Adventurers' monopolisation of trade.[249] In Reading, payments were recorded to representatives to attend their burgesses in the hope of attaining 'a free trade'.[250] In the Commons, these matters were discussed and debated by the committees for grievances and for trade. However, the permanent Commission for Trade also played an important role in this attack. In a debate held on 4 March, Sandys celebrated the active work of 'his Majesty's Commissioners', who had spent time and energy examining these issues.[251] The commissioners were invited to offer their opinions to the parliamentary committee for trade via the MP and fellow commissioner Sir John Suckling. The House proceeded to focus on the same grievances directed against the Company by clothiers, including their burdensome impositions, small numbers, and enhanced powers.[252] These debates led to decisive action. The Commons declared that, from henceforth, the Adventurers' monopoly was to be restricted to the export of white, undressed broadcloths only. All merchants were to be free to trade in dressed and dyed cloths to Germany and the Low Countries, and the impositions imposed by the Company were declared as a grievance.[253] Despite these significant changes, some wanted further action to be taken. On 11 May, knights in Gloucestershire went so far as petitioning for the export of white cloths to be made open to all, a move which would have rendered the Company's charter obsolete.[254]

The House included these recommendations in a petition of grievances to James. Outside of Parliament, the Commission for Trade continued to offer advice. A report by Sir Robert Heath in May noted that the Commissioners for Trade had advised James on how to respond to the Commons' opinions on the Adventurers' monopoly.[255] This ultimately led James to accept the recommendations that the Adventurers' powers needed to be restricted, leading him to agree that dyed and dressed cloths could be freely exported to Germany and the Low Countries, and the new draperies by any merchants to any location.[256] By 3 July, the Commission delivered a final report to the King and Council on these points.[257] The report made clear that the commissioners had been instructed to meet with the Staplers and Adventurers to negotiate the fine details of these agreements. The Commission had been actively consulting with them since its appointment. A surviving petition sent to the commissioners from the Adventurers reveals that Towerson had previously attended the Commission to negotiate the fine points of the parliamentary decisions against them, in an effort to retain the trade of coloured cloths, white cloths, and new draperies to the mart towns from the metropolis.[258]

In their final report, the Commissioners informed James and the Council of the net result of these negotiations. It was agreed that the Adventurers would receive all 'meere merchantes' into their fold, including the Staplers, for entrance fines to be set by the Council.[259] Their hated impositions were to be reduced by a third, placed on white cloths only, and issued for a maximum of three more years. Foreign impositions on cloth were best resolved via foreign treaties, to be made and directed by James. It was also agreed that the outports were to have the liberty to export dyed and dressed cloths, and significantly, the new drapery trade was made free to all, a move first proposed by the Council in the spring of 1622. The Commissioners justified their decision to keep the new drapery trade free from corporate regulation, suggesting that the costs imposed by any government for this trade would likely 'eate up the gaine' offered by these commodities.[260] Interestingly one draft document which appears to have been made by the commissioners even suggested bringing merchants of cloths other than whites under the government of the Staplers' Company for fees of five marks.[261]

The significance of these decisions was not lost on contemporaries. The letter writer Sir Francis Nethersole reported that the 'last deadly strike' had been delivered to the Company in the Commons.[262] This 'strike' had been inflicted not only by MPs, but through the continued work of the Commission for Trade, both by its continued investigations of the issue of free trade between 1622 and 1624 and through its chief role negotiating the practicalities of these decisions. Whilst Leng has identified such factors as the rise of new draperies, internal divisions, and parliamentary discontent for contributing to the decline of the Company's privileges, the Commission and the supplications presented to it were undoubtedly a crucial factor in the reduction of this monopoly.[263]

One final question remains: why were the commissioners prepared to give in to petitioning pressure and to reduce the Adventurers' monopoly? The answer must be sought in the make-up of the Commission. Many of the commissioners were merchants and thus, the collapse of the monopoly would allow them the freedom to enter the cloth export trade if they wished. Similarly, a decline in the overall influence of the Adventurers within London was already well underway: Robert Brenner has shown that the rise in import trades led to the replacement of the Adventurers with the growing East India–Levant merchant grouping, many of whom began to dominate the aldermanic bench.[264] Many of the commissioners were active members of the East India Company, including Wolstenholme, Digges, and Mun. For them, it was far better to sacrifice the Adventurers' stronghold on trade to appease anti-monopoly sentiment than to allow their own East India Company to fall. Ultimately, the anti-Adventurer grievances expressed within supplications and in Parliament provided them with an opportunity, to appear reactive to grievances whilst maintaining their own dominance in trade and in the city. Even the very personnel sitting in the Commission allowed it to emerge as a space for trading conflicts. It would take the arrival of a new monarch, who relied even more heavily on monopolies and companies, for the Adventurers to be restored to their former privileges.

## Conclusion

> The then Comissioners for Trade...making report unto the Lords of his Ma[jes]t[ie]s Privy Councell, that It was their opinion also That all the Subjects of this Realme should lawfully trade into any of those parts, except only in white Cloth, the same was then allowed and passed into an Act of State.[265]

Petitioning the Commons in 1641, the Adventurers constructed an elaborate narrative of the fortunes of their Company in James and Charles's reigns. In their suit, they acknowledged the role played by the Commission for Trade in the reduction of their privileges in 1624, complaining that this had opened the floodgates for interlopers to saturate their trade. This was not an exaggerated claim; by 1632 the number of merchants in the Company had tripled from totals in 1622.[266] Pre-existent narratives of the events of 1624 have often regarded Parliament or the Council as the key arena where discontent to the Company was articulated.[267] Ashton has argued that the Crown turned away from its long-standing alliance with the Adventurers, giving in to parliamentary pressure to allow a reduction in their privileges by 1624.[268] Brenner has instead argued that a larger alliance of interests between Buckingham, Prince Charles, and MPs in support of free trade allowed this attack to be successful.[269] More recently, Pennington has argued that the decision to open the Company was a compromise, triggered by twenty years of free trade protest in Parliament and by provincial lobbying activity.[270] This chapter has revealed the need to consider the role played by petitions and a broader public opinion in these events. The torrent of complaints directed against the Company, especially before the temporary and permanent Commissions, was essential in the decision to allow the permanent Commission to investigate corporate organisations like the Adventurers in the first place. This Commission in turn played an active role in Parliament, advising both the King and Commons on the need to restrict the Adventurers' privileges. Self-interest likely played a role in the commissioners' willingness to reduce the Company's powers, yet the continued calls for changes to trade articulated through petitions and reports from 1620 onwards were essential for these changes.

The depression of the 1620s had consequences and impacts beyond the outbreak of unemployment and the production of printed pamphlets. These events led to the creation of new avenues for petitioning activity, and in turn, facilitated the presentation of anti-monopoly grievances by clothiers, clothworkers, and merchants throughout the realm. These petitions provide further evidence of a theme developed throughout this book, demonstrating the ways in which the rhetoric and discourses utilised by petitioners were shaped by broader conceptual debates and concerns. Through their suits, clothiers tackled the issues of corporate regulation and free trade. Whilst this was certainly different from the more complicated mercantilist literature produced by figures such as Mun, clothiers and merchants still engaged in what we might term processes of economic *thinking*, as they discussed the need for regulation and expressed opinions on markets and overseas trade. Philip Stern and Carl Wennerlind have argued for the need for historians to broaden understandings of the processes of economic thinking and the types of subjects who participated in this activity.[271] Through manuscript petitions, we can trace these processes of engagement amongst a broader scope of subjects than those often considered in pre-existent studies of economic thought, moving away from a historiography of political economy which has so often focused on printed sources.[272]

This case also allows us to reflect more broadly on the processes of politicisation in early Stuart England, including clothiers as one subset of subjects who appear to have been particularly drawn into the political process. As noted, their interconnected trade and ability to hear and receive news contributed to their ability to mobilise. This chapter has shown that clothiers could unite across county boundaries, finding common cause whilst in the metropolis and when attending commissions. In the context of depression, with the government so eager to avoid any unrest by clothworkers, this process was intensified. The temporary Commission for Trade allowed the gathering of clothiers from different counties, allowing them to collectively discuss trade and industry. The Commons' investigation of trade in 1621 also brought clothiers to Westminster, which, when combined with the increased accessibility of Parliament and its proceedings as traced in Chapter 4, allowed clothiers to foster a deeper understanding of what others were saying about the depression. These processes facilitated the creation of a common, industrial identity amongst clothiers, formed and strengthened in town halls, Blackwell Hall, Westminster, and crucially, through commissions. As identified by Rollison, the rise of a national consciousness in the industry was therefore a prominent development.[273] By the late Elizabethan and early Stuart periods, this collective industrial interest found its chief expression not through riots or rebellions, but through petitions. In turn, corporate bodies like the Staplers were willing to make alliances with the clothiers, perceiving them as an interest group with a stake in debates.

The power of the petitions produced by these subjects is attested to by their institutional impacts. Complaints by clothiers in February–April 1622 ultimately triggered the creation of the temporary Commission in April, whilst supplications to this body contributed to the creation and agenda of the permanent Commission for Trade. This was intended to better streamline the process through which petitions pertaining to trade and commerce were heard by authorities, ultimately marking an important epoch in the history of both early Stuart petitioning practice and the making of economic policy. Early Stuart economic policy is often characterised as reactive, responding to short-term crises, and the Privy Council is presented as the pre-eminent institution for the formulation of policies.[274] Historians have often argued that it was the shift from conciliar to parliamentary policy-making by the end of the seventeenth century which created enhanced opportunities for a wider public involvement in the formation of policies.[275] However, the appointment of the permanent Commission complicates this narrative. As recognised by Supple and Slack, it reveals the importance of participatory spaces beyond the Council or Parliament for the formation of economic policy in the 1620s.[276] As we have seen throughout this book, commissions were important spaces facilitating dialogues and active negotiations with subjects. However, they were often temporary or limited in scope. Earlier in 1616, the Council had written to JPs in Wiltshire, calling for any examinations of problems in the cloth industry to be carried out quietly, to be 'not too publique to make a noyse amongst the people'.[277] By 1622, James and his Council had changed their position drastically. As argued by Slack, they had come to accept that they could not manage the economy without the advice of a wider body of opinion, creating a Commission which was designed to be permanent.[278] This was part of a broader trend and desire by governments throughout Europe to collect information, but as Slack argues, this information 'necessarily involved noise', as different interest groups pushed their own agendas.[279] As such, the Commission for Trade emerged as a new site for the politics of trade to manifest.

The pressures of the depression undoubtedly contributed to this change, but we also might point to the events of an earlier Parliament, that of 1621, which had revealed just how misjudged the advice James had received on patents and regulatory measures had been. The failures of bodies like the Commissions for Suits to properly examine projects had been highlighted by MPs and petitioners. As such, James was prepared to create a new institution to tackle not only the causes of the depression, but to consult with subjects on various issues in trade and industry, to avoid similar policy disasters moving forward. Similarly, the contests and conflicts generated by monopoly and corporatism played a role. Staplers and clothiers engaged with the issue of corporatism as a result of the Adventurers' new charter of 1617. Like so many others, this clashed with pre-existing rights (namely, that of the Staplers), and the changes wrought on the industry pushed clothiers to articulate their concerns with the Adventurers' enhanced powers. As such, it was necessary to create a Commission explicitly charged with the role of hearing disputes and controversies pertaining to companies, providing it with the power to review ordinances and to tackle the issue of free trade. The era of monopoly saw these issues rise to prominence, rendering it necessary to create a new institution to address them.

These events allow us to reflect on James's style of kingship. Cramsie stresses the importance of the city and the Court on progress as fundamental for the formulation of policies and advice-giving for a King who adopted such an open style of kingship.[280] Yet our analysis also invites us to consider how commissions allowed James to take advice from a wider remit of subjects than courtiers and councillors. It is possible that James's desire to appoint these commissions reflected his lack of willingness to deal with economic issues personally. In letters written to appoint the permanent Commission, for example, the King clearly expressed his wish that the body would deal with grievances pertaining to trade, and only refer these to the Council if no mediation could occur.[281] Similarly, in January 1625, James wrote directly to commissioners to praise their past work and to express his concern that they had been lax in meeting in recent months. He encouraged the commissioners to meet weekly, seeing that 'nothing cann Concerne the Wellfare of o[u]r Revennue in point of o[u]r Customes more then the due execution therof'.[282] In governing Scotland, James would similarly rely on commissions to investigate problems in industry.[283] For James, concerned with his revenues and personally preferring to focus his attention on religion and foreign policy, the appointment of the Commission perhaps reflected his wish to allow trade and commerce to be dealt with by others.

Regardless of James's motivations, the net effect of these Commissions was to create new points of contacts for the negotiation of economic policy. These spaces set the groundwork for the continued use of commissions under Charles. In 1638, commissioners were appointed to investigate problems in the cloth trade in the Cotswolds and Mendips.[284] Within their report, penned in 1640, the commissioners called for a permanent commission of 'able gentlemen Marchaunts, and Tradesmen' based in or near London, to sit weekly to hear grievances pertaining to the industry.[285] It is hard not to see subjects harkening for the creation of a body remarkably similar to that which had existed in 1622–25.

## Notes

1 BL, Add. MS 39,245, fo. 54v.
2 *Ibid.*
3 TNA, SP 14/127, fo. 109r.
4 *Ibid.*
5 For the best accounts, see Supple, *Crisis*, ch. 3; J. D. Gould, 'The Trade Depression of the Early 1620s', *Economic History Review*, 7:1 (1954), pp. 81–90.
6 TNA, SP 14/128, fo. 90r.
7 *Ibid.*
8 TNA, SP 14/128, fo. 65r; TNA, SP 14/128, fo. 25r; TNA, SP 14/128, fo. 66r.
9 Supple, *Crisis*; C. P. Kindleberger, 'The Economic Crisis of 1619 to 1623', *Journal of Economic History*, 51:1 (1991), pp. 149–75; C. Wilson, *England's Apprenticeship, 1603–1763* (London, 1971), chs 3–4.
10 J. O. Appleby, *Economic Thought and Ideology in Seventeenth-Century England* (Princeton, 1978); L. Magnusson, *Mercantilism: The Shaping of an Economic Language* (London, 1994), ch. 3; J. D. Gould, 'The Trade Crisis of the Early 1620's and English Economic Thought', *Journal of Economic History*, 15:2 (1955), pp. 121–33; Erikson, *Trade and Nation*; C. Suprinyak, 'Trade, Money, and the Grievances of the Commonwealth: Economic Debates in England During the Commercial Crisis of the Early 1620's', *History of Economic Ideas*, 24:1 (2016), pp. 27–55.
11 See Yerby, *Economic Causes*, ch. 8; T. Leng, '"His neighbours land mark": William Sykes and the Campaign for "Free Trade" in Civil War England', *Historical Research*, 86:232 (2013), pp. 230–52.
12 Suprinyak, 'Economic Debates', pp. 39–40; Patterson, *Urban Government*, pp. 156–7.
13 Supple, *Crisis*, p. 66. See also Friis, *Alderman Cockayne*, pp. 416–27; Lipson, *Economic History* (1956), iii, pp. 307–10; C. M. Andrews, *British Committees,*

*Commissions, and Councils of Trade and Plantations, 1622–1675* (Baltimore, 1908), p. 12; R. W. K. Hinton, *The Eastland Trade and the Common Weal in the Seventeenth Century* (Cambridge, 1959), pp. 27–31.

14 P. Slack, 'The Politics of English Political Economy in the 1620s', in M. J. Braddick and P. Withington (eds), *Popular Culture and Political Agency in Early Modern England and Ireland: Essays in Honour of John Walter* (Cambridge, 2017), p. 65.

15 C. Suprinyak, 'Dreams of Order and Freedom: Debating Trade Management in Early Seventeenth-Century England', *Journal of the History of Economic Thought*, 40:3 (2018), p. 406. Suprinyak focuses on the role these spaces played in helping to cement the ideas of thinkers, see Suprinyak, 'Economic Debates', pp. 28, 48.

16 Suprinyak, 'Debating Trade Management', p. 406.

17 Tazzara, 'Managing Free Trade', p. 527

18 Pennington, '"Free Passage"', pp. 297–9. Some analysis of the petitions has been made by G. Ramsay, *The Wiltshire Woollen Industry in the Sixteenth and Seventeenth Centuries*, 2nd edn (London, 1965), ch. 5.

19 R. H. Tawney (ed.), *Studies in Economic History: The Collected Papers of George Unwin* (London, 1927), pp. 137–45; G. F. Ward, 'The Early History of the Merchants Staplers', *English Historical Review*, 33:131 (1918), pp. 297–319.

20 A. F. Sutton, 'The Merchant Adventurers of England: Their Origins and the Mercers' Company of London', *Historical Research*, 75:187 (2002), pp. 25–46.

21 P. J. Bowden, *The Wool Trade in Tudor and Stuart England* (London, 1962), pp. 156–64.

22 BL, Hargrave MS 321, fo. 89r.

23 Bowden, *Wool Trade*, pp. 164–5.

24 Larkin and Hughes, I, pp. 317–19.

25 PA, HL/PO/JO/10/1/9, fos 209–15.

26 D. Stevenson, 'Erskine, Thomas, first earl of Kellie (1566–1639)', *ODNB* (2004), https://doi-org.ezproxy-prd.bodleian.ox.ac.uk/10.1093/ref:odnb/8872 (accessed 25 August 2023). For the patent, see Bowden, *Wool Trade*, pp. 166–73; E. E. Rich, *The Ordinance Book of the Merchants of the Staple* (Cambridge, 1937), pp. 78–86.

27 Bowden, *Wool Trade*, p. 168. Areas like Halifax had been made exempt from prohibitions on middlemen, see Heaton, *Yorkshire Woollen*, p. 120.

28 Larkin and Hughes, I, pp. 365–9.

29 Bowden, *Wool Trade*, pp. 169–73.

30 *CD 1621*, v, pp. 468–9, 486–7.

31 Supple, *Crisis*, p. 34.

32 The best account of the project remains Friis, *Alderman Cockayne*. For the Clothworkers' involvement, see Clothworkers' Court Books, CL, CL/B/1/4, fos 114v, 119v, 121v, 139r, 155v–157r; TNA, SP 14/72, fo. 146. For the Eastland Company, see Hinton, *Eastland Trade*.

33 Leng, *Fellowship*, pp. 221–2; Larkin and Hughes, I, pp. 371–3.

34 D. R. Bisson, *The Merchant Adventurers of England: The Company and the Crown, 1474–1564* (London, 1993), pp. 7–11. See for example, TNA, SP 12/161, fo. 65r; TNA, SP 12/161, fo. 63; TNA, SP 12/161, fo. 64.

35 PA, HL/PO/JO/10/1/19, fos 82–4; HRO, 44M69/L39/101, pp. 1–6; TNA, SP 14/120, fos 170r–171r; BL, Hargrave MS 321, fos 79v–84r. The Adventurers' response made a strong appeal to charter culture, see fos 84v–85r, 87r–95r.

36 HRO, 44M69/L39/101, p. 5.

37 *CD 1621*, iii, pp. 188, 443; *LJ*, iii, pp. 174, 184.

38 BL, Hargarve MS 321, fos 92v, 94r.

39 G. D. Ramsay, 'Industrial Discontent in Early Elizabethan London: Clothworkers and Merchant Adventurers in Conflict', *London Journal*, 1:2 (1975), pp. 227–39. For a recent consideration of the political consciousness exhibited within the Company, see E. Legon, 'The Lord Mayor's Show and the Politics of London's Clothworkers' Company in the Mid-Seventeenth Century', *London Journal*, 47:3 (2022), pp. 241–59.

40 TNA, SP 14/90, fo. 252v.

41 *Ibid.*

42 A. H. Johnson, *The History of the Worshipful Company of the Drapers of London* (5 vols, Oxford, 1915), iii; T. Girtin, *The Triple Crowns: A Narrative History of the Drapers' Company, 1364–1964* (London, 1964).

43 Girtin, *Triple Crowns*, p. 201.

44 Johnson, *Drapers*, iii, p. 90.

45 Girtin, *Triple Crowns*, p. 214.

46 Friis, *Alderman Cockayne*, pp. 21–3; G. D. Ramsay, *The English Woollen Industry, 1500–1750* (London, 1982), ch. 3.

47 Heaton, *Yorkshire Woollen*, pp. 91–2.

48 J. Thirsk, 'Industries in the Countryside', in F. J. Fisher (ed.), *Essays in the Economic and Social History of Tudor and Stuart England in Honour of R. H. Tawney* (Cambridge, 1961), pp. 70–89.

49 N. Bateman, 'From Rags to Riches: Blackwell Hall and the Wool Cloth Trade, c. 1450–1790', *Post-Medieval Archaeology*, 38:1 (2004), pp. 1–15.

50 T. Keirn, 'Parliament, Legislation and the Regulation of English Textile Industries, 1689–1714', in D. Lee (ed.), *Stilling the Grumbling Hive: The Response to Social and Economic Problems in England, 1689–1750* (Stroud, 1992), p. 4.

51 Walter, *Colchester Plunderers*, p. 243.

52 *Ibid.*, p. 245.

53 D. Rollison, 'Discourse and Class Struggle: The Politics of Industry in Early Modern England', *Social History*, 26:2 (2001), pp. 172, 187.

54 J. Walter, 'Authority and Protest', in K. Wrightson (ed.), *A Social History of England, 1500–1750* (Cambridge, 2017), p. 237.

55 Rollison, 'Discourse', pp. 175, 188.

56 C. G. A. Clay, *Economic Expansion and Social Change: England 1500–1700* (2 vols, Cambridge, 1984), ii, p. 121; *APC*, 33, pp. 457–8; TNA, SP 14/98, fo. 93r;

TNA, SP 14/97, fo. 249. For complaints during the Cockayne project, see *APC*, 35, pp. 2–4, 7–10, 10-12, 21–22; TNA, SP 14/88, fo. 70r; TNA, SP 14/88, fo. 71.
57 HRO, 44M69/L38/6; Ramsay, *Wiltshire Woollen Industry*, p. 76.
58 HRO, 44M69/L38/6.
59 *Ibid.*, n.f.
60 *Ibid.*; TNA, SP 14/115, fo. 28r.
61 HRO, 44M69/L38/6.
62 Peacey, *Public Politics*, p. 296.
63 TNA, SP 14/115, fos 86r–87r. Described by Ramsay as a 'tremulous' and 'lurid' petition, see Ramsay, *Wiltshire Woollen Industry*, p. 76.
64 TNA, SP 14/115, fo. 86r.
65 *APC*, 37, pp. 200–1, 205–6.
66 *CD 1621*, iii, p. 189.
67 HRO, 44M69/G2/13/1.
68 *Ibid.*
69 *Ibid.*
70 *CD 1621*, iii, p. 157.
71 Leng, *Fellowship*, p. 226.
72 BL, Hargrave MS 321, fo. 41r.
73 TNA, SP 14/128, fo. 25r.
74 *Ibid.*
75 TNA, SP 14/128, fo. 66r.
76 TNA, SP 14/128, fo. 65r.
77 *Ibid.*
78 *Ibid.*
79 *Ibid.*
80 TNA, SP 14/128 fo. 63r; TNA, SP 14/128, fo. 64r.
81 TNA, SP 14/128, fo. 66r.
82 *Ibid.*
83 Unwin, 'Industries', p. 265.
84 TNA, SP 14/128, fo. 90r.
85 Hinton, *Eastland Trade*, p. 24.
86 *APC*, 38, p. 223.
87 *Ibid.*, p. 224.
88 See Webb, 'Cloth Accounts', pp. 126–7; TNA, SP 14/131, fo. 53r.
89 TNA, SP 14/128, fo. 64r.
90 *Ibid.*
91 *Ibid.*
92 TNA, SP 14/128, fo. 90r.
93 *APC*, 38, p. 156; BL, Add. MS 39,245, fo. 59r.
94 TNA, SP 14/128, fo. 63r.
95 Their response to Gloucestershire has been misdated to 1635. TNA, SP 16/535, fos 82r–83v; TNA, SP 14/129, fos 16r–17v.
96 TNA, SP 16/535, fo. 82v.
97 *Ibid.*

98 *Ibid.*
99 TNA, SP 14/129, fo. 17r.
100 *Ibid.*
101 *Ibid.*
102 T. Leng, 'Interlopers and Disorderly Brethren at the Stade Mart: Commercial Regulations and Practices Amongst the Merchant Adventurers of England in the Late Elizabethan Period', *Economic History Review*, 69:3 (2016), p. 826.
103 TNA, SP 14/128, fo. 66r.
104 TNA, SP 14/129, fo. 16r.
105 *Ibid.*
106 *Ibid.*, fo. 16v.
107 *Ibid.*, fo. 17r.
108 TNA, SP 16/535, fo. 82r.
109 *Ibid.*
110 TNA, SP 14/129, fo. 16v.
111 Walter, *Colchester Plunderers*, p. 309.
112 TNA, PC 2/31, fo. 323r.
113 For reports see BL, Hargrave MS 321, fos 40r–47v, 51v–53v, 60v–61r, 66v–69r; TNA, SP 14/122, fo. 204r; TNA, SP 14/123, fo. 73; *APC*, 38, pp. 40, 71, 79–80; Slack, 'Political Economy', pp. 56–8. For standing committees, see R. Turner, 'The Origin of the Cabinet Council', *English Historical Review*, 38:150 (1923), p. 192.
114 Millstone, 'Sir Robert Cotton', p. 139.
115 C. Tazzara, *The Free Port of Livorno and the Transformation of the Mediterranean World* (Oxford, 2017), pp. 261–3.
116 TNA, PC 2/31, fo. 323r; TNA, PC 2/31, fo. 337r.
117 HRO, 44M69/L37/1.
118 TNA, SP 14/129, fo. 129r.
119 HRO, 44M69/G3/165.
120 *Ibid.*
121 TNA, PC 2/31, fos 335–6.
122 Patterson has argued that it reflected 'metropolitan' interests, see Patterson, *Urban Government*, p. 157.
123 R. Ashton 'Pindar, Sir Paul (1565/6–1650)', *ODNB* (2008), https://ezproxy-prd.bodleian.ox.ac.uk:2102/10.1093/ref:odnb/22291 (accessed 30 September 2024).
124 P. Gauci, 'Mun, Thomas (bap. 1571, d. 1641)', *ODNB* (2008), https://ezproxy-prd.bodleian.ox.ac.uk:2102/10.1093/ref:odnb/19527 (accessed 9 August 2022).
125 For Dawes and Pindar as customs farmers under Charles see TNA, SP 16/185, fo. 100.
126 See Chapter 4.
127 TNA, PC 2/31, fo. 336.
128 Larkin and Hughes, I, pp. 495–6, 519–21.
129 *APC*, 38, p. 153.

130 'The Clothiers' plan for the improvement of trade', April-May 1622, in J. Thirsk and J. P. Cooper (eds), *Seventeenth-Century Economic Documents* (Oxford, 1972), pp. 14–15.
131 BL, Stowe MS 354, fols. 63r–64v.
132 J. P. Cooper, 'Economic Regulation and the Cloth Industry in Seventeenth-Century England', *Transactions of the Royal Historical Society*, 20 (1970), p. 78; Gould, 'Crisis', p. 221.
133 'Clothiers' plan', *Seventeenth-Century Documents*, p. 14.
134 BL, Hargrave MS 321, fo. 80v.
135 'Clothiers' plan', *Seventeenth-Century Documents*, p. 15.
136 TNA, SP 14/129, fo. 129v.
137 'Clothiers' plan', *Seventeenth-Century Documents*, p. 15.
138 *Ibid.*
139 BL, Stowe MS 354, fo. 65r.
140 *Ibid.*
141 *Ibid.*
142 *Ibid.*
143 *Ibid.*, fo. 65v.
144 TNA, SP 14/130, fo. 188r; TNA, SP 14/130, fos 189r–191r. These have been noticed by Heaton, *Yorkshire Woollen*, p. 217.
145 TNA, SP 14/130, fo. 188r.
146 TNA, SP 14/130, fo. 189r.
147 Girtin, *Triple Crowns*, p. 214.
148 TNA, SP 14/130, fo. 189r.
149 BL, Cotton Galba E/1, fos 318r–323r.
150 For this in Europe, see Tazzara, *Free Port*, p. 262.
151 TNA, SP 14/130, fo. 189r.
152 *Ibid.*, fo. 189v.
153 *Ibid.*, fo. 190r.
154 TLA, COL/CC/01/01/032, fo. 125r.
155 *Ibid.*, fos 241, 267r.
156 TNA, SP 14/130, fo. 190v.
157 P. E. Kopperman, *Sir Robert Heath 1575–1649: Window on an Age* (Suffolk, 1989), pp. 114–20.
158 TNA, SP 14/130, fo. 190r.
159 *Ibid.*
160 Heaton, *Yorkshire Woollen*, p. 218.
161 TNA, SP 14/130, fo. 191r.
162 *Ibid.*
163 *Ibid.*
164 Johnson, *Drapers of London*, iii, p. 90; Girtin, *Triple Crowns*, p. 214.
165 In 1635 the Drapers launched a campaign with the Adventurers to monopolise the retail and wholesale of cloth in London, triggering protests by clothiers in counties. See Unwin, 'Industries', p. 266
166 TNA, SP 14/130, fo. 191r.

167 TNA, SP 14/130, fos 192r–193v.
168 *Ibid.*, fo. 192v.
169 BL, Cotton Galba, E/1, fo. 318r.
170 *Ibid.*
171 Larkin and Hughes, I, pp. 371–3.
172 Bisson, *Adventurers*, p. 10.
173 BL, Cotton Galba, E/1, fo. 318v.
174 *Ibid.*, fo. 319r.
175 *Ibid.*, fo. 322v.
176 *Ibid.*, fos 319v–320r.
177 *Ibid.*, fo. 319v.
178 *Ibid.*
179 *Ibid.*, fo. 320v.
180 *Ibid.*, fos 320v–321r.
181 *Ibid.*, fos 322v–323r.
182 TLA, COL/CC/01/01/032, fo. 267r.
183 TNA, SP 14/131, fos 73r–77v.
184 *Ibid.*, fo. 73r.
185 For a defence of the pretermitted customs in 1621 which attacked the Adventurers, see Oxford, Bodl., MS North A.2., fos 241r–242v.
186 TNA, SP 14/131, fo. 73v.
187 *Ibid.*, fo. 75r.
188 M. Zell, 'Walter Morrell and the New Draperies Project, c. 1603–1631', *Historical Journal*, 44:3 (2001), p. 669. For further considerations of this see BL, Hargrave MS 321, fos 76v–79r, 96v–98r, 98r–99v.
189 TNA, SP 14/131, fo. 75v.
190 *Ibid.*, fo. 75r.
191 *Ibid.*, fo. 74v.
192 Wrightson, *Earthly Necessities*, p. 253.
193 Larkin and Hughes, I, pp. 545–9.
194 *Ibid.*, p. 546.
195 TNA, SP 14/133, fos 38r–50r; TNA, SP 14/133, fos 61r–76r; *Seventeenth-Century Documents*, pp. 16–23.
196 TNA, SP 14/131, fo. 77r.
197 Larkin and Hughes, I, pp. 548–9. This also included the desire for them to work with Scottish commissioners to investigate the wool trade.
198 B. Quintrell, 'Montagu, Henry, first earl of Manchester (c. 1564–1642)', *ODNB* (2008), https://ezproxy-prd.bodleian.ox.ac.uk:2102/10.1093/ref:odnb/19020 (accessed 9 August 2022).
199 S. Handley, 'Cotton, Sir Robert Bruce, first baronet (1571–1631)', *ODNB* (2004), https://ezproxy-prd.bodleian.ox.ac.uk:2102/10.1093/ref:odnb/6425 (accessed 9 August 2022).
200 S. Wright, 'Paule, Sir George (1563–1635)', *ODNB* (2008), https://ezproxy-prd.bodleian.ox.ac.uk:2102/10.1093/ref:odnb/21610 (accessed 9 August 2022).

201 S. Kelsey, 'Digges, Sir Dudley (1582/3–1639)', *ODNB* (2004), https://ezproxy-prd.bodleian.ox.ac.uk:2102/10.1093/ref:odnb/7635 (accessed 9 August 2022); A. Davidson and B. Coates, 'SACKVILLE, Sir Edward (1590–1652), of South Berwick, Suss', *HoP*, vi.

202 A. McConnell and R. Brown, 'Garway [Garraway], Sir Henry (bap. 1575, d. 1646)', *ODNB* (2004), https://ezproxy-prd.bodleian.ox.ac.uk:2102/10.1093/ref:odnb/10405 (accessed 9 August 2022).

203 J. K. Laughton and H. V. Bowen, 'Wolstenholme, Sir John (1562–1639)', *ODNB* (2004), https://ezproxy-prd.bodleian.ox.ac.uk:2102/10.1093/ref:odnb/29857 (accessed 9 August 2022); Friis, *Cockayne's Project*, p. 424.

204 TNA, SP 14/135, fo. 112r.

205 TNA, SP 14/133, fo. 39r.

206 *Ibid.*

207 TNA, SP 14/133, fo. 61v.

208 TNA, SP 14/133, fo. 45r.

209 *Ibid.*

210 TNA, SP 14/133, fo. 68r.

211 This was the Ordinances of Corporations Act, 19 Henry VII, c. 7.

212 TNA, SP 14/133, fo. 45r.

213 Ibid., fos 45r–46r.

214 TNA, SP 81/27, fo. 164v.

215 BL, Add. MS 34,324, fo. 193r.

216 Slack, 'Political Economy', p. 64.

217 See Kopperman, *Sir Robert Heath*, p. 113 for his description of it as 'inactive'. Pennington cites agitation in the Commons and provincial lobbying with a brief mention to petitions to the temporary Commission, see Pennington, '"Free Passage"', pp. 298–9; S. Lambert, 'Committees, Religion, and Parliamentary Encroachment on Royal Authority in Early Stuart England', *English Historical Review*, 105:414 (1990), p. 64.

218 BL, Add. MS, 34,324 fo. 193r. For meeting notes, see fos 195r–196v, 197r–198v, 209r–210v, 211r–212v, 213r–214v. Other notes which appear to be from the Commission are in BL, Hargrave MS 321, fos 121v–123v.

219 BL, Add. MS 34, 324, fos 193r–v.

220 TNA, PC 2/32, fos 46–7; 'A further explanation', *Seventeenth-Century Documents*, p. 32. For their examination of the New Draperies, see BL, Add. MS 34,324, fo. 211r.

221 *APC*, 39, pp. 34, 53–4, 105, 115–16, 366, 389; TNA, SP 14/162, fo. 118; BL, Add. MS 34,324, fos 201r–202v; TLA, COL/RMD/PA/01/006, fos 14–15; TNA, SP 14/135, fo. 111v; BL, Hargrave MS 321, fos 76v–79r, 96v–98r. For continued investigations of corporations in 1625, see TNA, SP 14/184, fos 72r–73v; TNA, SP 14/185, fo. 20r. The Commission called for Morrell to be paid £40 a year for his services, see TNA, SP 14/184, fo. 79r.

222 'A further explanation', *Seventeenth-Century Documents*, p. 32.

223 TNA, SP 14/135, fo. 111v.

224 *Diary of the Corporation of Reading*, ii, pp. 153–4.

225 *Ibid*., p. 153.
226 BL, Add. MS 34,324, fos 199r–200v.
227 TNA, SP 14/140, fo. 133r; BL, Add. MS 39, 245, fo. 59r.
228 *APC*, 38, p. 156; TNA, SP 14/130, fo. 83r; TNA, SP 14/137, fo. 32.
229 TNA, SP 14/130, fo. 83r.
230 BL, Add. MS 34,324, fo. 211r.
231 TNA, SP 14/140, fo. 133r.
232 An undated document in the Hargrave papers might be a petition to commissioners from the Adventurers, blaming the decay of trade on Merchant Strangers, see BL, Hargrave MS 321, fos 112v–117r.
233 BL, Add. MS 34,324, fo. 199r. It is likely that this was part of a joint investigation between England and appointed Scottish commissioners on whether Scottish wool should be exported to England, see S. G. E. Lythe, *The Economy of Scotland in Its European Setting 1550–1625* (Edinburgh, 1960), pp. 221–2.
234 BL, Add. MS 34,324, fos 203r–208v.
235 *Ibid*., fo. 204r.
236 *Ibid*., fo. 204v.
237 *Ibid*., fo. 205v.
238 BL, Add. MS 34,324, fo. 209r.
239 GL, CLC/L/GH/B/001/MS11588/003, p. 239.
240 Patrick Wallis identifies this petitioning effort with protest launched by the Company in parliament in 1624, yet the references to the King's commission within the petition and its earlier date of 1623 suggests this was directed to the Commission for Trade. See P. Wallis, 'Medicines for London: The Trade, Regulation and Lifecycle of London Apothecaries, c. 1610–c. 1670' (unpublished DPhil thesis; University of Oxford, 2002), pp. 31–3. For the proclamation announcing these councillors as hearers of petitions, see Larkin and Hughes, I, pp. 568–70.
241 GL, CLC/L/GH/B/001/MS11588/003, pp. 242–3.
242 *Ibid*., p. 243.
243 TLA, COL/RMD/PA/01/006, fo. 15r; TLA, COL/CA/01/01/041, fo. 184r.
244 TLA, COL/RMD/PA/01/006, fo. 15r.
245 GL, CLC/L/GH/B/001/MS11588/003, pp. 250, 263.
246 *Ibid*., p. 249.
247 *Ibid*., p. 250.
248 '2 Mar. 1624' in *PP 1624*.
249 '19 Apr. 1624', '30 Apr. 1624', '25 May 1624' in *PP 1624;* TNA, SP 14/160, fos 83r–84v.
250 *Diary of the Corporation of Reading*, ii, p. 178. Earlier petitions by clothiers had complained of restraints on trade, see pp. 159–60.
251 '4 Mar. 1624', in *PP 1624*.
252 BL, Hargrave MS 321, fos 56r–57r.
253 '30 Apr', '10 May', '19 May' in *PP 1624*; BL, Hargrave MS 321, fos 56v, 85v.
254 '11 May', in *PP 1624*.

255 TNA, SP 14/165, fo. 126r. The commissioners were considering parliament's advice, see BL, Hargrave MS 321, fos 95r–96r.
256 TNA, SP 14/165, fo. 127r; Pennington, '"Free Passage"', p. 299.
257 *APC*, 39, pp. 268–9; BL, Hargrave MS 321, fos 57v–60v. Supple mentions the work of the Commission, see Supple, *Crisis*, p. 70.
258 BL, Hargrave MS 321, fos 86r–87r. This seems to refer to the parliamentary decisions of 1621.
259 *APC*, 39, p. 268.
260 *Ibid.*
261 BL, Hargrave MS 321, fos 95r–96r.
262 TNA, SP 14/165, fo. 64v.
263 Leng, 'Interlopers', p. 840.
264 Brenner, *Merchants*, pp. 3, 79–82; R. Brenner, 'The Social Basis of English Commercial Expansion, 1550–1650', *Journal of Economic History*, 32:1 (1972), pp. 361–84.
265 Whitelocke Papers, VIII, no. 29, microfilm XR 54/5 at the Institute of Historical Research (IHR), fo. 75r. Quotes included by kind permission of the Marquess of Bath, Longleat.
266 Brenner, *Merchants*, p. 60.
267 Leng, *Fellowship*, pp. 223–7; Supple, *Crisis*, p. 71.
268 Ashton, *City*, pp. 109–10.
269 Brenner, *Merchants*, pp. 211–13.
270 Pennington, '"Free Passage"', p. 299.
271 P. J. Stern and C. Wennerlind, 'Introduction', in P. J. Stern and C. Wennerlind (eds), *Mercantilism Reimagined: Political Economy in Early Modern Britain and Its Empire* (Oxford, 2013), p. 7.
272 Tazzara, *Free Port*, p. 15.
273 Rollison, 'Discourse', p. 187.
274 Supple, *Crisis*, pp. 227–30.
275 Keirn, 'Parliament, Legislation', pp. 2, 16.
276 Supple, *Crisis*, pp. 232–3; Slack, 'Political Economy', p. 64.
277 *APC*, 35, pp. 21–2.
278 Slack, 'Political Economy', p. 65.
279 P. Slack, 'Government and Information in Seventeenth-Century England', *Past and Present*, 28:184 (2004), pp. 54, 68.
280 Cramsie, *Kingship*, pp. 50–1.
281 TNA, SP 14/133, fo. 50r.
282 BL, Add. MS 12,496, fo. 121r.
283 Lythe, *Economy of Scotland*, pp. 94–5.
284 G. D. Ramsay, 'The Report of the Royal Commission on the Clothing Industry, 1640', *English Historical Review*, 57:228 (1942), pp. 482–93. For sewer commissions, see Robson, 'Edges of Governance', p. 178
285 Ramsay, 'Report', pp. 489–90.

# Conclusion: economics, politicisation, and the public sphere

> In truth the world doth euen grone vnder the burthen of these perpetuall patents, w[hi]ch are become so frequent, that whereas at the k[ing]s comming in there were complaints of some eight or nine monopolies then in beeing, they are now said to be multiplied to so many soures.[1]

In July 1620, the prolific news gatherer John Chamberlain complained to his companion Sir Dudley Carleton of the ubiquity of monopolies. Despite hopes that James's accession would render odious grants a distant memory, they remained a prolific sore on the body politic. Their effects extended beyond the confines of the Exchequer; the issues of monopoly and corporatism emerged as key drivers of politicisation in early modern England.

In this era of corporatism, patents and charters were granted to syndicates, companies, and individuals with increased intensity, clashing with pre-existent charters and established corporate bodies. Many subjects found themselves affected by monopoly policy, from alehousekeepers who were unfortunate enough to face the wrath of Mompesson, to clothworkers who sought charters to protect their interests. This policy led not only to the establishment of new institutions for overseas trade but also to domestic livery companies in both the metropolis and the localities. Often, the Statute of Monopolies has been seen as creating a loophole in its exemption of corporations from its purview, allowing the introduction of monopolistic schemes disguised as corporations in Charles's reign.[2] However, even before its passing, a host of companies were created, generating dialogues centred on the distinction between monopoly and legitimate corporation. Requests for charters gave rise to new disputes, whilst also infusing long-standing conflicts with new arguments centred around accusations of monopoly. These processes served to unsettle already unclear boundaries between monopoly and legitimate corporation, whilst myriad groups including glovers and leather dressers in the suburbs, glassmakers and starchmakers in London, and weavers in Wiltshire were exposed to, and engaged with, anti-monopoly discourses. Ideas of private interest and of restrictions to customary rights saturated complaints, whilst cries for 'free trade' were articulated. Amidst these calls were equally powerful demands for order and regulation, as appeals to corporatism remained strong.

This era of monopoly contributed to the politicisation of various subsets of subjects who were drawn into the political process. As Andy Wood demonstrates in his analysis of Derbyshire lead miners, popular politics existed in conflicts over customs and resources, and between interest groups.[3] Similarly, this book has identified a popular politics in the plethora of conflicts and alliances in different industries, contests which were driven by concerns with corporatism and monopoly. As the de-centralised state intruded on livelihoods through commissions, corporations, and patentees, negotiations between subjects and authority were increasingly necessary, and petitioning emerged as central for these dialogues.

By delving into these vibrant cases, larger insights into the processes and spaces where politicisation occurred, and the types of subjects exposed to them, have been gleaned. In London, freemen were brought into negotiations and discussions of proposed projects through commissions and via the Court of Aldermen. From the Brewers who were consulted on Drake's patent by Alderman Radcliffe, to the glovers and leather dressers who sought relief from their leatherselling brethren, these subjects were given a voice in affairs. Some petitioning subjects had the finances and connections to launch protest; they were not all members of the labouring poor. Thus, Isaac Bungard was able to supply London markets with glass well before Mansell's patent and was frequently described as using his monetary resources to finance campaigns. However, such subjects were still those usually pushed out of formal systems of policy-making, and thus, the ability of Bungard to campaign tirelessly with other glassmakers and glaziers to free the industry from Mansell's influence remains noteworthy.

Other campaigns were launched by members of London's livery companies, the yeomanry and livery, drawing on the resources of the wider company. The retailing grocers who fought both the Starchmakers' and the Apothecaries' Companies were able to use the Company chest whilst also attaining the support of the Lord Mayor and aldermen. By contrast, we have also met petitioners who conducted their activity outside of the auspices of company organisation. Jane Newe, Mary Fitche, Elizabeth Cockren, and Anne Mitchell, female spinners and apprentices, were drawn into Parliament by their monopoly concerns. For them and so many others, the effects of monopolies on their very livelihoods pushed them into the political process, in this case, directly into the chambers of Westminster. More widely and outside of the city, cutlers and knife-makers in Hallamshire, shopkeepers in Southampton, and clothiers in Wiltshire used petitions to push for, or challenge, economic policy. The issues of monopoly and corporatism fostered discontent and facilitated active dialogues beyond the metropolis, challenging previous assertions that in rural areas, patents made only 'rare appearances' and often had positive economic effects.[4]

Appearing frequently in these battles were clothmakers and clothiers. As Rollison has argued, participants in the trade were active lobbyists, and perceptions that they constituted a national interest triggered anxieties over their capacity to rise.[5] By 1642, clothiers and clothworkers were well integrated into a parliamentary political culture, persuaded by a popular anti-popery and by their experiences of yet another economic depression.[6] As Walter demonstrates, clothworkers articulated reasons for economic distress which were larger than concerns with the actions of their own employers.[7] This book has revealed that the emergence and development of a shared industrial interest amongst clothiers and even clothworkers was well underway, and indeed enhanced, by the late Jacobean period. This process was quickened not only by industrialisation but by the co-existence of both economic depression and monopoly policy. The latter caused clothiers to join, lamenting the effects of the Adventurers' new charter of 1617, but it also allowed clothworkers in areas like Reading, Bury, and Ipswich to reach for their own charters, triggering local 'conflicts of concessionary interest'.[8] The depression also heightened these processes as the appointment of specific commissions to hear their demands allowed clothiers a space to link their own problems with those affecting the wider realm, paving the way for their ability to join their own issues with wider, national problems by the 1640s. Again, this included a variety of subjects – from richer clothiers like Peregrine and Acton in Ipswich to poor weavers and spinners who scribbled their marks to petitions in Calne, Bromham, and Chippenham.

Where were people politicised, and in what sorts of spaces? This book has revealed the importance of commissions, both temporary and permanent, as a central aspect of crown financial policy. Whilst commissioners were experts drawn from within government and high-city circles, they collected information from a wider remit of subjects, beyond leading city merchants. Both the temporary and permanent Commissions for Trade facilitated the breaking down of county boundaries as clothiers were brought together to discuss problems in trade. Even temporary commissions such as the Commission for Glass created new points of contact for petitioning activity. Supplications were an important tool of governance, recognised as essential for the investigation of economic issues. The very process of investigating patents and projects was also highly participatory, offering opportunities for the advice of interested parties to be gleaned. The city authorities frequently received petitions in support or opposition from affected companies and subjects. In 1613, the Commissioners for Suits informed the city that they had received petitions from nail makers, blacksmiths, and shipmasters in support of a proposed patent to restrain the import of iron rods.[9] They requested that the city call before them the companies of Blacksmiths, Ironmongers, Carpenters, and the Masters and brethren of Trinity House to attest to its validity. This was just one of many examples of the ways in which subjects were brought into contact with the processes of government, allowing proposed policy to be negotiated and discussed more widely. Ultimately, this needs to be recognised as another part of the decentralised nature of the English state. Whilst subjects were vexed by patentees and their deputies, this very same system also saw a reliance on the advice and opinions of merchants, craftsmen, and artisans. Petitions were an integral aspect of England's participatory government, a recognised and necessary means through which subjects with knowledge of trade could advise on policy. Zaret has argued that these forms of petition were not a tool for protest, but an 'instrument of state', a means of administration to aid in the deployment of power.[10] It is possible to see them as both: a means by which subjects could negotiate with authorities, in a way which also saw them question the uses of prerogative power and its effect on local societies.

A range of spaces facilitated debate and activity beyond such central institutions. Crucial were livery company halls, where attendance at court meetings allowed members to present their demands and work with lawyers to produce supplications. As Archer and Ward have shown, company members frequently used petitions to inform leaders of their grievances.[11] In turn, they learned the processes necessary for engaging in this form of political action, which enabled them to move outside of their companies to produce collective petitions against monopolies. Thus, members of the Glaziers' Company could move against fellow brethren in the industry to petition Parliament against Mansell in 1621, whilst leather dressers and glovers were able to produce their petitions in support of Darcy, and for their own separate incorporation, despite the protests of their larger Company. Meanwhile, taverns provided an informal location where artisan skinners could pen petitions for a new charter, whilst local spaces such as Temple Hall in Wiltshire or the Crown in Sudbury allowed clothiers to meet with JPs and discuss the depression. Even the church was a political space; weavers in Reading were informed of the appointment of clothier overseers at Sunday services in 1623, whilst the Lords proposed that thanksgiving sermons announcing Mompesson's arrest be delivered throughout the realm. In the metropolis, Blackwell Hall was a key space where clothiers gathered and where news was spread, and more widely, the volume of government proclamations on monopolies brought information on developments in the industry to subjects. A variety of spaces beyond the Council and Parliament saw discussion of trade, allowing new alliances to be crafted, such as between clothiers and the Staplers, or between Eastland merchants and clothiers in Ipswich.

The petitions studied throughout this book were far from simple requests from deferent subjects to paternalistic authorities. Rather, they were part of broader dialogic cultures in which manuscript petitions were copied and circulated to interested parties, triggering the penning of counter-petitions and rebuttals. These documents were transmitted more widely than to the specific authority addressed, even if they were not as mobile as the large, printed documents which emerged during the Civil Wars. They demonstrate the blurred boundary between what one might constitute as a 'private' and a 'public' petition in an age where even specific industrial concerns could see petitioners reflect on larger political and constitutional issues.[12] This process of forwarding petitions amongst a limited circle of recipients facilitated a participatory culture, drawing other interest groups into debates as many were only too eager to defend themselves from accusations of misconduct. The survival of economic petitions in the papers of such figures as Sir Thomas Jervoise and Sir Robert Phelips attests to the production and circulation of these suits amongst MPs. Even if they were not printed, petitions could still be semi-mobile documents, tapped into larger networks of communication.

Company court records provide an important window into the mechanics of petitioning activity, revealing the centrality of lawyers and scribes, whilst also showing the ways through which aggrieved parties participated in the formation of their own complaints. Not all appeals to the law or custom were added by lawyers, and even the choice of legal counsel could be a deliberate strategy to infuse complaints with powerful arguments. Further, wardens' accounts reveal that some company members funded their own petitioning campaigns. Records from local archives also provide a tantalising glimpse into the processes through which clothiers met to discuss their demands, though there is certainly more room for future research to trace this political activism at a local level in what was an important period of economic change.

Just how successful were these petitioning campaigns? As we have seen, the degree of success petitioners achieved varied from campaign to campaign. Like lobbying activity more broadly, connections at Court and in Parliament greatly contributed to petitioners's successes. However, the variety of alliances made to promote or challenge patents meant that this was not always enough to guarantee success, and just as important was the degree of anxiety amongst authorities about the threat of popular unrest. In the 1590s, the city's relentless campaign against the leather sealing monopoly, combined with the Council's fear of the 'many-headed monster', ensured its cancellation in full. Later in the 1620s, clothiers in Suffolk, Oxfordshire, and Gloucestershire had vital backing from local JPs when questioning the Adventurers' monopoly. This, combined with a long-standing fear of unrest in the clothing counties, was enough to persuade the King and Council to appoint the temporary Commission for Trade. Concern that unruly clothworkers and clothiers in Bury and Ipswich had created monopolistic bodies saw their brief experiments in company organisation end. Other anti-monopoly petitioners had less success. The Grocers' failure to secure the cancellation of the Starchmakers' charter, despite Lord Mayor Rowe's support, was likely due to the involvement of powerful courtiers in the scheme. Only the concern with wheat supplies saw this corporation dissolved, something which again was generated by fears of potential disorder.

Petitioners sometimes found success in some institutions where they failed in others. The willingness of subjects to approach the same bodies on multiple occasions allows us an important glimpse into their own perceptions of the political process, and reflections on the values of certain spaces.[13] Thus, whilst the glassmakers successfully persuaded the Commons of their plight in 1614 and 1621, they were ultimately unable to overcome Mansell's domineering influence. Despite the time and effort Bungard and his allies spent petitioning, they continued to see supplicating Parliament as their best option for triggering change, revealing their own ideological perceptions of the role of the Commons as a protector of trades and liberties.

Beyond individual campaigns, it is helpful to think about the cumulative impact of this petitioning agitation. Time and again, anti-monopoly petitioning caused the Crown to announce changes in monopoly policy. Both Elizabeth and James used proclamations to cancel odious grants, whilst James also made the desire to rid the realm of monopolists a keynote of the first year of his reign. Whilst both monarchs ultimately continued to utilise this fiscal device, they had been forced to respond to public opinion. The eventual passage of the Statute of Monopolies stands as a pertinent example of the success continued agitation could have.

Petitioning affected political processes, generating institutional effects, and shaping the state from below.[14] It became easier for subjects to petition parliamentary standing committees across our period, and new institutions like the Commissions for Glass and for Trade were intended to hear petitions. Both were established to deal with clashes created by monopoly policy. In the former case, this involved contests between the Scottish and English glass patents. In the latter, it was expected that complaints against merchant companies would be articulated, allowing groups like the Staplers to contest the Adventurers' charter. Economic petitions were a powerful force, pushing the Crown and Council to create new spaces which only further contributed to the processes of politicisation outlined above. The establishment of these commissions demonstrates James and his Council's efforts to maintain a degree of consensus to contain trading disputes. However, by creating these bodies, yet more avenues were opened for the articulation of industrial disputes through dialogic petitioning campaigns. Appeals to them allowed subjects to engage with contentious issues as their ideological views emerged and developed.

This book has illuminated the practices of economic petitioning activity, enhancing our understanding of political culture at the turn of the century through an analysis heavily based on manuscript sources. The varied campaigns explored throughout this book have also shown the importance of including an analysis of language and discourse to this agenda and to our understandings of both late Elizabethan and early Stuart politics. Doing so allows insight into the degree to which conflict or consensus prevailed, especially within London. As Ashton has argued, the monopoly issue triggered conflicts of interest in numerous trades, generating transient alliances and fissures between the city and the Court and between and within companies.[15] Even below the level of business elites, the city was marked by a web of interconnections and alliances which were constantly shifted, negotiated, and contested. Thus, artisans like glovers and feltmakers proved capable of allying with courtiers, and physical spaces in the city like Blackwell Hall or Haberdashers' Hall (home of the permanent Commission for Trade) facilitated the making of broader alliances between clothiers from different counties. Language was a crucial way through which merchants and artisans tried to garner support from fellow subjects and the authorities. This discourse ultimately provides an important window into the values and ideas shaping political and economic culture within the metropolis. Even if they were not engaged in attempts to mobilise a wider body of public opinion, we can still see how different interest groups used similar discourses to present their rival 'truth claims', and their own perceptions of their rights and liberties.[16] Their petitions were heavily based around the language of rights, customs, and the city freedom, whilst the cries of opponents were shrouded in lamentations of corruption, collusion, and conspiracy.

At times, language was crafted and adapted to suit specific contextual circumstances. As such, complaints of poverty and beggary pervaded suits in the 1590s, as petitioners appealed both to authorities' concern with vagrancy and to their paternalistic duties to subjects. From 1603, references to James's perceived anti-monopoly agenda permeated petitions, and by 1621, the rhetoric of free trade was used as subjects sought to protect trades from undue interference.

Discourse was tailored, often tactically, yet underpinning this were genuine beliefs in the importance of rights to trade. These utterances, whilst sometimes tactical, were not always so. They represented real beliefs in the importance of such values as no taxation without consent and the unique privileges bestowed by the freedom, beliefs which caused supplicants to relentlessly fight their causes and even to face imprisonment for the same.

Subjects engaged with important issues of liberty and prerogative, acquiring crucial experience tackling the very same issues which would be pertinent during Charles's Personal Rule. This allowed their ideological beliefs to develop, ultimately leading to a range of subjects already well-versed in discourses of liberty and well-acquainted with the experience of protecting property in the face of arbitrary encroachments by 1625.

A recurring theme throughout our analysis has been that of social status; the 'language of sorts' permeated petitions.[17] Allegations that supplications had been presented by the 'meaner sort', or that new corporate bodies consisted of base and 'mechanical' men were common to campaigns. This was a concern in many ways designed to alarm authorities. The Leathersellers presented the glovers and leather dressers' potential incorporation as a dangerous precedent to 'all the Mechanick trades about London', the consequences of which could not be foreseen.[18] By contrast, the 'better sort' of tradesmen opposed the project.[19] This accusation was levied especially against new corporations of craftsmen, reflecting an awareness that the granting of charters to these institutions could instil them with significant powers of self-government. In a decentralised state, the existence of overlapping jurisdictions and forms of government meant the chartering of new companies could be seen as posing a threat to pre-existing companies and their systems of governance. Combining this with allegations of seditious campaigns spearheaded by named individuals was a useful way for opponents to question their legitimacy without undermining the entire corporate system. It also reveals that the boundaries between accepted and seditious petitioning, despite prescriptions in such documents as the *Book of Bounty*, were far from clear. This allowed rivals to present their foes as clamorous petitioners, repeatedly deploying this as an accusation in different contexts.

Despite the existence of conflicts in industries, disputes were ultimately articulated through shared discourses, showing the existence of consensus on such issues as property, the status of the freedom, and the value of customs. They also reveal the importance of such language for London's citizens. As explored in Chapter 1, Withington has argued for the importance of notions of 'civitas' for corporate speech and behaviour.[20] The petitions explored throughout this book show that ideas of the custom of London, the sanctity of oaths, and concerns with bondage, slavery, and tyranny were common to many supplications and articulated by subjects including retailers, weavers, and merchants. These sentiments were an essential aspect of the worldview and everyday lives of citizens, discourses learned in spaces such as the Guildhall, Common Council, and company halls.

On the issue of economic regulation, petitioners revealed their ability to articulate powerful ideas on how industries should be governed. This was clearly a source of debate and discussion throughout our period. The 1620s witnessed changes in economic ideas; money lending began to be accepted, 'improvement' rather than moral economy became a key driver of projects, and new theories like mercantilism flourished.[21] Pennington has argued that the previous Tudor consensus on economic policy had broken.[22] Many subjects called for a free trade, though as we have seen, for groups like the Staplers this was often tactical, whilst the clothiers who articulated these requests still sought forms of government regulation. Older ideas still endured. Slack has revealed that the values of charity and justice survived even as notions of improvement were articulated.[23] This was embodied in the Commission for Trade: it had the power to review the ordinances of companies, but it was still envisaged that they would remain pivotal for the organisation of trade. A consensus on the need for order and regulation endured. As such, groups like the Drapers or the Hallamshire cutlers could base their appeals for authority in the language of corporatism, which remained a powerful discourse.

However, within this broad framework, there was some dispute and debate as to *how* this desired order and regulation should be maintained in practice. In many ways, this is similar to Sommerville's assertion that, despite a broad desire to protect the English constitution, there were ideological divisions as to what this actually entailed in the early Stuart period.[24] For some individuals, like Walter Morrell, the erection of new clothing corporations was the only way to regulate the new drapery trade. For others, regulation through new statutes or officials was a necessity. Bodies like the Staplers believed wholeheartedly in corporatism but saw themselves as necessary figures in the cloth export trade. It was broadly accepted that monopolies were harmful in comparison to legitimate corporate bodies, a principle enshrined in the Statute of Monopolies. However, this definition was not fully fixed. As such, despite a broad agreement that monopolies were detrimental, the issue of what constituted a monopoly was still unclear, and it was this that triggered conflicts. As scholars have noted, the lack of a concrete definition of monopoly and exemption of corporate bodies in the statute allowed dubious bodies to be created well into Charles's reign.[25] Meanwhile, the corporate principle was to remain an enduring aspect of economic life, sitting uneasily beside this concern with monopolistic practices.[26] Ultimately, the monopoly issue raised real questions about how to organise trade at a time when new economic ideas, and new mercantile elites, were emerging and older perceptions of the need for regulation and the public good endured. These debates were engaged in not only by economic theorists, but by clothiers and artisans through petitions.

The net result of this activity was profound, bringing more subjects into active dialogues and negotiations with government as they moved to discuss not only their own hardships, but issues of prerogative power, liberties, and even national economic woes. This book has revealed that economic issues were a key feature of the pre-revolutionary public sphere, triggered especially by the age of monopoly between 1590 and 1625.[27] This generated new and loud discussions on trade and industry and pushed many to engage in political processes. Whilst the early 1620s have been seen as a period of development in economic thought, this book has shown that economic issues were widely discussed and facilitated political engagement even before the economic depression.[28] The pressures created by monopolies meant that a plethora of subjects, through their petitions and local trading conflicts, were discussing issues of regulation, customary rights, and corporatism much earlier, albeit in different ways from economic theorists such as Mun and Misselden. By the early 1620s, clothiers, Staplers, and the Drapers were able to link their concerns to broader national debates on economic regulation.

Hitherto, the discussion of political economy has been seen as a key feature of the post-Revolutionary public sphere as changing perceptions of wealth and trade necessitated the spread of economic information.[29] However, if we move to broaden our understandings of political economy to also consider how the day-to-day 'politics of trade' facilitated participation, then the role of economics in the late Elizabethan and early Stuart public sphere becomes evident.[30] In Bellany's model of the pre-revolutionary public sphere, a wider justification for the involvement of subjects in political discussion is seen as absent between 1610 and 1630.[31] However, as Slack notes, in the sphere of trade, the consultation of subjects appears to have become an accepted part of political practice.[32]

Ultimately, more attention needs to be paid to the role of economics in early modern popular politics. As Walter has argued, issues of religion, society, culture, and economics were far from 'discrete' subjects in the minds of contemporaries.[33] Customs, local politics and economic conditions in the lead industry were important for dictating the Civil War allegiances of miners, whilst clothworkers in Colchester remained concerned with issues in trade alongside their concern with popery in the 1640s.[34] These earlier anti-monopoly petitioning campaigns have similarly revealed the necessity of centring economic issues in analyses of late Elizabethan and early Stuart politics. Economic spaces, alliances, and ideas were key to politicisation and engagement, and for many subjects, just as pressing as concerns with religion or foreign policy. There is thus greater scope to analyse the 'politics of trade', particularly at the level of the corporation and locality, to further our understandings of the depth of political engagement and processes of decision-making, building on studies which have focused on reactions to particularly unpopular forms of taxation such as impositions, Ship Money, or the Forced Loan.[35] Just as 'new' social history has examined the interconnections between local conflicts, cultures, and economic relationships, it is necessary to integrate economic institutions and issues into our understandings of the development of a wider popular political culture. 'New political history' has similarly turned to include an analysis of linguistics and examination of a wider source base to understand political culture.[36] It is high time that scholars move towards advancing this further, to create a 'new economic history' which integrates economic realities and a study of discourse into analyses of subjects' perceptions of, and interactions with, high political culture and the realm of 'popular politics'. In this era of corporatism, the 'politics of trade' became charged with a new set of issues, creating contests, fissures, and alliances as subjects moved to bemoan the 'sores' inflicting a body politic vexed by bloodsuckers of the commonwealth.

## Notes

1 TNA, SP 14/116, f. 20v.
2 C. R. Kyle, '"But a New Button to an Old Coat": The Enactment of the Statute of Monopolies, 21 James 1 cap. 3', *Journal of Legal History*, 19:3 (1998), pp. 203–23.
3 Wood, *Social Conflict*, p. 254; Robson, 'Edges of Governance', p. 172.
4 Thirsk, 'Projects for Gentlemen', p. 286.
5 Rollison, 'Discourse', pp. 176, 187.
6 Walter, *Colchester Plunderers*, p. 284 and ch. 8. Ed Legon is currently producing important work on this topic, and I am grateful to him for permission to cite his paper, E. Legon, '"Rebells By Their Trade?" Revisiting Clothmaking and Parliamentarianism' (unpublished paper, delivered 24 April 2023, Britain in Revolution Seminar, University of Oxford).
7 Walter, *Colchester Plunderers*, p. 270.
8 Ashton, 'Conflicts'.
9 TLA, COL/RMD/PA/01/003, fos 100r–101r, 104r.
10 Zaret, 'Liminal Petitioning', p. 433.
11 Archer, *Pursuit*, ch. 4; Ward, *Metropolitan Communities*, ch. 4.
12 Waddell and Peacey, 'Introduction', p. 9.
13 *Ibid.*, p. 16.
14 *Ibid.*, p. 18.
15 Ashton, 'Conflicts'.
16 M. Braddick, 'Mobilisation, Anxiety and Creativity in England during the 1640s', in J. Morrow and J. Scott (eds), *Liberty, Authority, Formality: Political Ideas and Culture, 1600–1900. Essays in Honour of Colin Davis* (Exeter, 2008), pp. 233–56.
17 K. Wrightson, '"Sorts of People" in Tudor and Stuart England', in J. Barry and C. W. Brooks (eds), *The Middling Sort of People: Culture, Society, and Politics in England, 1550–1800* (Hampshire, 1994), pp. 28–50.

18 BL, Add. MS 12,504, fo. 158r.
19 *Ibid.*, fo. 159r.
20 Withington, *Politics.*
21 D. Pennington, 'Beyond the Moral Economy: Economic Change, Ideology and the 1621 House of Commons', *Parliamentary History*, 25:2 (2006) p. 230; N. L. Jones, *God and the Moneylenders: Usury and the Law in Early Modern England* (Oxford, 1989), p. 204; A. McRae, *God Speed the Plough: The Representation of Agrarian England, 1500–1660* (Cambridge, 1996), pp. 7, 18 and ch. 5; P. Slack, *The Invention of Improvement: Information and Material Progress in Seventeenth-Century England* (Oxford, 2014), ch 3.
22 Pennington, 'Moral Economy', p. 230.
23 Slack, *Improvement*, pp. 88–9.
24 Sommerville, *Royalists and Patriots*, p. 3.
25 Asch, 'The Revival of Monopolies', pp. 357–92.
26 Malament, '"Economic Liberalism"', p. 1354.
27 Bellany, 'Railing Rhymes', p. 1153.
28 Slack, *Improvement*, p. 82.
29 Pincus, 'State and Civil Society', p. 213.
30 Lake and Pincus, 'Public Sphere', p. 21.
31 Bellany, 'Railing Rhymes', p. 1154.
32 Slack, 'Political Economy', p. 65.
33 Walter, *Colchester Plunderers*, p. 8.
34 Wood, *Social Conflict*, pp. 254, 269; Walter, *Colchester Plunderers*, ch. 8. Sacks has demonstrated the importance of larger disputes between Bristol and the Merchant Venturers' Company for Civil War allegiances see Sacks, *Widening Gate*, ch. 7.
35 Walter, *Colchester Plunderers*, p. 314
36 Bellany, 'Railing Rhymes', p. 1141.

# Bibliography

## Manuscript sources


### *Bodleian Libraries, Oxford*

MS Bankes 11/2: Documents relating to patents, 1634–1635.
MS Bankes 12: Documents relating to charters, 1631–1640.
MS North A. 2: Miscellaneous Papers of Sir Julius Caesar, 1603–25.

### *Clothworkers' Company, London*

CL/B/1/4: Court Orders, 1605–23.

### *Drapers' Company, London*

WA6/1–4: Wardens' Accounts, 1604–1607.
WA7/5–7: Wardens' Accounts, 1621–1623.
WA8/1–2: Wardens' Accounts, 1623–1625.
Court Minutes and Records, 1603–1642.

### *Guildhall Library, London*

CLC/L/GH/D/001/MS11571/008–010: Grocers' Company Wardens' Accounts, 1601–1622.
CLC/L/GH/B/001/MS11588/001–003: Grocers' Company Court Orders, 1556–1639.
CLC/L/BF/B/001/MS05445/009: Brewers' Company Court Book, 1590–1597.
CLC/L/BF/D/001/MS05442/005: Brewers' Company Wardens' Accounts, 1582–1616.
CLC/L/SE/B/001/MS30708/001–002: Skinners' Company Court Books, 1551–1617.
CLC/L/SE/D/007/MS30727/004: Skinners' Company Wardens' Accounts, 1564–1596.

### *Hampshire Archives, Winchester*

44M69/G2: Political Papers, Sir Thomas Jervoise (1588–1654).
44M69/G3: Justices of Peace, Hampshire.
44M69/L37: Jervoise Papers, Sherfield Family: Mayor of Salisbury letters.
44M69/L38: Jervoise Papers, Salisbury, Wiltshire Sessions and Assizes.
44M69/L39: Jervoise Papers, Sherfield Family, Parliamentary Papers.

### *Hatfield House, Hertfordshire*

CP, The Cecil Papers.

### *Institute of Historical Research, London*

Whitelocke Papers VIII, Microfilm XR 54/5.

### *Leathersellers' Hall, London*

GOV 1/1: Court Minute Books.
Liber Curtes II: Wardens' Accounts and Inventories, 1584–1647.

### *Parliamentary Archives, Westminster*

#### *House of Lords, Main Papers*

HL/PO/JO/10/1/9.
HL/PO/JO/10/1/14.
HL/PO/JO/10/1/15.
HL/PO/JO/10/1/19.
HL/PO/JO/10/1/21.
HL/PO/JO/10/1/22.
HL/PO/JO/10/1/27.
HL/PO/JO/10/1/57.
HL/PO/JO/10/1/62.
HL/PO/JO/10/1/67.
HL/PO/JO/10/1/68.
HL/PO/JO/10/1/120.

#### *House of Lords, Main Papers (Parchment Collection)*

HL/PO/JO/10/2/2B.

#### *House of Lords, Main Papers Supplementary*

HL/PO/JO/10/13/7.
HL/PO/JO/10/13/9.

### *Suffolk Archives, Bury St Edmunds Branch*

BRO D9/1/1/A: Charter to Clothiers, Clothworkers, Weavers and Tailors' Company.
BRO D9/1/1/B: Ordinances.
BRO D9/1/1/C: Petition of objection.

### *Somerset Archives and Local Studies, Somerset*

DD PH/222/99–108: Phelips' Manuscripts.

### *The British Library, London*

Additional MS 10038: Papers of Sir Julius Caesar.
Additional MS 12496: Papers of Sir Julius Caesar.
Additional MS 34324: Papers of Sir Julius Caesar.
Additional MS 39245: Letter book of JPs.
Cotton MS Cleopatra F VI: Collections of Sir Robert Cotton relating to the revenues of the Crown.
Cotton MS Faustina C II: Collections of Sir Robert Cotton.
Cotton MS Galba E/1: Records and Papers concerning England, Germany and the Low Countries, 1603–1614.
Cotton Titus B/IV: Records and Papers relating to Royal Revenues.
Cotton Titus B/V: Records and Papers relating to Treaties, Musters, Loans and Projects.
Hargrave MS 321.
Harleian 6803: Alford Papers.
Harleian 1996.
Lansdowne MS 56, 62, 67, 69, 71, 73, 74, 152, 162, 487.
Stowe MS 354.

### *The London Archives, London*

#### *Court of Common Council*

COL/CC/01/01/024: February 1591–April 1595.
COL/CC/01/01/025: May 1595–September 1598.
COL/CC/01/01/028: February 1605–August 1609.
COL/CC/01/01/031: March 1616–September 1619.
COL/CC/01/01/032: August 1619–August 1621.
COL/CC/01/01/033: June 1622–June 1624.

#### *Remembrancia*

COL/RMD/PA/01/001–006: Remembrancia vols 1–6.

*Repertories of the Court of Aldermen*

COL/CA/01/01/024: November 1588–October 1592.
COL/CA/01/01/025: November 1592–October 1596.
COL/CA/01/01/026: November 1596–October 1599.
COL/CA/01/01/027: November 1599–July 1602.
COL/CA/01/01/028: July 1602–February 1604.
COL/CA/01/01/029: February 1604–April 1605.
COL/CA/01/01/030: April 1605–March 1607.
COL/CA/01/01/031: March 1607–March 1609.
COL/CA/01/01/036: November 1614–October 1616.
COL/CA/01/01/039: November 1620–October 1621.
COL/CA/01/01/041: November 1622–October 1623.

*The National Archives, London*

SP 12: State Papers Domestic, Elizabeth I.
SP 14: State Papers Domestic, James I.
SP 15: State Papers Domestic, Edward VI–James I: Addenda.
SP 16: State Papers Domestic, Charles I.
SP 46: State Papers Domestic: Supplementary.

*West Yorkshire Archives, Leeds*

WYL100/PO/6/XI/1–6: Temple Newsam Family and Estate Records: Legal Papers, Deeds, and Accounts: Starch.

*Wiltshire and Swindon History Centre, Chippenham*

G23/1/248: Salisbury Guild Records and ordinances.
G23/1/3: Salisbury City Ledgers, 1571–1640.

## Printed sources

*By the Queene. A Proclamation for the Reformation of Many Abuses and Misdemeanours*... (London, 1601).

Carr, C. T., *Select Charters of Trading Companies: A.D. 1530–1707* (2 vols, London, 1913), i.

*Chancery: Patent Rolls (C 66): Calendar and Index 1 & 2 Jas I*, ed. List and Index Soc., vol. 97 (Kew, 1974).

*Chancery: Patent Rolls (C 66): Calendar and Index 3–5 Jas I*, ed. List and Index Soc., vol. 98 (Kew, 1974).

*Chancery: Patent Rolls (C 66): Calendar and Index 6 Jas I*, ed. List and Index Soc., vol. 109 (Kew, 1975).

*Chancery: Patent Rolls (C 66): Calendar and Index 7 Jas I*, ed. List and Index Soc., vol. 121 (Kew, 1976).

*Chancery: Patent Rolls (C 66): Calendar and Index 9 Jas I*, ed. List and Index Soc., vol. 133 (Kew, 1977).

*Chancery: Patent Rolls (C 66): Calendar and Index 10–11 Jas I*, ed. List and Index Soc., vol. 134 (Kew, 1977).

*Chancery: Patent Rolls (C 66): Calendar and Index 12 Jas I*, ed. List and Index Soc., vol. 157 (Kew, 1979).

*Chancery: Patent Rolls (C 66): Calendar and Index 13 Jas I*, ed. List and Index Soc., vol. 164 (Kew, 1980).

Dasent, J. R. (ed.), *Acts of the Privy Council of England, New Series* (46 vols, 1890–1964), vols 20–39.

Dendy, F. W. (ed.), *Extracts from the Records of the Company of Hostmen of Newcastle-upon-Tyne* (Edinburgh, 1901).

Foster, E. R. (ed.), *Proceedings in Parliament, 1610* (2 vols, New Haven, 1966).

Green, M. A. E. (ed.), *Calendar of State Papers Domestic: James I: 1603–1610* (London, 1857–59).

Guilding, J. M. (ed.), *Reading Records: Diary of the Corporation* (4 vols, London, 1892–1896), ii.

*Her Maiesties Most Princelie Answere, Deliuered by her Selfe at the Court at White-hall...* (London, 1601).

Hinds, A. B. (ed.), *Calendar of State Papers Relating to English Affairs in the Archives of Venice* (37 vols, London, 1864–1947), xvii.

Historical Manuscripts Commission, *The Manuscripts of Lincoln, Bury St. Edmund's and Great Grimsby Corporations; And of the Deans and Chapters of Worcester and Lichfield, &c.* (Fourteenth Report, Appendix, Part VIII) (London, 1895).

Historical Manuscripts Commission, *Calendar of the Manuscripts of Major-General Lord Sackville preserved at Knole, Sevenoaks*, ed. A. P. Newton (2 vols, London, 1940), i.

Historical Manuscripts Commission, *Royal Commission on Historical Manuscripts: Report on the Additional Estate Papers of the Clavell and Mansel Families of Smedmore 1516–1874*, eds J. P. Ferris and E. Allen (London, 1977).

Jansson, M. (ed.), *Proceedings in Parliament 1614 (House of Commons)* (Philadelphia, 1988).

*Journal of the House of Commons: Volume I, 1547–1629* (London, 1802), *British History Online*, https://www.british-history.ac.uk/commons-jrnl/vol1 (accessed 27 September 2024).

*Journal of the House of Lords: Volume III, 1620–1628* (London, 1767–1830), *British History Online*, https://www.british-history.ac.uk/lords-jrnl/vol3 (accessed 27 September 2024).

Larkin, J. F. and Hughes, P. L. (eds), *Stuart Royal Proclamations* (2 vols, Oxford, 1973–83).

Martin R., *A Speach Deliuered to the Kings Most Excellent Maiestie...* (London, 1603).

Neal, S. R. (ed.), *Calendar of Patent Rolls 30 Elizabeth I (1587–1588): C 66/1304–1321* (Kew: List and Index Soc., vol. 297, 2003).

Neal, S. R. and Leighton, C. (eds), *Calendar of Patent Rolls 36 Elizabeth I (1593–1594): C 66/1405–1424* (Kew: List and Index Soc., vol. 309, 2005).

Notestein, W., Relf, F. H. and Simpson, H. (eds), *Commons Debates 1621* (7 vols, New Haven, 1935).

*Proceedings and Debates of the House of Commons in 1620 and 1621* (2 vols, Oxford, 1766), I, *Eighteenth Century Collections Online* (accessed 9 July 2020).

*Proceedings in Parliament 1624: The House of Commons,* ed. P. Baker (London, 2015–2018), *British History Online*, https://www.british-history.ac.uk/no-series/proceedings-1624-parl (accessed 27 September 2024).

*Proceedings in the Parliaments of Elizabeth I*, ed. T. E. Hartley (3 vols, London, 1995), iii.

Smith, C., Watt, H., Neal, S. R. and Leighton, C. (eds), *Calendar of Patent Rolls 40 Elizabeth I (1597–98): Part I (Calendar) C 66/1477–1492* (Kew, List and Index Soc., vol. 326, 2009).

Tawney, R. H. and Power, E. (eds), *Tudor Economic Documents* (3 vols, London, 1924), ii.

Thirsk, J. and Cooper, J. P. (eds), *Seventeenth-Century Economic Documents* (Oxford, 1972).

*The Charter of Incorporation of the Burgh of Bury St Edmund* (Bury, 1810), http://www.stedmundsburychronicle.co.uk/charter1606/chart1606.htm (accessed 27 September 2024).

*The English Reports* (178 vols, 1900–32), LXXX.

*The Lord Coke his speech and charge With a discouerie of the abuses and corruption of officers* (London, 1607)

Thomas, J. H. and Fraser, J. F. (eds), *The Reports of Sir Edward Coke, Knt. In Thirteen Parts, Volume IV. Parts VII–VIII* (6 vols, London, 1826).

Willson, D. H. (ed.), *The Parliamentary Diary of Robert Bowyer 1606–1607* (Minneapolis, 1931).

## Secondary Sources

Abrams, M. A., 'English Gold and Silver Thread Monopolies, 1611–1621', *Journal of Economic and Business History*, 3:3 (1931), pp. 385–94.

Allen, D. (ed.), *Ipswich Borough Archives 1255–1835: A Catalogue* (Woodbridge, 2000).

Andrews, C. M., *British Committees, Commissions, and Councils of Trade and Plantations, 1622–1675* (Baltimore, 1908).

Appleby, J. O., *Economic Thought and Ideology in Seventeenth-Century England* (Princeton, 1978).

Archer, I. W., 'The London Lobbies in the Later Sixteenth Century', *Historical Journal*, 31:1 (1988), pp. 17–44.

Archer, I. W., *The Pursuit of Stability: Social Relations in Elizabethan London* (Cambridge, 1991).

Archer, I. W., 'The Government of London, 1500–1650', *London Journal*, 26:1 (2001), pp. 19–28.

Archer, I. W., 'Spencer, Sir John (d. 1610)', *ODNB* (Oxford, 2004), https://ezproxy-prd.bodleian.ox.ac.uk:2095/10.1093/ref:odnb/26130 (accessed 18 February 2020).

Archer, I. W., 'Rhetorics of Metropolitan Incorporation. The Dialogue between City and Crown in Elizabethan London', in A. Roullet, O. Spina and N. Szczech (eds), *Trouver sa place: Individus et communautés dans l'Europe moderne* (Madrid, 2011), pp. 153–67.

Archer, I. W., *The History of the Haberdashers' Company*, 2nd edn (Bognor Regis, 2017).

Archer, I. W., 'Royal Entries, the City of London, and the Politics of Stuart Successions', in P. Kewes and A. McRae (eds), *Stuart Succession Literature: Moments and Transformations* (Oxford, 2019), pp. 257–81.

Asch, R. G., 'The Revival of Monopolies: Court and Patronage during the Personal Rule of Charles I, 1629–1640', in R. G. Asch and A. M. Birke (eds), *Princes, Patronage, and the Nobility: The Court at the Beginning of the Modern Age c. 1450–1650* (Oxford, 1991), pp. 357–92.

Ash, E., *The Draining of the Fens: Projectors, Popular Politics, and State Building in Early Modern England* (Baltimore, 2017), chs 2–4.

Ashdown, C. H., *History of the Worshipful Company of Glaziers of the City of London, Otherwise the Company of Glaziers and Painters of Glass* (London, 1919).

Ashton, R., 'Revenue Farming under the Early Stuarts', *Economic History Review*, 8:3 (1956), pp. 310–22.

Ashton, R., 'The Parliamentary Agitation for Free Trade in the Opening Years of the Reign of James I', *Past and Present*, 38 (1967), pp. 40–55.

Ashton R., 'Conflicts of Concessionary Interest in Early Stuart England', in D. C. Coleman and F. J. Fisher (eds), *Trade, Government and Economy in Pre-Industrial England: Essays Presented to F. J. Fisher* (London, 1976), pp. 113–31.

Ashton, R., *The City and the Court 1603–1643* (Cambridge, 1979).

Ashton, R., 'Pindar, Sir Paul (1565/6–1650)', *ODNB* (2008), https://ezproxy-prd.bodleian.ox.ac.uk:2102/10.1093/ref:odnb/22291 (accessed 30 September 2024).

Baker, J., *The Reinvention of Magna Carta 1216–1616* (Cambridge, 2017).

Bateman, N., 'From Rags to Riches: Blackwell Hall and the Wool Cloth Trade, c. 1450–1790', *Post-Medieval Archaeology*, 38:1 (2004), pp. 1–15.

Bellany, A., *The Politics of Court Scandal in Early Modern England: News Culture and the Overbury Affair, 1603–1660* (Cambridge, 2002).

Bellany, A., 'Railing Rhymes Revisited: Libels, Scandals, and Early Stuart Politics', *History Compass*, 5:4 (2007), pp. 1136–79.

Bellany, A. and Cogswell, T., *The Murder of King James I* (New Haven, 2015).

Bellany, A. and McRae, A. (eds), *Early Stuart Libels*, https://www.earlystuartlibels.net (accessed 27 September 2024).

Bisson, D. R., *The Merchant Adventurers of England: The Company and the Crown, 1474–1564* (London, 1993).

Bottomley, S., 'The Origins of Trade Secrecy Law in England, 1600–1851', *Legal History*, 38:3 (2017), pp. 254–81.

Bowden, P. J., *The Wool Trade in Tudor and Stuart England* (London, 1962).

Bowie, K. and Munck, T., 'Early Modern Political Petitioning and Public Engagement in Scotland, Britain and Scandinavia, c. 1550–1795', *Parliaments, Estates and Representation*, 38:3 (2018), pp. 271–8.

Braddick, M. J., *Parliamentary Taxation in Seventeenth-Century England: Local Administration and Response* (Woodbridge, 1994).

Braddick, M. J., *The Nerves of State: Taxation and the Financing of the English State, 1558–1714* (Manchester, 1996).

Braddick, M. J., *God's Fury, England's Fire: A New History of the English Civil Wars* (London, 2008).

Braddick, M. J., 'Mobilisation, Anxiety and Creativity in England during the 1640s', in J. Morrow and J. Scott (eds), *Liberty, Authority, Formality: Political Ideas and Culture, 1600–1900. Essays in Honour of Colin Davis* (Exeter, 2008), pp. 233–56.

Braddick, M. J. and Walter, J. (eds), *Negotiating Power in Early Modern Society: Order, Hierarchy and Subordination in Britain and Ireland* (Cambridge, 2001).

Brenner, R., 'The Social Basis of English Commercial Expansion, 1550–1650', *Journal of Economic History*, 32:1 (1972), pp. 361–84.

Brenner, R., *Merchants and Revolution: Commercial Change, Political Conflict, and London's Overseas Traders, 1550–1653* (London, 2003).

Broadway, J., 'Harrington, John, First Baron Harington of Exton (1539/40–1613)', *ODNB*, https://doi.org/10.1093/ref:odnb/12327 (accessed 1 December 2020).

Brooks, C. W., *Pettyfoggers and Vipers of the Commonwealth: The 'Lower Branch' of the Legal Profession in Early Modern England* (Cambridge, 1986).

Brooks, C. W., *Law, Politics and Society in Early Modern England* (Cambridge, 2008).

Brooks, C. W., 'Apprenticeship, Social Mobility and the Middling Sort, 1550–1800', in J. Barry and C. W. Brooks (eds), *The Middling Sort of People: Culture, Society, and Politics in England, 1550–1800* (Hampshire, 1994), pp. 52–83.

Burgess, G., *The Politics of the Ancient Constitution: An Introduction to English Political Thought, 1603–1642* (Hampshire, 1992).

Calhoun, C. J., *Habermas and the Public Sphere* (Cambridge MA, 1992).

Carlin, N., 'Levelling the Liveries: Some Aspects of the Outlook of Craftsmen in the London Livery Companies of the mid-Seventeenth Century', *Middlesex Polytechnic History Journal*, 1:4 (1984), pp. 3–25.

Cavert, W. M., *The Smoke of London: Energy and Environment in the Early Modern City* (Cambridge, 2016).

Cavill, P. and Gajda, A., *Writing the History of Parliament in Tudor and Early Stuart England* (Manchester, 2018).

Chan Smith, D., 'The Beginning of History for Corporate Law: Corporate Government, Social Purpose and *The Case of Sutton's Hospital* (1612)', *Seattle University Law Review*, 45:367 (2021), pp. 367–412.

Clarkson, L. A., 'English Economic Policy in the Sixteenth and Seventeenth Centuries: The Case of the Leather Industry', *Bulletin of the Institute of Historical Research*, 38:98 (1965), pp. 149–62.

Clarkson, L. A., 'The Leather Crafts in Tudor and Stuart England', *The Agricultural History Review*, 14:1 (1966), pp. 25–39.

Clay, C. G. A., *Economic Expansion and Social Change: England 1500–1700* (2 vols, Cambridge, 1984).

Cogswell, T., *The Blessed Revolution: English Politics and the Coming of War, 1621–1624* (Cambridge, 1989).

Coleman, D. C., 'An Innovation and Its Diffusion: The 'New Draperies', *Economic History Review*, 22:3 (1969), pp. 417–29.

Collinson, P., 'The Monarchical Republic of Elizabeth I', *Bulletin of the John Rylands University Library of Manchester*, 69 (1987).

Cooper, J. P., 'Economic Regulation and the Cloth Industry in Seventeenth-Century England', *Transactions of the Royal Historical Society*, 20 (1970), pp. 73–99.

Craig, J., *Reformation, Politics, and Polemics: The Growth of Protestantism in East Anglican Market Towns, 1500–1610* (Aldershot, 2001).

Cramsie, J., 'Commercial Projects and the Fiscal Policy of James VI and I', *Historical Journal*, 43:2 (2000), pp. 345–64.

Cramsie, J., *Kingship and Crown Finance under James VI and I, 1603–1625* (Suffolk, 2002).

Croft, P., *The Spanish Company* (London, 1973).

Croft, P., 'Free Trade and the House of Commons, 1605–6', *Economic History Review*, 28:1 (1975), pp. 17–27.

Croft, P., 'Parliament, Purveyance and the City of London 1589–1608', *Parliamentary History*, 4:1 (1985), pp. 9–34.

Croft, P., 'Fresh Light on Bate's Case', *Historical Journal*, 30:3 (1987), pp. 523–39.

Croft, P., 'Parliamentary Preparations, September 1605: Robert Cecil, Earl of Salisbury on Free Trade and Monopolies', *Parliamentary History*, 6:1 (1987), pp. 127–32.

Cust, R., 'News and Politics in Early Seventeenth-Century England', *Past and Present*, 112:1 (1986), pp. 60–90.

Cust, R., 'Anti-Puritanism and Urban Politics: Charles I and Great Yarmouth', *Historical Journal*, 35:1 (1992), pp. 1–26.

Cust, R. and Hughes, A. (eds), *Conflict in Early Stuart England: Studies in Religion and Politics, 1603–1642* (London, 1989).

Dean, D., 'Public or Private? London, Leather and Legislation in Elizabethan England', *Historical Journal*, 31:3 (1988), pp. 525–48.

Dean, D., 'Pressure Groups and Lobbies in the Elizabethan and Early Jacobean Parliaments', *Parliaments, Estates and Representation*, 11:2 (1991), pp. 139–52.

Dent, C., '"Generally Inconvenient": The 1624 *Statute of Monopolies* as Political Compromise', *Melbourne University Law Review*, 33:2 (2009), pp. 415–53.

Doran, S., '1603: a Jagged Succession', *Historical Research*, 93:261 (2020), pp. 443–65.

Downs, J. S., *Civil War London: Mobilizing for Parliament, 1641–5* (Manchester, 2021).

Duckworth, H., Bowler, J. and Freeth, S., 'The Early History of Feltmaking in London 1250–1604' (London, 2013).

Duckworth, H., Bowler, J. and Freeth, S., 'The Feltmakers' Wool Adventure 1610–24' (London, 2015).

Early Modern Research Group, 'Commonwealth: The Social, Cultural, and Conceptual Contexts of an Early Modern Keyword', *Historical Journal*, 54:3 (2011), pp. 659–87.

Erikson, E., *Trade and Nation: How Companies and Politics Reshaped Economic Thought* (New York, 2021).

Ewen, M., *The Virginia Venture: American Colonisation and English Society, 1580–1660* (Philadelphia, 2022).

Fisher, F. J., 'Some Experiments in Company Organisation in the Early Seventeenth Century', *Economic History Review*, 4:2 (1933), pp. 177–94.

Foster, E. R., *The House of Lords, 1603–1649: Structure, Procedure, and the Nature of Its Business* (London, 1983).

Foster, E. R., 'The Procedure of the House of Commons against Patents and Monopolies, 1621–1624', in W. A. Aiken and B. D. Henning (eds), *Conflict in Early Stuart England: Essays in Honour of Wallace Notestein* (London, 1960), pp. 57–68.

Fox, H. G., *Monopolies and Patents: A Study of the History and Future of the Patent Monopoly* (Toronto, 1947).

Friis, A., *Alderman Cockayne's Project and the Cloth Trade: The Commercial Policy of England in Its Main Aspects* (Copenhagen, 1927).

Gadd, I. A. and Wallis, P. (eds), *Guilds, Society & Economy in London, 1450–1800* (London, 2002).

Gadd, I. A. and Wallis, P., 'Reaching Beyond the City Wall: London Guilds and National Regulation, 1500–1700', in S. R. Epstein and M. Prak (eds), *Guilds, Innovation, and the European Economy, 1400–1800* (Cambridge, 2008), pp. 288–315.

Gajda, A., 'War, Peace and Commerce and the Treaty of London (1604)', *Historical Research*, 96 (2023), pp. 459–72.

Gajda, A. and Paterson, E., 'Prosperity, Petitions, and Parliament: Peace and Economic Debate in Early Jacobean England, c. 1604–1607' (forthcoming).

Gardiner, S. R., 'On Four Letters from Lord Bacon to Christian IV King of Denmark, With Observations on the Part Taken by Him in the Grants of Monopolies Made by James I', *Archaeologia*, XLI (London, 1867), pp. 219–69.

Gauci, P., 'Mun, Thomas (bap. 1571, d. 1641)', *ODNB* (2008), https://ezproxy-prd.bodleian.ox.ac.uk:2102/10.1093/ref:odnb/19527 (accessed 9 August 2022).

Girtin, T., *The Triple Crowns: A Narrative History of the Drapers' Company, 1364–1964* (London, 1964).

Giurato, R., 'The Language of Constitutionalism and the Royal Prerogative in the English Parliament of 1593: James Morice's Speech on the *Ex Officio* Proceedings and his Constitutional Thought', *Parliamentary History*, 37:3 (2018), pp. 327–49.

Godfrey, E. S., *The Development of English Glassmaking 1560–1640* (Oxford, 1975).

Goldie, M., 'The Unacknowledged Republic: Officeholding in Early Modern England', in T. Harris (ed.), *The Politics of the Excluded, c. 1500–1850* (Basingstoke, 2001), pp. 153–94.

Gough, J. W., *The Rise of the Entrepreneur* (London, 1969).

Gould, J. D., 'The Trade Depression of the Early 1620s', *Economic History Review*, 7:1 (1954), pp. 81–90.

Gould, J. D., 'The Trade Crisis of the Early 1620's and English Economic Thought', *Journal of Economic History*, 15:2 (1955), pp. 121–33.

Grassby, R., 'The Personal Wealth of the Business Community in Seventeenth-Century England', *Economic History Review*, 23:2 (1970), pp. 220–34.

Guy, J., 'The 1590s: The Second Reign of Elizabeth I?', in J. Guy (ed.), *The Reign of Elizabeth I: Court and Culture in the Last Decade* (Cambridge, 1995), pp. 1–19.

Handley, S., 'Cotton, Sir Robert Bruce, first baronet (1571–1631)', *ODNB* (2004), https://ezproxy-prd.bodleian.ox.ac.uk:2102/10.1093/ref:odnb/6425 (accessed 9 August 2022).

Harris, T. (ed.), *The Politics of the Excluded, c. 1500–1850* (Basingstoke, 2001).

Hart, J. S., *Justice Upon Petition: The House of Lords and the Reformation of Justice 1621–1675* (London, 1991).

Hartshorne, A., *Old English Glasses: An Account of Glass Drinking Vessels in England, From Early Times to the End of the Eighteenth Century* (London, 1987).

Hasler, P. W. (ed.), *The History of Parliament: The House of Commons 1558–1603* (London, 1981).

Hatcher, J., *The History of the British Coal Industry* (5 vols, Oxford, 1993), i.

Healey, J., *The First Century of Welfare: Poverty and Poor Relief in Lancashire, 1620–1730* (Suffolk, 2014).

Heaton, G., '"The Poor Man's Petition": Anthony Atkinson and the Politics of Libel', *Huntington Library Quarterly*, 69:1 (2006), pp. 105–20.

Heaton, H., *The Yorkshire Woollen and Worsted Industries: From the Earliest Times up to the Industrial Revolution*, 2nd edn (Oxford, 1965).

Heinze, R. W., 'Proclamations and Parliamentary Protest, 1539–1610', in D. J. Guth and J. W. McKenna (eds), *Tudor Rule and Revolution: Essays for G. R. Elton from his American Friends* (Cambridge, 1982), pp. 237–60.

Herbert, W., *History of the Worshipful Company of Skinners of London, Principally Compiled From Their Own Record* (London, 1837).

Hill, C., *The World Turned Upside Down: Radical Ideas During the English Revolution* (London, 1972).

Hill, L. M., 'Sir Julius Caesar's Journal of Salisbury's First Two Months and Twenty Days as Lord Treasurer: 1608', *Historical Research*, 45:112 (1972), pp. 311–27.

Hindle, S., *The State and Social Change in Early Modern England, c. 1550–1640* (Basingstoke, 2002).

Hinton, R. W. K., *The Eastland Trade and the Common Weal in the Seventeenth Century* (Cambridge, 1959).

Holmes, C., 'Drainers and Fenmen: The Problem of Popular Political Consciousness in the Seventeenth Century', in A. Fletcher and J. Stevenson (eds), *Order and Disorder in Early Modern England* (Cambridge, 1985), pp. 166–95.

Holmes, C., 'Parliament, Liberty, Taxation, and Property', in J. H. Hexter (ed.), *Parliament and Liberty: From the Reign of Elizabeth to the English Civil War* (Stanford, 1992), pp. 122–54.

Hopper, A., Appleby, D. J., Stoyle, M. *et al.*, 'Civil War Petitions', https://www.civilwarpetitions.ac.uk (accessed 27 September 2024).

Hoyle, R. W., 'Petitioning as Popular Politics in Early Sixteenth-Century England', *Historical Research*, 75:190 (2002), pp. 365–89.

Hoyle, R. W., 'The Master of Requests and the Small change of Jacobean Patronage', *English Historical Review*, 126:520 (2011), pp. 544–81.

Hoyle, R. W., 'The Sheffield Cutlers and the Earls of Shrewsbury: A New Interpretation', in R. W. Hoyle (ed.), *Histories of People and Landscape: Essays on the Sheffield Region in Memory of David Hey* (Hatfield, 2021), pp. 25–45.

Hunting, P., *The Leathersellers' Company: A History* (London, 1994).

Johnson, A. H., *The History of the Worshipful Company of the Drapers of London* (5 vols, Oxford, 1915), iii.

Jones, N. L., *God and the Moneylenders: Usury and the Law in Early Modern England* (Oxford, 1989).

Keirn, T., 'Parliament, Legislation and the Regulation of English Textile Industries, 1689–1714', in D. Lee (ed.), *Stilling the Grumbling Hive: The Response to Social and Economic Problems in England, 1689–1750* (Stroud, 1992), pp. 1–24.

Keller, V., *The Interlopers: Early Stuart Projects and the Undisciplining of Knowledge* (Baltimore, 2023).

Kelsey, S., 'Digges, Sir Dudley (1582/3–1639)', *ODNB* (2004), https://ezproxy-prd.bodleian.ox.ac.uk:2102/10.1093/ref:odnb/7635 (accessed 9 August 2022).

Kenyon, G. H., *The Glass Industry of the Weald* (Leicester, 1967).

Kilburn-Toppin, J., *Crafting Identities: Artisan Culture in London, c. 1550–1640* (Manchester, 2021).

Kindleberger, C. P., 'The Economic Crisis of 1619 to 1623', *Journal of Economic History*, 51:1 (1991), pp. 149–75.

Knights, M., *Representation and Misrepresentation in Later Stuart Britain: Partisanship and Political Culture* (Oxford, 2005).

Knights, M., *Trust and Distrust: Corruption in Office in Britain and Its Empire, 1600–1850* (Oxford, 2021).

Kopperman, P. E., *Sir Robert Heath 1575–1649: Window on an Age* (Suffolk, 1989).

Korda, N., *Labors Lost: Women's Work and the Early Modern English Stage* (Philadelphia, 2011).

Kramer, S., *The English Craft Gilds: Studies in Their Progress and Decline* (New York, 1927).

Kyle, C. R., '"But a New Button to an Old Coat": The Enactment of the Statute of Monopolies, 21 James 1 cap. 3', *Journal of Legal History*, 19:3 (1998), pp. 203–23.

Kyle, C. R., 'Attendance, Apathy and Order? Parliamentary Committees in Early Stuart England', in C. R. Kyle and J. Peacey (eds), *Parliament at Work: Parliamentary Committees, Political Power and Public Access in Early Modern England* (Woodbridge, 2002), pp. 43–58.

Kyle, C. R., 'Parliament and the Politics of Carting in Early Stuart London', *London Journal*, 27:2 (2002), pp. 1–11.

Kyle, C. R., *Theater of State: Parliament and Political Culture in Early Stuart England* (Stanford, 2012).

Kyle, C. R., 'Monarch and Marketplace: Proclamations as News in Early Modern England', *Huntington Library Quarterly*, 78:4 (2015), pp. 771–87.

Kyle, C. R. and Peacey, J. (eds), *Parliament at Work: Parliamentary Committees, Political Power and Public Access in Early Modern England* (Woodbridge, 2002).

Lake, P., 'Puritans, Popularity and Petitions: Local Politics in National Context, Cheshire, 1641', in T. Cogswell, R. Cust and P. Lake (eds), *Politics, Religion and Popularity in Early Stuart Britain: Essays in Honour of Conrad Russell* (Cambridge, 2002), pp. 259–89.

Lake, P., *Bad Queen Bess?: Libels, Secret Histories, and the Politics of Publicity in the Reign of Queen Elizabeth I* (Oxford, 2016).

Lake, P. and Peacey, J. (eds), *Insolent Proceedings: Rethinking Public Politics in the English Revolution* (Manchester, 2022).

Lake, P. and Pincus, S., 'Rethinking the Public Sphere in Early Modern England', in P. Lake and S. Pincus (eds), *The Politics of the Public Sphere in Early Modern England* (Manchester, 2007), pp. 1–30.

Lambert, S., 'Committees, Religion, and Parliamentary Encroachment on Royal Authority in Early Stuart England', *English Historical Review*, 105:414 (1990), pp. 60–95.

Laughton, J. K. and Bowen, H. V., 'Wolstenholme, Sir John (1562–1639)', *ODNB* (2004), https://ezproxy-prd.bodleian.ox.ac.uk:2102/10.1093/ref:odnb/29857 (accessed 9 August 2022).

Lee, S. and Kelsey, S., 'Mompesson, Sir Giles (1583/4–1651/63)', *ODNB* (2004), https://doi.org/10.1093/ref:odnb/18932 (accessed 29 July 2024).

Legon, E., 'The Lord Mayor's Show and the Politics of London's Clothworkers' Company in the Mid-Seventeenth Century', *London Journal*, 47:3 (2022), pp. 241–59.

Leng, T., '"His neighbours land mark": William Sykes and the Campaign for "Free Trade" in Civil War England', *Historical Research*, 86:232 (2013), pp. 230–52.

Leng, T., 'Interlopers and Disorderly Brethren at the Stade Mart: Commercial Regulations and Practices Amongst the Merchant Adventurers of England in the Late Elizabethan Period', *Economic History Review*, 69:3 (2016), pp. 823–43.

Leng, T., *Fellowship and Freedom: The Merchant Adventurers and the Restructuring of English Commerce, 1582–1700* (Oxford, 2020).

Letwin, W. L., 'The English Common Law Concerning Monopolies', *The University of Chicago Law Review*, 21:3 (1954), pp. 355–85.

Lindley, K., *Popular Politics and Religion in Civil War London* (Aldershot, 1997).

Lipson, E., *The Economic History of England*, 6th edn (3 vols, London, 1956), iii.

Lockyer, R., *Buckingham: The Life and Political Career of George Villiers, First Duke of Buckingham 1592–1628* (London, 1981).

Lythe, S. G. E., *The Economy of Scotland in Its European Setting 1550–1625* (Edinburgh, 1960).

McConnell, A. and Brown, R., 'Garway [Garraway], Sir Henry (bap. 1575, d. 1646)', *ODNB* (2004), https://ezproxy-prd.bodleian.ox.ac.uk:2102/10.1093/ref:odnb/10405 (accessed 9 August 2022).

Macpherson, R., 'Stuart [Stewart], Ludovick, Second Duke of Lennox and Duke of Richmond (1574–1624)', *ODNB* (2004), https://doi.org/10.1093/ref:odnb/26724 (accessed 6 June 2022).

McRae, A., *God Speed the Plough: The Representation of Agrarian England, 1500–1660* (Cambridge, 1996).
Magnusson, L., *Mercantilism: The Shaping of an Economic Language* (London, 1994).
Malament, B., 'The "Economic Liberalism" of Sir Edward Coke', *Yale Law Journal*, 76:7 (1967), pp. 1321–58.
Manning, B., *The English People and the English Revolution* (London, 1976).
Millstone, N., *Manuscript Circulation and the Invention of Politics in Early Stuart England* (Cambridge, 2016).
Millstone, N., 'Sir Robert Cotton, Manuscript Pamphleteering, and the Making of Jacobean Kingship During the Short Peace, ca. 1609–1613', *Journal of British Studies*, 62 (2023), pp. 134–60.
Milton, A., 'Marketing a Massacre: Amboyna, the East India Company and the Public Sphere in Early Stuart England', in P. Lake and S. Pincus (eds), *The Politics of the Public Sphere in Early Modern England* (Manchester, 2007), pp. 168–90.
Mishra, R., *A Business of State: Commerce, Politics, and the Birth of the East India Company* (Cambridge MA, 2018).
Money, W., 'The Guild or Fellowship of the Clothworkers of Newbury', *Journal of the British Archaeological Association, New Series*, 2 (1986), pp. 261–7.
Neale, J., *Elizabeth I and her Parliaments, 1584–1601* (London, 1957).
Nef, J. U., *The Rise of the British Coal Industry* (2 vols, London, 1932), ii.
Notestein W., *The Winning of the Initiative by the House of Commons* (London, 1924).
Ormrod, W. M, Dodd, G. and Musson, A. (eds), *Medieval Petitions: Grace and Grievance* (York, 2009).
Paterson, E., 'The Politics of Starch: Guilds, Monopolies, and Petitioning in Late Elizabethan and Early Stuart England', *London Journal*, 48:1 (2022), pp. 30–46.
Paterson, E., 'Corruption, Conspiracy and Collusion: Anti-Monopoly Petitioning in the Parliament of 1621', *Parliamentary History*, 42:3 (2023), pp. 289–308.
Patterson, C. F., 'Consensus, Division and Voting in Early Stuart Towns', in P. D. Halliday, E. Hubbard and S. Sowerby (eds), *Revolutionising Politics: Culture and Conflict in England, 1620–60* (Manchester, 2021), pp. 145–63.
Patterson, C. F., *Urban Government and the Early Stuart State: Provincial Towns, Corporate Liberties, and Royal Authority in England, 1603–1640* (Woodbridge, 2022).
Peacey, J., 'Print and Public Politics in Seventeenth-Century England', *History Compass*, 5:1 (2007), pp. 85–111.
Peacey, J., *Print and Public Politics in the English Revolution* (Cambridge, 2013).
Peacey, J., 'Parliament, Printed Petitions and the Political Imaginary in Seventeenth-Century England', *Parliaments, Estates and Representation*, 38:3 (2018), pp. 350–63.
Peacey, J., *The Madman and the Churchrobber: Law and Conflict in Early Modern England* (Oxford, 2022).
Peacey, J., '"The universal cry of the kingdom": Petitions, Privileges and the Place of Parliament in Early Modern England', in B. Waddell and J. Peacey (eds), *The Power of Petitioning in Early Modern Britain* (London, 2024), pp. 83–114.

Pearl, V., *London and the Outbreak of the Puritan Revolution: City Government and National Politics, 1625–43* (London, 1961).

Peck, I., 'The Great Unknown: The Negotiation and Narration of Death by English War Widows, 1647–60', *Northern History*, 53:2 (2016), pp. 220–35.

Peck, L. L., *Northampton: Patronage and Policy at the Court of James I* (London, 1982).

Peck, L. L., *Court Patronage and Corruption in Early Stuart England* (London, 1991).

Pennington, D., 'Beyond the Moral Economy: Economic Change, Ideology and the 1621 House of Commons', *Parliamentary History*, 25:2 (2006), pp. 214–3.

Pennington, D., '"Free Passage" for the "King's True Liegemen": The Meaning of Free Trade in a Corporate Age, 1555–1624', *Journal of British Studies*, 63:2 (2024), pp. 282–300.

Pettigrew, W. A. and Stein, T., 'The Public Rivalry between Regulated and Joint Stock Corporations and the Development of Seventeenth-Century Corporate Constitutions', *Historical Research*, 90:248 (2017), pp. 341–62.

Pettigrew, W. A. and Smith, E., 'Corporate Management, Labor Relations, and Community Building at the East India Company's Blackwall Dockyard, 1600–57', *Journal of Social History*, 53:1 (2019), pp. 133–56.

Pierce, H., *Unseemly Pictures: Graphic Satire and Politics in Early Modern England* (New Haven, 2008).

Pincus, S., 'The State and Civil Society in Early Modern England: Capitalism, Causation and Habermas's Bourgeois Public Sphere', in P. Lake and S. Pincus (eds), *The Politics of the Public Sphere in Early Modern England* (Manchester, 2007), pp. 213–37.

Pollard, A. and Kelsey, S., 'Villiers, Christopher, First Earl of Anglesey (d. 1630)', *ODNB* (2004), https://doi-org.ezproxy-prd.bodleian.ox.ac.uk/10.1093/ref:odnb/28287 (accessed 29 July 2024).

Power, M. J., 'London and the Control of the "Crisis" of the 1590s', *History*, 70:230 (1985), pp. 371–85.

Price, W. H., *The English Patents of Monopoly* (London, 1906).

Quintrell, B., 'Montagu, Henry, First Earl of Manchester (c. 1564–1642)', *ODNB* (2008), https://ezproxy-prd.bodleian.ox.ac.uk:2102/10.1093/ref:odnb/19020 (accessed 9 August 2022).

Rabb, T. K., 'Sir Edwin Sandys and the Parliament of 1604', *American Historical Review*, 69:3 (1964), pp. 646–70.

Rabb, T. K., *Enterprise and Empire: Merchant and Gentry Investment in the Expansion of England, 1575–1630* (Cambridge, 1967).

Ramsay, G. D., 'The Report of the Royal Commission on the Clothing Industry, 1640', *English Historical Review*, 57:228 (1942), pp. 482–93.

Ramsay, G. D., *The Wiltshire Woollen Industry in the Sixteenth and Seventeenth Centuries*, 2nd edn (London, 1965).

Ramsay, G. D., 'Industrial Discontent in Early Elizabethan London: Clothworkers and Merchant Adventurers in Conflict', *London Journal*, 1:2 (1975), pp. 227–39.

Ramsay, G. D., 'Clothworkers, Merchant Adventurers and Richard Hakluyt', *English Historical Review*, 92:364 (1977), pp. 504–21.

Ramsay, G. D., *The English Woollen Industry, 1500–1750* (London, 1982).
Rappaport, S., *Worlds within Worlds: Structures of Life in Sixteenth-Century London* (Cambridge, 1989).
Reed, M., 'Economic Structure and Change in Seventeenth-Century Ipswich', in P. Clark (ed.), *County Towns in Pre-Industrial England* (Leicester, 1981), pp. 87–142.
Rich, E. E., *The Ordinance Book of the Merchants of the Staple* (Cambridge, 1937).
Robson, E., 'The Edges of Governance: Contesting Practices and Principles of Justice in Seventeenth-Century Fen Petitions', in B. Waddell and J. Peacey (eds), *The Power of Petitioning in Early Modern Britain* (London, 2024), pp. 169–200.
Rollison, D., 'Discourse and Class Struggle: The Politics of Industry in Early Modern England', *Social History*, 26:2 (2001), pp. 166–89.
Russell, C., *Parliaments and English Politics 1621–1629* (Oxford, 1979).
Russell, C., 'The Nature of a Parliament in Early Stuart England', in H. Tomlinson (ed.), *Before the English Civil War: Essays on Early Stuart Politics and Government* (Basingstoke, 1983), pp. 123–50.
Sacks, D. H., 'Private Profit and Public Good: The Problem of the State in Elizabethan Theory and Practice', in G. Schochet (ed.), *Law, Literature, and the Settlement of Regimes: Papers presented at the Folger Institute Seminar on 'Political Thought in the Elizabethan Age, 1558–1603'* (Washington, 1990), pp. 121–42.
Sacks, D. H., *The Widening Gate: Bristol and the Atlantic Economy, 1450–1700* (Berkeley, 1991).
Sacks, D. H., 'The Countervailing of Benefits: Monopoly, Liberty and Benevolence in Elizabethan England', in D. Hoak (ed.), *Tudor Political Culture* (Cambridge, 1995), pp. 272–92.
Sacks, D. H., 'Freedom to, Freedom from, Freedom of: Urban Life and Political Participation in Early Modern England', *Citizenship Studies*, 11:2 (2007), pp. 135–50.
Seaborne Davies, D., 'Further Light on the Case of Monopolies', *Law Quarterly Review*, 48:3 (1932), pp. 394–414.
Seaward, P., 'Institutional Memory and Contemporary History in the House of Commons, 1547–1640', in P. Cavill and A. Gajda (eds), *Writing the History of Parliament in Tudor and Early Stuart England* (Manchester, 2018), pp. 211–28.
Sharpe, J., 'Social Strain and Social Dislocation, 1585–1603', in J. Guy (ed.), *The Reign of Elizabeth I: Court and Culture in the Last Decade* (Cambridge, 1995), pp. 192–211.
Slack, P., 'Government and Information in Seventeenth-Century England', *Past and Present*, 28:184 (2004), pp. 33–68.
Slack, P., *The Invention of Improvement: Information and Material Progress in Seventeenth-Century England* (Oxford, 2014).
Slack, P., 'The Politics of English Political Economy in the 1620s', in M. J. Braddick and P. Withington (eds), *Popular Culture and Political Agency in Early Modern England and Ireland: Essays in Honour of John Walter* (Cambridge, 2017), pp. 55–72.
Smuts, R. M., 'Howard, Thomas, Fourteenth Earl of Arundel, Fourth Earl of Surrey, and First Earl of Norfolk (1585–1646)', *ODNB* (2015), https://doi.org/10.1093/ref:odnb/13943 (accessed 15 July 2022).

Sommerville, J. P., *Royalists and Patriots: Politics and Ideology in England, 1603–164*, 2nd edn (Oxford, 2014).

Stater, V., 'Herbert, William, Third Earl of Pembroke (1580–1630)', *ODNB* (2008), https://doi.org/10.1093/ref:odnb/13058 (accessed 15 July 2022).

Stern, P. J., *The Company-State: Corporate Sovereignty and the Early Modern Foundations of the British Empire in India* (Oxford, 2011).

Stern, P. J., 'Companies: Monopoly, Sovereignty, and the East Indies', in P. J. Stern and C. Wennerlind (eds), *Mercantilism Reimagined: Political Economy in Early Modern Britain and Its Empire* (Oxford, 2013), pp. 177–91.

Stern, P. J. and Wennerlind, C., 'Introduction', in P. J. Stern and C. Wennerlind (eds), *Mercantilism Reimagined: Political Economy in Early Modern Britain and Its Empire* (Oxford, 2013), pp. 3–17.

Stevenson, D., 'Erskine, Thomas, First Earl of Kellie (1566–1639)', *ODNB* (2004), https://doi-org.ezproxy-prd.bodleian.ox.ac.uk/10.1093/ref:odnb/8872 (accessed 25 August 2023).

Stevenson, D., 'Hamilton, James, Second Marquess of Hamilton (1589–1625)', *ODNB* (2015), https://doi.org/10.1093/ref:odnb/12085 (accessed 6 June 2022).

Stobart, J., *Sugar and Spice: Grocers and Groceries in Provincial England, 1650–1830* (Oxford, 2013).

Supple, B., *Commercial Crisis and Change in England 1600–1642: A Study in the Instability of a Mercantile Economy* (Cambridge, 1959).

Suprinyak, C., 'Trade, Money and the Grievances of the Commonwealth: Economic Debates in England During the Commercial Crisis of the Early 1620's', *History of Economic Ideas*, 24:1 (2016), pp. 27–55.

Suprinyak, C., 'Dreams of Order and Freedom: Debating Trade Management in Early Seventeenth-Century England', *Journal of the History of Economic Thought*, 40:3 (2018), pp. 401–18.

Sutton, A. F., 'The Merchant Adventurers of England: Their Origins and the Mercers' Company of London', *Historical Research*, 75:187 (2002), pp. 25–46.

Tawney, R. H., *Business and Politics Under James I: Lionel Cranfield as Merchant and Minister* (Cambridge, 1958).

Tawney, R. H. (ed.), *Studies in Economic History: The Collected Papers of George Unwin* (London, 1927).

Tazzara, C., 'Managing Free Trade in Early Modern Europe: Institutions, Information, and the Free Port of Livorno', *Journal of Modern History*, 86:3 (2014), pp. 493–529.

Tazzara, C., *The Free Port of Livorno and the Transformation of the Mediterranean World* (Oxford, 2017).

Thirsk, J., 'Industries in the Countryside', in F. J. Fisher (ed.), *Essays in the Economic and Social History of Tudor and Stuart England in Honour of R. H. Tawney* (Cambridge, 1961), pp. 70–89.

Thirsk, J., *Economic Policy and Projects: The Development of a Consumer Society in Early Modern England* (Oxford, 1978).

Thirsk, J., 'Projects for Gentlemen, Jobs for the Poor: Mutual Aid in the Vale of Tewkesbury, 1600–1630', in J. Thirsk, *The Rural Economy of England: Collected Essays* (London, 1984), pp. 286–307.

Thrush, A. and Ferris, J. P. (eds), *The History of Parliament: The House of Commons 1604–1629* (6 vols, Cambridge, 2010), I.

Thrush, A., 'Mansell, Sir Robert (1570/1–1652)', *ODNB* (2008), https://doi-org.ezproxy-prd.bodleian.ox.ac.uk/10.1093/ref:odnb/17992 (accessed 19 November 2020).

Tittler, R., *The Reformation and the Towns in England: Politics and Political Culture, c. 1540–1640* (Oxford, 1998).

Turnbull, J., *The Scottish Glass Industry 1610–1750: 'To Serve the Whole Nation with Glass'* (Edinburgh, 2001).

Turner, H. S., *The Corporate Commonwealth: Pluralism and Political Fictions in England, 1516–1651* (Chicago, 2016).

Turner, R., 'The Origin of the Cabinet Council', *English Historical Review*, 38:150 (1923), pp. 171–205.

Tyacke, N. (ed.), *The English Revolution c. 1590–1720: Politics, Religion and Communities* (Manchester, 2007).

Tyacke, N., 'The Puritan Paradigm of English Politics, 1558–1642', *Historical Journal*, 53:3 (2010), pp. 527–50.

Tyacke, N., 'Collective Biography and the Interpretative Challenge of Early Stuart Parliamentary History', *Parliamentary History*, 32:3 (2013), pp. 531–54.

Unwin, G., *Industrial Organization in the Sixteenth and Seventeenth Centuries* (Oxford, 1904).

Unwin, G., 'Industries', in W. Page (ed.), *The Victoria History of the County of Suffolk* (2 vols, London, 1907), ii, pp. 247–300.

Upton, A. F., *Sir Arthur Ingram c. 1565–1642: A Study of the Origins of an English Landed Family* (Oxford, 1961).

Usher, R. G., 'Nicholas Fuller: A Forgotten Exponent of English Liberty', *The American Historical Review*, 12:4 (1907), pp. 743–60.

Veale, E. M., *The English Fur Trade in the Later Middle Ages* (London, 2003), *British History Online*, https://www-british-history-ac-uk.ezproxy-prd.bodleian.ox.ac.uk/london-record-soc/vol38 (accessed 22 January 2025).

Waddell, B. and Peacey, J. (eds), *The Power of Petitioning in Early Modern Britain* (London, 2024).

Waggett, R. W., *A History of the Worshipful Company of Glovers of London*, 2nd edn (Chichester, 2008).

Walter, J., *Understanding Popular Violence in the English Revolution: The Colchester Plunderers* (Cambridge, 1999).

Walter, J., 'Crown and Crowd: Popular Culture and Popular Protest in Early Modern England', in J. Walter (ed.), *Crowds and Popular Politics in Early Modern England* (Manchester, 2006), pp. 14–26.

Walter, J., 'Authority and Protest', in K. Wrightson (ed.), *A Social History of England, 1500–1750* (Cambridge, 2017), pp. 221–41.

Walter, J., '"A Foolish Commotion of Youth"? Crowds and the "Crisis of the 1590s" in London', *London Journal*, 44:1 (2019), pp. 17–36.

Walter, J., '"Law-Mindedness": Crowds, Courts and Popular Knowledge of the Law in Early Modern England', in M. Lobban and J. Begiato (eds), *Law, Lawyers and*

*Litigants in Early Modern England: Essays in Memory of Christopher W. Brooks* (Cambridge, 2021), pp. 164–84.

Ward, G. F., 'The Early History of the Merchants Staplers', *English Historical Review*, 33:131 (1918), pp. 297–319.

Ward, J. P., *Metropolitan Communities: Trade Guilds, Identity, and Change in Early Modern London* (Stanford, 1997).

Webb, J., 'An Ipswich Merchant's Cloth Accounts, 1623–24', *Proceedings of the Suffolk Institute of Archaeology and History*, 37:2 (1990), pp. 124–34.

Welch, C., *History of the Worshipful Company of Pewterers of the City of London: Based Upon Their Own Records* (2 vols, London, 1902), ii.

White, S. D., *Sir Edward Coke and the 'Grievances of the Commonwealth', 1621–1628* (Manchester, 1979).

Wilson, C., *England's Apprenticeship, 1603–1763* (London, 1971).

Winship, M. P., 'Freeborn (Puritan) Englishmen and Slavish Subjection: Popish Tyranny and Puritan Constitutionalism, c. 1570–1606', *English Historical Review*, 124:510 (2009), pp. 1050–74.

Withington, P., *The Politics of Commonwealth: Citizens and Freemen in Early Modern England* (Cambridge, 2005).

Withington, P., 'Company and Sociability in Early Modern England', *Social History*, 32:3 (2007), pp. 291–307.

Withington, P., *Society in Early Modern England: The Vernacular Origins of Some Powerful Ideas* (Cambridge, 2010).

Wood, A., *The Politics of Social Conflict: The Peak Country, 1520–1770* (Cambridge, 1999).

Wright, S., 'Nicholas Fuller and the Liberties of the Subject', *Parliamentary History*, 25:2 (2006), pp. 176–213.

Wright, S., 'Paule, Sir George (1563–1635)', *ODNB* (2008), https://ezproxy-prd.bodleian.ox.ac.uk:2102/10.1093/ref:odnb/21610 (accessed 9 August 2022).

Wrightson, K., '"Sorts of People" in Tudor and Stuart England', in J. Barry and C. W. Brooks (eds), *The Middling Sort of People: Culture, Society, and Politics in England, 1550–1800* (Hampshire, 1994), pp. 28–50.

Wrightson, K., *Earthly Necessities: Economic Lives in Early Modern Britain* (New Haven, 2000).

Wrightson, K., *English Society 1580–1640*, 2nd edn (London, 2003).

Yamamoto, K., *Taming Capitalism before Its Triumph: Public Service, Distrust, and 'Projecting' in Early Modern England* (Oxford, 2018).

Yerby, G., *The Economic Causes of the English Civil War: Freedom of Trade and the English Revolution* (New York, 2020).

Zaller, R., *The Parliament of 1621: A Study in Constitutional Conflict* (Berkeley, 1971).

Zaret, D., *Origins of Democratic Culture: Printing, Petitions, and the Public Sphere in Early-Modern England* (Princeton, 2000).

Zaret, D., 'Petition-and-Response and Liminal Petitioning in Comparative/Historical Perspective', *Social Science History*, 43:3 (2019), pp. 431–51.

Zell, M., 'Walter Morrell and the New Draperies Project, c. 1603–1631', *Historical Journal*, 44:3 (2001), pp. 351–75.

Zim, R., 'Sackville, Thomas, first Baron Buckhurst and First Earl of Dorset', *ODNB,* https://doi-org.ezproxy-prd.bodleian.ox.ac.uk/10.1093/ref:odnb/24450 (accessed 16 May 2025).

## Unpublished dissertations and papers

Clarkson, L. A., 'The English Leather Industry in the Sixteenth and Seventeenth Centuries (1563–1700)' (unpublished PhD thesis, University of Nottingham, 1960).

Legon, E., '"Rebells By Their Trade?" Revisiting Clothmaking and Parliamentarianism' (unpublished paper, delivered 24 April 2023, Britain in Revolution Seminar, University of Oxford).

Paterson, E., 'Bloodsuckers of the Commonwealth: Anti-Monopoly Petitioning in Late Elizabethan and Jacobean England' (unpublished DPhil thesis, University of Oxford, 2023).

Paterson, E., 'Approaching the "great Court of Justice now sitting": Petitioning and Parliamentary Memory in the Long Parliament (1640–1642) (unpublished paper, delivered 11 March 2025, Parliament, Politics, and People Seminar, IHR London).

Ross, C., 'The Development of the Glass Industry on the Rivers Tyne and Wear, 1700–1900' (unpublished PhD thesis, University of Newcastle, 1982).

Sgroi, R. C. L., 'The Language of Economic Debate and Public Policy in the Elizabethan Commonwealth' (unpublished DPhil thesis, University of Oxford, 2001).

Siegler, A. H., 'Royal Prerogative and the Regulation of Industry: Regulation of the Gold and Silver Thread Trade under James I and Charles I' (unpublished PhD thesis, University of Chicago, 1980).

Wallis, P., 'Medicines for London: The Trade, Regulation and Lifecycle of London Apothecaries, c. 1610–c. 1670' (unpublished DPhil thesis, University of Oxford, 2002).

# Index

EU authorised representative for GPSR:
Easy Access System Europe, Mustamäe tee 50,
10621 Tallinn, Estonia
gpsr.requests@easproject.com

www.ingramcontent.com/pod-product-compliance
Ingram Content Group UK Ltd.
Pitfield, Milton Keynes, MK11 3LW, UK
UKHW021840100926
8556IPUK00004B/457
* 9 7 8 1 5 2 6 1 8 9 0 8 0 *